AN ARSENAL FOR DEMOCRACY

Media Accountability Systems

edited by

Claude-Jean Bertrand

Université de Paris-2

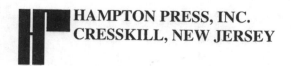

HAMPTON PRESS, INC.
CRESSKILL, NEW JERSEY

Printed in the United States of America.

Library of Congress Cataloging-in-Publication Data

An arsenal for democracy : media accountability systems / edited by Claude-Jean Bertrand
       p. cm. -- (Hampton Press communication series. Communication alternatives)
   Includes bibliographic references and index.
   ISBN 1-57273-425-6 -- ISBN 1-57273-426-4
    1. Mass media--Moral and ethical aspects. I. Bertrand, Claude Jean.
II. Series

P94.A755 2003
075--dc21

                         2002038879

Hampton Press, Inc.
23 Broadway
Cresskill, NJ 07626

CONTENTS

[1]When no author is listed, the chapter is by Claude-Jean Bertrand.

FOREWORD

In the 1970s after Watergate, there was much debate over "imperial media," the United States becoming a "newsocracy," the coming Information Age. The media had seized a central role in society. Then a disquieting thought loomed on my mental horizon: could the human race survive without quality media? Or, more clearly, could the human race survive without democracy? Considering the havoc caused over the last century by despotic ideologies (fascist, communist, or fundamentalist) and by ravenous irresponsible business behemoths, we may have some doubts about it.

No democracy can exist without the free communication of information, quality information. That is obvious. How can press freedom and quality be obtained or maintained? If news media are to avoid autocratic or bureaucratic enslavement, if they are to escape plutocratic bondage—or simply if they are to stop serving only the majority in a pluralistic society, it seems to me that the profession must take over, on behalf of the public, with public participation and under its control.

Media must serve the public first and only afterwards advertisers, shareholders, and news sources. Whether you call that "public service" or prefer to use terms like "social responsibility," "media ethics," or "quality control," does not matter. To achieve this, the intervention of the state is needed, but it should be kept to a minimum: for many centuries, the legislatures, the police, the courts, and officialdom have proved lethal to freedom of speech, without which there can be no quality media.

What then? Whoever has studied the news media in the United States, in Britain, or in the Nordic countries, has noted means and methods that have long been used in those countries to try to improve the services of the press, means and methods scorned in much of the rest of the world—even in countries that have shed their dictatorial regimes, for instance, in the Latin world. Those means and methods, with the assistance of the new technology, could achieve a true democratization of news media through a vast informal network of monitors, feedback purveyors, and access-makers

It was in the early 1970s that I became interested in what I did not yet call "media accountability systems," M*A*S—means to incite media to do all their jobs well (without intervention of government), mainly by exerting moral pressure. My research first focused on press councils, the national one in Britain and the several local ones in the United States. Then, with a fellowship granted me by the American Council of Learned Societies, I was able to widen my scope and include U.S. journalism reviews. Then came newspaper ombudsmen. Then codes of media ethics. Gradually the concept of M*A*S[1] developed: the notion that weapons for the good (democratic) fight existed—the arsenal was there but nobody seemed to know.

M*A*S are not some invention waiting to be materialized and tested. They exist—not everywhere, admittedly, but in many parts of the world. They have been tested and have usually given satisfaction. Some have been in existence since before World War II. Yet M*A*S are rare, overall. Why? One explanation is ignorance: the ordinary citizen has never heard about most of them. The other explanation is antagonism: when media people know about M*A*S, they usually have a wrong and negative idea of them.

That indifference and that animosity were obvious on 19 and 20 April 1991, on the occasion of a conference I organized in the elegant 17th-century Palais du Luxembourg in Paris. It was sponsored by the Institut français de presse (IFP), a department of the University of Paris-2, together with the Institut national de l'audiovisuel (INA), in charge of archives, research, and training for public broadcasting, and the daily Libération. With the official blessing of a dozen celebrities of the political, intellectual, television, and newspaper worlds, the conference was meant to publicize the M*A*S concept,[2] already well-known in the United States, though under different names. So U.S. experts, academics, and journalists had been invited to present various M*A*S with which they had been associated. Although Saddam Hussein had not been involved in the preparation of the conference, he started the Gulf War just at the right time to demonstrate the necessity for the media and the public to pay more attention to ethics.

Largely as a consequence of the war, media ethics attracted greater and greater interest in Europe in the 1990s. Everywhere in the world, the problem has been perceived to grow more serious as the commercialization and concentration of media accelerated from the 1970s onwards. More and more books have been devoted to the topic as well as conferences, programs on television and radio, and special issues of reviews. They have denounced media outrages as well as deep flaws; they have sought media vices and transgressions; they have expounded ethical principles and norms. What has never (or rarely) been done was to look for practical instruments to get the media to respect the rules, with no recourse to the government. Whining, invective, and wishful thinking accomplish little: the need is for action.

---

[1] See the list pp. 18-24.

[2] M*A*R*S in French for *Moyens d'assurer la responsabilité sociale des médias* (means to insure that media will be socially responsible).

THE PURPOSE OF THIS BOOK

The present book has the same purpose as the conference: to publicize a whole armory of available democratic means to improve news media. It provides data and informed opinion on major M*A*S. It thus stands as an extension of another book of mine that was published in the United States under the title *Media Ethics and Accountability Systems.*[3]

This volume offers a vast and precise panorama of "quality control" as applied to media, of the justification for it, and of its many methods. But its intent is not simply to depict an existing state of affairs. What the book describes certainly exists, but description alone is not enough. The book aims at promoting the M*A*S concept—which should not be confused with "media ethics," too often limited to books, speeches, and roundtables. Nor should M*A*S be assimilated with "self-regulation," which too often is no more than a promise of self-censorship by media wishing to avoid legal restraints. M*A*S involve not only the media, but the journalists and, crucially, the public, directly or indirectly. They mean doing, not talking They involve not just abstaining from certain (bad) things, but accomplishing necessary (good) things. It might be wise, in fact, to replace the moral concept of "media ethics" by a social concept like "public service" or an economic concept like "quality control"— or to use a combination phrase: "ethics & M*A*S."

The purpose is not to preach a panacea, but to inform on methods that have been used and have given some satisfaction in one or another part of the world. Some reasonable *via media* must be followed between two extremes, the jungle and the bureaucracy. We need to avoid the absolute rejection of ethics, of "social responsibility," of codes, and most M*A*S that characterizes libertarians and media moguls. We must also avoid the urge to force accountability on the media by law, an urge that seizes politicians occasionally (like, for instance, the British conservatives in the late 1980s). That middle course can be held if more and more M*A*S are used by more and more media. The improvement of just some media can cause the public to recover its confidence in journalists and to support them in their struggle for autonomy. Hopefully, a snowball effect will occur —and good journalism will shove bad journalism off the main road.

THE APPROACH

The material here has been fashioned by experts from journalism and from academe, laboring in various regions of the planet, who for many years have observed media with a critical eye and have participated in the creation of "the arsenal for democracy." Most of them are now free of any institutional involvement, so they can call the shots as they see them. They have no obligation to be careful or courteous.

---

[3]Piscataway (NJ) and London, Transaction, 2000.

Their approach, though quite critical at times, is positive: it deliberately differs from the usual cynicism of journalists and from the nostalgic pessimism of intellectuals. One cannot advocate ethics & M*A*S and, at the same time, believe that selfishness is the ultimate human quality, that money is the ultimate value, that democracy will be sacrificed to Mammon. Clifford Christians speaks of a social ethics "grounded in community, aiming at civic transformation and operating by the principle of mutuality." "We center," he says, "on the irrevocable status of universal human solidarity as a moral imperative."[4] In more prosaic terms, we must all work at making the planet a better place to live for as many humans as possible.

Ours is a pragmatic empirical approach. What experience has proven to be good for helping media provide good public service is all right—whatever some philosopher, ideologue, professor, publisher, editor, or press critic may have said to the contrary. Contributors to this book believe improvement is possible, with minimal state intervention, simply because improvement has already taken place. Whoever thinks that media are getting worse should have a look at newspapers of the 1920s, and at television programs of the 1950s. Awareness of the past always helps in preparing the future.

THE AREA COVERED

This book does not provide an exhaustive compendium of all M*A*S, their histories, and their operations now over the whole planet. One reason is that the history of media ethics, and of the arsenal needed to obtain respect for the rules, remains to be written. This book first presents some major concepts, including the fundamental one of a right to communicate. But most of the volume is devoted to the more controversial among the most important of the 60-odd M*A*S—such as codes, press councils, ombudsmen, critical reviews, journalism education, and mass communication research. In most cases, an overview by a professor precedes a presentation by someone who either created a M*A*S or worked on one. In the case of codes, the illustration comes in the shape of a series of codes from various parts of the world, which are not familiar to the U.S. reader.

The countries covered are primarily the United States, where many M*A*S were invented and most have been tried, Japan, Germany, France, and Britain—the next on the list of wealthiest democracies. The reason why enormous countries like Russia and China have been ignored is simply because at the turn of the millennium, they had not yet established press freedom. The rest of the world is represented by four small countries: Portugal (10 million inhabitants), Sweden (9 m.), Israel (6 m.), and Estonia (1.5 m.). Why these?

---

[4]Clifford Christians et al., *Good News: Social Ethics & the Press*, New York, Oxford UP, 1993, pp. 15-16.

Sweden was the pioneer in the establishment of press freedom (1766),[5] then later the pioneer of major M*A*S, with the first press council in 1916. Moreover, Sweden is typical of Sweden/Nordic countries, models of democracy with highly developed[6] and remarkably responsible media.

Portugal is the only Latin European country[7] to have set up a national press council, and the first after Spain to have appointed a newspaper ombudsman. One of those "readers' advocates," with a rich experience as reporter, editor, member of Parliament, and professor, has developed a vigorous and profound notion of that M*A*S, which should be an inspiration in many parts.

Israel? That nation, isolated in an undemocratic part of the planet, under constant threat of an annihilating war, has managed to maintain press freedom; it has equipped itself with M*A*S, the same ones as in the North Atlantic area. Thus it has demonstrated that even in extremely difficult circumstances, M*A*S can exist and do their job.

Little is said here about former communist states: in such countries, at the beginning of the 21st century, free media still found it hard to survive and they were only starting to think about accountability. One exception: the Baltic nations Estonia and Lithuania, the only former soviet colonies in Europe to have established a genuine press council in the 1990s.

Almost nothing is said about the regions that used to be known as the Third World. Countries there either possess few media and even less freedom of speech—or they have discovered press freedom so recently that they have not yet given much thought to protecting it. There, when you do find so-called press councils, they usually partake, in variable degrees, of state censorship—although there are more and more exceptions, mainly industrialized countries like India.

Again, do not expect to find here a history of communication ethics, or a dissertation on moral philosophy, or a textbook on media ethics, or an annotated collection of case studies, or a lamentation on media mediocrity, or a partisan pamphlet against the capitalistic press. Such books already exist.[8]. This volume deals with the crucial difficulty raised by media ethics, a problem that strangely is too often ignored: how to enforce ethical rules without governmental intervention. The aim is to inform journalists, future journalists, media consumers—but also to "convert" them and incite them to action. Here you will find tested ideas and methods: those weapons, like those of any arsenal, are meant not to be talked about, but to be used in the peaceful crusade for a better democracy.

Claude-Jean Bertrand

---

[5]In 1776 a Press Freedom Law was enacted and included in the Constitution.

[6]In the list of nations with the highest daily circulation per 1000 inhabitants, Norway is number 1, Japan number 2, Finland number 3 and Sweden number 4. *World Press Trends*, Paris, WAN, 2000.

[7]As regards Latin America, Chile has had a press council since 1991. See Table p. 131.

[8]See the bibliography, p. 395.

PART I
Introduction

CHAPTER 1
A Predicament
and Three Solutions

Globalization means everyone's life can be affected by events in faraway lands. Jobs, food prices, health in one part of the world depend on developments on the other side of the Earth. Globalization tends to cause conflicts by putting different cultures in contact. It increases the risk of wars, terrorism, economic depression, pollution, genetic manipulation, epidemics that could turn into disasters for the human race. So everyone now needs to be informed of what goes on in the world so as to be able to do something about it. A good example was provided by the support given all over the planet to the disturbers of the 1999 World Trade Organization conference in Seattle. The message was that globalization should not profit only big corporations: billions of men and women were involved whose welfare should come first. This requires that democracy spread all over the planet; hence it calls for media to serve society fully and honestly.

THE MEDIA ENVIRONMENT

A large part of the world is still deprived of press freedom or of viable media. In those regions, the media are enslaved to a dictatorial clique, to mafia-like businessmen, to political parties. Or the journalists are corrupt, mainly because they cannot survive on their salaries. Such is the situation in many former soviet colonies of southern Europe, in most countries of the Middle East and Africa, in some nations of Latin America and of South-East Asia. Media ethics there is irrelevant; journalists may like the idea, but for them it is utopian. Lack of free-

3

dom, fear for their lives, and dire need make it impossible for them to follow the standard rules or to set up accountability systems.

Everywhere else, over the last 20-25 years, the explosion of technology, and a little later the implosion of communism, have led to the privatization and commercialization of state media, to the deregulation of commercial media, and to the multiplication of new media—with increasing competition, concentration and prostitution.

In the 1990s, the Internet took off, fast becoming a news medium, but an anarchic, irresponsible one. On the Web, anybody can say anything. That is a totally unexpected democratization. But what computer science has achieved is what Jürgen Habermas has called "radical democracy," in which everyone has access to public opinion, however ignorant, stupid, insane, or malicious he/she may be. So more than ever citizens need a guarantee of authenticity, a quality label on the news they get. There is an ever greater need for competent, honest journalists to filter, check, and comment upon the information available.

WHAT'S WRONG WITH MEDIA

Whatever the pompous declarations about democracy, press freedom, the First Amendment, and the Fourth Estate—facts and figures indicate concentration of ownership, public distrust of the media, decreasing sales and ratings. Something is rotten in the realm of media. Everywhere. Problems do differ a little from country to country: in Japan, it is the intermingling of banks, industrial corporations, political parties, and media; in Russia or Latin America, the custom for media to sell editorial space, for journalists to sell their pen; in England, the national tabloid press, so vile that it has become the focus of all British books on media ethics. But all over the globe, apart from the dictatorial areas, the core issues are the same.

Commercialization

Almost everywhere, the privatization of state-owned media and the deregulation of commercial media have turned former propaganda machines into entertainment factories. The business logic and the obsession with short-term profit have taken over and they cannot co-exist well with public service.

Regardless of what journalists believe would be good journalism, they find it hard to resist the pressure put on them by management, by sources, even by peers. "Our profession still tries to maintain its ethical standards, but I see the task becoming more and more difficult. . . . There is nothing wrong with high ratings or huge profits or healthy circulation. But economic performance is one thing; journalistic integrity is another," writes Helen Thomas, long-time

White House correspondent, at the end of her career.[1] The climate has changed since the days when U.S. news media reported on the Civil Rights movement, on anti-war demonstrations, on the Pentagon Papers, on the Watergate. Morale has gone down.

Columnist William Pfaff[2] expresses concern that the United States is becoming a plutocracy, with one billion dollars being spent on media in the 2000 electoral campaign, itself described by Senator John McCain as "an influence-peddling scheme in which both parties compete to stay in office by selling the country to the highest bidder."

Concentration

Unchecked since the deregulating 1980s, concentration has inevitably increased. In Britain now, 85% of the national daily press (which accounts for two thirds of total circulation) is in the hands of four groups. And the corporate oligopoly has established an ideological monopoly: in Britain as in Sweden, most of the press is conservative, while at least half of the popular votes go to the social-democrats.

In the United States, according to Ben Bagdikian in the 2000 edition of *The Media Monopoly*,[3] six companies control most of the media: AOL-Time Warner, General Electric, Viacom, Disney, Bertelsmann, and News Corporation (Murdoch). In the first edition of the book (1983), the number was 50. "Corporate and agency consolidations make all major media dependent on a reduced number of decision-makers who produce an ever-larger share of total ad billings," says Leo Bogart.[4] Obviously, concentration cannot co-exist well with information pluralism.

Conglomerates own more and more media of all kinds and they are in a position to make their newspapers, magazines, networks, and stations, serve the interests of their other corporate components instead of serving the public interest—to say nothing of exposés or campaigns that might cause harm to sister companies.[5]

Decline of News

Greed has caused deregulated media to concentrate on only two of their functions: entertainment and the sale of advertising. The trend for some years has

---

[1]In *Front Row at the White House,* New York, Scribner, 1999.

[2]*International Herald Tribune*, 15 July 1999.

[3]Boston, Beacon, 6th ed.

[4]"Church and State" in *Media Studies Journal*, Spring-Summer 2000, p. 129.

[5]An indication: in June 2000, *Brill's Content* (p. 23) reported that ABC (part of the Disney empire) killed a story about a pedophile at Disney World.

been to reduce news staffs, to produce infotainment so as to seduce customers[6] and advertisers—cheap fun instead of public service. During the year 2000 presidential campaign, the FOX and NBC networks did not carry the debates, whereas they had covered the murder of Italian couturier Versace for nine days: violence, (gay) sex, jet set, big business—great for titillation. Before that, all media had spent months focused on O.J. Simpson, on JonBenet Ramsey[7] and on Monica Lewinsky.

The "wall" supposed to exist between editorial and business departments has started crumbling and journalism regrettably combines with entertainment, public relations, and advertising. "Much of what is perceived as 'news' is little more than free advertising."[8] And toxic material invades the news-hole, like sleazy stories about the sex life of celebrities, movie stars, or statesmen.

Bad media results in declining news audiences and an under-informed population. "Americans know less about current events than any of the [8] nationalities polled; asked a series of five questions, 37% of the Americans polled got all five wrong, while only 3% of the Germans failed all five."[9]

Silence

The "bullet" theory according to which any message of the almighty media will have an impact on the receiver is no longer accepted. But no one doubts that media do have a great effect through what they do not tell. Their worst sin is omission, because the reader/listener/viewer cannot react to it. One hears constant harping on inaccuracy, bias, libel, invasion of privacy, political incorrectness—but little is said about the big omissions of the past, such as famine in Ethiopia, mad cow disease in the 1980s, or the many taboos of the Japanese press. Let me give you two striking examples.

Everyone has heard of the genocide of Tutsis by Hutus in Rwanda in the 1990s. But who knows that 20 years before, in the neighboring country Burundi, the Tutsis killed 300,000 to 500,000 Hutus? Fearing to lose power as had just happened to their cousins in Rwanda, they preempted the strike and decimated the Hutus. At that time Western media preferred to report on South African police brutality: racism can take strange forms.

---

[6]Yet, in reaction to a cover story on the Lewinsky scandal, *Time* magazine received 1,454 letters asking it to drop gutter journalism and 39 letters awarding the magazine a medal for good journalism (*Time*, 30 March 1998).

[7]A six-year-old beauty queen murdered in Boulder, Colorado in December 1996.

[8]James Curran and Jean Seaton, *Power Without Responsibility,* London, Routledge, 5th ed., 1997, p. 278.

[9]The *Los Angeles Times,* 16 March 1994, reporting a study by the Times Mirror Center for the People and the Press.

Another case. Everybody over 40 has heard about a South Korean airliner shot down by soviet fighters over the sea of Japan in August 1983. But who has heard of the other one, in 1978. That Korean plane, flying to the United States, lost its bearings over the pole, flew south into the Soviet Union, was spotted, shot at by fighters, and then lost in the clouds. It flew on for some 500 km then landed on a frozen lake. Why the silence? Would it not be because the incident indicated that the USSR was not at all the fortress it was claimed to be—bad news for some on both sides of the Iron Curtain?

Media, for reasons numerous and diverse, will hide or down play big stories that reveal major phenomena (see p. 239).

WHAT'S WRONG WITH JOURNALISTS

What is wrong mainly is the definition of journalism. It would be better to stop chanting about the Truth,[10] Objectivity, the Right to Information—and keep in mind the functions of journalism: to report on what is happening, on and under the surface of reality, that it is important for the public to know; to provide a forum where all sections of the people can debate issues and work out a consensus; to give an image of the world beyond the range of each individual's experience; to transmit the culture of the land to the next generation; to help people pursue happiness by entertaining them. It seems, unfortunately, that quite a few media people do not well understand (or refuse to accept) what their many, now crucial, functions are in society.

An Archaic Tradition

On the threshold of the third millennium, the general journalistic tradition seems terribly out-of-date, with its coverage only of the emerged part of the information iceberg; its concentration on politics and "human interest stories"; its love of events, entertaining events, preferably sensational; its obsession for scoops;[11] its neglect of context and explanation; its language difficult to decipher for under-educated people, and so on.

Journalists most often fashion a mosaic of the obvious occurrences of the day before, isolated in time and space and hard to understand—including pseudo-news fabricated by whoever intends to profit from it. Journalists concentrate on covering interesting "news" rather than discovering long, obscure

---

[10]Absurdities are common, like "Journalism is telling the truth" (in M. Kiernan [ed.], *Media Ethics,* New York, Routledge, 1998, p. 9). Everything in the world that happens to be true?

[11]Made worse by the new technology; reporting live from anywhere leaves no time for reflection, checking, and editing.

but important processes. And everywhere one finds the same mosaic of events because reporters move in packs. So certain aspects of reality are over-covered while others are covered very little (e.g., overpopulation).

"Good news is no news": in deference to that regrettable myth, journalists tend to give priority to conflicts, scandals, declines, failures, threats, accidents, and deaths—and in general to see only the half-empty glass.[12] That systematic distortion seems able to instill in the public an unfounded pessimism about the state of the world, dangerous in that it can desensitize and cause withdrawal from social affairs.

By tradition, the journalist is reluctant to explore unconventional fields: at least up to the last years of the last century, for instance, little effort was made to bring out from the labs the discoveries and thoughts of scientists. In the media world, there seems to be a fear of new, unconventional, extreme ideas—a fear of change. Added to this is an old usage, re-enforced daily by personal contact: the journalist addresses decision-makers, the elite, and his peers far more than he/she speaks to the public. And yet it is indispensable that a large majority of citizens get a correct perception of the world.

Incompetence

Human affairs grow more complex. And journalists are no longer supposed just to cover the routines of a small town. In order to report accurately, they need far more knowledge, general and specialized, than they used to. However, their competence is not checked by an entrance examination to the profession (as is the case in Italy), contrary to that of physicians or attorneys. And their incompetence is commonly aggravated by assignments to sectors about which they have no knowledge.

Even eminent reporters betray incompetence: that was clear during the Gulf War, although they had had months to gather knowledge on the region, its history, its culture, and its religion. And arrogant pundits can turn out to be totally wrong; as when they dogmatically forecast a quick end of the Clinton administration at the start of the Lewinsky scandal. This is all the more disturbing at a time when, because of the Internet, there is an ever-greater need for competent journalists, for reliable guides as a niagara of information keeps pouring out.

Journalists are crucial to any improvement of media, but because they are not numerous and not self-employed, they cannot achieve much without public support. Surveys show that readers/listeners/viewers notice the errors and the blunders (especially when they have been involved in the events reported). The dishonesty of a few journalists, the low abilities of a few others, and their

---

[12]Of Americans, 60.1% believe the press makes conditions in America seem worse than they really are (18% better). *Brill's Content*, March 2000, p. 78.

laziness, arrogance, submissiveness, or rule-breaking, undermine the prestige of all and they antagonize consumers.[13] In nearly all democracies, journalists are held in low esteem. In France, 60% of the people do not believe that journalists are independent from political or economic forces.[14] In the United States, three quarters of the people think "reporters are biased, inaccurate and prying."[15] Evidently, to some extent, that reputation reflects the bad image of news media—but the overall effect is the same.

Ethics Misunderstood

In Europe, one cause of misunderstanding is the frequent confusion of ethics with law and regulation, linked to the confusion between the sins of media and the sins of journalists. The confusion also exists between media accountability systems (M*A*S) and self-regulation, because many media people would rather do without that great source of power: the public. In the United States, the misleading confusion is of professional ethics with morals (and with philosophy): ethics belongs within the conscience of each individual. His/her accountability to the public is discounted—and so is the accountability of media.

Some journalists, even in the West, have no sense of right and wrong: they believe that if it sells it's OK. They practice journalism with no idea of its social function, with no more ethical awareness than if they peddled potted plants or leather belts. Others, more numerous, know something about ethics but do not distinguish well between three types of ethical violations: the big scandals that get a lot of publicity; the thousands of daily little failings; and media faults involving omission and long-term distortion. The third does not attract a fraction of the attention that the other two get, the first in the media themselves and in books, the second in seminars and workshops.

Few people know much about M*A*S. Most journalists in France have no idea what a press council is. Before *Le Monde* appointed one in 1992, they had never heard of an ombudsman. In every country, as a consequence, when accountability systems become part of the agenda, the same debates start all over again, with the same groundless arguments bandied around. When in 1999 Niger wanted to give itself a press council, it ignored what had been done before in neighboring Nigeria and Ghana.

News people usually consider M*A*S not as means to increase the quality of journalism and their independence, but as direct threats to their free-

---

[13]See Christine D. Urban, *Examining our Credibility: Perspective of the Public and the Press,* ASNE Survey, 1999.

[14]Annual survey by SOFRES for the daily *La Croix* and the TV magazine *Télérama,* 26 January 2000, p. 30.

[15]From a survey by the Scripps Survey Research Center at Ohio University, reported in *Editor & Publisher,* 27 February 1999.

dom. For centuries, they fought so hard to be free to do their job that they now consider their freedom as a supreme value instead of a means to serve the public well. And besides, they do not realize how limited their freedom is, limited mainly because their status, their income, and career is controlled by management. Can a reporter afford to lose his job by respecting an ethical rule or by violating one of a long list of taboos affecting advertisers and the powers-that-be? In the United States, most often, they are not even protected by a union.

THE THREE SOLUTIONS

If you observe the state of the economy in nations like Russia, a land of huge natural resources that, for lack of decent media, endured for 70 years one of the most destructive dictatorships that ever existed; or if you consider the state of human rights in nations like Saudi Arabia or North Korea that have no Fourth Estate—then it is clear why nations need quality media.

The quality of news media and of journalists is now better than it has ever been (contrary to the nostalgic wail of many critics), but even in industrialized democracies, media are not as good as they need to be for civilized society to survive. How can they be improved? That is the crucial question.

But first, what are quality media ? Media that serve the citizens first. Media that assume all their functions (not just report yesterday's events) towards all the groups in the population—not only towards the majority, or the rich, or some caste, or noisy minorities. To make sure that they provide adequate services, the media must study and survey the many groups within their public. They must supply the people with important and interesting information, in an attractive shape. Not only must they satisfy their desires, but also (on a longer-term basis) satisfy their needs. Then, after delivery, the products must be evaluated with critical input from consumers.

A controversial form of journalism spread in the United States at the end of the 20th century, called "public journalism": at best, it consists in keeping in close touch with the local citizenry, in stimulating their civic sense, in helping them find solutions to their problems. By such devotion to the welfare of the public, media take part in the improvement of society,[16] as indeed they should.

Traditionally, two approaches are advocated for bettering the media. Some claim that freedom alone, the "marketplace," can take care of problems; letting customers, the people, decide what they like and need. Others argue that only law and regulation can be trusted; the market alone can produce nothing but trash and exploitation. However, in recent years, a third theory has been emerging, the notion that quality must come from a combination of market and

---

[16]See Clifford Christians et al., *Good News: Social Ethics and the Press,* 1992: a communitarian approach to media ethics, quite different from the individualistic or collectivistic ones.

law and ethics: a triple solution to a crucial problem; a three-pronged offensive towards excellence; three pillars to sustain the media edifice.

It might be useful now to recall the advantages and disadvantages of each of the three approaches, because champions of one are often hostile to the others and ignorant of their virtues.

THE LAW AND THE COURTS

The law, voted by a democratic Parliament, then interpreted by competent, independent magistrates, expresses the will of a majority of the people, not the arbitrary whim of a Leviathan State. In their denunciations of "government," libertarians often ignore what happens when the rule of law breaks down, when government is snuffed out and society turns into a jungle. Even in functioning democracies, lack of legal regualtion can produce regrettable situations, as in Australia where R. Murdoch owns 60% of the daily press, or in Britain where over half the national daily press belongs to foreign groups.

The law, national or international, is the only quick efficient protection against the power of corporate giants. This is a truth too often ignored in the United States, where "freedom" usually means freedom from political restraint and rarely freedom from economic restraint. Fortunately, in the 21st century globalization can sometimes restore balance: the European Commission "provides a needed counterweight to the American tradition of keeping government out of the marketplace—a practice that has let the market go too far at times."[17] At the turn of this century, it was the European Union that intervened to protect privacy on the Internet on both sides of the Atlantic and to regulate the mergers of some multinational communication companies.

Democratic Law creates an environment, determines basic duties, and sets up independent supervisory institutions in the interest of the general public. To the extent that media, being companies, cannot have a moral conscience, laws are required to force them into fulfilling their community obligations. The law will endorse international agreements, and set national rules for the business of running media, the same for all. And it can limit concentration of ownership. More specifically, it will deter a newspaper from committing libel or a TV network from interfering with a trial. It can impose obligations with respect to children (like no ads aimed at kids in Sweden). Only the law can keep in check unscrupulous rags like the London daily tabloids and prohibit pedophile magazines or nazi hate sheets.

In the United States as in most democracies, citizens favor legal limits to the activities of media: "substantial majorities would like to restrict press freedom to protect military secrets, stamp out terrorism and cut down stories

---

[17]S-G. Richter in the *New York Times* (A 31), 21 September 2000.

dripping with sex and violence."[18] There are human rights to be protected other than press freedom. Besides, media managers themselves request a level playing field, which they should be given, if only to avoid that the worse pull down the better, as happened in the British popular press in the 1970s.[19]

The law does much to insure the respect of individual rights, those of journalists and those of citizens. Take the European Convention on Human Rights. It has exerted great influence on former soviet colonies that want to become members of the European Union at a time when they equipped themselves with democratic institutions. Even a country like Britain finally had to integrate the Convention within its constitutional documents (in 1998), thus officially giving her citizens the Bill of Rights they did not have. Article 10 (on freedom of expression) will now protect journalists against British courts.

With the full power of the state to enforce the rules, to carry out court decisions and the requests of regulatory agencies, the law also grants rights to the media and professionals, like the Freedom of Information Act in the United States or the "conscience clause" in France (which makes it possible for a journalist to leave a publication if it changes its nature or political orientation, and yet not lose any benefits). And then there is the extraordinary press law of Sweden, incorporated in the constitution, whose provisions include: no censorship even in time of war; the appointment by each publication of an official scapegoat, usually the editor (thus shielding all journalists from the justice system); the illegality of asking a journalist about his/her sources; open governmental archives; and special jury treatment[20] in case of a trial.

Unfortunately, the legal system also has drawbacks. It tends to favor the interests of a ruling elite, or just the government (in the wide U.S. sense), or only the central executive.[21] Laws are passed by politicians and interpreted by magistrates—and few are the nations where the judiciary is fully independent. Letting the so-called State rule the media has proved atrocious in the 20th century both in fascist and communist regimes. Indirectly, it has caused millions of deaths and massive destruction.

Even in democracies, the Law can be dangerous. At the beginning of the 21st century, the press in Britain, in spite of its reputation worldwide, was one of the least free in Europe. That was the effect of the Official Secrets Act,

---

[18]According to an 8-country survey by the Times-Mirror Center (*Los Angeles Times*, 16 March 1994).

[19]When, after buying the *Sun*, R. Murdoch turned it into a shameless rag, thus increasing its circulation by several million copies, and forced the other tabloids to follow suit.

[20]Trial by jury does not normally exist in the Scandinavian judicial system.

[21]Although they sometimes cover the same ground, ethics has nothing to do with the law, contrary to what some politicians seem to think and many lawyers, too, who believe that they can and should help solve all problems.

the Rules of contempt of court, the Libel laws, the Police and Criminal Evidence Act, plus a series of laws on terrorism, trespassing, copyright etc. Many of them were enacted to satisfy the middle-classes disgusted by the popular press.

Generally speaking, the law does not find it easy to adapt to continuous change. The law is slow, expensive, and so complicated that it scares off the common human being. For wealthy rogues, on the contrary, it can, in some countries, turn into a gold mine, allowing them to pocket thousands, even millions of dollars from libel suits—or to muzzle their opponents, as in the famous thalidomide case[22] in Britain.

In France, as in other Latin nations, many people (including media people) believe that the law, upheld by the police and the courts, will ensure quality media. So they rely on the very detailed 1881 General Law on the Press, which actually is not often enforced because it is largely out-of-date. But it is a constant threat, together with various other laws that affect social communication. Politicians both wish to restrain the press and are afraid of offending it—and so they dare not revise, liberalize and energize the 1881 instrument.

The laws do not seem to have much effect on the quality of French dailies, which are (with a few exceptions in Paris) quite mediocre (see p. 345) compared to newspapers in sister countries Spain and Italy. And they have not had much effect on the confidence the public has in media. As regards broadcasting, the French have had a succession of laws, which all turned out to be unsatisfactory except for the one in 1982 that put an end to state monopoly on radio and television and started deregulating the industry. Besides, because the law is supposed to take care of all problems, almost no major "media accountability systems" ever developed in the country.

In the United States, although the country is supposed to be a paradise for lawyers, one finds extreme hostility to the law: the media hate it as the great enemy of freedom. They wish broadcasting (largely deregulated in the 1980s) were made as free as the print media. They claim that the only law they need is the First Amendment (1791) to the Constitution. It says "Congress shall make no law abridging the freedom of speech or of the press," and the absolutists claim that "no law means no law," Taken literally, it is extremely limited in that it mentions only Congress, not the Executive and Judiciary at federal level, nor any of the three political powers at the State or municipal level. Beginning in the 1920s a body of interpretation has grown around the amendment, and some would like it to mean that none of the three branches of government at any of the three levels should interfere with any operation of the media.

---

[22]Distillers Co. had sold a drug that caused babies to be born without limbs. For over 10 years, it refused to pay decent damages to 450 families. In 1972, the *Sunday Times* took the serious risk of exposing the case, still sub judice. The courts blocked the series but the first installment was enough to cause a public outcry and eventually make Distillers pay up.

The Market

The law alone, or simply too much of it—that is, an excess of State intervention, can lead to authoritarian rule. That is why Americans trust the market.
Undoubtedly, a free market can have a positive influence on the media; it was
striking in France to witness the improvement in broadcast news after the state
monopoly was lifted, when government censorship and direct manipulation
ended, when new largely unregulated voices were heard.

Market rivalry keeps media people on their toes. Competition boosts
creativity; that was clear in the late 1950s in Britain when BBC television was
suddenly rejuvenated by ITV, its commercial competitor. Although it is true
that commercial media produce a lot of garbage, Soviet-style media produce little but garbage. Generally speaking, the market goads media into reacting fast
both to new technology and to the changing tastes and needs of the public.
Media that are unable to obtain an audience have to fold, which happened to the
French television network La Cinq in the 1980s and also to the daily *Info-
Matin*, in spite of very wealthy shareholders.

Lastly, what is often ignored by left-wingers is that media moguls are
not all megalomaniacal crooks like Robert Maxwell. The people who made the
New York Times, *El Pais*, or *The Economist* into superb newspapers were businessmen fighting in a competitive environment. Even Axel Springer, vituperat-
ed in Germany because of his trashy reactionary *Bild Zeitung*, had created a
quality daily, *Die Welt*.

The drawbacks of the market, however, are great too, as can be seen
from the somber description that opened this chapter. Europeans have never
trusted free enterprise to deliver good media. Up to the 1980s, every country in
Europe had imposed a state monopoly on broadcasting (with the exception of
Spain, which authorized private radio before World War II, and Britain, which
in 1954 allowed commercial television). Nowadays, all European countries (and
Japan) have a large "public" broadcasting sector, financed entirely or largely by
an annual tax. Moreover, France and Italy shield the daily press from competition by subsidizing small opinion papers. So do the Scandinavian countries,
except Denmark—to avoid the local monopolies that the market would bring
about, as happened in Denmark.

In any country, private operators pilot their media in their company's best
interest, which may or may not agree with that of the general public. They are
inclined to yield to the pressure of advertisers, of politicians, of the elite, of the puri-
tan, of the politically correct. Their natural aim is not to provide public service, but
to make money, if possible quick money. So they save on expenses; for instance,
the print media omit to invest in information and rely on press releases and news
services rather than hire more reporters and establish new bureaus. Experience
clearly shows that dailies that are not profit-oriented, like the *Frankfurter
Allgemeine Zeitung* or the British *Guardian*, benefit the public far more than rival

dailies run by big corporations, such as *The Times* and *Die Welt*. As far as news is concerned, the U.S. commercial television networks, even in their heyday of the 1960s, could not compare with the BBC or the Japanese NHK.

And operators strive to increase revenues. Commercial electronic media especially are inclined to turn into prostitutes; they pander to the lowest tastes, with infotainment and brutal and/or dumb entertainment. They ignore ethical rules to please advertisers or politicians, or the elite, or any sufficiently militant group. On the right and the left, observers denounce the vast amounts of rubbish produced by many of the commercial media and also their policy of manipulating public opinion by omission, distortion, and lies. Because of competition, even public television networks feel the need to program the same low-brow material as the private nets. Quality media become more expensive and thus restricted to well-off people.

Probably, the United States best illustrates what is wrong with the market. Many Americans believe that the free market, plus a dose of ethics, will ensure good service. Foreign visitors have doubts about it on discovering that most dailies consist for the main part in a blend of municipal bulletin board, press releases, 60% to 70% advertising, and cheap stuffing bought from syndicates. They may also have doubts when they watch U.S. network television, which does almost nothing for the education of children, which piles silly games over reality shows over soap operas over bizarre talk shows and brutal series—with commercial interruptions every 9 or 10 minutes, adding up to 17 minutes per hour in prime time (1999). In the words of a U.S. columnist: "with honorable exceptions, American newspapers, magazines and television are today mainly concerned with stories and gossip about stars, including athletes and public figures, with backstage film and television reports and with promotional material on films and television programs."[24]

Foreign observers were amazed in the 1980s by the discretion of U.S. media regarding the Savings and Loans scandal, said to have cost the federal government an estimated 500 billion dollars, about $6,000 per household. And they were amazed in the 1990s by the central importance the U.S. media gave to two murders attributed to the former football star O.J. Simpson, while ignoring hundreds of thousands of people then being slaughtered in Rwanda.

To wield the law or yield to the market? Legislation counters abuse by merchants. Free enterprise counters abuse by the state. But many failings of journalists (like incompetence, arrogance, bias, cowardice, mendacity) or of the media (like parochialism, infotainment, self-censorship, masked advertising) cannot be cured by the law and the courts.[25] As for the market, it causes many of the faults and cannot cure the others. There is a need for a third force.

---

[24]William Pfaff in the *International Herald Tribune*, 18 December 1997.

[25]They can even be encouraged by them: see the Chiquita suit against the *Cincinnati Enquirer* (1998), which caused other media not to echo the well-documented case against the company.

Of the many groups involved in social communication, in my opinion only two are entitled to control quality in journalism: news processors and news consumers, journalists and public. Obviously, neither commerce nor a governmental agency can produce quality media. They can only come from experts addressing and mobilizing communities of citizens.

MEDIA ETHICS AND ACCOUNTABILITY SYSTEMS

For some years now, new ideas have been slowly making their way: what if press freedom was put in the service of the citizens to whom it belongs (a fact that news people tend to ignore)? What if democratic quality control was used? What if professionals and consumers took over social communication?

Everywhere, and in the United States maybe more than elsewhere, media ethics is highly appreciated by (nearly)[26] all. Most media people appreciate it, especially since the 1960s. They love the rhetoric about freedom, truth, the right to information, public service. It gives the media a good image in the eyes of the public—and does not cost anything. It is a panacea systematically used to fend off the menace of restrictive laws and regulations. When the media commit some outrage and public hostility reaches a disturbing degree, then a profusion of workshops, seminars, conferences, articles, books, radio and television programs debate ethical issues. After a few months, the debate usually winds down and vanishes. At best, one concrete step has been taken: a list of rules was drafted. In all countries in the world now, you find at least one code of press ethics.

Nevertheless, at the turn of the millennium, the environment seemed unfavorable to ethics. People, including journalists, are obsessed with rights and not much interested in duties. Media are obsessed with profits and not much interested in service. It should not come as a surprise that ethics is highly praised only so long as it remains on the level of talk. The tune changes, the climate of unanimity dissolves, when rhetoric gives way to action, when practical means are considered to enforce the rules devised by consensus, when the focus turns to "media accountability systems" or M*A*S. What are they? They are any nongovernmental means used to insure that media provide good public service and they deserve a chapter of their own.

---

[26]"Journalism and Ethics: Can They Co-exist?" is the title of the first chapter, by Andrew Belsey, in Matthew Kieran's *Media Ethics*, 1998.

CHAPTER 2
The Arsenal
of the M*A*S

M*A*S? Any means of improving media services to the public that function independently from the government. M*A*S are expected to achieve their purpose by increasing the competence of journalists; by discovering (through observation and analysis) what media do and don't do, as compared to what they should do. And, mainly, M*A*S enable media to hear the consumers' views, what they like, dislike, might like. And they enable media to discover, correct, explain their errors and mistakes, and apologize for them. M*A*S are a mix of quality control, customer service, continuing education—and much more, certainly not just self-regulation. To the citizens, M*A*S give back human rights that a media caste is inclined to confiscate.

The concept embraces close to 60 of those means. All of them have been used, somewhere at some time—from correction box to in-house critic, from viewers' association to university fellowship. We can expect quite a few other M*A*S to be invented in the future. The originality of the concept resides in that very diversity of the means available to pursue a one and only goal. It is unusual to assemble such different instruments, probably because it is unusual for attention to be focused on the welfare of the public.

The wealth of the armory can be appreciated better if its weapons are diversely distributed into categories. The first, most obvious, classification is into three groups by the nature of the M*A*S : (1) documents, printed or broadcast; (2) people, individuals or groups; and (3) processes, long or short.

A Text or a Broadcast Program

- A written code of ethics, a set of rules that media professionals have discussed and/or agreed upon—preferably with input by the public, and which is made known to the public.
- An internal memo that reminds the staff of ethical principles (perhaps even the "tradition" of the paper)[1] and provides it with guidelines as to behavior in particular circumstances.
- A correction box, published, in a visible spot or time taken to correct an error on the air.
- A regular "Letters to the Editor" column/program, including messages critical of the newspaper/ magazine/ station.
- Other means of public access, such as an on-line message board or a forum for immediate feedback.
- An accuracy-and-fairness questionnaire, mailed to persons mentioned in the news or published for any reader to fill out.
- A public statement about media by some eminent decision-maker, abundantly quoted in the news.[2]
- A space or time slot purchased by an individual, a group, or a company to publish an "open letter" about some media issue.[3]
- An occasional "Letter from the editor" or a sidebar, explaining some editorial decision.
- A newsletter to readers, inserted or mailed, to keep them informed of what goes on at the newspaper or station.
- A regular media column, page, section in a newspaper, newsmagazine, trade review—or a program on radio or television, that does more than just mention new appointments and ownership changes.
- A web site systematically posting corrections of media errors[4]—or the grievances of working journalists.[5]
- An alternative periodical or station, which publishes facts and gives viewpoints that regular media ignore, including criticism of said media.

---

[1]To its Standards & Ethics code, the *Washington Post* appends Eugene Meyer's (its former owner) 1933 "Principles."

[2]A huge ballyhoo greeted VP Spiro Agnew's two 1969 speeches against "liberal" media.

[3]Like the one against toxic popular culture published in newspapers all over the United States by 56 eminent Americans in July 1999.

[4]Like www.slipup.com in the United States.

[5]Like, the News Mait site maintained in the United States by Maurice Tamman for 3 years until 1999.

- A journalism review, on paper or the air or the Web, devoted principally to media criticism, exposing what media have distorted or omitted, and whatever other sins reporters or media companies have committed.
- "Darts and Laurels," a page of short stories in criticism or praise of some media action, such as most journalism reviews have.
- An article, report, book, film, or TV series about media, informative about media and, to some extent at least, critical.
- A petition signed by hundreds or thousands to put pressure on media directly or via advertisers or via some regulatory agency.

> ### Individuals or Groups

- An in-house critic, or a contents evaluation commission (like the *shinsa-shitsu* set up by Japanese dailies in the 1920s) to scrutinize the newspaper or monitor the station for breaches of the code—without making their findings public.
- An ethics committee or a staff review group (a rotating panel of journalists) set up to discuss and/or decide ethical issues, preferably before they occur.
- An ethics coach operating in the newsroom occasionally to raise the reporters' ethical awareness, to encourage debate, and advise on specific problems.
- A media reporter assigned to keep watch on the media industry and give the public full, unprejudiced reports.
- A whistle-blower who dares to denounce some abuse within the media company.
- A consumer reporter to warn readers/viewers against misleading advertising and to intervene on their behalf (such as the "Action Line" teams common in the 1970s).
- An ombudsman, paid by a newspaper or station, to listen to complaints from customers, investigate, obtain redress if need be, and (usually) report on his activities.
- A complaints bureau or customer service unit to listen to grievances and requests (such as that of the BBC in Britain).
- A disciplinary committee set up by a union or other professional association to assure that its code be respected—under pain of expulsion.
- A liaison committee set up jointly by media and a social group with which they may occasionally clash (for example, the police or some ethnic minority).
- A citizen appointed to the editorial board, or several invited to attend the daily news meeting.

- A panel of readers/listeners/viewers regularly consulted.[6]
- A club to which a medium (most often a magazine) attracts readers/listeners[7]/viewers with gifts of various kinds, then leads them into a dialogue about its services.
- A local press council, that is, regular meetings of some professionals from the local media and representative members of the community.
- A national (or regional) press council set up by the professional associations of media owners and of journalists, which normally includes representatives of the public, to speak up for press freedom and to field complaints from media users.
- A watchdog agency set up by a media-related industry (such as advertising) to filter contents—and ask that some not be made public, for ethical reasons.
- A militant association dedicated to media reform (such as FAIR in the United States) or to helping persons with grievances against media (such as PressWise in Britain).
- A media-related institution, national (such as AEJMC[8]) or international, that has a direct or indirect interest in promoting media quality (such as the International Press Institute or the World Association of Newspapers) through conferences, seminars, publications and so forth.
- An NGO that trains personnel and provides free services to media in emerging democracies (Eastern Europe) and under-developed nations.
- A citizen group (such as a labor union, a parents' association) that, for partisan and/or public interest reasons (for example, the welfare of children), monitors the media.
- A consumers' association, especially one of media users,[9] using awareness sessions, monitoring, opinion polls, evaluations, lobbying, mail campaigns, even boycotts to obtain better service.
- A representative group of journalists in the newsroom, endowed with some rights, as allowed by law in Germany or required in Portugal.
- A *société de rédacteurs,* an association of all newsroom staff, that demands a voice in editorial policy and preferably owns shares in the company so as to make itself heard. The first was at the French daily *Le Monde* in 1951.

---

[6]In Mexico, the four newspapers of the Reforma group listen to the daily opinion of panels of up to 150 readers.

[7]Radio clubs have long been an institution in rural parts of Niger where they help broadcasters serve the audience better and help listeners use the material broadcast.

[8]Association of Educators in Journalism and Mass Communication.

[9]Such as People For Better TV, a U.S. broad-based national coalition.

- A *société de lecteurs*, an association of readers that buys, or is given, shares in the capital of a media company and demands to have a say, as is the case at *Le Monde* (of which it owns about 11%).

Reluctantly, I also place in this category three types of institutions that some experts would rather leave out of the M*A*S concept altogether. To the extent that they do not take orders from government, to the extent that their purpose is to improve media service to the public, it does not seem possible to leave them out completely. They might be called para-M*A*S.

- The regulatory agency, set up by law—again, provided it is truly independent—especially if it takes complaints from media users: like the Italian *Ordine dei giornalisti* (Order of Journalists) or the French *Conseil supérieur de l'audiovisuel* (the equivalent of the FCC in the United States).
- The non-commercial broadcasting company (such NHK in Japan or ARD in Germany) whose sole purpose is to serve the public and which, by its mere existence, constitutes implicit criticism of commercial media.
- The international broadcasting company, public or private, using short wave radio or satellites, that makes it difficult for national media to hide or distort the news, such as the BBC World Service or CNN.

Processes

- Higher education, a crucial M*A*S. Quality media should only hire people with a university degree, preferably (though this is controversial) one in mass communications.
- A separate course on media ethics required for all students in journalism.
- Further education for working journalists: one-day workshops, one-week seminars, six-month or one-year fellowships at universities. Such programs, quite common in the United States (such as the Knight fellowships at Stanford), are very rare elsewhere.
- A "media at school" program to train children from an early age in the understanding and proper use of media.
- A media[1] literacy campaign to educate and mobilize the public.
- An in-house awareness program to increase the attention paid by media workers to the needs of citizens, especially women and cultural, ethnic, sexual, or other minorities.

- The regular encounter of news people with ordinary citizens in a press club, on the occasion of town meetings, or even on a cruise![10]
- A listening session: once a week or irregularly, editors man the phones to answer calls from readers, as is done at some Brazilian papers.
- An internal study of some issue involving the public (such as a newspaper's relations with its customers).
- An ethics audit: external experts come and evaluate the ethical awareness, guidelines, conduct within the newspaper or station.
- A regular opinion survey, commissioned by the media, to get feedback from the person-in-the-street; also a questionnaire on a newspaper or station website.
- A nation-wide survey of public attitudes towards all or some media (for example, towards public broadcasting).
- Non-commercial research, done mainly by academics in the universities, but also in think tanks or scientific observatories,[11] studies of the contents of media (or the absence of them);[12] or of the perception of media messages by the public, or of the impact of those messages.
- An annual conference bringing together media decision-makers, political leaders and representatives of citizens' groups of all kinds.[13]
- International cooperation to promote media quality and accountability, such as the European Alliance of Press Councils or the Ibero-American Federation of Ombudsmen.
- A prize, and other tokens of satisfaction, to reward quality media and quality journalists—or an anti-prize.[14]

Internal, External and Cooperative

Another classification of M*A*S depends on who is involved: some M*A*S function inside the newspaper or broadcast station exclusively; some exist outside of it and escape its control; others require that media and non-media people work together. Those boxes, however, are not air-tight: they allow variants of one M*A*S to slip from one into either of the other two.

The internal M*A*S constitute self-regulation proper, quality control in the narrow sense. External M*A*S prove that accountability can be applied

---

[10]The Belgian daily *La Libre Belgique* has organized such cruises.

[11]Such as the European Institute for the Media in Düsseldorf (Germany).

[12]Such as Project Censored. See p. 239.

[13]Such as the "Université de la communication" in late August, in Carcans-Maubuisson, later in Hourtin, SW France.

[14]Such as the Silver Sewer Award bestowed by Empower America, a conservative media watchdog.

to the media without their acceptance; their aim is not reparation to aggrieved individuals but benefit to the public as a whole. Cooperative M*A*S are certainly the most interesting, because they imply that press, professionals and public can join together for quality control.

Internal M*A*S

Media page/program	Ethics coach
Letter from the editor, sidebar	Internal memo
Newsletter to customers	Awareness program
Correction box	Code of ethics
Media reporter	Whistle-blower
Consumer reporter	Ethics committee
In-house critic	Disciplinary committee
Evaluation commission	Newsroom committee
Filtering agency	Company of journalists
Internal study of issues	[Public broadcasting]
Readership survey	[International broadcasting]
Ethics audit	

External M*A*S

Alternative media	Non-profit research
Journalism review	Opinion survey on media
"Darts and laurels"	Media literacy campaign
Critical book/report/film	Media-at-school program
Media-related website	Consumer group
Petition to pressure media	Association of militant citizens
Public statement by VIP	Media-serving NGO
Higher education	
Required ethics course	[Independent regulatory agency]

Co-operative M*A*S

Letters to the editor	Club of readers/viewers
On-line message board	Local press council
Ombudsman	Annual conference
Complaints bureau	National press council

Listening session by editors	Liaison committee
Accuracy and fairness	Media-related association
questionnaire	International cooperation
Paid advertisement	Training NGO
Encounter with public	Continuous education
Panel of media users	Prize or other reward
Citizen on board	

Other Classifications

Several other classifications are possible. One is according to the method used by a given M*A*S: criticism (such as a book-form pamphlet), monitoring (such as a research laboratory), feedback (such as a complaints bureau) or training (such as a week-long seminar). Many M*A*S, however, use a combination of approaches: an ombudsman, for instance, listens, monitors, criticizes, and coaches.

M*A*S can also be distinguished according to the level at which they operate: national, regional, or local. Many M*A*S are capable of functioning at all three levels: most can function at local level as required when the media system is largely local, as in the United States. But they can also work at a fourth level, the international one: scientific observatories can cover all the nations on a continent;[15] international codes exist (see p. 126); critical books get translated into diverse languages;[16] the conferences of world-wide media-linked associations take place all over the planet (ICA, IAMCR, IIC,[17] etc.).

Another distinction depends on the effect produced by the M*A*S. Some cause an immediate impact, such a correction box or a letter to the editor. Some act on a short-term basis, such as a code of ethics or a liaison committee. And others exert only a long-term influence, such as departments of journalism on campus or research centers.

M*A*S also differ quite a lot in their costs. Few can be profitable, such as a newspaper page sold to a group wishing to express a (usually negative) opinion on media. Some M*A*S are inexpensive, such as a code of ethics or a citizen on the board: any medium can afford them. Some can be quite costly, such as an interactive website or an ethics audit. And some can require great expense, such as a full-time ombudsman or regular in-depth readership surveys.

Lastly, M*A*S differ clearly in their present-day presence on the media scene. Some have become so common, so much part of the environment, as almost to escape attention—such as a correction box, a critical book, or a journalism school. Some are not unusual, such as a media reporter, a public statement about media by some VIP, or a media-at-school program. And then

[15]Such as the European Audiovisual Observatory in Strasbourg.

[16]My little book on ethics has been translated into five languages.

[17]International Communication Association, International Association for Media and Communication Research, International Institute of Communications.

some are exceptional such as an accuracy-and-fairness questionnaire, a local press council, or an ethics audit.

M*A*S are still relatively rare. Indeed, the rarity of some is amazing. In 2000, quite a few democracies, big or small, still did not have a press council (among them Brazil and Japan, France and Ireland), very few had journalism reviews, not many had ombudsmen: there is not a single one in Germany. How many local press councils are there in England or Sweden? Is there much continuing education for journalists in Spain or Britain? Where, outside the United States, do big media companies finance media research and education? Reasons abound to explain the scarcity.

THE VICES OF M*A*S: REAL OR IMPUTED

M*A*S face many obstacles and much resistance, mainly the indifference or hostility of media proprietors and of journalists. Here are the major criticisms made of them.

PR Ploys.   When commercial media do consider establishing some major M*A*S, such as a press council or an ombudsman, it is not normally with the idea of serving the public better, but rather to dispel the memory of some scandal, to avoid court actions, or to dissuade a Parliament from voting restrictive regulation. When media managers approve of a M*A*S, it means they intend to include it in their PR strategy.

So on the left, social-democrats look upon M*A*S merely as a cosmetic trick to avoid regulation: media pretend to care about the public, but their passion remains maximum profit and/or propaganda. Marxists and militants in the cultural-critical movement tend to regard ordinary human beings as puppets manipulated by corporate media. Ethics and M*A*S are part of the manipulation or, at least, can do nothing against it.

Similarly, fascists and communists dismiss ethics and M*A*S as despicable inventions of naive democrats. They do not believe in press freedom: for the good of "the nation" or "the people," they advocate control of the media by police censorship or through state ownership.

If such opinions were justified, if M*A*S were nothing but PR gimmicks, then it is amazing that there are so few of them, especially as the public has greeted them favorably wherever they have been tried.

Threats to Freedom.   On the ultra-liberal side, which considers all media laws and regulations superfluous, ethics and M*A*S are presented as a bolshevik plot against freedom of speech and free enterprise.[18] Libertarians

---

[18]See J. C. Merrill, *The Imperative of Freedom: A Philosophy of Journalistic Autonomy* (New York, Hastings House, 1974). In former soviet colonies, there is indeed much distrust of "social responsibility," which reminds people of the rhetoric of communist censors.

judge that a journalist has a right to be irresponsible: he/she should only be guided by his/her conscience. If a medium does not serve the public well, they say, the market will get rid of it. These opponents seem generally blind to the constant economic interference with media freedom.

Also right of center, there are people who fear that governments could take over the M*A*S, turn them by law into regulatory agencies,[19] and even use them to muzzle the press.[20] They might, for instance, turn a press council into a Star Chamber. These opponents are encouraged in their hostility by a regrettable tendency, especially in Europe, even among advocates of media ethics, to mix the concepts of regulation (by state agencies) and of self-regulation.[21]

Illegitimate. The law of the land is established by an elected parliament. Any other rule carries the suspicion of illegitimacy. Owners tend to look upon a M*A*S as a violation of their property rights. Besides, M*A*S tend to increase the autonomy of reporters, who might turn from docile employees to active servants of the public—a little like physicians and lawyers.

Claiming it was a question of principle, the *New York Times* refused to have anything to do with the National News Council (1973-1984) and thus hamstrung it. Three reasons were given by the chairman of the *Presserat,* the German press council, for not admitting lay members: (1) the public is ignorant of media matters; (2) it is impossible to find candidates who are not the agents of a cause or some special interest; (3) a press council partakes of self-control, regulation by media people, only.[22]

The belief is common that the public is not to poke its snout into media business: if it is not pleased with what it is given, let it stop consuming or sue. That belief is becoming dangerous both for the profession and for society, but quite a few journalists also seem attached to it.

Most journalists deep down disapprove of accountability and M*A*S. They judge common citizens as incompetent to evaluate media products and production and consider university experts to be out of touch with reality. Both media owners and journalists feel endowed with the special grace of running the Fourth Estate and cannot see any reason to share that privilege.

The profession closes ranks against external critics who cannot be anything but ignorant, vindictive, partisan, deranged. The first French code of ethics adopted in 1918 by the national union of journalists (SNJ) stresses that a journalist "recognizes only the jurisdiction of his peers, which is sovereign in

---

[19]Denmark actually did so with its press council but without opposition from the media.

[20]This occurred in India where the council was set up by Parliament. More than half the complaints it gets come from journalists and are aimed at elected officials and civil servants.

[21]See books by K. Nordenstreng (1995) and G. von Dewall (1997). Bibliography p. 409.

[22]At the 30 September 2000 conference of the Alliance of Independent European Press Councils in Bonn.

matters of professional honor." An echo is provided by the 1954 (rev. 1986) code of the International Federation of Journalists (see p. 126) "the journalist shall recognize in professional matters the jurisdiction of colleagues only, to the exclusion of every kind of interference by governments or others."

Such clannishness is not surprising, but journalism seems to be the only profession not to have set up effective means of self-discipline. Violators of the code are rarely cited before a disciplinary commission set up by a union or a professional association; their transgression is disclosed neither to management or to the public. Even the criticism of peers is not tolerated;[23] who are they to judge? The appointment of an ombudsman is usually opposed by the newsroom. Experience shows that, in general, journalists oppose M*A*S more than management.

New and Untested.   In no profession is change or novelty appreciated, especially when it puts at risk the power or the prestige of people. But in journalism, it goes further than that: it goes against an old tradition. So for journalism to reform itself, a strong pressure must be exerted, even threats. Quite often, only the fear of a state legislative intervention can shock media proprietors and professionals into pre-empting the move by self-regulation.

The media people's reaction is partly knee-jerk antagonism. Actually, they are ignorant of most M*A*S and at best indifferent to them because they have never given them much thought. This obstacle could easily be swept aside. Within and without the media world, everyone has heard about ethics on the occasion of some scandal, but most people have never heard about the many quality control systems that have been invented, tested, and proved to be both efficient and harmless.

The media themselves are to blame for that ignorance; they have made no effort to find out about the M*A*S and they have refused to publicize their activities. For instance, the *St Louis Post-Dispatch*, in spite of its liberal reputation, never mentioned the *St Louis Journalism Review* for about 20 years. Up to recently, most media even refused to discuss ethics. Now when they do mention M*A*S, it is to dismiss them as evil.

Useless.   For many, M*A*S are useless. Politicians and lawyers, of course, consider that nothing can give results except the law. M*A*S may function as a disinfectant on a scratch but cannot cure the deep ills of the media, meaning control by Big Business. Undeniably, the British PC did not cure Britain from having probably the vilest popular daily press in Europe. Employing an ombudsman did not save the *Washington Post* from the Janet Cooke scandal.[24] The United States probably has the best journalism education

---

[23]A good example was provided by Serge Halimi's *Les nouveaux chiens de garde* (Paris, Liber, 1997), which became a best-seller in spite of the bitter silence of the media.

[24]The *Washington Post* reporter who had to give back her Pulitzer prize (1981) when it was revealed that she had invented her report on a 8-year-old heroin addict in a ghetto.

system in the world, yet that did not prevent its news media from wasting more than a year on O.J. Simpson and then another on Monica Lewinsky.

The old saw is that "good" media do not need quality control and "bad" media will not accept it unless forced to. [The same British popular press that slowly destroyed the Press Council then accepted the Press Complaints Commission, only because it became afraid that Parliament was about to set up a statutory council.]

British tbloids

Unworkable. M*A*S are often dismissed as worthless: they don't work, they can't work. Here are a few quotes on codes from recent books: "No code can anticipate every situation" . . . "codes do not agree even on basic principles" . . . "Journalists never agree on ethical issues" . . . "what does it mean to be ethical?" . . . "the difficulty is in defining journalistic misbehavior" . . . "codes are not worth the paper they are written on."

Enforcing the rules without recourse to the law demands that all groups involved apply themselves to it whole heartedly. But none of the three groups is willing and able, especially not media users. The public is heterogeneous, unorganized, apathetic, and feels powerless. It does not have the time, the knowledge, the motivation to get involved in media improvement.

Power is in the hands of media owners—and they wish to keep it. They believe the law is quite enough for them and they pressure legislators to be given as little law as possible. Their natural policy is to make as much money as possible. Most judge that if their acts are to be evaluated, the verdict of sales and ratings or of the courts is quite enough. They do not feel they are accountable and have no time to waste.

media owners— as little law as pos QUOTE

In affluent democracies, journalists cannot afford to antagonize their employers for ethical reasons. To thrive (or merely stay) in the profession, they must do favors and yield to entreaties—unless they are well-protected by law, well-organized, or well-supported by the public, which is not often the case. Unless you are an expert or a celebrity, hence precious to your employer, you must obey orders. In poor democracies such as India or Russia, ethics is something most journalists cannot even consider. Their central concern is to keep their job, to make survival money, by fair means or foul. Direct corruption or a second job can hardly be refused.

The top 100 or 200 well-known journalists who, in every country, work close to the centers of power, believe they stand above ethical concerns. They exploit their position for the money and for the influence, claiming that a professional's conscience is quite sufficient to guide him/her. Alas, they constitute a model for the rank and file.

Anyway, the real world is so complex, situations are so diverse, that general rules cannot be any use or special rules cannot provide for every possible case. News people don't always agree among themselves about what should be done. A code is inevitably too short and vague, whereas the mass of a press council's judgments, after a few years, is too vast. The reporter in a hurry cannot go and look through a book of rules when he/she has to make a decision.

Expensive. ⌈Many M*A*S (though not all) are expensive, if they are to do their job well—that is, quickly and visibly. An ombudsman, for instance, must be a highly respected veteran, hence very well-paid. A press council absolutely needs funds to deal with complaints fast, contrary to law courts, and to exert all its other functions[25]—and to publicize all its activities.⌉

Journalists do not have money to spare. It is considered preferable not to ask anything of the state.[26] Outside the United States, there are few philanthropic foundations. So it seems almost impossible to do without financing by owners who are reluctant to pay. Some simply do not have the money.[27] It is all very well to forbid junkets but what if the newspaper cannot cover the reporters' trips? Recommending better coverage is all very well, but it translates into heftier payrolls.

As for owners who could afford them, they rightly suspect M*A*S of hindering the easy accumulation of profit. In their eyes, the law is quite enough, and it rarely forces any media to serve the public. It is not much of an impediment, because one can most often avoid being taken to court.

Actually, M*A*S are a good investment, not only by improving quality, which always pays, but also by improving image: all big (non-media) companies spend fortunes to improve their image in the eyes of the public, the government, and the courts. Business, some years back, discovered the appeal and profitability of ethics, yet many media prefer to invest in equipment or to increase dividends.

Time-Consuming. The worst, because the most real, of the obstacles comes in a triple shape. On the one hand, quality control consumes time, which is always in short supply in the media world. Can one imagine a reporter having to answer all the email messages he/she receives? Besides, serving the public well is not a reporter's only purpose in life: quite naturally, he/she seeks excitement, influence, fame, promotion, money. As for the media owner, he/she has much else to do than set up means of accountability: primarily, he/she must keep the company alive and make it prosper.

On the other hand, M*A*S function on a long-term basis: probably the best method to improve journalism is through education, which bears fruit only after many years. And most M*A*S require that professionals and public get used to them, which also takes a long while.

---

[25]The late British Press Council took 8 to 12 months to adjudicate a complaint.

[26]Although the German and Finnish councils are subsidized.

[27]U.S. media have an advantage over those in many parts of the planet: they can afford ethics. It might decrease their profit margin, but that is far above what is considered decent in the rest of the world.

Ill-Targeted.   The drawbacks just mentioned add up to little, in my opinion, compared to what can be considered as the deep flaw of ethics: it can, and often does, divert attention away from those forces that truly determine what media do and don't do. In any firm, the main decisions are made by the managers not by the underlings, and taken for economic, not moral, reasons. In other words, the important responsibilities are not in the hands of journalists.

Journalists do commonly commit many sins, some very visible, from sexism to invasion of privacy, from inaccuracy to plagiarism. But can those sins be compared in terms of social damage to the wrongdoing by media companies, such as not giving reporters the means to do their job fully or ethically, or ignoring information that might offend advertisers, or publishing material that will please them? Are journalists responsible if in the United States more than two-thirds of a daily are devoted to advertising and only some 2% to foreign news? Are they responsible for the silence of the media on the lethal effects of tobacco from the 1930s to the 1960s—the probable cause of thousands of deaths? Are they responsible for the media's systematic hostility towards labor unions and strikes—and overwhelming endorsement of conservative candidates in presidential elections?

The difference between the faults of journalists and the faults of the media is the difference between venial and mortal sins. Yet, traditionally, the ethical focus is on journalists, if only because a corporation has no moral conscience. The result is to turn them into scapegoats.

THE VIRTUES OF M*A*S

Now the case for the defense. What most people do not know, mainly because the media seldom mention it, so that in country after country, when a M*A*S is introduced, the same debate takes place with the same objections, which have repeatedly proved unjustified. In my view, M*A*S possess qualities that make all criticisms and obstacles negligible and should, ultimately, get them all accepted everywhere.

To appreciate those qualities, one must clear one's mind of some common biases. One is cynicism, common among journalists: only the naive, credulous, idealists can believe that human beings might obey their better instincts, might serve the public interest without being forced to. Another is absolutism: either you opt for regulation or for ethics; either the media are good or they are bad; either the M*A*S prove efficient or they do not. Another bias I would call "intellectualist"; it consists of quibbling about the true meaning of "public interest," or "quality journalism," or "freedom," or "accountability" and so forth. It also causes the submersion of the practical issue (finding ways to improve the service of the media) in philosophical debate on universal values and human nature. In the eyes of someone who has been observing them for about 30 years, and who tends to be empirical and pragmatic, the M*A*S have great qualities.

Harmless.   M*A*S present no danger for anybody; except maybe some decrease in the power of owners who must let journalists have a say or a limited invasion of the journalists' professional sphere as they must let the public have a say. There is probably also some risk for both of seeing their failings publicly exposed and their egos suffer.

Democratic.   M*A*S are certainly so. Many of them involve both professionals and citizens, quite a few gather the three major groups of actors in social communication. M*A*S are voluntary: with few exceptions, mainly in the Third World, the government or the State bureaucracy are never directly involved. At most, the state pays part of the budget.

Diverse, Flexible, and Cooperative.   M*A*S can easily adapt to circumstances. Compare, for instance a code of ethics and a piece of legislation: how easy it is to amend the former and how difficult it is to get rid of an outdated law. The extremely diverse M*A*S are complementary. Although every one is useful, none is sufficient—but they can all operate together. The ideal would be if they all existed and if they were associated into a vast, loose, network dedicated to quality control, thus reinforcing each other. Conflict between them is unlikely: their immediate objects and methods are different, they function at different levels, in different areas, in different time-frames.

Efficient.   Another essential advantage of M*A*S is that they can operate where other means cannot, especially when the obstacle to quality is the journalistic tradition, as shackling as political censorship or economic manipulation but rarely mentioned.[29] Iceberg journalism which supplies a mosaic of isolated events, a superficial, very incomplete, largely fabricated, negative report on the world mixed with an unacceptable dose of entertainment which is no longer acceptable.
  Against those flaws, the law and the market cannot do much. And they neither can do much against many of the sins of newspeople. Ethics and M*A*S can cause journalists to become aware of their failings and of media flaws, to start thinking and discussing what quality journalism should be. After rules have been written down and endorsed by news people, the resulting code gives each of them the power of the whole caste to resist the unethical demands of employers and sources—and to resist their own temptations. Accountability through M*A*S provides them with public support to defend their autonomy.

Inexpensive, Profitable, and Prestigious.   Many M*A*S are within reach of most media and some are affordable by all media. And what's a correction and an apology compared to a libel suit ? Not that they should be looked

---

[29]For a more developed presentation, see my "The Media in 2045," in *Public Relations Review*, Winter 1995, reprinted in *The Impact of Mass Media*, R.E. Hiebert (ed.), New York, Longman, 1999.

upon merely as cheap means of getting rid of complaining customers, as some publishers do. More importantly, M*A*S increase the credibility, the attractiveness of a medium, and hence the loyalty of its customers—and so increase sales and advertising income. Quality control pays.

Quality also pays in terms of prestige and influence, even when the profits remain low. In the 1930s in England, the very serious and responsible (Manchester) *Guardian* sold fewer than 50,000 copies and enjoyed great influence. The popular dailies which were pushing their circulation up to over 2 million by all means (from fabricated sensations to free insurance), lost all political weight.

Quite a few critics of M*A*S[30] seem to have started from the premise that they were cure-alls, and so were disappointed by their actual achievements. That they cannot cure all does not mean they are inefficient. As they have slowly proved over many years, they are not a simple, quick, and global solution to all media problems, but they could provide immense improvement if they were better supported, better financed—or simply better known.

Mainly, M*A*S are mighty yet gentle weapons to be wielded together with high journalistic competence (the two being intimately linked anyway) to insure both that a better public service is provided by media and that journalists thus recover public confidence and support.

QuoTE

---

[30]See, for example, David Pritchard (ed.), *Holding the Media Accountable*, Bloomington, Indiana UP, 2000.

PART II
Principles and Rules

CHAPTER 3
Right to Communicate in the Internet Age

Jim Richstad

The inspiration for a right to communicate for everyone was born in the fertile and imaginative mind of Jean d'Arcy in the late 1960s and has been emerging as a global human rights concept since—without clear success. The concept, as developed by Unesco and others in debates and papers in the 1970s, envisioned an overarching right to communicate for everyone as a basic human right.

The new right was seen as encompassing the freedoms and rights of expression over the centuries, and adding such aspects as a right to participate, a right to communication privacy and the need for cultural sensitivity in communication. Another element added was a right to the communication resources needed to use a right to communicate, and the means of access to the information needed for such a right.

Under d'Arcy's vision, earlier established rights of expression were seen as restricted by the outmoded, one-way mass media technology and communication culture of the 20th century. And it was time to recognize the possibilities of a truly global right to communicate for everyone. He said the mass media communication systems limited the rights of people to really communicate with each other and that the technology of the Information Age makes much more possible a revolutionary right to communicate.

D'Arcy saw the possibilities of broader communication means through the era of the direct broadcast satellites and related developments. The opportunities were there, however unclearly, for a new way to structure communication, with a focus on people's participation rather than professional communicators. One early example was the emergence of the Citizen's Band radio, which

many thought could open people-to-people communication in a way not possible under the mass media system. But, as events showed, the CB development
soon found a narrow communication niche, providing some important services
and exchanges but far from what was seen as a right to communicate.

D'Arcy saw the potential of the new technology and of the right to
communicate for demystifying and for deprofessionalizing the news media and
for letting people take a larger, more active role, and thus be better able to raise
ethical questions and to demand media accountability. The excitement generated by d'Arcy's initiative on the right to communicate filtered through Unesco
meetings and papers and into other forums. It was picked up by many as a possible way to break a decades-long cold war lock on information rights—as well
as to help the emerging New World Information and Communication Order.
Deeper than the cold war positions, of course, were the centuries of restrictive
cultural and political controls on communication that were in place.

This chapter takes a first look at how the right to communicate, as
envisioned and developed, could be enhanced by the burgeoning capacities of
the Internet. Conversely, some of the uses of the Internet can be seen as contrary to such concepts as the right of privacy and cultural sensitivity.

DEVELOPMENT OF THE RIGHT TO COMMUNICATE

The conceptual origins of the right to communicate go back to the beginning of
communication and through centuries of struggles by humans to communicate
with other humans. Although free expression is an individual human right, it is
also (as Sommerlad and others in the right to communicate debates have
argued) a right of human communities. Communication rights developed into
specialized areas such as freedom of the press in mass communication. As populations grew and communities became less closed, simple face-to-face communication rights proved inadequate, and rights of mediated communication were
fought over since the invention of moveable type and printing press in the
1400s. That area is still evolving as the new communication technologies
emerge, one after the other, and combine and merge as they grow.

The development of the mass media created powerful voices, especially for those who governed the media, either directly or through financial or
political controls. And with the rush to globalization in the 1990s, with larger
and larger media organizations, the voice of the individual finds it almost
impossible to be heard, to make a difference. D'Arcy credits his inspiration
from reading what Bertolt Brecht wrote in the "Theory of Radio," published in
1932: Radio must be changed from a means of distribution to a means of communication. Radio would be the most wonderful means of communication
imaginable in public life, a huge linked system—or it would be such if it were
capable not only of receiving but of transmitting, not only of letting the listener
hear but speak; if it did not isolate him but brought him into contact with others.

D'Arcy noted that Brecht's vision saw "the need for man to communicate, the need to use the right technology, and the disrupting effects of one-way transmission." D'Arcy, a former program director of French television (1952-1959), at the time president of the International Institute of Communication (IIC), was well-versed in audio-visual communication. He wondered why the pioneers in the development of radio communication saw radio as a distribution system rather than as a communication system. One of his answers was that maybe "this need of communication for man was not clear enough to become a goal in itself at a time when it was still orally fulfilled at the community level in closed and still homogeneous societies."[1] D'Arcy first proposed "the right of man to communicate" in a 1969 article in the *EBU Review*.[2] He later called it "an as yet inchoate concept, a concept of the future, still in the making."[3] He saw it as pulling together many individual rights to information and communication and putting them in a modern context under "the right to communicate" in the rapidly developing world of communication technology.

The new technologies made possible the "blending of emerging technologies with the age-old traditions of two-way, interactive, participatory communication."[4] D'Arcy's call for a right to communicate was concurrent in 1971 with the report *Instant World* in Canada[5] for which more than 40 studies had been undertaken: "there were extended discussions on how to deal with the 'right to communicate.'" The 1971 Canadian communication statement examined what were then the parameters of the right to communicate: freedom of knowledge and freedom of speech are among the most valued privileges of a democratic society. The rights to hear and be heard, to inform and to be informed, may be together regarded as the essential components of a right to communicate. The report added that such communication should be available to all Canadians, regardless of where they lived in that vast country, and that telecommunication services should be available "on a non-discriminatory basis and at a reasonable price."

The concept was the theme for the 1973 meeting of the International Broadcast Institute in Nicosia, with d'Arcy giving the keynote address. In summer 1974, E. Lloyd Sommerlad took leave from Unesco to be a Senior Fellow at the East-West Communication Institute in Honolulu, and he worked closely

---

[1]From D'Arcy's Foreword to *Evolving Perspectives on the Right to Communicate*. L.S. Harms and J. Richstad (eds.), Honolulu, University Press of Hawaii, 1971. (Many early articles on right to communicate)

[2]"Direct Satellite Broadcasting and the Right to Communicate," *EBU Review,* 118 (1969), pp. 14-18.

[3]"The Right to Communicate," International Commission for the Study of Communication Problems, document 36, Paris, Unesco, 1980.

[4]L.S. Harms, Jim Richstad, and Kathleen A. Kie (eds.), *Right to Communicate: Collected Papers*. Honolulu, University of Hawaii, 1977.

[5]Canadian Telecommunications Commission, *Instant World*, Ottawa, Information Canada, 1971.

with Harms, Richstad, and Kie to develop a draft resolution on the right to communicate. The draft embodied the key elements of the right, and eventually made its way as one of the documents Sweden used to formalize its resolution at the Unesco in 1974, and again in 1976, when it passed. The right then emerged as a global topic, and was taken up by many other organizations.[6]

As the debates and papers and publications continued, wider views were brought in from around the world, and inevitable differences emerged as to what the right meant and how it could be applied. It soon became clear that although there might be a universal right to communicate, how it was applied in different cultures depended on different priorities. How could such a right be applied universally, when there are so many cultural, social, and political differences in the world? Another liberal, idealistic concept going nowhere? Maybe not. Developing a new human right, a universal human right to communicate, was never viewed as the work of a year or even a decade but, as Harms noted early on, it could take decades, or perhaps a lifetime or more of work.

The conditions for a new right were clear and strict. The right to communicate should be developed, d'Arcy and the pioneers said, with processes and structures that provided

1. Participatory communication
2. Interactive communication
3. Horizontal communication
4. Multi-way communication

Other key elements in a right to communicate developed in the first decade included the need to have a balanced system of communication where free flow of communication means free flow for everyone, and a culturally sensitive system. Canadian contributions added a "right to be informed, the right to inform, the right to privacy, the right to participate in public communication . . ." (*Instant World*). And, as Sommerlad said, "The 'right to communicate' presupposes the availability of and access to resources, and this in turn depends on policy decisions and planning and organization of a communication system—on the international no less than the national level. . . ."[7]

The publication of *Many Voices, One World*, in 1980, gave further global recognition to the right to communicate, and many saw it as a hope for improved communication for individuals, groups (and especially news media organizations), and nations. The report said communication "is a matter of human rights" and "is increasingly interpreted as the right to communicate,

---

[6]"Towards a Definition of the Right to Communicate: An Expert Meeting," Unesco, Stockholm, 8 to 12 May 1978.

[7]"Free Flow of Information, Balance, and the Right to Communicate", in *New Perspectives in International Communication*, Jim Richstad (ed.), Honolulu, East-West Center, 1978 (2nd printing).

going beyond the right to receive communication or to be given information."
Communication was seen as a two-way process involving partners (senders and
receivers) carrying on a "democratic and balanced dialogue" (p. 172). The
MacBride Commission said: "Extension of [. . .] communication freedoms to a
broader individual and collective right to communicate is an evolving principle
in the democratization process," and charged the media with a "defense of all
human rights . . ." (p. 265).[8]

It said that the right to communicate had not then received its final
form or its full content. Time was needed to explore potential applications and
determine what "intrinsic value such a concept possesses." An early definition
of the right to communication, developed by Harms, was cited "to show the
variety of its elements and vision of its intentions. Everybody has the right to
communicate: the components of this comprehensive Human Right include but
are not limited to the following specific communication rights: (a) a right to
assemble, a right to discuss, a right to participate and related association rights;
(b) a right to inquire, a right to be informed, a right to inform, and related information rights; and (c) a right to culture, a right to choose, a right to privacy, and
related development rights. [. . .] The achievement of a right to communicate
would require that communication resources be available for the satisfaction of
human communication needs" (p. 173).

Renewed attention to communication rights and the role of the media
in promoting democratic communication was sparked by the end of the cold
war and the great political changes that swept across Eastern Europe and the
former Soviet Union, and was apparent wherever the democratization process
was active. In Asia, the economic breakdowns starting in mid-1997 brought further demands for transparency in information and economic organizations and
governments. Concurrent with all this were the constant advances in communication technology and the bursting of the Internet age around the world. The
opportunities for communication and the right to communicate appear daily in
reports of the world's newspapers as new and expansive ways of communicating are developed. And, towards the end of the 20th century, there did not seem
to be a way to seriously restrict global communication.

In the 1980s, the right to communicate found its way into constitutions
and other documents but, despite what Fisher and Harms had forecast in their
1982 book,[9] it had not really emerged. Unesco, battered over its "free flow" and
NWICO activities, devised a "New Communication Strategy" for reaching its

---

[8]International Commission for the Study of Communication Problems, *Many Voices,
One World*. Paris, Unesco, 1980. The report for Unesco of the so-called MacBride
Commission (after its president Sean McBride), part of a compromise between blocs, the
West desiring "free flow" and the Soviet bloc/Third World demanding a "New World
Information and Communication Order" (NWICO).

[9]Desmond Fisher and L.S. Harms (eds.), *The Right to Communicate: A New Human
Right*, Dublin, Boole Press, 1982.

goals of "the free flow of information at international as well as national level, and its wider and better balanced dissemination without any obstacle to freedom of expression" in 1989.

This new strategy left aside the broader issues in communication rights and a new communication order, so as to focus on more specific areas such as "media development and democracy, women's access to decision-making and expression in the media, public service broadcasting, violence on the screen, promotion of media independence and pluralism, new communication technologies, conflict prevention and post-conflict peace-building." Unesco wished to "emphasize the need for a diversity of solutions to the problems of communication, promoting press freedom and the independence, pluralism and diversity of the media, in response to the needs and values of each people and society."

A much broader effort was undertaken by an ad hoc group in their proposed People's Communication Charter. The charter states that the "rights of communication professionals need to be secured, but that also the information and communication rights of the public need to be protected," and that the group is "determined to take new steps towards securing a basic human right to communicate for all people." The draft charter goes on to list such communication rights as "freedom of expression of opinions, information, and ideas, without interference by public or private parties . . . to receive opinions, information and ideas . . . to gather information . . . to distribute information . . . to reply . . . to a diversity of languages . . . to protect their cultural identity . . . to knowledge . . . to participate in public decision making . . . to acquire needed skills to participate fully in public communication."[10]

Privacy was to be protected, and wide transparency of information was proposed. Other provisions concern biased reporting, coverage of criminal cases, consumer information, and more detailed concerns. Article 20 addresses the right to communicate directly: "People's fundamental right to communicate under international human rights law can only be restricted if limitations are prescribed by international law and are necessary in democratic societies."[11]

INTERNET AND THE RIGHT TO COMMUNICATE

The Internet, developed at about the same time as the right to communicate, is a dazzling display of ingenuity, bringing possibilities of interactive communication on a scale that was not foreseen at the start of the right to communicate movement. The potential for such a right is clearly emerging, and also opportunities for the abuse of communication rights. With free and open communication among people, the wind blows from all directions through the open windows, as Gandhi under-

---

[10]*People's Communication Charter* (4th draft). Dated 23 October 1994.

[11]The fourth draft of the charter, coordinated by Cees J. Hamelink. See www.pccharter.net

stood well. There are few windbreaks in the Internet. The open windows bring in the smell of roses as well as the stink of human sewage, and sometimes the annoying and disease-carrying bugs, as a Singapore leader noted.

Demands for, and outlines of, controls on the content and structure of the Internet are multiplying around the world. From the United States and elsewhere comes the countermove, a demand of no or very limited restrictions: let the communication flow freely across borders, across classes. The structure of the Internet itself makes control difficult without closing down the whole system. Kleinwachter calls cyberspace an invitation for "millions of individual to come and to communicate, a new dimension of the human right to free expression has occurred in the history of international communication."[12] The past 40 years of technology development have greatly reduced the restrictions of time, capacity, cost, and distance in communication. Yet in magnitude the Internet goes far beyond all previous increases in communication power. Although, as Kleinwachter notes, the Internet is not the first new system to challenge political and legal controls on communication, "it represents the most radical change." The "decentralized Internet," he says, "is to a certain degree the most organized chaos in the history of humankind," and is largely "unmanageable and uncontrollable." "It is a new dimension, a new culture, a new way of communication. For the first time in history, everybody gets (theoretically at least) the opportunity 'to seek, receive and impart information and ideas of all kinds regardless of frontiers', to use the language of the Article 19 of the Universal Declaration of Human Rights."

The Internet is not, of course, unmanageable and uncontrollable. Some controls are already in place and others surely will follow. The Internet will grow around the world; that seems inevitable. And many governments will continue to control news and information within their countries and internationally. Some see that those efforts will in the end fail—and others, such as Leonard Sussman of Freedom House, see attempts to control the Internet as simply a continuation of centuries-old censorship and control of communication with many of the same arguments: to protect citizens from pornography, from blasphemy, from national security breaches, from becoming confused by unauthorized information. Sussman, an advocate for world press freedom, noted that Russia forced servers to install surveillance equipment, and other countries permit only government servers and have policies to bar a range of materials. Yet, he said, "The Internet [. . .] is the most formidable challenge to the censor."[13]

An open Internet is also threatened by private interests, both regulatory and corporate, according to McChesney, Bagdikian, and Zittrain. Bagdikian notes the continuing trend to concentration of media ownership and control in

---

[12]Wolfgang Kleinwachter, "Is There a Need for the Right to Communicate in Cyberspace?" *Javnost (The Public)* 2:1, 1995, pp. 107-113.

[13]"The Internet and Press Freedom 2000," introduction to the Freedom House Report, 3 May 2000, at www.freedomhouse.org.

the United States and sees it spreading to the Internet services.[14] In 2000, he wrote, "the country's most widespread news, commentary, and daily entertainment are controlled by six firms that are among the world's largest corporations, two of them foreign." Bagdikian praised the emergence of new sources of news and information but said it had been "overblown" as advertising and other corporate communication "on the Internet seem to grow exponentially. . . ." McChesney, reinforcing Herbert Schiller's earlier work, sees danger of growing control of communication by giant corporations.[15] Another dynamic is the growing development of "private rule making and enforcement," as opposed to government regulation, in the United States.[16]

Governments around the world are facing the task of regulating the Internet, with mixed results. China, for example, in early October 2000, published regulations for the Internet that, "if enforced, could markedly slow development of the industry here," Craig S. Smith of the *New York Times* wrote from Beijing. Under the new licensing rules, Internet companies would be held responsible for the content, and there could be no foreign investment. Government rules on content, already in place, were repeated. A wide range of content would have to be vetted by various government departments before it can go on the Internet.[17] In Japan, the political content and criticisms on the Internet present problems for a government not used to such open political comment. Singapore, too, is seeking ways to integrate the Internet while retaining controls on some kinds of materials. Government controls will be a continuing reality for open use of the Internet.

Other concerns restrict open communication for everyone: they include access to computers and servers, the cost involved in equipment and service, and knowledge of how the Internet can be used. The dominance of English is another factor in global access to the wealth of information and potential links. New concerns are rampant, such as the authenticity of information, privacy, cultural sensitivity; some sinister like child pornography, hate speech, and criminal use of the system. All of these will have to be dealt with.

A special concern for everyone is how to manage the immense amount of information available through the Internet. Scarcity of information can create a dependency on who controls information, which was a major issue in the NWICO debates. That problem seems to be deconstructing into a series of different problems, including too much information. The overabundance of information provided by the Internet can create a dependency on whoever knows

[14]Ben H. Bagdikian, *The Media Monopoly*, 6th ed, Boston, Beacon Press, 2000.

[15]Robert McChesney, *Corporate Media and the Threat to Democracy.* New York, Seven Stories Press, 1997.

[16]Jonathan Zittrain, "Balancing Control and Anarchy on the Internet," *Chronicle of Higher Education,* 13 October 2000, p. B20.

[17]Craig Smith, "Tough New Rules Don't Faze Chinese Internet Start-Ups," *New York Times*, October 4, 2000, p. C2. Also: Kavita Menon, "Controlling the Internet: Censorship Online in China," *Quill,* September 2000.

how best to find and manage the flow. For journalists, this new abundance, the wide range of access to the Web, and the difficulties of authenticating information is creating a whole new environment.

Ethical issues of authenticity in the new Internet context were dramatically raised during the Clinton-Lewinsky controversy in early 1998. Whereas the first publication on the Internet was by Matt Drudge, a single person running his own Drudge Report site, the mainstream media apparently felt compelled to jump in with reports that were not verified as the story grew, breaking their own rules on news-checking and the use of anonymous sources. A New York Times Service report by Janny Scott traced how the story developed from Drudge's report on the Internet, and said reporters and editors were trying to authenticate rumors that "seemed to catapult into truths by simply bouncing back and forth from one medium to another."[18]

There is some major rethinking among American media people concerning how to handle the flow of Internet items that come from non-traditional sources. This occurs at a time when Americans are increasingly seeking news from Internet sources. One study showed a readership increase from 6% to 20% in two years, although much of the news-seeking was supplementary to traditional news media.[19]

The Internet fits clearly in the right to communicate's emphasis on media accountability. The concept of communication as a participatory process is reflected in the interactivity: "everyone" connected to the Internet can participate in communication in a wide variety of ways—from fully active to a passive seeker and viewer of information on the Web. Participation is not required, but it is there in the system for everyone. The system can link thousands of people, or a few people, in virtual real-time face-to-face exchanges. Horizontal and multi-way communication are of the essence of the Internet. The decentralized flow can be one to many (centralized sender to many receivers), as in mass media communication, but more likely is the whole array of communication patterns—many to one, many to many, one to one, one to a few, and so on—and vice versa.

Culturally sensitive systems are being developed within cultural groups, on the one hand, and insensitive systems are being developed (sometimes intentionally so), on the other hand. For example, the Internet is very open for members of cultural groups to cyber-meet and strengthen their cultural ties. "Forgotten languages," in another example, can be kept alive through the Internet, thus keeping a culture alive. The negative aspects are clear; for example, when hate groups of any kind, whatever they are called, use the Internet to support and unite supporters.

---

[18]*International Herald Tribune*, 2 February 1998.

[19]Ted Bridis, Associated Press, "More Americans Getting Their News on Internet," *Seattle Times*, June 8, 1998.

Individual privacy is a basic principle of the right to communicate, but with the Internet there seems to be an almost complete loss of privacy. In May 1998, the Vice President of the United States called for "an electronic bill of rights" to protect privacy. Continuing efforts are expected. The direction, however, seems to be heavily toward a loss of privacy. Many of the same concerns the NWICO debates raised in the 1970s about the world news system remain highly relevant. The concerns then were that the world "haves" controlled the news systems as they now control the Internet. The "have nots" can argue, as they did in the 1970s, that the Internet and other communication developments simply promote communication imperialism through domination by the United States and other Western countries, and through the use of English as the primary Internet language.

All these concerns are real. As the Web continues unfolding, however, with new use after new use appearing almost daily, these concerns should be lessening rapidly. As Rupert Murdoch is fond of saying, "Anybody can do it." Obviously, not everybody can do it now, but the direction seems clear. A May 1998 article in the *International Herald Tribune*, for example, described how Jim Lowenthal was establishing Internet nodes through local phone calls in the fringes of the global communication system in Africa. He has already established nodes in Madagascar, Mozambique, and Guinea, as well as in that cliche for remoteness, Timbuktu in Mali. "If you don't factor the Web into your analysis of Africa, you're going to miss something. We're just two years away from large numbers of people in Africa being able to tell their own story . . . ", Lowenthal said. This in a continent that is at the bottom of world communication development. Although Africa may be slow at gaining more access to the Internet, an *Article 19* report titled "The Right to Communicate: The Internet in Africa" said that journalists and human rights groups and others had been quick to utilize Internet connections, and government authorities were trying to maintain control of the medium.[20]

Another example is from the Pacific Islands. From the late 1960s on, there was a renewed effort by the island countries and territories to learn more about each other (most are separated by hundreds and thousands of miles of ocean) by exchanging news from their media. Exchanging newspapers or clippings was tried and then faxes were sent to a central location, and reworked into news bulletins and sent back out. PEACESAT, an audio satellite system, was used for both news and other kinds of exchanges such as health and agriculture. New Zealand and Australia were at times collection points for other news exchange systems. The telephone was used. Radio services were able to get bulletins from around the Pacific and the newspapers could transcribe them for print. Yet all this proved difficult, given the resources in island journalism.

---

[20]For details, see *IFEX report*, March 16, 1999 or e-mail <article10@gn.apc.org>. See also Paul A.V. Ansah, "The Right to Communicate: Implications for Development," *Media Development* 1/1992, pp. 53-56; and Cecil Blake, "Traditional African Values and the Right to Communicate," *Africa Media Review* 7:3, 1993, pp. 1-17.

Then came the Internet. As the Pacific joined the Web, the exchange of news became, or could become, an almost automatic function, built into the newspapers' computer system. A simple code could send designated stories to designated newspapers, or they could all be gathered and re-netted from another point. Instead of one or two short items, virtually the entire content of relevant Pacific news could be sent to other Island newspaper and broadcasting, as well as outside the Pacific. And the Pacific Islands News Association (PINA) was able to alert its members and others to press dangers in the region, as in the case of forwarding an International Freedom of Expression Exchange Alert on Samoa on 22 May 1998. And in early 2000, the Pacific Islands News Association and others used the Internet to report almost daily the attempted coup in Fiji and the concurrent armed disorders in the Solomons.[21]

On a grander, global scale, the same use of computer capacity is giving editors more choices, a wider selection of news. The Reuters chief in Singapore, for example, a few years ago described how the Asia wire worked, to a class of journalism students. There is so much capacity with the computer systems, he said, that Reuters didn't have to pick and choose what went on the Asia wire from the global wires. It could just dump the whole thing into the Asia wire, giving editors a wider selection.

The increase in sources of news through the Internet have in large measure turned control over information from the producer and processor of the information to the user of information. The news media are now held accountable to the public for their reports by a public that can itself access a variety of sources (media and non-media) on the same news event, from around the world. There are, for example, about 500 on-line services by American daily newspapers, numerous ones in Asia and other parts of the world.[22] The problem for the public as well as the news media is determining the authenticity of the many sources now available.

Examples of the Internet as a guide to readers in U.S. newspapers are plentiful. A journalist may put his or her e-mail address at the end of the story, for example, if readers want to ask for more information, or give additional information or insight, greatly expanding the resources of the reporter. Reporters also cite Web sources where readers can go for more information, or later information on a story. Letter-writers can include their own e-mail address for other readers to comment or challenge their views. Or the writer can include Web sources to back arguments or simply to provide more information.

Numerous other uses of the Internet for innovative communication are described in a 30 April 1996 report in *USA Today* by Joe Urschel. He describes how students from all over the United States used e-mail on the Internet to organize a campaign against PepsiCo for continuing to operate in Burma, a country

---

[21]E-mail PINA for more information at <pina@is.com.fj>

[22]See for example, Brian S. Brooks. *Journalism in the Information Age*, Boston, Allyn & Bacon, 1997.

ruled by military dictators. "The e-mails were burning up the Internet [. . .] as a modern-day student rebellion celebrated its accomplishments not with bullhorns and fist-pumping, but with the furious clatter of fingers on the keyboard." In describing how the younger generation is seizing the potential of the Internet, Andrew Brownstein cites the example of 12-year-old Craig Kielburger using the Internet to mobilize volunteers and to establish the 100,000-member Free the Children after reading a news account about a Pakistani boy his age sold into bondage and murdered.[23]

Another developing use came when reporters for a FOX network television station, apparently unable to get their story on questionable practices in milk production on the air, took to the Net to make their suppressed story and all the legal documents of a court suit against FOX available to concerned editors, reporters, and others.[24] D'Arcy spoke for the deprofessionalization and demystification of the mass media, and this can be seen in example after example of people getting on the Net to spread the word, often beating the news media when they cover it. Examples came out of the besieged radio station in Bosnia during the turmoil there in the late 1990s; the anti-Chinese attacks during the Indonesian upheaval in early 1998; and early reports on working conditions in manufacturing plants in Asia for an American shoe and sporting goods company. The early reports of the situations came through the Internet and alerted the news media as well as the world. The opening of chat lines with officials lets people ask direct questions, and the *Washington Post* set an example by having their foreign correspondents come on the Internet to respond to people's inquiries, whatever they are. And these openings are just the beginning of a new, often difficult journalism, with much more involvement of people.

Jack Shafer, deputy editor of the on-line magazine *Slate,* noted that pursuit of the Clinton-Lewinsky story "shattered the ethical barrier" but said the new media were being over-blamed. Technology is neutral, he said, and the Internet is no more to blame for journalistic mistakes than the telephone. Shafer reminds his readers that journalism is still about being first, beating the competition. The example "shows that anybody who has an Internet connection and something original to say can reach a global audience." And Shafer shows the need for a variety of sources with fresh information and opinions that haven't had the life pecked out of them "by editors and lawyers who identify with the bow-tie-and-braces brigade that runs the Government and corporate America." And why, he asks, did the great mainline American and foreign press in Washington not produce the story before Drudge put it on the Internet? Similar "outbreaks of news" around the world can validate the right to communicate.[25]

---

[23]"The Next Generation," *Chronicle for Higher Education,* October 13, 2000.

[24]"Reporters File Suit to Thwart Fox-TV Coverup," at www.foxbghsuit.com/home.htm

[25]Jack Shafer, "The Web Made Me Do It," *New York Times Magazine,* February 15, 1998.

This seems a propitious time to join in the debate on the running of the Internet, and to shape it to the extent possible in the ideals of the right to communicate.

WHITHER THE RIGHT TO COMMUNICATE?

There are different ways of achieving a right to communicate, as there are of developing a new world communication order. The new communication technology might, this time, do what d'Arcy hoped the direct broadcast satellite would do—open up communication and communication rights for everyone.

Many of the early advocates of the new right felt that it had to be clearly defined, that its relationship had to be shown to earlier rights, to communication issues at local, national, and international levels, as well as individuals, groups, and national entities communicating with other countries. Other saw it as enshrined in laws, codified at all levels, and in constitutions and other controlling instruments. Yet others saw it more as a moral and ethical construct, something that was right, something that would be fair for all people and communities.

Another possible way is to take an inventory of the elements of the right to communicate and compare their achievement country by country, region by region. The much simpler Unesco standard of so many newspapers sold per 100 people, so many television receivers, so many radios and so on, proved an arbitrary but effective standard for achieving communication-resource comparability among nations, and is still in use today. It is much more revealing and perhaps more useful concerning the state of world communication than annual surveys of how "free" the press is in various countries.

A global survey on the right to communicate attributes for the 21st century would, very likely, show that some of the key elements of the right to communicate are in fact in place and thriving in some countries and in some international and subnational areas.

In a world of diversities, a neat and tidy right to communicate is unlikely ever to achieve full and universal implementation. There are encouraging signs. It is not an all-or-nothing game. The concept's lack of strict formalization can be a plus in the age of indeterminacy, and although it was born during the cold war, it owes most of its appeal to principles developed over centuries and to the continuing surges in communication technologies. The advance toward economic transparency and wider political participation have an essential symbiotic relationship with the right to communicate.

The draft People's Communication Charter provides a comprehensive starting point to assess the progress of the right to communicate. A key idea in much of the discussion is that the world's cultural, political, and social diversities must be taken into account. There are likely to be many exceptions in a universal right to communicate, at least at the operational level. This is entirely appropriate; the ideal is that everyone has the right to be heard, to participate in communication, to help formulate a right to communicate. The ideal, of course, is that only "good" people would use the right to communicate, but, as on the Internet, lawlessness is the dark side of communication rights.

Although it is easy to get excited about the potential and actual use of the Internet in opening up the right to communicate around the world, it is not a magic wand. The speed of the Internet, its immense reach and accessibility, stir up many of the traditional ethical concerns in communication and journalism, and it will take time to reform into a global ethic. The standards of the right to communicate provide an important guide for the media and the whole of communication.

CHAPTER 4
Social Responsibility, Corporate Morality, and Codes of Ethics

Clifford C. Christians

After two years of debate, the Commission on Freedom of the Press published its report, *A Free and Responsible Press*, in March 1947. Henry B. Luce of Time, Inc., financed the study with a $200,000 contribution. Robert Maynard Hutchins, president of the University of Chicago, served as chair. He assembled 13 of America's leaders for 17 meetings to hear 225 interviews and 58 testimonies and to study 176 documents. What we call the social responsibility theory of the press emerged from this potent mixture,

The Hutchins Report insisted on the media's duty to serve *society*, rather than the interests of business or government. Believing that the press was over-committed to its own "individual rights," the Commission stood both terms on their head by advocating the "social responsibility" of the press. The complications of a post-war world, in the Commission's view, demanded more "truthful, comprehensive, and intelligent" reporting than was generally available from a press co-opted by the demands of profit. Insisting on independence from government intrusion was insufficient by itself.

Positive freedom is social responsibility's most enduring theoretical concept. However, this axis of a socially responsible press was not articulated adequately in terms of corporate structures. The Hutchins Commission worried about the media becoming big business enterprises and warned against the dangers of monopoly ownership so obvious more than half a century later. But in social responsibility's central theorist, William Hocking, positive freedom is integrated with inter-subjectivity rather than with institutional structures. Therefore, what remains on our intellectual agenda is demonstrating why *corpo-*

49

rate entities ought to be socially responsible and not simply a corporation's individual decision-makers. This argument in turn entails a viable notion of corporate morality. Once the concept of corporate morality is established, we have an appropriate framework for understanding how codes of ethics operate as an internal mechanism for keeping an organization socially responsible.

HOCKING AND POSITIVE FREEDOM

William Earnest Hocking had recently retired as chair of Harvard's Philosophy Department when he began serving on the Hutchins Commission.[1] Within his astonishing variety and quantity of scholarly materials, three books have emerged as classics in the philosophical literature: *The Meaning of God in Human Experience, Human Nature and its Remaking,* and *Freedom of the Press: A Framework of Principle* (published in 1947 as a background document for the Hutchins Commission's deliberations).

The organizing concept in *Freedom of the Press* is positive liberty. Hocking developed in this volume a definition of freedom distinctive from classical liberal theory in which a negative conception of liberty equates freedom with the absence of arbitrary restraint. In the political theory underlying classical liberalism, individuals possess an inner citadel that is inviolate, and therefore they must be left alone to pursue those ends each considers right or sacred. To contravene these natural rights, from this perspective, is to violate the self's autonomy.

In Hocking's view, negative freedom was bankrupt. As he argued in a 1935 symposium on "The Future of Liberalism" called by the American Philosophical Association, for all its importance historically in political matters, deficiencies in this wholesale commitment to autonomy had become obvious to him on both conceptual and empirical levels. He recognized that John Stuart Mill's argument for freedom from coercion, for example, provided a significant constraint against undue government encroachment. But Hocking was concerned that a theory of free expression anchored in individual rights does not resolve or even advance certain fundamental disagreements that have arisen in Western democratic history. For instance, to what extent should defenders of free expression appeal to long-term benefits as the paramount consideration?

Against an intellectually and historically disabled negative freedom, Hocking contended that the state bears responsibility for fostering social justice. He argued for a pro-active state that would develop the moral character of its citizens by creating a social environment in which those who wish to live justly

---

[1]For a detailed account of Hocking's biography with particular reference to his work on the Hutchins Commission, cf. P. Mark Fackler, "The Hutchins Commission and the Crisis in Democratic Theory, 1930-1947," PhD dissertation, University of Illinois-Urbana, 1981, ch. 7.

can act on their principles. Part of that service, in Hocking's view, was enabling public discourse, a function classical liberals left to the private sphere. Instead of the unrestrained liberty of the weed, as Hocking put it, he preferred the constrained liberty of the garden that "builds a strong, organic, and fertile culture." Hocking concluded in *The Lasting Elements of Individualism*:

> In every point, men must be free; and in every point they must be subject to a sobering objective judgment which checks that freedom. The new state must do two things where the Liberal state attempted but one. It must restrict liberty for the sake of liberty. [. . .] Liberty is a positive thing and demands tools to work with and food to grow on, a mental capital of working beliefs to begin life with. Minds cannot grow in a vacuum.[2]

Out of this more complicated view of freedom—and consequent belief in an active state to promote the conditions of liberty—the Hutchins Commission argued for the opposite of classical liberalism's negative freedom and limited state. Through Hocking, the Hutchins Commission contended in its report that a philosophically different view of freedom was needed for an economically powerful press to prosper in the post-war era. Hocking had insisted, to the agreement of the commissioners as a whole, that liberty cannot be distinguished from the conditions of its existence. In his role as the Commission's principal philosopher, Hocking contended that freedom of expression should no longer be considered an inalienable natural right but an earned moral right. Hocking's *Framework of Principle* is a carefully reasoned argument that freedom—given our status as social beings—is not unconditional, but involves the necessity to assume and perform duties toward others. Although errors are inevitable, what cancers the ground of freedom

> . . . is deliberate or irresponsible doing-wrong adopted as an individual policy. Here the good will of the claimant, which is his good faith with society, is purposely put aside; the resulting errors are not the tolerable errors incident to a process of learning.[3]

True to his ongoing integration of universals with experience, Hocking understood positive freedom as conditional. He recognized it as a defining feature of our humanness, but he faced squarely our tendency to serve ourselves rather than use our freedom for the common good. In fact, Hocking concluded that if one takes seriously the history of ideas and culture, freedom's limited scope has never been seriously contradicted. He reminds us that even Mill accepted restraints, such as forcibly preventing someone from crossing a collapsing bridge if no time is left for a warning. Thus he warned political theorists in the tradition of Locke, Mill,

---

[2]William E. Hocking, *The Lasting Elements of Individualism*, New Haven, CT, Yale University Press, 1937.

[3]Ibid., p. 66

Constant, and Tocqueville not to misrepresent the positive conception as a spe-
cious disguise for tyranny. Admittedly positive freedom can be seen as encouraging government interference, though *Freedom of the Press: A Framework of
Principle* itself never condones political intervention. And the Hutchins Report,
which reflects its argumentation, views the government only as a "residual legatee"
of last resort in case of gross negligence by the press.

Hocking grounds positive freedom ontologically. He provides a philosophical basis on which to rest both freedom and responsibility. Rather than
patchwork and synthesis, Hocking demonstrates that a social theory of liberty is
required that fundamentally reconceptualizes the issues and conclusions. Rather
than a doctrine of individual autonomy, Hocking substitutes communitarian inter-
subjectivity. By emphasizing positive freedom, he seeks to replace the protectionism of autonomy. But he does not defend his alternative as merely salutary at this
historical moment; he develops a theoretical rationale for positive freedom.
Consistent with his philosophical orientation throughout, he contradicts the
assumptions that no metaphysical truth exists and that no "ought" can be derived
from "being." He aimed to demonstrate that irrespective of our belief in divinity,
position on justice, naturalistic fervor, or political power, we are bound to the cat-
egorical imperative of using our freedom responsibly. One's only escape is the
absurd notion that our starting point is nothingness rather than existence.

Hocking is correct that building a theory of freedom is an arduous,
complicated, and multi-leveled enterprise; but justifying a basis for moral judgments and public policy must be accomplished nonetheless. He is not content to
debate freedom in a juridical context where constitutional guarantees and shield
laws and court decisions control the parameters of our understanding. Endless
fussing over functional matters such as government intrusion, he concludes
appropriately, prevents a more fundamental analysis of liberty's character.
Freedom needs, in his view, an intellectual home within the nature of being
itself. He develops through the concept of positive freedom a rigorous philosophical context in which responsibility becomes not just an archaic survivor
from a pre-scientific age, but a constituent part of a metaphysics of human
being. Hocking shows that when rational agents take responsibility for their
actions, this is not delusion or a foolish imposition. With great subtlety, he
thereby frees us from the dilemma inherent in the negative-liberty model—
under the guise of self-realization, does it actually entail self-abnegation?

Certainly our moral possibilities are grounded in our freedom; actions
cease to be moral if humankind is not free. True enough. The debate revolves
around the nature of freedom, not its centrality. What Hocking develops is the
foundation for an accountable freedom, human freedom with responsibility as its
integrating center. Responsible humanness should be compelling to us because
history and theory permit us no alternative framework with equal comprehen-
siveness. Graham Haydon refers to this moral outlook in the Hocking tradition
as an "ethic of responsibility," a view of virtue-responsibility required of human
beings without reference to roles. Advocates of an ethic of responsibility.

. . . treat the requirement of responsibility as an ever-present moral demand, necessarily incumbent on any person as a person prior logically to particular responsibilities.[4]

Thus obligations to fulfill our task or role duties are not the fundamental element in the moral life as many thinkers suggest. We are not required to act responsibly first of all because we are professional journalists, but because we are human beings. Our humanity has primacy over our roles.

Corporate Moral Agency

Hocking's conceptual work on positive liberty is a major achievement. But it must be recognized that inter-subjectivity was the fundamental orientation for his understanding of freedom. Inter-subjectivity was Hocking's label for contending that all persons, as subjects of one divine being, are interrelated by the very fact of their common integration prior to any communication. Inter-subjectivity is the fountain of all the arts and the ground of communication. Underneath humankind's communal existence is

. . . a common, persuasive, constant experience of an active, creative other mind, which, by virtue of its scope and power, we recognize as the mind of God.[5]

The human predilection to communicate presumes a region beyond our individual selves possessed in common with others. The drive is innate; Hocking's very definition of persons presupposes that they "inhere in a common life."[6] And this dimension of our humanity cannot be examined by sociology, but by philosophy. The novelty of Hocking's method is connecting his idealism with everyday experience.

Hocking shared classical liberalism's concern for the person, and protested with equal vigor the escalating dehumanization of political power. However, in his view, there is a stronger foundation for personal rights and dignity than rights-oriented individualism. Hocking's inter-subjectivity, built around community and a universal life force, is a deliberate alternative to the atomistic insistence in classical liberalism on the individual's sacred rights to life, liberty, and property. Hocking viewed a bankrupt individualism as fundamentally undermining an interest in ethics and public philosophy. Through inter-subjectivity he posed the community as the gateway to understanding per-

[4]Graham Haydon, "On Being Responsible," in *Philosophical Quarterly*, 1978, pp. 46-51.

[5]Leroy S. Rouner, *Within Human Experience: The Philosophy of William Ernest Hocking*, Cambridge, MA, Harvard University Press, 1969, p. 104.

[6]William E. Hocking, *Man and the State*, New Haven, CT, Yale University Press, 1926, p. 344.

sons. He was thus a distinctive advocate of what is now labeled the communitarian view in which the self and community and universal humanness are interdependent and all equally important. What he offers through inter-subjectivity is a conceptually rigorous view of the human species in which, at the highest level, being is fundamentally personal.

But in centering positive freedom on a philosophy of the personal, Hocking leaves for us a monumental agenda. In order to integrate the Hutchins Commission's big-business concern with its concept of positive freedom, the latter must be developed in terms of the former. The present-day task of social responsibility theory is to anchor positive freedom in corporate morality rather than assume that Hocking's inter-subjectivity is adequate in a secular age. And in order to develop that connection successfully, we must establish the idea of corporate moral agency. A judge once bemoaned that corporations have "no pants to kick or soul to damn," and concluded, "by God, they ought to have both."[7]

Unlike a real person, the corporation has no conscience to keep it awake all night, no emotions for the psychiatrist to analyze, and no body to be thrown into jail. It is a *persona ficta*, and its fictional nature, coupled with remarkable down-to-earth power, makes it a thoroughly puzzling object of moral understanding.[8] Obviously, institutions are more than impersonal machines. They do resemble a complicated package of gears, engines, and levers; but like people, corporations write contracts, meet deadlines, take precautions, act incompetently, issue reports, pay taxes, own property, and incur financial liability.

But is an opposite view sustainable? Are organizations equivalent to the persons who embody them? Because corporations act intentionally, the Moral Person theory concludes:

> Corporations can be full-fledged moral persons and have whatever privileges, rights, and duties as are, in the normal course of affairs, accorded to moral persons.[9]

However, although it is plausible to draw suggestive parallels between corporations and persons, no one argues that institutions should register for the draft and are entitled to retirement benefits or investiture. As Thomas Donaldson concludes correctly: "Can corporations have a right to worship as they please? To pursue happiness? [They] fail to qualify as moral persons . . . in any literal sense of that term."[10]

---

[7]Th. Donaldson, *Corporations and Morality,* Englewood Cliffs, NJ, Prentice-Hall, 1982, p. 1.

[8]Th. Donaldson, *Corporations and Morality,* p. 1.

[9]P. French, "The Corporation as a Moral Person," in *American Philosophical Quarterly,* 16 (1979), p. 207. For historical background, see Frederick Pollock and F. W. Maitland, "Corporation and Person," in *Anthropology and Early Law,* Lawrence Krader (ed.), New York, New York University Press, 1965, pp. 300-336.

[10]Th. Donaldson, *Corporations and Morality,* p. 23.

The solution to the machine-person dichotomy is the rational agent model, which considers the corporation a moral *agent,* but not a moral *person.* Institutions use moral reasoning in their organizational decision-making, but that does not mean they have all dimensions of personal morality, such as pleasure and guilt.

Corporate decisions arise from a loosely aligned combination of power centers, though normally coordinated by a leadership team and formalized by standard operating procedures. And in order to qualify as moral decision-making above the level of machine operations, the process must involve a capacity for structuring the very policies that guide rational action. Obviously, some institutions are so thoroughly fragmented or so imprisoned by technicalities that they are analogous to sick or insane persons who cannot tell right from wrong. But in any rich definition of institutional structure is the capacity for clear deliberation, careful implementation, and empathy for others. Individuals who make decisions carefully and show respect for others are morally responsible. By extension, those institutions whose planning, policy, and performance are based on rational deliberation and respect for others can also be said to be morally responsible.[11] As moral agents they resemble formally the legal notion that corporations are artificial persons, or juristic beings, created as such by the law in order to assign responsibility to corporate activity. U.S. Chief Justice Marshall initiated this definition in 1819: "A corporation is an artificial being, invisible, intangible, and existing only in the contemplation of law. Being the mere creation of law, it possesses only those properties which the charter of its creation confers upon it, either expressly, or as incidental to its very existence."[12]

Objections to this view typically locate ethics in a system outside the institution. Milton Friedman, for instance, argues that businesses are responsible only for making profits and obeying laws. Given the sanctity of voluntary agreements—in this case between management and stockholders who brought the company into existence—employers are duty bound to increase earnings. The common good will result not by conscious corporate policies—corporations are ill-designed for achieving social justice anyhow—but rather through the checks and balances of unbridled competition in the marketplace.[13] John Kenneth Galbraith takes a different stance by arguing that the locus of ethics resides in laws and governmental policies.

---

[11]Cf. K. E. Goodpaster and J. B. Matthews, Jr., "Can a Corporation Have a Conscience?" in *Harvard Business Review,* 60 (January/Feb. 1982), pp. 132-141.

[12]*Dartmouth College v. Woodward,* 4 Wheat 518.636 [1819].

[13]Milton Friedman, "The Social Responsibility of Business Is to Increase Its Profits," *The New York Times Magazine,* 13 Sept. 1970; see also his *Capitalism and Freedom* (University of Chicago Press, 1962). Friedman's sharp separation between ethics and economics actually reflects 19th-century Social Darwinism more than Adam Smith's *Wealth of Nations.* Smith was suspicious of commercial motives and never championed the pursuit of profit with the blanket endorsement of a Milton Friedman.

Despite the importance of the marketplace and the government, theories that locate ethics outside the corporation exaggerate the differences between individuals and institutions, and they permit a double standard between one's private and one's nine-to-five values and behavior. Furthermore, an institution cannot choose not to establish ethical policies because all activity has moral dimensions. As Goodpaster and Matthews observe, "The issue in the end is not whether corporations (and other organizations) should be 'unleashed' to exert moral force in our society but rather how critically and self-consciously they should choose to do so."[14]

Of course, defending a meaningful sense of corporate moral agency involves complicated issues in organizational theory. The dominant tradition has been functionalist in character. Functionalism employs elegant statistical strategies for understanding organizational processes. Prediction and control of projected outcomes are sought by carefully calibrating the relevant variables and testing all conceivable hypotheses. Mainstream functionalism seeks that technical knowledge which enables institutions to operate efficiently, and success depends on creating organizational models that enable managers to achieve company objectives. However, in order to specify the logic and content of institutional accountability in terms of positive freedom, I believe that we should adopt the framework of organizational culture instead.

Organizations are understood as cultures in the sense that their members engage in producing a shared reality. Through organizational symbolism— myths, awards, stories, rites, policy statements, logos, legends, architecture—an institution's practice is exhibited and made meaningful.[15] Whereas traditional research investigates sending and receiving networks to make information flows more effective, communication in the cultural paradigm emphasizes the construction and reproduction of symbolic meaning systems.

> Thus communication is not just another organizational activity that occurs inside an organization rather it *creates* and *recreates* the social structure that makes organization.[16] (Italics in original)

---

[14]Goodpaster and Matthews, "Can a Corporation Have a Conscience?" p. 140.

[15]Dennis K. Mumby, *Communication and Power in Organizations: Discourse, Ideology, and Domination,* Norwood, NJ, Ablex, 1988, p. 5. Mumby summarizes why organizational culture has become "a major theoretical rallying point": continuing impact of Max Weber's writings on bureaucracy, rediscovery of the American symbolic tradition, disaffection among mainline organizational theorists, the impact of European intellectuals (Heidegger, Schutz, Gadamer, Habermas), and the influence of organizational communication theorists such as Deetz, Pondy, Morgan, Frost, and Dandridge (ch. 1).

[16]Linda Smirchich and Marta B. Calas, "Organizational Culture: An Assessment," in Frederick M. Jablin et al. (eds.), *Handbook of Organizational Communication: An Interdisciplinary Perspective,* Beverly Hills, CA, Sage, 1987, p. 231.

Organizations, therefore, manifest human consciousness. They are visible expressions of worldviews, organized understandings "of what constitutes adequate knowledge and legitimate activity."[17] And the metaphors for interpreting these shared beliefs derive from the humanities rather than the natural sciences, . . . more and more from the contrivances of cultural performance than from those of physical manipulation—from theater, painting, grammar, literature, law, play.[18]

And in any sophisticated understanding, an organization's discourse must be seen as representing various disputes over terrain and authority within organizational sub-units. The workplace is not merely created in symbolic form, but it is a site for fundamental human struggles over the meaning of vocation. And the institutional infrastructure—particularly its technological dimension— is stitched into the conceptual whole. It cannot be ignored in a cultural analysis or summarily dispatched to political economists.

> Cultural theorists are fond of bandying about this artifact from sports: three umpires disagreed about the task of calling penalties in soccer. The first one said, "I calls them as they is." The second one said, "I calls them as I sees them." The third and cleverest umpire said, "They ain't nothin' till I calls them."[19]

The shrewd number three recognizes that language plays a critical role in creating reality. Calling a penalty does not merely label an objective event; the umpire's naming interconnects a player's action with that overall pattern of meanings we know as soccer. J. B. Thompson is correct that interpretive theory has highlighted the symbolic construction of social worlds, while neglecting the role of language in repression, deformation, subterfuge, and distortion.[20] Yet ideological masking is impossible except on the presumption that humans continually enact and recreate their realities just like umpires do. This is what we mean by time-and-space existence. Organizations create themselves in similar fashion. In that sense, organizations, by definition, are also intermeshed value systems accountable as moral agents. Dominant power interests do not bring organizations into being *de novo*, but coerce, sediment, and re-direct an inescapable process for antihuman ends. Stuart Hall makes the same distinction

---

[17]Linda Smirchich, "Concepts of Culture and Organizational Analysis," in *Administrative Science Quarterly*, 28 (1983), pp. 347-350.

[18]Clifford Geertz, *Local Knowledge*, New York, Basic Books, 1983, pp. 22-23.

[19]Quoted in K. Weick, *The Social Psychology of Organizing*, 2nd ed., Reading, MA, Addison-Wesley, 1979, p. 1. In a more serious version, see Richard White's *Inventing Australia*, in which he argues there was never an Australia waiting to be uncovered; national identity is an invention.

[20]J. B. Thompson, *Studies in the Theory of Ideology*, Berkeley, CA, University of California Press, 1984, p. 10.

from a different direction: "It does not follow that because all practices are [. . .] inscribed by ideology, all practices are *nothing but* ideology" (italics in original).[21] Thus, social responsibility theory can insist on the same type of accountable freedom for corporations that Hocking established for persons. It would be nonsense for umpires to deny accountability for their decisions, and likewise so for humans in everyday life and for corporations.

CODES OF ETHICS AS ORGANIZATIONAL DISCOURSE

A rich notion of accountable freedom will resonate in an organization's consciousness only through its discourse. Presuming that institutions constitute their reality through language, narrative forms enable organizations to structure themselves almost *ad infinitum*—toward *laissez faire* freedom, collegiality, profit, responsibility, innovation, quality products, public service, civic transformation or whatever. Because organizational language legitimates particular philosophies of life while excluding others, discourse systems are a primary resource for ensuring that media institutions serve the public interest. Two discursive forms—company stories and codes of ethics, one informal and the other formal—are especially powerful vehicles for defining an institution's moral contours.

Moral Dramas

The narratives that dominate institutional memory encapsulate a company's value system and create its pattern of ethical compliance or deviance. Stories encapsulate organizational culture. They "punctuate and sequence events in such a way as to privilege certain interpretations of the world." They represent "a signification system" that accents "certain meaning formations and hence interests over others."[22] And such narratives are always moral dramas—they make a point, they interpret events in terms of a moral imperative, they animate an ideal. "Where narrativity is present, we can be sure that morality or a moralizing impulse is present too."[23] Leaders who shape organizational reality in terms of their own agendas understand the powerful character of a company's discourse.

A classic story out of the communications company IBM illustrates further that narratives are as central to understanding organizational life as are its products, employee files, or bank accounts. Apparently a young female security guard stopped Thomas Watson, Jr., IBM's chairman, from entering a security

---

[21]Stuart Hall, "Signification, Representation, Ideology: Althusser and the Post-structuralist Debates," in *Critical Studies in Mass Communication*, 2 (1985), p. 103.

[22]Mumby, *Communication and Power in Organizations*, pp. 108-109.

[23]H. White, "The Value of Narrativity in the Representation of Reality," in *Critical Inquiry*, 7 (1980), p. 24.

room without proper identification. Watson silenced his entourage of white-shirted engineers and waited patiently at the doorway until an aide returned with a badge.

The story crystallizes IBM's commitment to rules. No one is above company policies. The story is easier to remember than arid corporate directives. This moral drama has impact because of the immense disproportion in social status between the actors. And in its retelling, it exalts Watson's heroic gentlemanliness rather than exposing him as the lawgiver himself who extracts strict obedience to maximize efficiency and to maintain IBM's core rules about company secrecy in a technological race with competitors for its market share. Meanwhile, the male-dominated corporate structure remains intact and unexamined.[24]

Regrettably, rather than these moral dramas enabling critical self-reflection, empirical studies indicate that typically the company's intention and employee understanding coalesce. Given the concurrence-seeking tendency social-psychologist Irving Janis identified in his *Victims of Group Think*, organizational narrative ordinarily becomes framed in similar terms from top to bottom. In principle, all linguistic constructions have multiple meanings, but in cohesive cultures they fall into a unified semantic field. Organization members retell the narratives with pride and commitment. Jacques Ellul despairs that the propagandized generally welcome it. And Antonio Gramsci argues that hegemony succeeds because subordinates actively reiterate the worldview of élites.

Codes of Ethics

Given this conceptual framework, it is apparent that ethics codes serve a systematic role in creating an organizational conscience. Self-regulation has long stood in classical liberalism as the only control mechanism acceptable to the news enterprise itself. And the press' fixation with negative freedom continues to hinder it from intelligently considering all inside mechanisms for increasing responsibility. But various broadcasting and newspaper companies are now adopting codes at a mushrooming pace—though frequently for the misguided reason that they supposedly enhance press credibility. Too often codes serve as a public relations tool like paint over bad plaster. Many press leaders have reservations, fearing that codes could be used against them in courts.

Although a code of ethics alone cannot improve corporate conduct, M. Cash Mathews insists that it can be an effective component in a broad strategy to institutionalize ethical behavior. This broad strategy requires wholesale institutional commitment; a code of ethics that is ancillary will be as useful as a sixth toe or an appendix. One structural modification would be a company ethics committee, a sort of collective ombudsperson, with authority to examine all corporate operations. It would be composed of representative professionals

---

[24]For interpretive details on the Watson story, see Mumby, *Communication and Power in Organizations*, pp. 115-125.

throughout the organization—editors, reporters, photographers, clerical staff, advertising salespersons. In order to help gain breadth and critique, it is also imperative that moral philosophers be included from outside the company. And, as a matter of fact, both the *Philadelphia Inquirer* and *Louisville Courier Journal* have experimented successfully with ethics coaches.

Such a task force could establish a binding code of ethics integral to daily corporate practice, arrange periodic ethics workshops, grapple with the ethical issues that employees raise, and reward those employees who contribute positively to the corporate culture. As Mathews suggests, the ethics committee would not only help to resolve ethical quandaries, but it would also participate in corporate planning. In this way ethics would be built into the institution, not just added as window dressing or afterthought.[25]

Codes of ethics are not rules to foist upon the rank and file, with exemptions for the boardroom. An organization can self-consciously develop a code of ethics in which all parties participate and which is as binding on editors and publishers as on reporters. The mutuality model necessarily involves all workers in the interpretation and articulation of the professional values that govern their work. Just as codes of ethics are not handed down, enforcement of codes is not the lonely role of top management exerting judicial power over their juniors.

Communities with explicit functions cannot be maintained successfully without attaching specific rebukes for failing to meet obligations. People cannot be called into account without a visible process whereby agreed-on principles function as arbiters of innocence or guilt. Written codes force corporate leaders to declare and explain themselves and allow fair negotiation of claims. Surprises are less frequent and quixotic, enforcement more foreseeable, if codes are taken from the inscrutable reserves of managers' psyches and summarized in a document that all can read and critique. In the best settings, the document becomes a symbol of mutual trust born of the difficult process of repartee in a demanding profession.

Even in small news shops, written codes have the effect of building a tradition of respect for professional norms and even-handed fairness in dealing with unfriendly news and outside wolves. Written codes provide moral continuity from case to case. Written codes widely discussed in a community make the arm-twisting of local politicos less of an embarrassment on either end of a protesting phone call. The document serves as a third-party around which discussion can proceed and, on occasion, a principled exception be formulated. For Adolf Hitler, Idi Amin, and Al Capone, the case is shut. Ordinarily the corporate conscience refuses to tolerate outright lies, breaking and entering, and physical assault. But frequently the moral dimension is not obvious or all the choices have tragic consequences. Everyday journalism in a complicated world often

---

[25]M. Cash Mathews, *Strategic Intervention in Organizations: Resolving Ethical Dilemmas,* Newbury Park, CA, Sage, 1988, p. 137.

leaves us with a forked tongue or a double mind. Media institutions are not an amalgamation of individuals making free and unbiased decisions; presuming autonomous action situation-by-situation inevitably results in minimalism. Modifying our codes by mutual agreement through a communal process sustained over time enables a sense of center and periphery when concrete moral judgments must be made. Stations and papers who struggle through ongoing ethics committees with suicide coverage or rape victims, for example, guarantee higher level responses at the crisis moment than when individual practitioners shoot from the hip.

The issue is not codes or no codes, but the type of codes news organizations adopt. Hortatory codes insisting that journalists tell the truth, promote justice, act honorably, and keep faith with their readers are vacuous rhetoric. Only explicit, practical, itemized, and carefully nuanced codes establish a company mystique, while decreasing quandaries and resisting flagrant misjudgment. The Springfield (Massachusetts) *Republican,* for example, makes inaccurate quotations unpardonable: "When people are quoted, the quoted passage is literally spoken." The *Louisville Courier Journal* refuses all advertisements that "attack, criticize, or cast reflection on any individual, race, religion or institution." CBS has explicit news standards for "demonstrations, riots, and other civil disturbances." The Society of Professional Journalists' code has helped make freebies outmoded: "Nothing of value shall be accepted." The Roanoke (Virginia) *Times-World News* has exacting guidelines regarding anonymous sources.

However, even though institutional codes are generated through democratic participation and contoured with finesse, conceiving of them as rules is counterproductive. This traditional perspective is entrenched in our thinking. We tend to think that a panoply of guidelines improves a company's productivity if obeyed automatically. In fact, professional ethics generally presumes mainstream organizational theory, and conceives of ethics in rule-oriented terms. In its own way, it reflects the emphasis on external constraints in classical liberalism. When facing dilemmas, we tend to believe, right action depends on following prescriptions.

However, as Karen Labacqz has argued convincingly, situation ethics has put all rule morality in jeopardy. Rules are never independent of particulars. "Rules take situations seriously and definitions of situations already incorporate moral notions."[26] And the organizational culture approach also refuses to reduce linguistic structures (well-polished ethical tenets, for example) to information strings in the imperative mood. Instead, codes of ethics crafted in mutuality are understood to stimulate the moral imagination. Codes keep supple the organizational conscience. They are not to be reduced to a set of barriers that impede our freedom. Codes do not merely represent organizational values, but constitute

---

[26]Karen Lebacqz, *Professional Ethics: Power and Paradox*, Nashville, TN, Abingdon Press, 1985, p. 24.

them. Since Aristotle, discernment has been recognized as the axis around which morality revolves. Ethical codes orient our discernment constructively, but that is something other than a fail-safe mechanistic rule system.

Signifying forms such as moral dramas and codes of ethics inspire our moral awareness. They activate the company's conscience. But without a normative foundation, narratives and codes are ingrained with daily pressures or encumbered by authority and economic interests. They are surface-level formulations whose longevity and legitimacy presuppose deeper philosophical justification. The nearly intractable problem with moral dramas is establishing a critical dimension so they empower rather than oppress. When codes of ethics are issued by fiat and exclude upper management from their restrictions, they are not emancipatory either. But even participatory codes do not automatically guarantee ethical enlightenment. A finely honed normative ethics on which codes can rest remains a nonnegotiable priority. And the academy need not play an exclusive role. Reflective ombudspersons, media critics, news councils, philosophically inclined and well-read news directors, journalism reviews, and ethical specialists in newsrooms—these options prevent organizational culture from turning in on itself. Abstract theorizing is inappropriate for them, and meta-ethics alien territory for their readers and viewers. However, they can contribute credibly to the necessary intellectual work, especially by integrating cognitive substance with the avalanche of practical dilemmas. What we codify, and how we codify it, necessitates a reservoir of value theory and informed ethical inquiry.

Organizational discourse anchored to a normative center does not merely solve problems one-by-one. The moral point of our institutional story or a prescription from a code of ethics is trivialized if primarily used to extinguish a fire or patch a rut in the company road. Moral dramas, codes, and theoretical claims actually fulfill the more noble but elusive role of establishing a socially responsible organizational culture.

CHAPTER 5
Codes of Media Ethics
An International Comparative Approach

Benoît Grévisse[1]

At the beginning of the 21st century, the ethics code constitutes an element of journalistic self-regulation that is essential, though not sufficient by itself. It stands together with ombudsmen, press councils and other M*A*S. The code is the only place where the ethical norm is specified, made concrete and public. Too often otherwise it belongs to the sphere of usage and is kept within the profession.

The recent proliferation of codes in every part of the world is often explained by the decline of the credibility of journalists. The abundance of codes creates problems; it makes for repetitions and vagueness, even contradictions. The coexistence of norms applicable to the firm that formulates them, to a nation or to a group of countries contributes to a regrettable haziness. However, it is a sign of a diversity of cultural, legal, commercial, and political conditions to which the international handling of information needs to adapt as journalists seek common values. Comparative media ethics has the advantage of suggesting improvements in each nation depending on its peculiarities.

The drafting of a set of ethical rules is closely associated to the issue of the journalist's professional identity and the fragility thereof. In France, the creation of the National Union of Journalists (SNJ) derived from an awareness of that fragility. One of the first acts of the union, in July 1918, was to compose a charter of the professional duties of journalists, which was revised and augmented in 1938 and has remained the ethics code of the profession.[2]

---

[1]All the texts that were not originally written in English were translated by C-J. Bertrand, who assumes full responsibility for any imperfections.

[2]See C. Bellanger et al. (eds.), *Histoire générale de la presse francaise,* Vol. III, Paris, PUF, 1972, p. 40.

In that kind of genesis, the code is presented as a stage in the union struggle. The protection of journalists against their employers belongs to that historical legacy. It is thus described in the *Munich Declaration of the Duties and Rights of Journalists* (1971):[3] "The journalist's responsibility towards the public exceeds any other responsibility, particularly towards employers and public authorities." The protection took concrete shape notably in the "conscience clause" introduced in the French law of March 29, 1935:[4] it underlines the ambivalent nature of the journalistic profession, torn between corporate demands and the requirements of the public. By the principle of a quest for truth, expressed by all codes, journalists and public enter into an essential contract: it gives that responsibility precedence over that which a journalist has towards his/her employers, or even towards the authorities. The same principle is also essential to the credibility and the identity of the journalistic profession. The *Munich Declaration* expresses it thus :

> The right to information, to freedom of expression and criticism is one of the fundamental rights of man. All rights and duties of a journalist originate from this right of the public to be informed on events and opinions. . . .

> The essential obligations of a journalist engaged in gathering, editing and commenting news are: 1. To respect truth, whatever be the consequences to himself, because of the right of the public to know the truth.

Latin languages have a choice of words: ethics and "deontology,"[5] the latter referring to professional ethics, the practical ethics within a given profession—what Daniel Cornu calls "daily morality." A necessary complement to "ethics" proper, which "functions as a force to question the whole process of information, *deontology* has the more limited range of a morality applied to journalistic activity. It refers to professional rules that set the conditions usually accepted for a correct information, in the pragmatic sense."[6]

The great number of codes and their diversity (in spite of many similarities) puts a limit on a comparative approach. What follows is meant merely as a content analysis. The purpose is twofold. The first is to do an inventory of the issues mentioned by codes. At a time when, in many newsrooms and professional associations, people are undertaking the writing or the updating of a

---

[3]Approved in 1971 by representatives of the journalists' unions of six countries of the European Community, meeting in Munich (Germany). Adopted by the International Federation of Journalists (IFJ-FIJ).

[4]It provides that if a publication is sold, if it changes its nature or political orientation, a journalist may leave with all the severance allowances he/she would get if dismissed.

[5]The word exists in English. It seems to have been first used in 1826, by Jeremy Bentham.

[6]See D. Cornu, *Journalisme et vérité. Pour une éthique de l'information,* Geneva, Labor et Fides, 1994, p. 48.

code, I wish to offer a pragmatic organization of contents.
aims at pointing out the various cultures and philosophies th
istic self-regulation.

THE FOUNDATIONS OF PROFESSIONAL MEDIA ETHICS

Texts show great diversity as to the values on which their legitimacy is founded.
Sometimes the foundation is tautological: the French *Charte des devoirs professionnels des journalistes*[7] simply ignores the need for a foundation by considering the professional as the alpha and omega of self-regulation: "A journalist
worthy of the name. . . ."

Others consider the special conditions of production as the source of a
desire for self-regulation. The foundation can then consist in the particular
responsibility of a dominant medium: "We fully recognize that the power we
have inherited as the dominant morning newspaper in the capital of the free
world carries with it special responsibilities" (Standards and Ethics [S&E] of
the *Washington Post,* 1989).

Or again the foundation lies in the responsibility of a particular sector
of journalism. Thus, the regional press can highlight its responsibility towards a
readership that is close to it. "The regional daily press is, first and foremost, a
local medium, conscious of its daily responsibility to inform" (*Règles et usages
du syndicat de la presse quotidienne régionale,* France, 1995).[8]

A majority of codes of ethics and similar texts place their foundation in
the democratic values inherited from the past, especially the British, American,
and French revolutions. Those values may sometimes seem rather abstract. The
public does not know them well and does not fight for them enough. That
makes it possible for journalists to use a particular rhetoric and thus appropriate
collective freedom of speech to the sole benefit of the press, shrunk to its individual or guild dimensions.[9]

Among the great values mobilized by codes and other ethical texts is
freedom of the press. "A journalist shall at all times defend the principle of the
freedom of the press and other media" (*Code of Conduct* of the British union
NUJ). Another is the right to inform, to which the German press code
(*Pressekodex*) refers, taking the public into account: "Respect for the truth,
observance of human rights and accurate informing of the public are the over-
riding principles of the press."

---

[7]*Charter of Professional Duties of French Journalists,* drafted by the SNJ union in 1918,
revised in 1938.
[8]*Rules and Usages of the Society of Regional Daily Newspaper Publishers.*
[9]See B. Libois, *Ethique de l'information: essai sur la déontologie journalistique,*
Brussels, Éd. de l'Université de Bruxelles, 1994.

Freedom of information and freedom of opinion are defined by the national constitutional and legal regime. Some texts invoke the very basis of the social contract contained in the constitution. That is the case in Italy, where the *Carta dei doveri del giornalista*[10] mentions in its preamble that "the work of a journalist is inspired by the principles of freedom of information and opinion established by the Italian Constitution." Also to be noted is the specific U.S. assertion of the freedom of expression: "The First Amendment, protecting freedom of expression from abridgment by any law, guarantees to the people through their press a constitutional right, and thereby places on newspaper people a particular responsibility. Thus journalism demands of its practioners not only industry and knowledge but also the pursuit of a standard of integrity proportionate to the journalist's singular obligation" (*Statement of Principles*, ASNE, 1975).[11]

Another value is the right to information deriving from freedom of speech: here the 1954 *Bordeaux Statement* could be quoted,[12] which mentions the right of the public to know the truth. The duty of respecting that right is there defined as essential for the journalist. But the *Munich Declaration* (1971) states the same idea even more bluntly by grounding it in the right to information: "The right to information, to freedom of expression and criticism is one of the fundamental rights of man. All rights and duties of a journalist originate from this right of the public to be informed on events and opinions. The journalist's responsibility towards the public excels any other responsibility, particularly towards employers and public authorities."

Another generation of texts, rather more modern, tends to place the public at the forefront of self-regulatory thinking. Journalists do not claim press freedom for themselves. On the contrary, they assert a right to information, which brings the public into the picture. It is because of the freedom of expression, which belongs to all of us, that the right to information is exercised by journalists on behalf of the public. *The Unesco Mass Media Declaration* (1978) is a fully fledged instance of that.

Two variants are worth quoting: recourse to the notion of public opinion and the mention of democracy as a fundamental value. There is a clear appeal to public opinion in the 1973 text of the SDX[13] code: "We believe in public enlightenment as the forerunner of justice, and in our Constitutional role to seek the truth as part of the public's right to know the truth" (SDX, 1973). *The Italian Charter of Journalistic Duties* offers a similar approach. More globally, democracy can serve as a fundamental value: "a free and independent press constitutes one of the most important bases of a democratic society" (*Code of Ethics of the Norwegian Press*, 1994).

---

[10]*Charter of the Duties of Journalists.*

[11]American Society of Newspapers Editors.

[12]A text adopted at the 1954 conference of the IFJ in Bordeaux, and revised in 1986.

[13]Sigma Delta Chi, now known as the Society of Professional Journalists (SPJ).

Last among foundations are social responsibility and professional identity: the latest generation of texts mentions a social responsibility of journalists within a clearly defined and evolving professional context. The self-regulating process is then rooted in an ultimate responsibility towards citizens. This is noted in the quite special case of the 1996 *Professional Code of Ethics for Quebec Journalists* of the FPJQ:[14] "The role of journalists is to accurately report, analyze, and in some cases, comment on the facts that help their fellow citizens understand the world in which they live. Complete, exact and diverse information is one of the most important guarantees of freedom and democracy. [. . .] Since it takes into account the specific nature of the journalistic environment, this is not a Code in the strictest sense of the word."

That comprehensive concept of foundations makes possible a pragmatic approach of self-regulation. Thus, the *Code of Practice* and the Quebec code determine a corpus of well-defined, enforceable norms. The traditional foundations (the quest for truth, the right to information, the defense of freedom of speech, respect for the human person) are now unchallenged. So the normative texts now focus on a description of usages. The British option is linked to the existence of a body (the Press Complaints Commission) whose job it is to make sure the norms are respected.

THE RANGE OF ETHICAL NORMS

Origin of the Process and Area of Application

The many different codes can be classified by area of application, from small to very large. It can cover just one newsroom: many newsrooms have adopted their own list of rules, so many that no inventory can be taken here. As a symbolic example, the S&E of the *Washington Post* can be noted. The text was introduced in 1989 by editor Ben Bradlee and inspired many later initiatives. The obvious advantage of those internal charters is that they take into account real conditions and their evolution.

A special field of activity may be defined by the kind of responsibilities assumed: the APME[15] code offers the example of managing editors assuming ethical accountability. Certain kinds of practices, like those of the regional press, can also determine the area of application. This is the case with the *Vademecum,* or guide, published by the Society of Publishers of the French Regional Daily Press (SPQR). One can also find codes of ethics specific to professional activities related to, but distinct from, traditional journalism—for example in the United States the code of the National Press Photographers Association.

---

[14]Professional Federation of Journalists in Quebec, Canada, see p. 98.

[15]Associated Press Managing Editors—the association of ME of newspapers that are members of the cooperative wire service AP.

The national sphere is the domain of a professional association and it is the most common (for example, the British *Code of Conduct* or the SPJ-SDX code in the United States). But the national sphere can also be the domain of a joint action by reporters and publishers. Such is the case of the *Pressekodex,* drafted by the German Press Council, itself established by the professional organizations of proprietors and journalists.

Some texts, though they aim at a national jurisdiction, do take into account the need to adapt to the realities of each newsroom. Thus the APME code allows that "common sense and good judgement are required in applying ethical principles to newspaper realities. As new technologies evolve, these principles can help guide editors to insure the credibility of the news and information they provide. Individual newspapers are encouraged to augment these APME guidelines more specifically to their own situations."

In the international area, there is clearly a desire to bring the norms into harmony. This can be seen in the *Declaration of Principles by the International Federation of Journalists,* known as the *Bordeaux Declaration,* as well as in the *Declaration of Rights and Obligations of Journalists,* known as the *Munich Declaration,* a basic text in Europe.[16] Lastly, some observers consider the *Unesco Mass Media Declaration* as "the most recent and most ambitious international document on practical ethics because it is the only one that has a truly global scope. However, it was not meant to be directly applied: rather it was meant to guide professional groups in the drafting of their codes of ethics."[17] The transnational aim of all these texts has led their authors to stress general principles at the expense of a more practical approach.

Who is to Respect the Norms

The historical and technological evolution of the jobs within journalism has multiplied the tasks fulfilled in the production of news. By defining the people they aim at, codes of ethics take this fact into account. A restrictive definition is content to refer to "a journalist worthy of the name. . ." (French *Charte des devoirs*), "a journalist has a duty to . . ." (British *Code of Conduct*).

Wider, yet limited, definitions use a generic term: "We believe the agencies of mass communication are carriers of public discussion and information" (SDX, 1973). They can aim explicitly at some professional categories; for example the Polish *Media Ethic Charter*: "Journalists, editors, producers and broadcasters." The extensive definition covers all contributors: "Editors and publishers must ensure that the code is observed rigorously not only by their staff but also by anyone who contributes to their publications" (*Code of Practice* of the British PCC).

---

[16]See Daniel Cornu, *Codes et chartes de déontologie,* Lausanne, CRFJ, 1995, p. 4.
[17]See C.J. Bertrand, *Media Ethics and Accountability Systems,* 2000, p. 79.

Lastly, the open definition acknowledges the principle of freedom of expression for all and posits that no one can escape ethical responsibility:

> Neither the title of journalist nor the journalistic act are reserved for a particular group of people. The journalistic world is open, and that is the way journalists want it to be. [. . .] The term "journalist" in this Code refers to all people who exercise a journalistic function for a news organization. In the context of publicly disseminating information or opinions, this includes one or several of the following tasks: researching, reporting, interviewing; writing or preparing reports, analyses, commentaries, or specialized columns; translating or adapting texts; press photography, filmed or electronic reports; assignment, the desk (headlines, lay-out . . .), editing; caricatures; information drawing and graphics; animation, producing and supervising current affairs programs and films; managing news, public affairs or other comparable departments. *(Professional Code of Ethics for Quebec Journalists)*

Some codes of ethics present not only the duties of journalists, but also their rights. That is useful, both to reassure journalists and to warn their employers and also legislators. But here let's only consider duties (the social responsibilities) of professional news workers.

Duties

Two types of duties are to be distinguished. They are directly linked to the philosophy behind the norms. Some reflect great principles; others specify "standards of practice" (SDX). That dichotomy appears in that some codes are brief and some are detailed. Thus, the British *Code of Practice*[18] is original in that it contains no mention of great principles and many very pragmatic rules. The APME *Code of Ethics* proposes the same approach, based on a case law concept of evolution and adaptation: "No statement of principles can prescribe decisions governing every situation. Common sense and good judgement are required in applying ethical principles to newspaper realities."

The acknowledgement of the primacy of the public's right generally appears as a fundamental duty. The ASNE *Statement of Principles* sums up the principle neatly: "Freedom of the press belongs to the people." The *Charter of Duties of the Italian Journalist* is one of the most explicit texts as regards responsibility towards the public. It lists various pragmatic measures to be taken in order that true interaction take place with the readers.

The defense of the freedom to inform implies, as the *Swiss Declaration of the Rights and Duties of the Journalist* specifies, the duty to defend "the independence and dignity of the profession." That crucial nuance places ethical rules in the realm of collective accountability.

---

[18]Used by the British Press Complaints Commission, PCC, 1991.

A journalist is under the obligation to seek and respect truth: "to respect" (*Munich Declaration*, German *Pressekodex*) and "to seek truth, because of the public's right to know it, whatever the consequences for the journalist" (Switzerland). That commitment, with its serious possible consequences, is defined as follows by *Code of Conduct* (NUJ-GB) as an unceasing struggle: "He/she shall strive to eliminate distortion, news suppression and censorship."

There is a limit to the quest for information and its ultimate form, investigative reporting, which is clearly expressed by the French journalists' *Charter of Professional Duties*: "A journalist worthy of the name [. . .] does not confuse his function with that of a policeman."

The SDX code, when it defines press freedom, brings an extra element into play, by reminding us how complex truth is: "Journalists uphold the right to speak unpopular opinions and the privilege to agree with the majority." The *Washington Post* puts the principle of a quest for truth in the same perspective. But it puts more stress on the importance of the public to which journalists are responsible: they must "listen to the voiceless, avoid any and all acts of arrogance, face the public politely and candidly."

What are the means to find truth? First, systematic skepticism. *The Quebec Code of Ethics*, in proposing "fundamental journalistic values," brings in an element that is absent elsewhere: "The fundamental values of journalists include: a critical viewpoint, so they methodically doubt everything; impartiality, so they research and expose the diverse aspects of a given situation. . . ." The ASNE *Statement of Principles* offers another operating principle: "Good faith with the reader is the foundation of good journalism."

Another obligation: the naming of the source and "double-checking." A journalist is bound "to report only on facts of which he knows the origin" (Munich, Bordeaux, Switzerland). The *Pressekodex* is more precise: "The publication of specific news and information in word and picture must be carefully checked in respect of accuracy in the light of existing circumstances." It is proper "to give very explicitly as such the news that have not been confirmed," states the Swiss *Declaration*. It is to the credit of the *Pressekodex* and the Quebec *Code* that they also consider the case of rumors: "Unconfirmed reports, rumors or assumptions must be quoted as such," "A rumor cannot be published unless it originates from a credible source and contributes to the understanding of an event. It must always be identified as a rumor." It is in the U.S. codes (e.g., *Washington Post*) that one finds the most complete treatment of the issue of naming sources.

A journalist will only use "fair means to obtain information, photos and documents" (Bordeaux). Similarly, the Munich text, the Swiss, German, and British (NUJ) codes condemn "unfair methods." That principle stems from the duty to seek justice that conditions the quest for truth. The *Code of Practice* (GB) condemns recourse to payment for information; it also condemns clandestine listening devices. This explicitness is in reaction to the methods used by the popular tabloids in Great Britain. The *Code of Practice* adds that "Documents or photographs should be removed only with the consent of the owner [. . .] Subterfuge can be justified only in the public interest and only when material cannot be obtained by any other means."

The Québec text, even more precise, lists clandestine methods and the limits to their use: "false identities, hidden microphones and cameras, imprecise information about the objectives of their news reports, spying, infiltrating." Always very practical, that same code deals with the "rules of conversation": "If there is no explicit agreement, journalists are not obliged to follow the rules of conversation ('off the record,' 'background,' 'publication without naming the source'). These kinds of rules must be established before the conversation—not after. To avoid being manipulated by their sources, journalists must limit these rules to the best of their ability. [. . .] Journalists should not seek sources' approval before publishing or broadcasting their stories."

The title or quality that one claims to possess appears as a means to obtain information: "A journalist worthy of the name will refrain from using some invented title or quality, from using unfair means, to obtain a piece of information or abuse the good faith of anyone" (*Charter of Professional Duties of French Journalists*). The *Code of Practice* (PCC-GB) posits that: "Subterfuge can be justified only in the public interest and only when material cannot be obtained by any other means." The *Code of Conduct* adds that "The journalist is entitled to exercise a personal conscientious objection to the use of such means."

Journalists have a duty "not to suppress essential information" (Munich, Bordeaux, Switzerland, etc.) nor "falsify" (Bordeaux), "alter" (Munich), or "distort" (Switzerland) texts or documents. To that commonly mentioned duty, the *Pressekodex* adds that "its sense must not be distorted or falsified by editing, title or picture captions." The Italian *Charter* is even clearer: "Headlines, menus, photographs and captions must neither distort nor exaggerate the content of news or features." The Québec *Code* adds that "Quotations, editing, sound effects, etc., and the sequence in which they are presented, must not distort the meaning of people's words."

The Swiss *Declaration* mentions the obligation to "label photomontages for what they are." The Québec *Code* demands that "Photographs, graphics, sounds and images that are published or broadcast must represent reality as accurately as possible. Artistic concerns should not result in the public being deceived. Edited images and photographs must be identified as such." The German *Code* goes further, about the meaning of photos: "When reproducing symbolic[18] photographs, it must be clear from the caption that these are not documentary pictures." The Swiss *Declaration* also considers the case when responsibility is pinned on a third party, a common argument because of the

---

[18]"Substitute or auxiliary illustrations (i.e. similar motive, different time, or different motive at the same time etc.); symbolic illustrations (reconstructed scene, artificially reconstructed events to accompany text, etc.)." See Guideline 2.2, p. 83.

common use of photos from agencies: "not to manipulate pictures or get them to be manipulated by third parties so as to falsify them." The Italian Charter deals with the manipulation of photos linked to "human interest stories": "Besides, the journalist must not publish, in relation to people involved in 'human interest stories' any pictures or photos likely to inspire repulsion, or in any way offensive to the dignity of the human person."

The Québec *Code* is exceptional in that it deals in detail with reenactments and dramatizations. It lays down as a principle that "Whenever possible, journalists should use real events in their reports rather than reenactments by diverse artificial means."

The German texts seem the more exhaustive as regards violence. The *Guidelines*[19] specify that "the threshold of acceptability in reports on accidents and catastrophes is exceeded when the suffering of the victims and their dependants is not respected. Victims of misfortune must not be made to suffer a second time by their portrayal in the media."

Faithful to its policy of being specific as to commended behavior in sensitive circumstances, the *Pressekodex* requires that "reports on medical matters should not be unnecessarily sensationalist since they might lead to unfounded fears or hopes on the part of some readers." The *Guidelines* add that "critical or one-sided reports on controversial opinions subject to debate should not make seriously ill persons unsure and thus raise doubts about the possible success of therapeutic measures." The *Italian Charter* contains similar rules. In a related field, hospitals, the *Code of Practice* (GB) considers that "journalists or photographers making enquiries at hospitals or similar institutions should identify themselves to a responsible executive and obtain permission before entering non-public areas."

The notion of fairness, as defined in the S&E of the *Washington Post*, helps to define the practical rules relative to the respect of truth: "Reporters and editors of *The Post* are committed to fairness. While arguments about objectivity are endless, the concept of fairness is something that editors and reporters can easily understand and pursue. Fairness results from a few simple practices: No story is fair if it omits facts of major importance or significance. Fairness includes completeness. No story is fair if it includes essentially irrelevant information at the expense of significant facts. Fairness includes relevance. No story is fair if it consciously or unconsciously misleads or even deceives the reader. Fairness includes being honest with the reader. No story is fair if reporters hide their biases or emotions behind such subtly pejorative words as 'refused,' 'despite,' 'quietly,' 'admit,' and 'massive.' Fairness requires straightforwardness ahead of flashiness."

Facts and comments must be kept separate. An explicit mention of this principle is found in the British *Code of Conduct*: "A journalist shall strive to

---

[19]Most articles of the page-long *Pressekodex* are accompanied by one or several guidelines giving explanations and details (see p. 82).

ensure that the information he/she disseminates is fair and accurate, avoid the expression of comment and conjecture as established fact." The *Washington Post* posits that principle as a distinctive feature of the newspaper: "On this newspaper, the separation of news columns from the editorial and opposite-editorial pages is solemn and complete." The ASNE introduces a nuance that is useful in apprehending the principle of separation, which can be too absolute: "To be impartial does not require the press to be unquestioning or to refrain from editorial expression."

As regards the correction of violations of the truth, rarely do codes state from the outset the principle of journalistic responsibility, which the French *Charte des devoirs professionnels des journalistes* does: "A journalist worthy of the name accepts responsibility for his writings."

A journalist will strive by all means to "rectify any published item of news that has proved inaccurate and harmful" (Bordeaux). The *Munich Statement* omits the "harmful" component, as does the *Swiss Declaration*, which specifies "factually inaccurate." For the *Pressekodex*, "Published news or assertions which subsequently turn out to be incorrect must be promptly rectified in an appropriate manner by the publication concerned." The *Italian Charter* provides for rectification "even in the absence of any explicit request." It adds a preventive provision: "In all cases, before publishing the news that a person is involved in legal proceedings, he/she must make sure by all means that the person has been informed of it." Lastly, a number of codes, including the British *Code of Conduct* (NUJ) and *Code of Practice* (PCC) mention the right of reply and the option of publishing apologies.

A journalist must "observe professional secrecy and not divulge the source of information obtained in confidence" (Munich, and also Bordeaux, *Swiss Code, Charter of French Journalists*, British *Code of Conduct* and *Code of Practice, Italian Charter of Duties*). Note that professional secrecy is or is not mentioned depending on the legal recognition of the principle in the country. The *Pressekodex* and the *Guidelines* that go with it are probably the most precise text on secrecy and confidentiality. The Québec *Code* states the same principles and makes clear what behavior journalists should adopt on that issue with the judiciary. As a logical extension of professional secrecy concerning respect for an agreement (even though tacit) with a source, the embargo is rarely mentioned, although it is part of journalistic usage. There again, the German *Guidelines* define the notion clearly.

Respect for the Individual

In my view, ASNE offers the clearest foundation for that principle: "Journalists should respect the rights of people involved in the news, observe the common standards of decency and stand accountable to the public for the failings and accuracy of their news reports."

"The journalist will beware of the risks of discrimination that might be spread by the media and will do his/her utmost not to facilitate such discrimination, founded on race, gender, sexual preferences, language, religion, political and other opinions, national or social origin" (Bordeaux, 1986 revision). Those principles are to be found in many codes. The German *Guidelines* add: "When reporting on crimes, it is not permissible to refer to the alleged perpetrator's religious, ethnic or other minority membership unless this information is directly relevant to the event." Note the addendum in the *Code of Practice* to the list of people usually mentioned as victims of discrimination, when it condemns "prejudicial or pejorative reference to [. . .] any physical or mental illness or disability"—a principle also present in the *Italian Charter*.

The journalist must "restrict himself to the respect of privacy" (Munich). The same provision is in the *Pressekodex*. The *Swiss Declaration* contributes a crucial restriction: "Respect the privacy of people, to the extent that public interest does not require not to." The British *Code of Practice*, again influenced by the practices of the popular press, is very specific: "Everyone is entitled to respect for his or her private and family life, home, health and correspondence. A publication will be expected to justify intrusions into any individual's private life without consent."

The use of long-lens cameras to photograph persons secretly in private areas is unacceptable. "Private areas" means any private property, but also public places where some amount of privacy can reasonably be requested. The death of Lady Diana caused a revision of the *Code of Practice*. The latest version[20] explicitly mentions agencies that employ paparazzi. "Editors must ensure that those working for them comply with these requirements and must not publish material from other sources which does not meet these requirements."

The Duty to Show Compassion

The *Code of Conduct* (NUJ) mentions this principle in general terms: "Subject to the justification by over-riding considerations of the public interest, a journalist shall do nothing which entails intrusion into private grief and distress." The *Code of Practice* (PCC) is more precise: "In cases involving personal grief or shock, inquiries should be carried out and approaches made with sympathy and discretion. Publication must be handled sensitively at such times but this should not be interpreted as restricting the right to report judicial proceedings." The German Guidelines usefully supplement the principle of respect for privacy with practical norms concerning the publication of the names or the pictures of criminals and victims.

Victims must be protected. "In most cases, journalists can reveal the names of victims of accidents and criminal acts. This information is of public

[20]Ratified by the PCC on November 26, 1997.

interest," with exceptions (Québec). The *Italian Charter* is precise: "The names of the victims of sexual violence shall not be published or any data that might lead to their identification, unless the victims themselves asked that that the publication be made for reasons of predominant general interest." Under the influence of Diana's death and reckless media assaults on the royal family, the *Code of Practice* defines the rules relative to the treatment of children, and especially to the protection of children caught in some sexual scandal.

The *Pressekodex* deals with offenses committed by young people: "When reporting on crimes committed by young persons and on their appearance in court, the press must exercise restraint out of consideration for their future."

Like the *Italian Charter*, the *Pressekodex* and *Guidelines* supplement the notion of respect for the individual with provisions concerning presumption of innocence. The *Guidelines* consider, among others, the case of "a person mentioned by name or identifiable to a large circle of readers" or again the pictorial representation of criminals, victims, or suspects. We may also note that the Québec *Code* establishes a duty to "follow up": "When media organizations have covered an incident where individuals have been incriminated and prosecuted, they must continue to follow the story as closely as possible, and ensure the public is informed of the end result."

To my knowledge, only the *Italian Charter* includes a clause relating to the protection of witnesses and of security forces: "A journalist shall always be extremely careful when publishing the names, or data that can lead to the identification, of persons that collaborate with the judiciary authorities or with public security forces, if that can put them or their families in danger."

"Journalists must tell sources who are unfamiliar with the media that their remarks may be published or broadcast and thus communicated to a large group of people" (Québec).

Lastly, the *Washington Post* mentions that as a newspaper it "respects taste and decency, understanding that society's concepts of taste and decency are constantly changing."

The notion of public interest often appears as the ultimate value, mentioned when an exception is considered to a particular rule. That principle is the only way to draw the line between behavior that is socially acceptable and behavior that is not. However, the principle of public interest can be used as an excuse for the worst journalistic practices. When scandal sheets are taken to court, that is the argument they never tire of using. So the latest version of the *Code of Practice* presents a clear formulation of the principle. The great number of clauses in the *Code of Practice* where this principle is mentioned shows the importance of public interest as the fundamental factor in ethical judgement.

Professional Sins

Violating the Principle of the Quest for Truth. That kind of misbehavior comes in many shapes: plagiarism, proscribed by many texts; malicious

distortion (Bordeaux), or malignant gossip, slander, libel, unfounded accusations (Bordeaux, Munich, Switzerland).

The Breach of Professional Integrity. That principle is set under the
authority of the editor: "To resist every pressure and to accept editorial orders
only from the responsible persons of the editorial staff" (Munich).

Illicit Benefit Drawn From One's Function. The Québec *Code* sets
the most complete and concrete definition of conflict of interest: "When journalists serve or seem to serve specific interests, there is a conflict of interest.
These interests may be their own or those of other individuals, groups, unions,
companies, political parties, etc. The conflict of interest can occur through
diverse contracts, favors or public commitments. Public interest should be the
only principle that guides a journalist's choice to publish information."

The *Code of Practice* devotes a section to financial journalism and to
insider trading. The *Italian Charter* contains similar clauses. But the
Washington Post's S&E show greater pragmatism by specifying how to proceed
concretely in order to limit risks: "All members of the Business and Financial
staff are required to disclose their financial holdings and investments to the
assistant managing editor in charge of the section." Such transparency seems
difficult to impose in a European culture where knowledge of someone's personal fortune is lodged in the private sphere.

The Confusion of the Job of Journalist and Other Functions That
are Incompatible With It. Some codes are remarkable by their relative
restraint, their mere evocation of general principles. It is the case of the *French*
Charter. Some texts aim at relationships with the government and the State
bureaucracy: "Connections with government are among the most objectionable"
(*Washington Post*). Others (APME) mention the giving of lectures outside
work. The Québec *Code* makes its position very clear regarding public relations: "Journalists must refrain from working in any form of communications
that is outside the field of journalism; this includes public relations, publicity,
promotions, courses on how to deal with the media, staged news conferences to
prepare spokespeople for their dealings with journalists, etc."

Most ethical texts condemn any confusion of the jobs of the journalist
and of the advertiser. The *Pressekodex* "requires that editorial publications be
not influenced by the private and business interests of third parties or by the
personal commercial interests of journalists." But German *Guidelines* go even
further by pointing to "surreptitious advertising" included in editorial matter.

As regards the acceptance of gifts, a delicate issue, some texts
(Bordeaux, Munich, *Code of Conduct*) decided to define general principles.
Other texts, more pragmatic in their inspiration, list common customs that
involve pressure on the journalist and they clearly set the boundaries of what is
acceptable. That is the case in the norms of the *Washington Post*: they devote a
lot of space to conflicts of interest and go so far as to set journalism clearly

apart from the rest of the business world, some of whose practices create much ethical confusion. The Quebec Code and that of the APME set very strict prohibitions as regards travel, gifts and other advantages.

Some U.S. codes even consider the issue of journalism prizes, for example, the APME code: "Stories should not be written or edited primarily for the purpose of winning awards and prizes."

The *Washington Post* clearly disapproves of "active involvement in any partisan causes [. . .] that could compromise or seem to compromise our ability to report and edit fairly." Another point, sometimes linked to that one, is denounced in the same text: the confusion between the role of a journalist and that of a media star. The *Italian Charter* specifies that "a journalist cannot belong to secret societies or other groups proscribed by Article 18 of the Constitution," that is, paramilitary factions.

To end this comparative panorama, let us note that a few codes denounce lapses in confraternity: "Journalists and publishers are expected to promote a spirit of cooperation among colleagues, between reporters and publishers" (*Charter of the Duties of the Italian Journalist*); "A journalist worthy of the name [. . .] will not apply for the job of a colleague, nor will he/she cause his/her dismissal by offering to work at a lower rate" (*Charter of Professional Duties of French Journalists*). However elementary they may seem, these principles remind the profession that self-regulation cannot be implemented unless there is solidarity within the group.

CHAPTER 6
A Selection of Non-U.S. Codes
(IFJ, Japan, Germany, Sweden, Canada)[1]

IFJ DECLARATION OF PRINCIPLES ON THE CONDUCT
OF JOURNALISTS

[Adopted by 1954 World Congress of the IFJ. Amended by the 1986 World Congress. IFJ claims to represent 450,000 journalists in 100 countries]

This international Declaration is proclaimed as a standard of professional conduct for journalists engaged in gathering, transmitting, disseminating and commenting on news and information in describing events.

1. Respect for truth and for the right of the public to truth is the first duty of the journalist.
2. In pursuance of this duty, the journalist shall at all times defend the principles of freedom in the honest collection and publication of news, and of the right of fair comment and criticism.
3. The journalist shall report only in accordance with facts of which he/she knows the origin. The journalist shall not suppress essential information or falsify documents.

---

[1]For U.S. codes, see the websites indicated at the end of this chapter.

4. The journalist shall use only fair methods to obtain news, photographs, and documents.

5. The journalist shall do the utmost to rectify any published information which is found to be harmfully inaccurate.

6. The journalist shall observe professional secrecy regarding the source of information obtained in confidence.

7. The journalist shall be aware of the danger of discrimination being furthered by the media, and shall do the utmost to avoid facilitating such discrimination based on, among other things, race, sex, sexual orientation, language, religion, political or other opinions, and national or social origins.

8. The journalist shall regard as grave professional offences the following: plagiarism; malicious misrepresentation; calumny, slander, libel, unfounded accusations; acceptance of a bribe in any form in consideration of either publication or suppression.

9. Journalists worthy of the name shall deem it their duty to observe faithfully the principles stated above. Within the general law of each country the journalist shall recognize in professional matters the jurisdiction of colleagues only, to the exclusion of every kind of interference by governments or others.[2]

| JAPAN |

THE CANON OF JOURNALISM

[On 21 June 2000, Nihon Shimbun Kyokai (NSK—the Japan Newspaper Publishers and Editors Association) created a new comprehensive code of ethics not only for journalists but also for everyone engaged in newspaper work]

Aware afresh of the important mission of newspapers on the threshold of the 21st century, and pledging their continued effort toward an affluent and peaceful future, members of the Nihon Shimbun Kyokai have formulated this new Canon of Journalism.

The public's right to know is a universal principle that sustains a democratic society. That right cannot be ensured without the existence of media, operating with the guarantee of freedom of speech and expression, while being totally committed to a high moral standard and fully independent of all powers. Member newspapers resolve to retain their role as the fittest standard-bearers in this regard.

---

[2]Those unfortunate two last words would limit ethics to self-regulation.

In a modern society flooded with a vast range of information, the public is constantly required to make correct and swift decisions on what is true and which information to select. It is the responsibility of member newspapers to respond to such requirements and fulfill their public and cultural mission through accurate and fair reporting, and through responsible commentaries.

All newspapermen and women engaged in duties including editing, production, advertising, and circulation should uphold freedom of speech and expression. They should also conduct themselves with honor and decency in such a way as to ensure this responsibility is duly performed, and to strengthen the readers' confidence in the newspapers.

Freedom and Responsibility

Freedom of expression is a fundamental human right, and newspapers have that absolute freedom in both their news coverage and editorial comment. In exercising that freedom, however, member newspapers must be duly aware of their heavy responsibility and be constantly mindful not to impair public interests.

Accuracy and Fairness

Newspapers are the first chroniclers of history, and the mission of reporters lies in the constant pursuit of truth. Reporting must be accurate and fair, and should never be swayed by the reporter's personal conviction or bias. Editorial comment should be an honest expression of the writer's belief, not to court popularity.

Independence and Tolerance

Member newspapers uphold their independence in the interests of fair comment and free speech. They must reject interference by any outside forces, and resolve to remain vigilant against those who may wish to use the newspapers for their own purposes. On the other hand, they should willingly give space to opinions that differ from their own, provided such opinions are accurate, fair and responsible.

Respect for Human Rights

Member newspapers should pay utmost respect to the dignity of human beings, put a high value on individuals' honor and give serious consideration to their right to privacy. They should also acknowledge errors and correct them promptly, and in cases when an individual or a group has been unjustly maligned, adequate steps should be taken to rectify the situation, including the provision of an opportunity to reply.

Decency and Moderation

In the performance of their public and cultural mission, member newspapers must be available for anyone to read anytime, anywhere. They should maintain decency both editorially and in the area of advertising, and in their circulation practices they should at all times exercise moderation and good sense.

GERMANY

JOURNALISTIC PRINCIPLES (PRESS CODE)

[Drawn up by the German Press Council in collaboration with the press associations and presented to the Federal President on 12 Dec. 1973 in Bonn. Guidelines clarify and develop the meaning of the articles when the need appears.]

Preamble

The freedom of the press guaranteed in the Basic Law of the Federal Republic of Germany embraces independence and freedom of information, expression of opinion and criticism. Publishers, editors and journalists pursuing their profession must remain constantly aware of their responsibility towards the general public and their duty to uphold the prestige of the press. They must perform their journalistic duties to the best of their ability and belief and must not allow their work to be influenced by personal interests or extraneous motives.

The journalistic principles embody the professional ethics of the press. These ethics encompass the duty, within the framework of the constitution and the constitutional laws, to maintain the standing of the press and to be committed to the freedom of the press.

These professional ethics grant everyone affected the right to complain about the press. Complaints are justified if professional ethics were infringed.

Clause 1: Respect for the truth, observance of human rights and accurate informing of the public are the overriding principles of the press

Guideline 1.1—Exclusive Agreements
The informing of the general public about events and happenings which, because of their importance, weight and significance, are of general interest and importance for political formation of public opinion and intent, must not be

restricted or prevented by exclusive agreements or protective measures with the informant. Those who seek the monopoly of information prevent the rest of the press from acquiring the use of this import and thus impinge upon the freedom of information.

Guideline 1.2—Electioneering Events
It is a matter of journalistic fairness, serves the citizen's right to freedom of information, and upholds the equality of opportunity of democratic parties, when newspapers and magazines, in their reports on elections, also include opinions which are not those shared by themselves.

Guideline 1.3—Press Releases
Press releases compiled by authorities, parties, associations, clubs or other interest groups must be clearly defined as such when they are published without being edited.

> Clause 2: The publication of specific news and information in word and picture must be carefully checked in respect of accuracy in the light of existing circumstances. Its sense must not be distorted or falsified by editing, title, or picture captions. Documents must be accurately reproduced. Unconfirmed reports, rumors, or assumptions must be quoted as such. When reproducing symbolic photographs, it must be clear from the caption that these are not documentary pictures.

Guideline 2.1—Opinion Poll Results
The German Press Council recommends news agencies, newspapers, and magazines to give the number and representative nature of persons approached, and to state the time when the poll took place, as well as the commissioner, when publishing findings by public opinion-poll institutes.

If there is not commissioner, it should be pointed out that the poll was carried out on the private initiative of the institute itself.

Guideline 2.2—Symbolic Photographs
Should an illustration, in particular a photograph, be taken to be a documentary picture by casual reader, although this is not the case, the situation must be clarified. For this reason,

- substitute or auxiliary illustrations (i.e., similar motive, different time, or different motive at the same time etc.),
- symbolic illustrations (reconstructed scene, artificially reconstructed events to accompany text, etc.),
- photomontages or other changes

must be clearly marked as such for the casual reader, either in the caption or in the accompanying text.

Guideline 2.3—Advance Reports

A newspaper or magazine bears full journalistic responsibility for advance reports published in a compressed form which announce a forthcoming publication. Anyone who further distributes advance reports by press organs by stating the source must, basically, be able to rely on their validity. Abridgements or additions must not lead to a situation where the basic elements of the publication are given a new slant or prompt incorrect conclusions which may damage the justifiable interests of third parties.

Guideline 2.4—Interviews

An interview is completely journalistically fair if it has been authorized by the interviewee or his representative. If time is scarce, it is also correct to publish unauthorized interviews, if it is clear to both the interviewer and the interviewee that the statements made therein are to be published either verbatim or in an edited version. Journalists must always declare themselves as such.

If the text of an interview is reproduced in full or in part the newspaper or magazine concerned must state its source. If the basic content of orally expressed thoughts is paraphrased, it is nonetheless a matter of journalistic honor to state the source.

In the case of advanced reports of an interview in the form of an abridged version, care must be taken to protect the interviewee against any distortions or impairments which may jeopardize his justified interests.

Guideline 2.5—Embargoes

The imposition of the embargoes during which the publication of certain information is held over is only justifiable if it is vital for objective and careful reporting. In principle they represent a free agreement between the informant and the media. Embargoes should only be observed if there is a justifiable reason, such as in the case of speeches still to be held, advance copies of company reports or information on a future event (meetings, resolutions, honors' ceremonies, etc.). Embargoes must not be used for publicity purposes.

Guideline 2.6—Readers' Letters

1. By means of readers' letters, insofar as they are suitable in terms of form and content, readers should have the chance to express their views and thus participate in the opinion-forming process. It is in line with the journalistic duty of care to observe the journalistic principle when publishing readers' letters.

2.   Correspondence with the publisher or editorial department of a newspaper or magazine may only be printed as readers' letters if it is clear, due to form and content, that this is in accordance with the sender's wishes. Consent may be assumed if the letter refers to articles published by the newspaper or magazine concerned or to matters of general interest. The authors of such readers' letters have no legal right to have them published.

3.   It goes without saying that readers' letters are also subject to the usual practice of publishing the author's name. Only in exceptional cases can another designation be used, upon the wish of the author. If there is any doubt about the identity of the sender, the letter should not be printed. The publication of bogus readers' letters is not compatible with the duties of the press.

4.   Changes or abridgements to letters from known authors are basically impermissible without the author's consent. Abridgements are possible if the column contains a permanent reference to the editor's right to shorten letters. Should the author expressly forbid changes or abridgements, the editor must comply with his wish, even if he has the right to abridge, or else refuse to publish the letter.

5.   All readers' letters sent to the editor are subject to confidentiality. They must never be passed on to third parties.

Clause 3: Published news or assertions which subsequently turn out to be incorrect must be promptly rectified in an appropriate manner by the publication concerned.

Guideline 3.1—Correction

The reader must be able to recognize that the previous article was wholly or partly incorrect. For this reason a correction publishing the true facts must also refer to the previous incorrect article. The true facts are to be published even if the error has already been publicly admitted in another fashion.

Clause 4: Dishonest methods must not be used to acquire news, information or pictures.

Guideline 4.1—Research

Research is a legitimate part of journalistic activity. In principle, journalists must identify themselves. Untrue statements by a researching journalist about his identity and employer are irreconcilable with the reputation and function of the press.

Undercover research may be justifiable in individual cases if in this way information of particular public interest is gained which cannot be procured in another fashion.

In the event of accidents and natural disasters the press must take note that emergency services for the victims and those in danger have priority over the public right to information.

Guideline 4.2—Research Vis-à-Vis People Requiring Protection

When conducting research vis-à-vis people requiring protection, particular reticence shall be called for. In particular, this concerns people who are not in full possession of their mental or physical powers or who have been exposed to an extreme emotional situation, as well as children and young people. The limited strength of mind or the special situation of these people must not be deliberately exploited in order to gain information.

Clause 5: Confidentiality is to be adhered to in principle.

Guideline 5.1—Confidentiality

Should an informant stipulate, as a condition for the dissemination of his/her statements, that he/she remain unrecognizable as a source and thus protected from danger, this condition shall be respected. Confidentiality may only be lifted if the information concerns the planning of a crime, in which case the journalist is obliged to inform the police. It may also be lifted if, after careful assessment of the considerations and property and interests, important reasons of state are predominant, which may be the case where the constitutional order is affected or jeopardized.

Confidential events and plans may be reported upon if, after careful consideration, it is seen that the public right to information has a higher priority than the reasons advanced for secrecy.

Clause 6: All those employed by the press shall observe professional secrecy, make full use of the right to refuse to give evidence and shall not disclose the identity of informants without their express consent.

Guideline 6.1—Separation of Functions

Should a journalist or publisher exercise another function in addition to his journalistic activity, for example in a government, an authority or in an economic enterprise, all those concerned must take care to clearly separate these functions. The same applies vice versa. A conflict of interests harms the standing of the press.

Guideline 6.2—Secret Service Activities
Journalists or publishers who engage in secret service activities damage the credibility of the press and destroy the basis of trust enjoyed by journalism.

> Clause 7: The responsibility of the press towards the general public requires that editorial publications are not influenced by the private and business interests of third parties or by the personal commercial interests of journalists. Publishers and editors must reject any attempts of this nature and make a clear distinction between editorial texts and publications for commercial reasons.

Guideline 7.1—Distinction Between Editorial Text and Advertisements
Regulations under advertising law apply to paid publications. According to these regulations publications must have such a form that the reader can recognize it as advertising.

Guideline 7.2—Surreptitious Advertising
Editorial publications that refer to companies, their products, services or events, must not fall prey to surreptitious advertising. The danger of this is especially great if the publication goes beyond justified public interest or the reader's interest in information.

The press's credibility as a source of information requires particular care in dealing with PR texts and in producing separate editorial comments.

This also applies to unedited advertising texts, advertising photographs and advertising illustrations.

Guideline 7.3—Special Publications
Special publications are subject to the same editorial responsibility as all other editorial publications.

> Clause 8: The press shall respect the private life and intimate sphere of persons. If, however, the private behavior of a person touches upon public interests, then it may be reported upon. Care must be taken to ensure that the personal rights of uninvolved persons are not violated.

Guideline 8.1—Publication of Names and Photographs
1.   The publication of names and photographs of accused persons and victims in reports on accidents, crimes, investigations and court cases (cf. Clause 13 of the Press Code) is in general not justifiable. The public's right to information

must always be weighed up against the personal rights of those involved. The need for sensation cannot justify the public's right to be informed.

2.   Victims of accidents or crimes have a right to special protection of their name. It is not necessary to identify the victim in order to better understand the report of the accident or crime. Exceptions can be justified if the person concerned is famous or if there are special accompanying circumstances.

3. In the case of dependents and other people who are affected who have nothing to do with the accident or the crime, the publication of names and pictures is in general impermissible.

4.   The publication of the complete name and/or the picture of suspects accused of a capital crime is justified in exceptional cases if this is in the interests of solving the crime and an arrest warrant has been issued or if the crime was committed in public.

If there is any reason to believe that a perpetrator has no criminal capacity, no names or pictures should be published.

5.   In the case of crimes committed by juveniles, names and identifying pictures should not be published with deference to the future of the juveniles, insofar as no serious crimes are concerned.

6.   In the case of officials and elected representatives, the publication of names and pictures can be permissible if there is a connection between the office or mandate and a crime. The same applies to famous people if the crime they have committed is contrary to the image that the public has of them.

7.   The names and pictures of missing persons may be published; however only in agreement with the authorities concerned.

Guideline 8.2—Re-socialization
In the interests of re-socialization, the publication of names and pictures is to be omitted in reporting following a criminal trial.

Guideline 8.3—Illness
Physical and mental illness or injuries fall within the private area of the person concerned. The press, out of consideration for those involved and their dependents, should refrain from naming and including pictures of persons in such cases, as well as avoiding deprecating remarks concerning the illness or hospital/institution, even if such remarks are to be heard among the general public. Historical or famous persons are protected by law against discriminating revelations even after their death.

Guideline 8.4—Suicide
Reporting on suicide cases requires restraint. This particularly applies to the publication of names and the detailed description of the circumstances. Exceptions are only justifiable if the case is taken from current history and for which there is a public interest.

Guideline 8.5—Opposition and Escapes

In reports on countries where opposition to the government can mean danger for life and limb, consideration must always be given to whether, by publishing names or photographs, those involved may be identified and persecuted in their home country. The same applies to reports on refugees. Furthermore, it must be remembered that the publication of details about such persons, the preparation and execution of escapes and routes may result in remaining relatives and friends being endangered or in existing escape routes being eliminated.

Guideline 8.6—Anniversary Dates

The publication of anniversary dates of such persons as are otherwise not in the public eye requires that the editor confirms in advance whether those involved consent to publication or would prefer protection from public scrutiny.

> Clause 9: It is contrary to journalistic decorum to publish unfounded claims and accusations, particularly those likely to injure personal dignity.

> Clause 10: Publications in word and image which could seriously offend the moral or religious feelings of a group of persons, in form or content, are irreconcilable with the responsibility of the press.

> Clause 11: The press will refrain from an inappropriate sensational portrayal of violence and brutality. The protection of young persons is to be given consideration in reports.

Guideline 11.1—Inappropriate Portrayal

A portrayal is inappropriately sensational if in the report the person is reduced to an object, to a mere thing. This is particularly the case if reports about a dying or physically or mentally suffering person go beyond the public interest and the information interest of the reader.

Guideline 11.2—Reporting on Acts of Violence

In reporting on threats of violence and violent acts, the press should carefully weigh up the public's interest in information against the interests of the victims and other parties involved. It shall report on such things in an independent and authentic way, but shall not serve as the tool of criminals, nor shall it undertake independent attempts to mediate between criminals and the police.

Interviews with perpetrators during the act are not allowed.

Guideline 11.3—Accidents and Catastrophes
The threshold of acceptability in reports on accidents and catastrophes is exceeded when the suffering of the victims and their dependents is not respected. Victims of misfortune must not be made to suffer a second time by their portrayal in the media.

Guideline 11.4—Co-ordination With the Authorities/News Embargo
In principle the press does not accept news embargoes. Co-ordination between the media and the police shall only occur if the action of journalists can protect or save the life and health of victims and other involved persons. The press shall comply with police requests for a partial or total news embargo in the interests of solving crime, if the request is convincingly justified.

Guideline 11.5—Criminal Memoirs
The publication of so-called criminal memoirs infringes the journalistic principles if crimes are justified or qualified with hindsight, the victims are inappropriately affected and if only the demand for sensation is satisfied by a detailed description of the crime.

Guideline 11.6—Drugs
Publications in the press must not play down the use of drugs.

> Clause 12: There must be no discrimination against a person on racial, ethnic, religious, social or national grounds or because of his/her sex.

Guideline 12.1—Reports on Crimes
When reporting on crimes, it is not permissible to refer to the alleged perpetrator's religious, ethnic or other minority membership unless this information is directly relevant to the event.

It must be particularly born in mind that any such mention could awaken prejudices against groups in need of protection.

> Clause 13: Reports on cases or investigations which are still sub judice must be free from prejudice. For this reason, before and during legal proceedings, all comment, both in portrayal and headline, must avoid being one-sided or prejudicial. An accused person must not be described as guilty before final judgment has been passed.

Guideline 13.1—Prejudice—Subsequent Reporting
Reports on investigations and court cases are designed to inform the public in a careful and unbiased way about crimes, their prosecution and judgment.

Suspects must be assumed innocent until they are proved guilty by the court, even if they have confessed. Also in cases when the guilty person is obvious to the public, the person concerned cannot be portrayed as guilty within the meaning of a judgment until judgment has been made.

Prejudicial portrayals and allegations are contrary to the constitutional protection of human dignity, which also applies to criminals without limitation.

In a state guided by the rule of law the aim of court reporting must not be that of socially punishing convicted criminals by using the media as a pillory. There should, therefore, be a clear distinction in reporting between suspicion and proven guilt.

Should the press report on the unconfirmed conviction of a person mentioned by name or identifiable to a large circle of readers, journalistic fairness dictates that an ensuing, legitimately confirmed acquittal or quashing of proceedings also be reported on, insofar as the determinable interests of the person affected do not dictate to the contrary. This recommendation also applies to the suspension of investigations.

Criticism and commentary pursuant to a case must be easily distinguishable from the report on the case itself.

Guideline 13.2—Crimes Committed by Young Persons
When reporting on crimes committed by young persons and on their appearance in court, the press must exercise restraint out of consideration for their future. This also applies to young victims.

Clause 14: Reports on medical matters should not be of an unnecessarily sensationalist nature, since they might lead to unfounded fears or hopes on the part of some readers. Research findings which are still at an early stage should not be portrayed as if they were conclusive or almost conclusive.

Guideline 14.1—Medical or Pharmaceutical Research
Articles on alleged successes or failures in medical or pharmaceutical research on the fight against serious illnesses require circumspection and a sense of responsibility. Neither text nor presentation should thus include anything which might awaken unfounded hopes of cure in the foreseeable future in ill readers and their dependents, if this does not coincide with the actual state of medical research. Conversely, critical or one-sided reports on controversial opinions subject to debate should not make seriously ill persons unsure and thus raise doubts about the possible success of therapeutic measures.

Clause 15: The acceptance or granting of privileges of any kind which could possibly influence the freedom of decision on the part of publishers and editors are irreconcilable with the prestige, independence, and responsibilities of the press. Anyone accepting bribes for the dissemination of news acts in a dishonorable and unprofessional manner.

Guideline 15.1—Invitations and Gifts

The acceptance of invitations and gifts which exceed the usual level in social intercourse and the level necessary in the line of duty may lead to an impairment of the freedom of decision and independent judgment on the part of newspaper companies and their staff. Even the appearance that the freedom of the publishing house and the editor to make decisions can be impaired by accepting invitations and gifts is to be avoided.

Gifts are economic and ideal benefits at any time. The acceptance of advertising goods for everyday use or other low-value objects on ritual occasions is not considered.

Research and reporting must not be influenced, hindered or prevented by the giving or accepting of gifts, discounts or invitations. Publishing houses and journalists should insist that information be given regardless of the acceptance of a gift or an invitation.

Clause 16: It is considered fair reporting when a public reprimand issued by the German Press Council is published, especially by the newspapers or magazines concerned.

Guideline 16.1—Publication of Reprimands

The following applies to the newspaper or magazine concerned:
The reader must be informed of the false nature of the reprimanded publication and of the journalistic guideline violated by it.

SWEDEN

CODE OF ETHICS FOR THE SWEDISH PRESS, RADIO AND TELEVISION

[Issued by the Joint Committee of the Press, founded by the leading media organizations in Sweden: the National Press Club, the Union of Journalists, the Newspaper Publishers' Association. This text is the revision of 1999]

The press, radio and television shall have the greatest possible degree of freedom, within the framework of the Freedom of the Press Act and the constitutional right of freedom of speech, in order to be able to serve as disseminators of news and as scrutinizers of public affairs. In this connection, however, it is important that the individual be protected from unwarranted suffering as a result of publicity.

Ethics does not consist primarily in the application of a formal set of rules but in the maintenance of a responsible attitude in the exercise of journalistic duties. The code of ethics for the press, radio and television is intended to provide support for this attitude.

I. Rules On Publicity
Provide accurate news

1. The role played by the media in society and the confidence of the general public in them require accurate and objective news reports.
2. Be critical of news sources. Check facts as carefully as possible in the light of the circumstances even if they have been published earlier. Allow the reader/listener/viewer the possibility of distinguishing between statements of fact and comments.
3. Newsbills, headlines and leads must be supported by the text.
4. Make sure of the authenticity of pictures. See to it that pictures and graphics are accurate and are not used in a misleading way.

Treat rebuttals generously

5. Factual errors are to be corrected when requested. Anyone wishing to rebut a statement shall, if this is legitimate, be given the opportunity to do so. Corrections and rebuttals shall be published promptly in appropriate form, in such a way that they will come to the attention of those who received the original information. It should be noted that a rebuttal does not always call for an editorial comment.
6. Publish without delay statements of censure issued by the Swedish Press Council in cases concerning your own newspaper.

Respect individual privacy

7. Be careful in giving publicity where it can trespass upon an individual's privacy. Refrain from such action unless it is obviously in the public interest.
8. Exercise great caution in publishing notices concerning suicide and attempted suicide, particularly out of consideration for the feelings of relatives and in view of what has been said above concerning the privacy of the individual.
9. Always show the greatest possible consideration for victims of crime and accidents. Carefully check names and pictures for publication out of consideration for the victims and their relatives.

10. Do not emphasize race, gender, nationality, occupation, political affiliation, religious persuasion or sexual disposition in the case of the persons concerned if such particulars are not important in the context or are disparaging.

Exercise care in the use of pictures

11. Where applicable, these rules also apply to pictures.
12. Doing a montage, retouching a picture electronically, or writing the caption of a picture should not be done in such a way as to mislead or deceive the reader. Always state, close to the picture, whether it has been altered by montage or retouching. This also applies when such material is filed.

Listen to each side

13. Endeavor to give people who are criticized in a factual report the opportunity to reply to the criticism simultaneously. Endeavor also to state the views of all parties involved. Keep in mind that the sole objective of some reports may be to cause harm to the subjects of the reports.
14. Remember that, in the eyes of the law, a person suspected of an offence is always presumed to be innocent until proven guilty. The final outcome of a case that is described should be reported.

Be cautious in publishing names

15. Give careful thought to the harmful consequences that might follow for people if their names are published. Refrain from publishing names unless it is obviously in the public interest.
16. If a person's name is not to be stated, refrain from publishing a picture or particulars of occupation, title, age, nationality, gender, etc., which would enable the person in question to be identified.
17. Bear in mind that the entire responsibility for publication of names and pictures rests with the publisher of the material.

II. Professional Rules

The integrity of the journalist

1. Do not accept an assignment from anyone outside the editorial staff leaders.
2. Do not accept an assignment or an invitation, a free trip or any other benefit either in or outside your job, that could bring in question your status as a free and independent journalist.

3. Do not use your position as a journalist in order to exert pressure for your own or someone else's profit or in order to acquire personal benefits.

4. Do not utilize, for your own or someone else's profit, unpublished news concerning economic conditions or measures by state, municipalities, organizations, companies or private persons.

5. Bear in mind the provision in the Collective Contract for Journalists according to which a journalist cannot be ordered to write against his/her conviction or to carry out humiliating assignments.

Obtaining of material

6. Comply with reasonable wishes from persons interviewed to find out beforehand how and where their statements will be published.

7. Show particular consideration with people not used to being interviewed. Inform him/her whether the conversation is intended for publication or only for background.

8. Do not falsify interviews or pictures.

9. Show consideration in taking photographs and in procuring them, especially in connection with accidents and crimes.

10. Do not yield to outside pressure intending to prevent or restrict justified publishing.

11. Observe copyright as well as quotation rules and rights to photographs.

12. Indicate the source when the published material is mainly based in information from other parts.

Time of press releases

13. Respect the agreed times of releases (embargoes).

III. Rules Against Editorial Advertising
Main rule

Protect the public's trust for the press, radio and television as well as their integrity. Do not make the general public suspicious that anybody might improperly influence the content of a program or story. Therefore do not publish or present within editorial material anything that is not motivated by journalism. This implies that material published must not have an advertising purpose: it must have informative qualities or be motivated by entertaining or artistic reasons.

General regulations

1. Frame the material only in accordance to journalistic and/or program-related decisions. Your intention must never be to give publici-

ty to any products or services; neither can the presentation of the material be such that the audience think it is commercial by nature. Beware that the commercial material should not be mixed with the editorial material, in the slightest.

2. Dismiss ideas and proposals of articles and programs if they include in return, as a favor, advertisement in any form. As a principle, also dismiss offers of free or heavily subsidized trips. Reject gifts and other benefits. Never promise beforehand that you are going to publish anything.

3. Articles and programs informing consumers put specially heavy demands on journalistic integrity. Therefore show how the choice of the products/services in the article/program has been made. Make it clear how the products/services have been compared or tested. Be particularly careful and critical when dealing with reviews of products. Avoid bias in informing about limited groups of products or only about one provider of products/services, warehouses, shops, restaurants, etc.

4. Put information about theatre shows, concerts, films, art exhibitions, sport events and such through a normal journalistic evaluation to determine the value of it as news. Look critically through the material and make sure that it is given in a journalistically motivated form. Consider carefully whether information and pictures about new companies and shops or such have news value.

5. If a company or an organization takes part in some undertaking, like a competition, party or a charity ball, by providing prizes, as sponsor or organizer, the name of the company shall not be mentioned if there are not very strong journalistic reasons to do so.

6. Do not publish/present on editorial space information about the rights and obligations of individuals and other public messages that state or municipal authorities demand or wish to see published. Broadcasting companies are subject to the rules on messages by the authorities that may exist in contracts between the broadcasting company and the State and in internal instructions related to that. Reject from the editorial space data about companies and organizations, such as opening hours, product demonstrations, prize competitions or other arrangements that are not journalistically motivated.

7. Advertisements by newspapers or broadcasting companies for their own products and services shall be presented as advertisements.

8. When using material (cars, boats, clothing, furniture, kitchen equipment, etc.) for photographing purposes, only mention the names of the producers or retailers if there are journalistic reasons for it.

9. Special editorial pages and supplements in newspapers must be journalistically motivated. Overviews such as "the job market," "the boat market," "the house market," "the car market" and such, which might be

considered as advertisements or which imply that the products and services are offered for sale; must be presented as commercials.

10. Lists of entrepreneurs and suppliers at building companies presented in the newspaper must take a form of an advertisement.

CANADA—QUEBEC

PROFESSIONAL CODE OF ETHICS FOR QUEBEC JOURNALISTS

[This is the first professional Code of Ethics created for all Quebec journalists. Discussed at the 1994-96 annual meetings of the Fédération professionnelle des journalistes du Québec (FPJQ), the Code was formally adopted at the FPJQ's general assembly on November 24, 1996]

Preamble

The role of journalists is to accurately report, analyze, and in some cases, comment on the facts that help their fellow citizens understand the world in which they live.

Complete, exact and diverse information is one of the most important guarantees of freedom and democracy.

When information is of public interest, it must always circulate freely. Facts and ideas must be communicated without constraint or obstacle. Knowing that a free press acts as an indispensable watchdog over authority and institutions, journalists must defend the freedom of the press and the public's right to information; they must fight any restrictions, pressures, and threats that aim to limit the gathering and dissemination of information.

Journalists serve the public interest—not personal or specific interests. As such, they have a responsibility to publish everything that is of public interest. This obligation must override any desire to serve information sources or to favor the financial and competitive needs of news organizations.

Journalists must take their role very seriously. They must demand of themselves the same ethical qualities they demand of newsmakers; in other words, they cannot denounce other people's conflicts of interest, and at the same time, accept their own.

This Code establishes the ethical rules that should guide journalistic work. These rules lay the foundation for a journalist's most precious asset: credibility.

Since it takes into account the specific nature of the journalistic environment, this is not a Code in the strictest sense of the word. There is no professional body in Quebec to which journalists must belong. Neither the title of journalist nor the journalistic act are reserved for a particular group of people. The journalistic world is open, and that is the way journalists want it to be. Since there is no disciplinary board with the necessary legal authority to sanction breaches of ethics, journalists are subject to the body of laws that govern the lives of all citizens.

In its current form, this Code has no disciplinary powers. Yet it remains indispensable for journalists, news organizations and the public. Journalism is increasingly practiced outside of large newsrooms; as a result, it is becoming more difficult to transmit journalistic culture—ethical norms—from one generation to the next. As some journalists work in isolation throughout their entire careers, they do not benefit from a newsroom environment. This Code can thus serve as a pertinent reference point.

It will also serve as a useful reminder for journalists, editors and managers who work in newsrooms and who may sacrifice ethics to the demands of competition. Without the support of management, the application of these ethical norms would be difficult. This Code must serve as an inspiration as much for large national media as for regional and smaller media.

The review board of the Conseil de presse du Quebec [Quebec Press Council] can also use this Code to support its decisions when it investigates complaints.

Finally, both the public and information sources would benefit from a more precise knowledge of the ethical norms that should guide journalistic work. This Code will help them better judge journalistic behavior. It will also demonstrate journalists' desire to better serve the public.

1. Definition

The term "journalist" in this Code refers to all people who exercise a journalistic function for a news organization. In the context of publicly disseminating information or opinions, this includes one or several of the following tasks: researching, reporting, interviewing; writing or preparing reports, analyses, commentaries, or specialized columns; translating or adapting texts; press photography, filmed or electronic reports; assignment, the desk (headlines, lay-out. . .), editing; caricatures; information drawing and graphics; animation, producing and supervising current affairs programs and films; managing news, public affairs or other comparable departments.

2. Fundamental Journalistic Values

The fundamental values of journalists include: a critical viewpoint, so they methodically doubt everything; impartiality, so they research and expose the diverse aspects of a given situation; fairness, so they view all citizens as equal before the press as they are before the law; independence, so they maintain their distance from authority and lobby groups; public respect and compassion, so they demonstrate moderation; honesty, so they display a scrupulous respect for facts and are open-minded. This in turn demonstrates a receptiveness to unfamiliar realities, and an ability to report on these realities without prejudice.

3.   Truth and Rigor

3a. Accuracy: Journalists must rigorously gather and verify information to ensure their facts are accurate. They must correct their mistakes diligently and appropriately with regard to the harm they have caused.

3b. Context: Journalists must put their facts and opinions in their proper context so they are understandable, without exaggerating or diminishing their scope.

3c. Headlines: Headlines and introductions of articles and news reports should not exaggerate or lead to misinterpretation.

3d. Personal opinions: So as not to confuse the public, journalists must carefully distinguish between personal opinions, analysis and factual information. Above all, they must give a precise account of the facts. In the case of editorials, columns and opinion pieces, or in advocacy journalism where opinions dominate, journalists must also respect the facts.

3e. Rumors: A rumor cannot be published unless it originates from a credible source and contributes to the understanding of an event. It must always be identified as a rumor. In the judicial field, the publication of rumors is prohibited.

3f. Quotations: Journalists must give an accurate account of what people say. Quotations, editing, sound effects, etc., and the sequence in which they are presented, must not distort the meaning of people's words.

3g. Images: Photographs, graphics, sounds, and images that are published or broadcast must represent reality as accurately as possible. Artistic concerns should not result in public deception. Edited images and photographs must be identified as such.

3h. Plagiarism: Journalists must never plagiarize. If they use an exclusive piece of information that has just been published or broadcast by another media organization, they must identify the source.

4.   Gathering information

Journalists exercise their profession openly by always identifying themselves as journalists. They gather information by established journalistic methods: interviews, bibliographic research, consultation of files and contacts, etc.

4a. Undercover procedures: In certain cases, journalists are justified in obtaining the information they seek through undercover means: false identities, hidden microphones and cameras, imprecise information about the objectives of their news reports, spying, infiltrating.

These methods must always be the exception to the rule. Journalists use them when:

- the information sought is of definite public interest; for example, in cases where socially reprehensible actions must be exposed;

- The information cannot be obtained or verified by other means, or other means have already been used unsuccessfully; the public gain is greater than any inconvenience to individuals.

The public must be informed of the methods used.

4b. Sources who are unfamiliar with the media: Journalists must tell sources who are unfamiliar with the media that their remarks may be published or broadcast and thus communicated to a large group of people.

4c. Harassment: Journalists must show compassion and respect for people who have suffered tragedies, and for those close to them; they must avoid harassing people to obtain information.

5. Dissemination of information

5a. Reenactments and Dramatizations: Whenever possible, journalists should use real events in their reports rather than reenactments by diverse artificial means. Although reenactments of events and dramatizations may be used in journalism to illustrate and support a report, journalists must use caution to avoid deceiving the public. Before resorting to these techniques, journalists must evaluate if they are the best and only way to help the public understand a situation. The public must thus be clearly informed when reenactments or dramatizations are used.

Reenactments should be limited to reproducing as accurately as possible the facts, opinions, and emotions that surround the re-created event.

When journalists ask the people they are filming to speak on the telephone, for example, it is a harmless dramatization. As long as it does not modify the content of the report, it has no impact. This kind of staging does not have to be identified in the news report.

Yet in the case of more elaborate reenactments, journalists must demonstrate extreme prudence. They must avoid manipulating reality, for example, by inciting demonstrators to use violence in front of their cameras.

When invited to raids organized by the police or to reenactments orchestrated by sources, journalists must maintain a critical perspective.

If there is an attempt to portray these reenactments as spontaneous events, journalists must ensure the public knows the truth.

Archival documents must be identified as such, and should indicate the date and place.

5b. Rules of conversation: If there is no explicit agreement, journalists are not obliged to follow the rules of conversation ("off the record," "background," "publication without naming the source"). These kinds of rules must be established before the conversation—not after. To avoid being manipulated by their sources, journalists must limit these rules to the best of their ability.

5c. Sources' approval: Journalists should not seek sources' approval before publishing or broadcasting their stories.

5d. Publicity: When journalists disseminate information, they should not be influenced by their sources; in addition, they must refuse to disseminate information in exchange for advertising for their news organizations or for any other benefit. There must a clear separation between information and publicity. Journalists must not write info-mercials. If they are obliged to do so, they never sign them.

Infomercials must be clearly identified so they are not in any way confused—even by their lay-out—with information. Journalists must cover events sponsored by their own media with the same rigor they apply to every other event.

In all cases, journalists must judge the pertinence of their stories by their merit, public interest, and any other available information.

5e. Identification of suspects and the accused: Journalists must respect the presumed innocence of all citizens. When an arrest warrant has been issued, or there has been an arrest or the start of formal judicial procedures, journalists can identify citizens. Nonetheless, they must ensure they do not present them as criminals; for example, they should use the conditional.

If there have been no arrest warrants or judicial procedures—and unless their suspicions stem from rigorous journalistic work that aims to shed light on socially reprehensible acts—journalists must be cautious about revealing the identity of suspects.

5f. Follow-up: When media organizations have covered an incident where individuals have been incriminated and prosecuted, they must continue to follow the story as closely as possible, and ensure the public is informed of the end result.

5g. Identification of victims: In most cases, journalists can reveal the names of victims of accidents and criminal acts. This information is of public interest; its disclosure is especially important when the victim is a public figure or when the facts may affect the social responsibilities or public mandates of the individuals in question.

Unless there are exceptional circumstances, journalists must not identify the victims of sexual aggression or the people close to them.

6.   Protection of Sources and Journalistic Material
Journalists must identity their sources so that the public can best evaluate their competence, credibility and interests.

6a. Anonymity: In some cases journalists cannot gather and disseminate important information without guaranteeing their source's complete anonymity. Yet some people may use this anonymity to manipulate public opinion with impunity or to cause harm to individuals without assuming responsibility.

Anonymity should be granted only as a last resort and in exceptional circumstances:

- when the information is important and there are no other identifiable sources to provide it;

- when the information is of public interest;
- when the sources seeking anonymity could suffer prejudice if their identities were revealed.
- In these cases, journalists should explain the justification for anonymity, and without identifying the sources, provide a sufficient description so that the public can appreciate the sources' skills, interests and credibility.

6b. Promise of confidentiality: Unless they have been intentionally deceived by their sources, journalists must always respect a promise of anonymity. Journalists can reveal the identity of a confidential source to their superiors, but only if the latter also agree to respect the promise of confidentiality.

6c. Journalistic material: Whether published or not, journalistic material (notes, photographs, videos, etc.) should only be used to inform the public. Journalists should not provide material for any other purposes.

6d. Journalists as witnesses: Journalists must not act as police informers. In court, they should only reveal information that has already been made public in the media.

6e. Paying sources: Journalists and news organizations must not pay people who act as information sources.

7. Private Life and the Right to Information

Journalists must respect an individual's right to privacy. They must also defend the right to information; this is a fundamental individual right which enriches the private life of citizens by permitting them to broaden their horizons and knowledge. Yet these two rights may conflict. When private information is of public interest rather than simple public curiosity, journalists must give precedence to the right to information. This is of particular importance:

- when public figures or individuals who have public responsibility are involved, and when certain elements of their private lives shed light on the way they exercise their public duties, or when they place their public lives or public behavior in proper perspective;
- when an individual makes his or her private life public;
- when private affairs take place in the public domain.

8. Individual Rights

Journalists must treat all people fairly. Characteristics such as race, religion, sexual orientation, disabilities, etc., are to be mentioned only when they are pertinent.

Yet journalists must also be aware of the scope of their stories. They must avoid: generalizations that harm minority groups; incendiary remarks; non-pertinent allusions to individual characteristics and prejudices; systematically unfavorable angles that encourage discrimination. They must be particularly attentive to anything that could provoke reactions that are racist, sexist, homophobic, etc.

9. Conflicts of Interest

Whether monetary or not, journalists must avoid situations that could create a conflict of interest, or that could even have the appearance of a conflict of interest. They must avoid any behavior, commitment or job that could weaken their independent stance, or that could sow doubt in the mind of the public.

When journalists serve or seem to serve specific interests, there is a conflict of interest. These interests may be their own or those of other individuals, groups, unions, companies, political parties, etc.

The conflict of interest can occur through diverse contracts, favors or public commitments. Public interest should be the only principle that guides a journalist's choice to publish information. Facts should not be suppressed in order to preserve or enhance the image of a particular individual or group. By breaking the indispensable link of confidence between journalists and their public, conflicts of interest cast doubt or may appear to cast doubt on a journalist's choice to disseminate information.

The fact that journalists may be deeply convinced they are honest and impartial does not make a conflict of interest acceptable. The appearance of a conflict of interest is as damaging as a true conflict.

9a. Public relations: Journalists must refrain from working in any form of communications that is outside the field of journalism; this includes public relations, publicity, promotions, courses on how to deal with the media, staged news conferences to prepare spokespeople for their dealings with journalists, etc. These tasks serve specific interests and aim to transmit a partisan message to the public. Journalists cannot communicate partisan information one day and impartial information the next. This confuses the public and casts doubt on a journalist's credibility and integrity.

9b. Privileges: Journalists should not use their professional status or the information gathered in the exercising of their duties for their own benefit or to help the people close to them.

In the same way, journalists must not lie or publish information to help themselves or the people close to them.

When applicable, journalists should give their employers a list of assets and interests, including those held in corporations.

9c. Gifts and other rewards: Journalists must refuse gifts and other rewards that may be offered as a result of their duties. Gifts should be returned to the senders with an explanation.

Accepting gifts compromises journalistic impartiality or the appearance of impartiality. Gifts do not constitute a normal benefit of the journalistic profession.

Gifts are only acceptable when they serve a direct purpose in journalistic work: books; records; free tickets to cover exhibits and shows; in the case of consumer journalism, certain objects, etc. After being used, and unless they are being kept for reference purposes, these objects should be given to community or public organizations whenever possible.

A gift can also be acceptable when its value is of little importance, and when the cost of returning it to the sender exceeds the cost of the object.

9d. Journalism contests: Journalists can compete in journalism contests or act as jury members as long as the contests serve their profession.

Contests serve the interests of journalism when the jury is independent of any sponsors, when the majority of people serving on the jury are journalists, and when the work is judged according to recognized journalistic criteria. In these cases, a journalist's credibility cannot be used to support or invalidate a cause; as well, the awards will only serve the future work of journalists.

9e. Paid trips: Journalists and media must pay the costs associated with covering their stories. They must not accept free trips or financial aid from public or private organizations that are seeking media coverage.

Trips that are paid by sources can distort coverage by favoring wealthy interest groups. They can also—at least in appearance—limit journalists' freedom of expression.

A trip offered by a source can nonetheless be accepted:

- when there is no other way of obtaining information or no other way of travelling to the site. In this case, the media organization should evaluate and reimburse the cost of the trip;
- when the trip provides professional training and is not used to gather stories.

If—in exceptional circumstances and as a last resort—media organizations accept a trip paid by a source, journalists must protect their professional freedom while covering the story. In addition, they must explicitly inform the public that their trips were paid by a source.

10. Conscience Clause

Journalists are responsible for their own acts, and cannot blame others for what they have done. They must not be forced to resort to unethical practices, or to put their names on stories that have been substantially modified.

The (English) texts of other codes can be found in books:

Bertrand, Claude-Jean, *Media Ethics and Accountability Systems*, Piscataway, NJ, Transaction, 2000.

Bruun, Lars (ed.), *Professional Codes in Journalism*, Prague, IOJ, 1979 [IOJ was a soviet front].

Cooper, Thomas W. (ed.), *Communication Ethics and Global Change,* New York, Longman, 1989.

Crawford, Nelson A., *The Ethics of Journalism*, New York, Knopf, 1924; new ed. 1969 [Contains several early U.S. codes].

Jones, G. Clement, *Mass Media Codes of Ethics and Councils,* Paris, Unesco, 1980 [marxist bias].

By far the best sources of media codes of ethics are on the web, and many of the following sites have links to other possible sources:

- www.presscouncils.org
  British Press Complaints Commission
- www.presswise.org.uk
  has about 60 codes from all over the world.
- www.asne.org/ideas/codes
  has about 40 U.S. national codes and codes of individual newspapers.
- www.ijnet.org/code.html
  has about 35 codes from various parts of the world.
- www.uta.fi/ethicnet
  has about 40 European codes.
- http://www.uow.edu.au/crearts/journalism/ajnet/AJNet.html
  has more than 10 codes from the Asian region.
- http://csep.iit.edu/codes/media.html
  has about 50 codes from all over.
- http://www.usp.ac.fj/journ/docs/ethics.html#MEDIA
  has a dozen codes from the Pacific islands.

See also the bibliography (p. 416).

PART III
Press Councils

CHAPTER 7
Press Councils

As the third millennium started, there were press councils in the whole world *press* *council* from Austria to Australia, from Iceland to Indonesia, from Turkey to Taiwan. With the exceptions of a few Latin countries, all industrialized democracies had *in nearly* one, or had had one, in one shape or another. Even under-developed countries *all countries* experimented with them in the 1960s and 1970s. Those early councils quickly vanished (as in Burma or Pakistan)—but others have re-emerged in the 1990s, as in Ghana or have appeared for the first time, as in Senegal or Tanzania.

Yet most people outside the media world do not know what a press council is and many have never even heard of one. One reason might be that the institution is relatively new. Though the first press council was set up by the Swedes in 1916, councils only started multiplying in the 1960s. Half were born after 1970 and a quarter in the 1990s.

A better explanation, however, is that the media, both commercial and "public," greeted councils with no enthusiasm and gave them minimal publicity. Many journalists still often mistake them for governmental control bodies. And media bosses seem to consider them as a possible sign of an evolution towards the participation of producers and consumers (i.e., professionals and public) in the control of media.

The first press councils that included non-media members, that were more than disciplinary committees within a union or joint commissions of publishers and reporters, were those of Turkey and South Korea in the early 1960s. Yet the few people who have heard about press councils know the original British one (1953), which admitted lay members (5 out of 25) only in 1963. It was set up by national associations of newspaper proprietors, editors, and reporters. When it was terminated in December 1990 (see p. 137), it consisted of 18 representatives from the associations, 18 lay members (indirectly) co-opted by the former group, and a non-media person as president. Because it operated for 37 years and enjoyed (relative) visibility, that London institution long served as an inspiration for many creators and reformers of press councils throughout the world.

Nevertheless, a mere description of it would not provide a definition of the ideal, or even the typical, press council. For one thing, it turned out that the British Press Council did not win support at home. But, mainly, such a definition would fit very few of the existing councils.

Admittedly, press councils have appeared in countries that shared many of the same values and the same concerns for democracy—or in countries that have been under the colonial or cultural influence of Western democracies. Everywhere the need has been felt for an institution that would help media be more "socially responsible" without yielding any of their freedom. To some extent, that explains the similarity of press councils all over the world. Another factor of resemblance was the existence of the British model. Yet another was the publicity given to the notion of press council by several international organizations: Unesco, the International Press Institute, the International Federation of Journalists, and the Council of Europe. But, inevitably, in every country circumstances and local needs have fashioned a different institution. The councils in Peru or Indonesia have very little in common with the early European models.

The concept is not easy to define, except negatively. A press council is *not* an office of governmental censorship, *nor* an internal self-censorship bureau, *nor* a lobby serving media owners, *nor* a union of professional journalists, *nor* an arbitration agency to settle disputes among media, *nor* a branch of a media users association.

Press councils are found under so many different guises that to include them all in a single sentence, one would have to define a council as "a group of people whose concern for the quality of media has led them to use their moral authority with the intent of improving them." Such a definition is too vague to be meaningful.

More useful would be to identify the fundamental purposes of all councils. They aim at preserving press freedom against direct and indirect threats of government. They strive to help the press assume all its functions in society and thus to mobilize public opinion in support of its fight for independence. Who exactly is going to do that job and how? On those two points, the initiators of press councils rarely agree.

TYPES OF COUNCILS

To acquire a clear perception of the strange institution, the best way is to have a look at the 40-odd councils that exist. So as better to distinguish among them, I think it useful to distribute them into several categories. But before doing so, let me make three points.

The first unoriginal point is that media make up a large part of the nervous system of a modern nation. Hence, the health of the social body is predicated on their satisfactory operation. Another consequence: the media have given every member of the social body new means of intervention. A press council is a way of using public opinion, which is stronger than ever, in order to pressure media into serving society better. A council is unthinkable in a dictatorship, be it fascist, communist, or religious. And a council finds it difficult to operate in an under-developed country, where media also are under-developed.

The second (unoriginal) point to underline is that in a democracy, the press is at the same time an industry, a public service, and a political institution, the fourth of the political "estates". This triple nature generates most of the problems of the press because it gathers four potentially antagonistic groups: citizens, journalists, equipment owners and the elected (or appointed) leaders of the nation.

The public is certainly capable, through apathy, ignorance, stupidity, or narrow-mindedness, of jeopardizing the freedom or the quality of the press. Journalists may do so, too, through incompetence or dishonesty. Yet neither of those groups can be considered as a major danger.

For four centuries at least, the main threat to freedom of expression has come from political leaders jealous of their power. So it is unimaginable that an acceptable and effective press council include representatives of the government. The second most serious threat emerged at the turn of the 20th century, when the press turned into a big business: this is the threat of proprietors more interested in profit than in public service. Ideally, it would be preferable that they, too, be kept out of a press council. But if it is to be efficient, a council needs money and publicity. It depends on media owners for its funds and for access to its only source of power—the public.

The third and last point I wish to stress before classifying press councils is that the media world is vast and diverse. The scope of a council's action will depend on the size of the region and of the media in its jurisdiction. The area can be anything from a small town to a continent-size country like the United States—or even a multinational community such as the English-speaking Caribbean. The media involved can be a single local weekly newspaper or all the print and electronic media in a country.

With these three remarks in mind, one can appreciate a first distinction between three main categories of existing councils.

A. Pseudo-Councils

These self-styled "press councils" include agents of the government, unofficial as in Egypt, or official as in Sri Lanka, where the chairman of the council is appointed by the president of the country. An extreme case is when all members are appointed by the government, as in Indonesia until 1999, where the council

meetings were chaired by the Minister of Information. Those councils are totally contemptible: their only mission is to muzzle the press.

Regrettably, in the 1990s, a so-called World Association of Press
Councils (WAPC), launched in Australia, with honorable concerns for the Third
World, admitted as members some pseudo-councils (Egypt, Bangladesh)—thus
giving them respectability and, in the process, damaging the image of the true
press councils. Most of the genuine press councils have never joined, or have
left, the WAPC, including all the European councils.

Let's note that it is not unacceptable, though hardly recommended, that
a small minority of the members of a council represent a democratically elected
Parliament, as in India. History, after all, proves that legislators often show
great support for press freedom.

B. Semi-Councils

These councils can assume some, but only some, of the functions of a press
council, because they do not include people from outside the media, except an
independent chairperson, which nearly all councils have. At best, these councils
are bipartite: they have been created jointly by owners and journalists, as in
Austria. More often, they represent only one group, like the journalists in
Switzerland (until 2000). These semi-councils come in three types: the German,
the Japanese, and the Italian.

In Japan, a *shinsa-shitsu*, or "contents evaluation commission," was set
up by the *Nihon Shinbun Kyokai* (NSK), the association of newspaper publishers (see p. 305). The veteran journalists who work on it scrutinize all dailies and
report any violation of the NSK code of ethics. The NSK then remonstrates
with the editors and publishers involved. That is certainly a M*A*S, but not
really a press council.

In Italy, an Order, the *Ordine dei giornalisti*, established by law in
1963 yet independent from the state, includes all the journalists in the country.
To enter journalism, as any other profession, you need to be admitted into the
Order by taking an exam organized by the Order. Violations of its code of ethics
fall within the jurisdiction of 19 autonomous regional orders[1] to which complaints should be addressed. Their sanctions (oral or written reprimand, suspension, expulsion) can be appealed to the national council before they become
effective.[2] Afterwards an appeal can be made to the court.

Far closer to the press council concept stands the German *Presserat*. It
was based on the original, bipartite version of the British General Council of the

---

[1]For example, in the first 10 months of 2000, the *Ordine* in Milan processed 63 disciplinary actions.

[2]Over the years, 20 such appeals were made and 17 rejected, the journalists then being
expelled from the profession.

Press, of 1953.[3] Publishers and journalists moved into action to avoid federal regulation and more or less stopped there. The *Presserat* keeps in regular contact with regional and central governments as a representative of the press industry. And now it is more concerned with the ethics of the profession and with grievances of the public—yet one third of the complaints it receives come from politicians and institutions.

C. Genuine Councils

All include both media people and non-media people, though in various proportions. The press members usually represent their professional associations (though they did not in the late U.S. National News Council). Media owners participate most often; otherwise they are represented by editors. In the Press Complaints Commission (Great Britain, 1991), editors *de facto* "represent" journalists, who do not participate.

True councils can operate at three levels: national, regional, and local. Actually, some regions such as Minnesota or Quebec are larger than nations such as Israel or the Netherlands, and their councils are almost identical to national ones. In contrast, local councils form a separate breed, because they function neither as lobbies, nor as alternative courts. Their purpose is to establish and maintain direct contacts between the media and the citizens of a community (see p. 147).

Ideally, a press council (national or regional) should use a whole arsenal of methods to improve the media. Among other things, it should permanently monitor the evolution of media and publicize any unethical trends. One of its missions should be to watch the government's communication policies and also the evolution of media ownership. It should serve as a forum for an ongoing debate of issues pertaining to mass communication. It should take some interest in journalism training and media research, and so forth. See Clause 2 of The Articles of Constitution of the British Press Council (1963-1990).

The Objects of the Council are:
1. To preserve the established freedom of the British Press;
2. To maintain the character of the British Press in accordance with the highest professional and commercial standards;
3. To consider complaints about the conduct of the Press or the conduct of persons and organisations towards the Press; to deal with these complaints in whatever manner might seem practical and appropriate and record resultant action;

---

[3]The British press was reluctant to implement the suggestion of the first Royal Commission on the Press (1947-1949) and to set up the council—with the result that Parliament passed the very severe 1952 Defamation Act.

4. To keep under review developments likely to restrict the supply of information of public interest and importance;

5. To report publicly on developments that may tend towards greater concentration or monopoly in the Press (including changes in ownership, control and growth of Press undertakings) and to publish statistical information relating thereto;

6. To make representations on appropriate occasions to the Government, organs of the United Nations and to Press organisations abroad.

7. To publish periodical reports recording the Council's work and to review from time to time, developments in the Press and the factors affecting them.

And yet, up to now, press councils have usually pursued only two missions, sometimes only the second of the two: (1) they have tried to help the press in its struggle against the traditional enemy of its freedom, the government and its bureaucracy; and (2) they have tried to get the news media to render accounts to the public. Most councils have both a commission on freedom of information and an ethics commission—but the second is always far more active, or at least more visible.

The first aim is easy to achieve. The council has merely to publish warnings to public opinion about any abuse of power by the State. In fact, that function is often assumed by other organizations, older and more powerful. Not in India, however, where about half the complaints lodged are aimed by journalists at public officials.

The second aim is more elusive. Two obvious ways to reach it are either to wait for the public to complain and then to denounce possible abuse of power by a media outlet; or to take the initiative which, except in case of some flagrant violation of ethics, implies monitoring. One problem is that media users lodge few complaints and that their grievances often are quite futile compared to the real sins of media, meaning omissions and long-term distortion, of which the person-in-the-street is not aware.

A Finer Distinction. At this point, a finer distinction is called for between types of councils—and also a hierarchy based on participants. In the eyes of all four social groups involved (proprietors, professionals, public, politicians), media are crucially important. The "tribunal" that is supposed to evaluate their behavior can include one or more of those groups. Mathematically, there are sixteen possible combinations.

Practically, some possibilities would be absurd. How could a council not include members of the profession when its major purpose is to contribute to media self-regulation? How could media owners and professionals open a council to politicians (whom they distrust) and close it to the public (whose support they need). Similarly, it is difficult (though not quite impossible) to imagine that proprietors would let both politicians and lay people criticize their products and would keep out their employees.

Actually, there are only eight reasonable combinations—seven of which have been realized, as of the year 2000:

- publishers (or their agents) only, as in Japan;
- publishers and journalists, as in Luxembourg;
- publishers and public, as in Britain since 1991;
- journalists only, as in Slovenia;
- journalists and public, as in the Netherlands;
- publishers, journalists, and public, as in New Zealand, the classic model;
- publishers, journalists, public, and legislators, as in India.

As for the eighth possibility, an alliance of journalists, media users, and politicians, it would imply an end to the commercial control of media. Because government ownership of media is unacceptable to most participants, this would have to be a "public" ownership of media, such as the Britisher Raymond Williams suggested years ago: the technical equipment would be owned by an independent regulatory agency (such the FCC in the United States or the CSA in France or ITC in Britain), which would entrust a printing plant or a broadcast station to a team of journalists for a (renewable) period of time, just as a theater is entrusted to a company of actors. Even the advocates of such a revolution look upon it as utopian—and even anachronistic in the cyber-world.

Considering that the right to be informed belongs to the public, considering that the talent to inform belongs to journalists, considering that the means to inform belong to media owners—and, lastly, considering that politicians have an inclination to disinform—so a hierarchy of press councils can be determined (see the following chart).

A.1.   Tripartite mixed councils include representatives of proprietors, journalists and public—as in Australia;

A.2.   Bipartite mixed councils, consisting of proprietors and public—as in GB since 1991; or journalists and public—as in the Netherlands;

B.   Bipartite professional councils, including proprietors and journalists—as in Germany.

And then, on the margins of the concept:

C.1.   Councils limited to journalists, as in Switzerland until 2000, which are more like disciplinary committees;

C.2.   Councils limited to proprietors (or their agents), as in Japan, which are more like quality control units.

The Evolution.   Psychologically and historically, the evolution has been from C2 to A1. As soon as journalism started becoming a profession in a commercial environment, some journalists found it hard to accept that some of their peers behaved in opposition to the public interest. As they refused external regulation, they often sought self-discipline by forming ethics commissions. In Italy and formerly in Chile, those bodies were turned by law into Orders of Journalists.

A little later, the authorities made proprietors understand that, with the growing monopolization of media, the decreasing number of outlets and of owners, profit-motivated sensationalism or private propaganda were not tolerable any more. To avoid interference by legislators, the media started taking action. In 1945, Japanese newspaper publishers formed an association, the NSK, adopted a code, the "Canon of Journalism," and set up a commission to scrutinize the press and report violations. There again, dirty linen was to be washed out of public sight.

The next stage was a union of proprietors and journalists to pillory the sinners in their own ranks. Sweden in 1916 and Norway in 1938 had been pioneers, but very discreetly—and without much effect. Then in 1953, the British Parliament pressured a reluctant press into forming a "General Council of the Press"—which was hardly more efficient, as it was strictly proprietorial and professional.

A few years later, in 1960, with Scandinavian help, obtained via the International Press Institute (IPI), the Turks set up a *Basin Seref Divani* (Honor Court of the Press) which included non-media members—though these could hardly be considered representatives of the general public. The undiplomatic harshness of that council soon offered Turkish newspapers a pretext to rebel and ignore the council. It faded away.

In 1961, again with the help of IPI, the South Koreans innovated by creating a Press Ethics Commission. It consisted of representatives of publishers, journalists, parliamentarians, and public. It adjudicated complaints, British style, and it also monitored the press, Japanese style. But soon press freedom vanished as the military seized power. In Western democracies, little attention was paid to those short-lived experiments, made in what was then looked upon as the Third World.

In 1963, the British Press Council (again under the pressure of Parliament) admitted members from outside the media world and really got down to work, to the apparent satisfaction of all concerned. It was as if it had given an expected signal. Mixed councils appeared where before only professional councils existed—and in places where no council existed before. Some improved on the model, by increasing the number of lay members, by widening the scope of action, or by adding new missions. A good example is the Quebec press council: it gave equal representation to owners, journalists, and public; it covered the print and the electronic press; and it used its power to initiate inquiries, in the absence of a complaint.

Lastly, in 1973, further enriching the press council concept, a National News Council was created in the United States by a foundation, without any participation of professional organizations. It assumed its functions honorably for ten years. Its closure in 1984 seems to have been due to bad management and poor morale rather than to low efficiency.

This quick historical overview shows the kinship of Type C (Italian or Japanese) and Type B (German) and Type A (Australian) councils—although some commentators (like me) are very reluctant to bestow the name "press council" on the ethics committees of the *Ordine dei Giornalisti* and the NSK or even to such bodies as the journalists alone set up in Belgium or in Switzerland (before 2000) that sometimes use the name. Types B and A differ mainly in their scope.

The single element in C becomes one of two elements in B, which themselves make up two of the three elements in A. What C can do, B can do better and A better still. What C does, B does too and adds the defense of press freedom. What B does, A does too and adds (in theory at least) several other functions.

How a Council Emerges. A genuine press council normally (but not exclusively) appears, and can develop, only in a particular environment, in an urbanized, industrialized nation, a pluralistic democracy with developed media and truly professional journalists. The country, geographically or culturally, belongs to the Western world and, more specifically, to the North Atlantic liberal tradition—or has close links to them. In that country, there is neither a morbid distrust of government nor a blind trust in the law and the courts. That excludes vast regions of the planet such as Russia, China, the Arab world, most of black Africa and, to some extent, the United States and the Latin world.

The project emerges within groups angered by the behavior of media: militant journalists, academics, or politicians of the democratic Left. From their ranks will come one or several champions whose passion is needed to energize the movement leading to the creation of a council.

In the case of the very first councils, the process was long and divided into several stages. Take, for instance, the Norwegian *Pressens Faglige Utvalg*: it was successively an arbitration committee of publishers and journalists (1910), an internal disciplinary commission (1928), an ethics committee examining complaints from the outside (1938), and lastly a (practically) tripartite council since 1972.[4] On the contrary, most of the councils that were born after 1960 appeared in their final shape. A variant, common in the under-developed world but not limited to it, is for media organizations first to adopt a code of ethics and then to form a council to enforce its rules, as in Japan, Pakistan, and Catalonia (Spain).

---

[4]Only editors and reporters sit on the council, not the publishers, but the two editors can be considered representatives of management. Besides, all three categories are represented in the Norwegian Press Association (NPA). The NPA founded the council and its executive committee appoints council members.

The original impulse usually comes from journalists, or rather their unions. When a democratic State was involved in the creation, it acted under pressure from journalists—but that only in developing nations (India). In North America councils have been set up by private individuals (Honolulu, National News Council in the United States), or by individual publishers (Ontario, Alberta).

Many obstacles stand in the way of those who wish to develop a press council. The first, maybe the worst, is psychological. A press council, being a new concept, can be disturbing. Resistance is so strong that a council is rarely, if ever, set up without direct or indirect pressure being exerted by a government or parliament—usually through the threat of establishing a council by law.

Composition.   The membership of press councils differs widely, from 5 in Iceland to 52 in Israel—but the average is 18. Between a dozen and a score of members makes it possible for a council to be both efficient and representative. In some cases, responsibility is delegated to a smaller unit. In the Netherlands, every case is examined by 3 only out of the 18 members. In Israel, an executive committee of 19 deals with all the business and reports to the plenum only once a year.

The members are elected or appointed for terms of one, two, or three years—in staggered terms to insure stability. Councils, are institutions that depend on volunteer participation. They usually recruit eminent personalities, very busy people, who most often serve without pay. So, to guarantee a smooth operation, many councils provide for substitute members.

Two problems come up immediately. First, what proportion of non-media people should be admitted? The more media people there are in a council, the faster it gets to influence the media—and the less credibility it enjoys in public opinion. Conversely, the more non-media people there are, the less media people feel inclined to cooperate.

Except in regional councils (Ontario, Minnesota), the distinction between management and rank-and-file journalists is always made—although it is quite often blurred by the presence of editors, as in the (British) Press Complaints Commission. Representatives of the media are appointed by their respective associations/unions, which usually correspond either to levels of the hierarchy or to areas of the media industry (newspapers, magazines). That was well illustrated by the distribution of seats in the late Press Council of Britain.[5]

The distribution can also reflect geographical divisions: the national and the provincial press in Britain; the press of the various provinces in Australia; the press of the several linguistic areas in Switzerland. Only regional

---

[5]They went to members of the NPA (proprietors of the national press), the Newspaper Society (provincial publishers), the Periodical Publishers Association (magazines), the Scottish Newspaper Proprietors Association, and the Scottish Newspaper Proprietors Association, the Guild of Newspaper Editors, and the NUJ (union of journalists) and the IoJ (Institute of Journalists).

councils sometimes limit their jurisdiction to participating newspapers (Alberta, Ontario): then the papers appoint representatives to the council. The National News Council in the United States was unique in that its media members were not representative of the profession and co-opted their successors.

The second question is how to select non-media members. Usually, lay members are appointed, directly or indirectly, by the founding bodies (Norway) or by their representatives in the council, or by the chair they have elected (Caribbean), or again, after the original appointments, by the council itself. However, in the first Turkish council they were appointed by outside institutions (University, Bar Association) and in Britain until 1990 they were chosen by an Appointments Commission, itself appointed by the council. The following chart illustrates comparative non-European membership distribution.

Distribution of Members in a Few Mixed Councils*

Nation	Total	Managt.	Journalists	Public	Institutions**	Parliam.
Australia	21	10	3	8	0	0
India	28	13	7	0	8	5
Israel	60	18	18	24	0	0
Minnesota	25	12	***	13	0	0
N. Zealand	11	3	2	6	0	0
Quebec	19	6	6	7	0	0
Ontario	21	6	4	11	0	0
Taiwan	11	2	***	8	0	1

* For European councils see Table, p. 135.
** Bar Association, University, Churches, etc.
*** Those councils do not distinguish.

What criteria should be used to select non-media members? The Quebec press council seeks people who represent various groups in the population. The NNC in the United States wanted people from various fields of activity (businessmen, feminists, Blacks, politicians, clergy, etc.) The Israeli council wants eminent people. The Minnesota council wants people likely to be efficient. With non-media VIPs chosen at random, the risk is elitism, like choosing like. If the chosen are representatives of social categories (whether or not they are actually chosen by a Church, a union, etc.), the council may become too large and be manipulated by pressure groups.

Nevertheless, although in theory it does not work, in practice it can. Informal attempts are worth making so as to produce a panel broadly representative of the public in age, gender, education, occupation, geography, religion, and so forth. Thus did the British press council obtain 18 public members of widely differing backgrounds and opinions who worked surprisingly well together.

In most councils formed or reformed since the 1970s, the presidents do not belong to the media world. More than half are elected from within the council. Others are appointed by the founding bodies, one third of which choose a former magistrate, such as a retired Supreme Court judge. The reason for that is that he/she can insure a fair trial and arbitrate among supposedly hostile factions.

Financing. Whatever the policy the council chooses, it needs means to apply it, money especially. It is better not to ask the State. Journalists do not have enough resources to finance a council properly. Sources of funds such as the Ford or the Rockefeller Foundations are rare outside the United States. As for media owners, they are reluctant to fund an institution because they often cannot see what benefit they can get out of it.

A local council, or Advisory Board, will have few problems; it can use the logistics of the town's newspaper. But the efficiency of a regional or a national council will be judged from its budget. The average 1998 budget, for about 30 councils, was US $ 218,000, but the gap is wide between the Icelandic council ($3,000) and the British Press Complaints Commission ($1,920,000).[6] The money normally comes from the founding institutions: most often owners provide either the lot (99% in Australia) or the largest part (75% in Sweden). In the (mainly Canadian) case when the council was set up by some newspapers only, those publications finance it in proportion to their circulation.

Some funds do come from other sources; foundations (100% for the NNC in the United States) or private corporations (40% in Minnesota).[7] The State gives subsidies when it has participated in the creation, as in India (88%), but also where it played no direct role, as in Finland, where it provides half the budget of the council, and in Germany (30%). It is possible for a council to demand a fee from plaintiffs (as formerly in Turkey and Switzerland). The advantage of such payment is that it deters pranksters and eccentrics—but also the poor, regretfully, so it is never required anymore. Only the Swedish council finds part of its budget by fining guilty newspapers—as did the South African when it existed.[8]

Once a council has secured more or less (usually less) sufficient funds to function, it then needs to acquire visibility and moral authority. In the best of circumstances, that takes years of unstinting effort, both to educate the public and not to alienate media people.

Polity and Scope. The purpose of any M*A*S—and particularly of a press council (this cannot be overstressed) is to protect freedom of speech by

---

[6]These figures need to be set beside the one or two million dollars that the larger U.S. dailies spend every year on market research.

[7]And only about 25% from media sources.

[8]It is worth noting that in the days of the apartheid, when the press was far from free, its press council, set up by law, protected the media by saving them from court actions that would have been far more damaging.

enabling news media to keep or to recover public trust—by improving both their quality and their social accountability. To reach that goal, a council can follow four paths.

1. It can fight against violations of ethical rules, pointed out by the public. The rules can consist in the unwritten usage of the profession or can gradually emerge from the council's accumulated decisions (as in India or in Britain before 1991). Most often, however, the rules have been gathered into one or several codes, either written before the council was born or drafted by the council. In the latter case, the council can compose a code straight away (Israel) or wait until it has accumulated experience (17 years in Germany).
2. The council can fight for freedom of expression, against state indifference or antagonism. The council strives to improve the relations between the Fourth Estate and the other three, gives its opinion on desirable laws, and mobilizes public opinion against restrictive bills and any encroachments on the part of the Executive.
3. It can also fight for the freedom to inform about, and against, all limitations to, or the manipulation of, the news flow by mercantile forces. To that purpose, the council keeps under review the evolution of media, particularly concentration of their ownership and links with other commercial interests. And it warns the public about any alarming phenomenon.
4. Lastly, it can fight for the improvement of media by promoting high quality teaching and research.

When you examine the history of press councils, you discover that their first concern has been media ethics, in the narrow sense of the word. Most councils have certainly shown a vague interest in the improvement of journalistic products by, for instance, denouncing an act of censorship or contents solely motivated by greed or again, for a few councils, by trying to improve professional training and media research—but those activities never expanded.

Practically, councils focused all their energies on those sins of the press about which they received complaints from citizens. Compare what the Articles of Constitution of the British press council said (see p. 113) and what that body did—remembering that that council was considered as a model from 1963 onward. It only dealt seriously with one of its seven assigned missions.[9] For lack of imagination or courage, and mainly for lack of funds and support, nearly all councils have been content with letting outside amateurs watch the media for them haphazardly, content with listening to the grievances of a few consumers and giving them access to the press.

---

[9]It is fair to recall that at the time they set up the (original) General Council of the Press, which was expected to deal with training, the same organizations launched the National Council for the Training of Journalists.

In the case of obvious violations of ethical rules, the council should initiate a case; most of them never do it (Ontario) or do it rarely (Great Britain)—unless they employ an ombudsman (Sweden) or a monitoring team, which is exceptional. As for the kind of serious sins that do not attract attention, such as omission, obviously a council cannot expect them to be reported: so it should be equipped to spot them by its own means. Taking the initiative implies monitoring, which is very expensive. Only one national self-regulatory institution practices monitoring nowadays, that of Japan[10]—but then it does not take complaints.

Ideally, a press council should keep an eye on all informative activities of all media. In fact, very few councils cover news agencies. The reasons that used to be given for not covering electronic journalism were that it was watched by the state,[11] or that there was a specialized regulatory authority (like the FCC or the CSA in France), that those media already had a complaints bureau, or that they were too different. Starting in the 1970s, however, the trend has been to include broadcasting, from the start (Québec) or as an addendum (Minnesota). In 2000, this was the case for 60% of them—but not, of course, those that had been set up by groups of newspapers (as in Canada).

Procedure. For the defense of media, whatever the relative importance given to that mission, the procedure is quite simple: the council is expected to act as a mouthpiece: to make direct representations to the various institutions whose activities affect journalists and the media; and to publish statements. Usually, a special committee is in charge of those problems. In Sweden, the function is assumed by another body created by the same press organizations that set up the press council. In Japan, the function is entrusted to the NSK itself, the association that provided itself with a "contents evaluation commission."

Because most councils have been content with acting as arbitrators, their procedural rules are quite important. Normally, a (written) complaint can be lodged by any private individual or any organization that considers that a medium has violated media ethics. For half the councils, it does not matter whether the plaintiff himself/herself suffered any damage. Most often, however, the involved person/s must at least be informed (Sweden) or give permission.

Complaints must be aimed not at a particular journalist, but at a publication or broadcast station. That restriction has not been adopted by some professional councils (Austria). Nor does it arise, of course, when the council is the disciplinary arm of an organization of journalists, as in Italy.[12]

[10]That of the NSK at national level. The *shinsa-shitsu* of individual newspapers do take complaints.

[11]Yet in Finland, the *Julkisen Sanan Neuvosto* covers broadcasting, which for a long time was a State monopoly.

[12]In Switzerland, however, before 2000, a journalist incriminated could claim that he had obeyed orders: then the case was transferred to a joint commission of publishers and journalists.

Quite a few complaints are futile or foolish. Some winnowing is needed if the council, a voluntary institution, is to be able to deal seriously with important cases. The selection is entrusted to one or several filterers. Complaints may have already been transmitted to the council by a local section of the founding body (as formerly in Switzerland), or by an ad hoc committee formed for each particular case, or by an ombudsman to whom the council delegates the authority to settle minor complaints (Sweden). All those methods, however, are exceptional. In one third of the councils, a permanent secretary (Norway) or a legal adviser (Israel), who are not members of the council, do the sifting—or, more commonly, a complaints committee, made up of council members.

The filtering body can reject the complaint for various reasons: if the complaint is unsubstantial; if the events are too distant in time; if the grievance does not belong within the field defined by the statutes of the council, its code, or its case-law; if the case is being dealt with by a court of justice—also, if the plaintiff refuses to waive his/her right to go to court later with the case. About half the councils demand that waiver; the others either do not wish to require it (Germany) or cannot legally. That condition is important because it prevents a council from slowly being absorbed into the judicial system. It guarantees its independence while saving media the huge expense of damages, especially in libel cases.

That being said, a press council is supposed to be not simply an alternative tribunal, but mainly a mediator, an educator, a guide. So, if a grievance seems justified, it will first seek a settlement. The plaintiff is asked to send the complaint to the media outlet—or the council will do it for him. If necessary, a meeting is held of both parties to seek conciliation. Very often, the plaintiff obtains satisfactory explanations or a correction is published: then the complaint is withdrawn or discontinued. Otherwise, the filtering agency starts an investigation, sometimes holds a hearing after which the case is closed, or (more often) it is forwarded to the council with statements by both parties and its own opinion.

Councils normally meet at regular intervals, once a month on average, some twice a month (Chile, Cyprus, Iceland). Regional councils meet less often, five times a year on average, only three times in Canada.

The Swedish council examines only the written file but most other councils can hold hearings, usually not public. Most have adopted flexible procedural rules so as to act faster, more efficiently, more fairly. Many councils, however, accept the principle that judicial usage be respected, that the parties can be assisted by witnesses and counselors. Nearly half of them even tolerate the use of lawyers, though they usually discourage it. Only councils established by law (as in India) are entitled to summon witnesses and make them testify under oath.

That done, unless it feels the need for further information, the council debates and then votes. More than 8 councils in 10 use a code of ethics as a reference; even the British Press Council had finally adopted one in the last year of its existence. Councils in North America do not have their own code, but can use the many codes drafted by professional associations.

The decision is usually taken by a simple majority; sometimes, as in Germany, by a two-thirds majority. Rarely does the council, as in Sweden, seek unanimity. Lastly, the council drafts its adjudication; it recalls the facts and then either expresses and explains its judgment or limits itself to a general statement.

The number of complaints lodged being anything between 10 and 1,500—and as most Canadian councils systematically seek conciliation—it is difficult to determine a realistic average in judgments. At the end of the 1990s, the Press Complaints Commission in London received some 1,500 complaints a year and the *Pressens opinionamnd* in Sweden up to 400. The Japanese NSK *shinsa-shitsu* generates about as many. Not counting those three, the annual average for national councils in 1998 was 180. The figure had doubled in ten years. But the gap was wide between the 1,213 complaints in India or 600 in Korea—and the 8 in Iceland or 3 in Manitoba.

About one third of complaints are amicably settled; a little more than 10% cause the council to censure the defendant; and the rest are rejected, directly or after examination. There again, differences can be important: in 1998, negative judgments amounted to 0 out of 60 complaints in the Atlantic Provinces (Canada) and 0 out of 41 in Austria—but 34 out of 36 in Turkey, and 87 out of 99 in Quebec.

With one exception (Sweden), the only conceivable sanction is the publication of a moral condemnation. Such a publication is automatic in the council's report, which can be monthly, quarterly, annual, or irregular. It normally is done by the periodical of the association that sponsors the council—a weekly in Japan, a monthly in Switzerland. It often appears in professional or trade reviews: for many years, the weekly *UK Press Gazette* published in full all the adjudications of the British Press Council. In the United States, *Editor & Publisher* used to report regularly on the decisions of Canadian councils. Sometimes, the council's decision is only made known to the two parties to protect the victim. But in other cases, publicity is entrusted to a national wire service.

Nearly everywhere, the judgment is published in the daily press for the general public. For the newspaper or station that was found guilty, it is a moral obligation. In many countries, it is understood that it must publish without any comments. When media owners support the council, publication is rarely refused. Even in Britain in the 1980s, the scandal sheets, often condemned by the council, continued publication in full—but sometimes they counter-attacked with scathing editorials, which contributed greatly to the demise of the Press Council. In Germany, the popular daily *Bild Zeitung*, which is the target of a full 25% of complaints, never publishes reprimands by the *Presserat*.

When the council is closely linked to some press organization, the accused, whether a press firm (Japan) or a journalist (The Netherlands before 1960), can be warned, reprimanded, or even suspended or excluded. Exclusion can be a very serious punishment when many professional advantages depend on membership. The Italian Order of Journalists can close the profession to a guilty reporter. Actually, councils in general look upon such sanctions as unacceptable.

If the filtering unit gives a negative opinion, the plaintiff can usually appeal. Thus, in Sweden, one can appeal a decision of the ombudsman to the council itself. When there is a hierarchy within the council, one can appeal a decision made at a lower level, such as from the "grievance committee" to the full council (Quebec). In rare cases when there is a hierarchy of councils, one can appeal a regional decision to the national body (Italy). In Switzerland before 2000 you could appeal to the professional association that sponsored the council. That said, most councils refuse any kind of appeal—but are ready to revise a decision.

HOW HAVE COUNCILS FARED?

After observing press councils for about 25 years, I have reached the conclusion that the concept is excellent. I have sung its praises in articles published in many languages[13] and have never stopped lecturing on the topic. That entitles me to say, at the dawn of the 21st century, that councils have not reached their assigned goals.

Exactly half the councils were created in the 1960s and early 1970s. Twenty years later, either they had disappeared, like those in Pakistan, the Caribbean, Portugal, or the NNC in the United States; or they had never acquired much influence, as those in Austria or Switzerland (before 2000), or again they had generated great dissatisfaction, as in Britain. There were only two councils in Latin America, a couple in black Africa, and not one in the Arab world. Only about half a dozen operated in the whole of the Third World. In the United States, there were only 3 for 50 States. In Europe, not a single mixed council had been created between the mid-1970s and the mid-1990s. Elsewhere, in the 1980s, four only were started, three of them in Canada. Globally, only one nation in seven has a press council.

In the north of Europe and in the former British dominions, press councils do exist but they cannot be said to play a major role. What have the Dutch, Danish, German, or Norwegian councils done to improve media? Has the Australian council prevented the concentration of 60% of the dailies in the hands of the Murdoch group? Did the British council play any part in the revolution of the 1980s, in the sudden collapse of reactionary labor unions and in the birth of new papers, such as *The Independent*? A few years ago, when I asked the councils themselves what their greatest achievement was, their replies were depressing; nowhere could a council pride itself on having clearly participated in the progress of media.

---

[13]In English: "Press Councils: An Evaluation," *Gazette* (Amsterdam), Winter 1977, reprinted in *Readings in Mass Communication*, M.C. Emery and Ted C. Smythe (eds.), Dubuque, Brown, 1979, 1983; "Press Councils of the Commonwealth," *Commonwealth Press Union Quarterly*, March 1978; "Press Councils: Unraveling a Definitional Dilemma," *Journalism Quarterly*, Summer 1978, and so on.

Why Such Lack of Impact?[14] A first factor resides in the definition of a press council. As mentioned before, it can only prosper, or even survive, in particular environments. It requires a liberal press regime and media that are not state-controlled. Media need not be commercial, but they need to be at least rich enough to finance the many activities that a council should have. Working journalists need to be true professionals, conscious of their duties and endowed with strong self-confidence. The country must not be split between two fiercely hostile ideological blocks. Also it must harbor a minority of enlightened citizens concerned with media. Lastly, among media owners, there must be people aware that the best long-term guarantee of profitability and expansion is quality control.[15]

Obviously, a council cannot exist in a soviet-style regime where all media are part of the state machine. But it has been very difficult, almost impossible, for a council to be set up in the United States; proprietors would not give up an ounce of their power. Also a council looks too much like a tribunal in a country whose media fear more than anything an intrusion of "government" in their affairs. On the contrary, in Latin nations, like those of southern Europe (e.g., France, Italy), people rely on legislators and magistrates to force the media into good behavior—and conversely, they do not trust NGOs very much. As for the Third World, its media are under government control and when they do break free, they do not have the means to improve their services much.

A second cause of failure is that wherever the creation of a press council was considered, it was perceived as dangerous and useless. Even in countries where a council was actually set up, it met with strong resistance. None of the dangers it was accused of carrying has ever materialized, and yet in one nation after another the same fears were expressed, the same endless debates took place as soon as the project was announced.

The press council was perceived as an instrument of government. Admittedly, in some rare cases, it was—but then it usurped its name. In the Spain of Franco, for instance, the central censorship agency was called *consejo de prensa*. In the Philippines under Marcos, the press council was designed as a counterfeit. In Egypt at the beginning of the 21st century, under Mubarak's authoritarian regime, there was a Supreme Press Council. Actually, the government can become the worst enemy of a council: in India, one of the first acts of the Prime Minister in 1975 when she decreed a state of emergency (read "seized dictatorial powers") for two years, was to terminate the Press Council, thus paying it a major compliment.

Others fear that a council might be used by the State merely to the extent that courts could take its opinions into account at the expense of media.

---

[14]See also Chapter 20 of the Report of the Royal Commission on the Press, London, HMSO Cmnd. 6810, 1977.

[15]The heyday of the British Press Council coincided with the dominance of the newspaper market by two respectable moguls, Lord Thomson and Cecil King—in the pre-Murdoch era.

And so, it seems, because of the very stringent libel laws in their country, the Irish media decided not to set up a council. Quite differently, it has happened that a council was perceived as a tactical move on the part of proprietors to shift public hostility away from media and thus avoid the creation by law of a regulatory body—which was often the case.

A third cause of failure resides in some built-in abnormality, such as when one of the three groups that should always be represented on the council has kept the other two out—or when two joined in keeping the third out. In Germany, owners and journalists have refused to let lay members in. In Switzerland for many years, journalists insisted on running the council by themselves.

Certainly publishers perceive a council as a limit to their right to use the press as they wish simply because they own it. They anticipate that the council will ask them to curb their appetite for profit so as to improve the public service. Besides, media proprietors do not enjoy being criticized by their employees and even less, of course, by non-media people. So, even if they accept a council, they are not inclined to give it the needed support. As for the journalists, they, too, do not appreciate any interference by consumers: they see it as a violation of the sanctuary where they, the high priests of news, pursue their calling.

A press council can also be handicapped by the refusal of some major publication to recognize it. The National News Council in the United States was badly hurt by the arrogant scorn of the *New York Times*. The British Press Council was badly hurt by the aggressive opposition of large circulation tabloids such as the *Daily Mail* and the *Sun*, which were the worst ethical offenders.

More serious because more general: because proprietors and journalists are reluctant to let it do more, a press council usually limits itself, as I said, to examining complaints and to making its judgments public (too often in periodicals that the ordinary person never reads). And so it misses many of the worse sins committed by media, especially sins of omission. Again, a council should also monitor the contents of media, commission surveys and investigations. It should assume every one of the functions required by the goals it is supposed to pursue. Restraint cannot kill but it does paralyze.

The most serious cause of failure is linked to that diffidence, that indolence of councils, their lack of imagination and energy. There is the source of their obscurity, which can be such that one council gets only three complaints a year. Their deficiency in visibility, in credibility, is such that many do not even realize they suffer from it.

You meet few people who express hostility to press councils after you have explained what they are about: some merely doubt that a council can produce any effect. Actually, the general public has never heard about press councils, does not know what they are and could become. That is a fatal flaw, because the founding idea is that a council must mobilize media users to fight for their freedom and quality. Only the power of the masses, guided by media professionals, can successfully oppose political or commercial interference.

ASSESSMENT: ADVANTAGES AND PROSPECTS
OF COUNCILS

Can those obstacles be eliminated? How can a council be made capable of doing its job? To start with, there are some prejudices and myths to be dispelled, especially the following:

- The press council is not the only M*A*S, even though it may be the most controversial.
- The former British Press Council was not the best in the world and the new one is even less so—hence they should no longer be held up as models.[16]
- A press council should not limit its scope to print media (or even to newspapers) as 40% of councils still do, at a time when most people get most of their news from electronic media and when television is the medium most inclined to be unethical.
- A press council should not consider that its one function is to adjudicate complaints: that might not even be its most important mission.
- A press council is not necessarily toothless. From its birth, some media cooperate with it—and many others are so sensitive to any negative publicity that they finally join the former and respect the rules. Quality can be contagious. Besides, in the days of the Internet, a council has no trouble finding inexpensive means of exposing unethical operators.
- Strictly speaking, few press councils have been set up voluntarily: as mentioned before, most often, there first had to be debates in Parliament on the possible need to regulate the media by law. If resistance proved too strong, here and there, why should not an independent press council be created by law, as in Denmark, an unquestionable democracy. One should keep in mind that the existence of a council has never led a government to restrict press freedom. On the other hand, a council can intimidate a government that harbors evil intentions: in Korea and in Germany, a council prevented the passing of restricting laws; in Britain and in Hawaii, a council contributed to the passing of laws favorable to the media.

Once those assumptions are out of the way, an important condition of success lies in obtaining enough money for the council to operate correctly, enough money for it to assume all its functions and to publicize its existence. That requirement may seem obvious, but it has not been for all the people involved.

---

[16]See my "The Ideal Press Council" in *The Media Reporter* (GB), Winter 1984, and *Quill* (USA), June 1985. It was also published in Spanish and Japanese.

For a council to function properly, it must be well known to the public: its main source of power must be support by media consumers. A press council must devote a large part of its funds and efforts simply to getting known.[17]

Media owners are the most obvious source of financing and most councils get from them most of their budget, but that means little. So money must be sought from other sources, as diverse as possible so as to maintain independence: public or private international organizations, governmental agencies, foundations, unions, universities, and corporations external to the media.

One way for councils to get more visible is to become more numerous. Another is to break the isolation of the council. First, the national council should not ride alone; it should stimulate the creation of other councils at every level where social communication takes place: local, regional, and even international. It can thus share the work, increase its influence, and be supported by associates within the country and internationally.

The press council could in the future become the best of M*A*S. Why? First, because it is a permanent, independent institution that gathers, and represents, the people who own the power to inform, those who possess the talent to inform, and those who have the right to be informed. As a council cannot force anyone to do anything, its efficiency depends entirely on the cooperation of owners, journalists, and public. Their association is probably as important by what it implies as by what it can do: it implies that no longer is it considered normal that a news medium be used as a cash register or a propaganda fountain by people who happen to own it or to possess political power. By participating in a press council, owners acknowledge that their employees have a word to say in production. And journalists acknowledge that media users also have a right to make their views heard—a great step for democracy.

A press council is capable of adapting to various contexts at every level of society, provided only that there is a minimum of economic, political, and journalistic development. It is democratic, but not linked to a particular type of democracy or press regime. The Finnish council covers both privately owned newspapers and State-controlled broadcasting. Even if all media were "public," a press council would be needed just as much as it now is in the United States where nearly all media are private.

A press council is multi-functional. As a master in ethics, it deals not with abstract concepts but with everyday experience; it teaches not out of ancient folios but from the columns of newspapers and magazines. As an alternative court of justice, it is competent, flexible, and fast; and it provides simple and inexpensive services. As a protector of press freedom, because of its independence and of the respect it can get from the public, it could enjoy an influence both strong and totally harmless.

---

[17]In the 1990s, many British dailies appointed ombudsmen without telling their readers—nothing but ploys to assuage a Parliament where support was growing for a privacy law to muzzle the press.

All those qualities clearly appear in the very concept of a true press council—but no longer is a press council a vague project. Some councils have been operating for over half a century and evidence exists now that a large part of the original criticisms of the concept was unfounded. A press council is not an anti-media machine: lay members show no knee-jerk hostility. Actually, a council proves that most complaints are unjustified. And it saves the honest media from being tainted by the misbehavior of a few. A council does not intimidate media: it is not concerned with their published opinions; and, as far as news is concerned, it distinguishes between documented and slanderous accusations, between a well-researched report and a sensationalized story. It does it better than a court of law. Thus it promotes vigorous journalism.

Neither a council nor any other M*A*S can have an immediate, spectacular impact. But all together, they can have a great long-term influence. Each M*A*S reinforces the others—whereas one that does not expand tends to wilt. It should be a mission of councils to strive for the multiplication of M*A*S and for their loose alliance in a network in which councils could serve as major intersections.

Press councils, together with the other M*A*S, reflect not just an evolution but a soft revolution. Remember the rabid protests or glacial indifference that greeted the first great manifesto of that subversive movement, the 1947 report of the Hutchins commission on freedom of the press (see p. 49). Among other recommendations, it suggested "the establishment of a new and independent agency to appraise and report annually upon the performance of the press."[18] Two years later, the first of the three British Royal Commissions on the Press recommended in its report[19] that a council be voluntarily established by the press, which should include non-press members, and that its functions go much further than merely to deal with complaints. Some 50 years later (true revolutions are slow), there are press councils in a majority of democratic countries that give journalists and lay people a real right (even though it is unofficial and limited) to evaluate how well the media serve the public and to pressure them into improving their quality.

In the year 2000, two genuine councils were born in Switzerland and Indonesia. As the year ended, the news was that others were about to be created or to begin operating in either part of Belgium, in Bosnia, in the Czech Republic, in Slovenia, and in Slovakia. Hopefully, the ethical snowball has started rolling.

---

[18]*A Free and Responsible Press,* University of Chicago Press, 1947, 7th ed. 1974, p. 100.

[19]*Royal Commission on the Press (1947-1949) Report,* London, HMSO Cmnd 7700, 1949, p. 173.

PRESS COUNCILS IN THE WORLD (4/2002)

Mixed Councils
(including non-media members)

National Councils

Country	Creation	Modifications
Sweden	1916	modified in 1969
Finland	1927	modified in 1968
Norway	1928	modified in 1972
Netherlands	1948	modified in 1960
Great Britain	1953	modified in 1963; transformed in 1991
Turkey	1960	dead in 1968; recreated in 1988
South Korea	1961	*
Israel	1963	
Taiwan	1963	modified in 1971 and 1974
Iceland	1963	
Switzerland	1972	revived in 1984; transformed in 2000
New Zealand	1973	
Australia	1976	
(Greek) Cyprus	1990	still-born; recreated in 1997
Estonia	1991	
Chile	1991	
Fiji	1993	relaunched in 1996
Peru	1997	**
Tanzania	1997	
Indonesia	2000	
Hong Kong	2000	***
Bosnia	2001	

The media in seven countries of francophone West Africa (Benin, Burkina Faso, Ivory Coast, Mali, Niger, Senegal, and Togo)[1] have in recent years set up "media observatories" which intend to serve as press councils but also to monitor media ethics. Lack of funds and an unfavorable political climate make their development problematical.

---

*The Korea Ethics Commission (set up by the press) is overshadowed by a statutory Commission of Press Arbitration (1981) that covers all media and can demand corrections.

**Special cases: the press council (Ethics Tribunal) in Peru consists entirely of non-media VIPs who are appointed by media professionals from the organizations that set up the PC.

***The two major newspaper groups have not endorsed the council.

[1]For more information on the observatories, see *Media Ethics* (Emerson College, Boston, MA), Fall 2001, pp. 12-13, 43-44.

National Councils Set Up by Law, Yet Non-State

Country	Creation	Modifications
Denmark	1964	recreated in 1992
India	1965	forbidden in 1975; revived in 1978
Lithuania	1996	mixed since Oct. 2000

Regional Councils

Country	Region	Creation
Europe	Cataluna (Spain)	1997
Canada	Quebec	1971
	Ontario	1972
	Alberta	1972
	Maritimes	
	(Atlantic)	1980
	British Columbia	1983
	Manitoba	1984
United States	Honolulu	1970
	Minnesota	1971
	Washington	1998

Professional Councils
(comprising only media people)

Set up by publishers and journalists		
Germany	1956	
Austria	1961	modified in 1963
Luxemburg	1979	
Set up by journalists alone		
Italy	1963	Professional Order created by law
Belgium	1988	
Slovenia	1995	Ethics Committee
Set up by publishers alone		
South Africa	1962	mutated in 1997[1]

[1] The council was replaced with an ombudsman, backed by an appeal committee.

Councils Whose Activity or Independence Could Not Be Ascertained (2002)

Country	Creation	Modifications
Ghana	1968	dead in 1970; recreated in 1993
Nigeria	1992	
Thailand	1997	
Russia	1998	
North Cyprus	1999	

The above table suffers from a lack of precise information, either on the council or on the degree of press freedom in the country. Some councils seem to be genuine, but it has proved impossible to obtain external evaluation of them. Besides, in developing nations, a council created by government may include journalists and enjoy a certain amount of independence.

Dead Councils

Country	Creation	Modifications
Burma	1962	dead in 1964
Pakistan	1965	dead in 1968
Philippines	1965	modified in 1972; recreated in 1988; dead in 1989
U.S.A. (NNC)	1973	dead in 1983
Portugal	1975	dead in 1990
West Indies	1976	dead, at unknown date
Namibia	1991	still-born

INTERNATIONAL BODIES

The Alliance of Independent European Press Councils. Website: www.aipce.org

World Association of Press Councils. The WAPC gathers about 20% of the councils listed here, none from Europe and many of a questionable independence.

Réseau des instances africaines d'autorégulation des médias (RIAAM; set up in July 2000) gathers the "observatories" in francophone West Africa.

PRESS COUNCILS IN EUROPE

Nowadays, Europeans tend to be shy about their achievements because there have been so many and everybody knows about them. However, there's one invention they should boast about, because so few people know about it: Press councils. They originated in Europe.

Half the press councils of the world operate in Europe (19 out of 38 genuine councils, as of 2002), on a continent where only 5% of the world's population lives. Not only was the first press council set up in Sweden in 1916, but the model of most PCs in the world was the British Press Council. After half a century of experimenting, every kind of council can be found on the Old Continent.

The 18 nations in Western Europe have 13 councils, as contrasted to 3 in the United States for 50 States. If Cyprus, Turkey, and Malta are joined to the list, then it adds up to 16 councils in 20 nations. Admittedly, there are only 2 councils (in the Baltic states) in the 14 nations of Eastern Europe (not including Russia) that, for half a century, were part of a totalitarian empire. With a little help from their friends, that situation is changing: at the end of 2000, several new ones were in the planning stage.

A major cause is that Europe is the one region of the planet where press freedom is prevalent; there can be no media accountability without freedom. Also, media in Europe have not been so thoroughly commercialized as those in the United States; they have kept an ideal of public service. Or, put in a negative light, European media need to self-discipline because governments on the Old Continent are prone to legislate regulation.

European Press Councils (2000)

Country	Range[1]	Freed[2]	Broadcast[3]	Composition[4]	No. Members	Code[5]	Complaints[6]	Initiatives[7]	Budget (US $)[8]
Austria	N	Yes	No	M-J	24 (12-12)	Yes	41 (0)	Rarely	26 500 (0%)
Belgium	N	Yes	Yes	J	11	Yes	12 (6)	Rarely	100 000 (0%)
Cyprus	N	No	Yes	M-J-P	13 (6-3-4)	Yes	25 (10)	Rarely	20 000 (85%)
Denmark	N	No	Yes	M-J-P	8 (2-2-4)	Yes	184 (28)	Rarely	220 000 (0%)
Estonia	N	Yes	Yes	M-J-P	15 (7-3-5)	Yes	33 (11)	Occasionally	5 000 (0%)
Finland	N	Yes	Yes	M-J-P	10 (4-2-4)	Yes	122 (16)	Rarely	156 000 (50%)
France	-								
Germany	N	Yes	No	M-J	20 (10-10)	Yes	401 (73)	Rarely	450 000 (30%)
Great Britain	N	No	No	M-P	16 (7-9)	Yes	1 510 (34)	No	1 920 000 (0%)
Greece	-								
Iceland	N	Yes	Yes	M-J-P	5 (1-2-2)	Yes	8 (2)	No	3 000 (0%)
Ireland									
Italy									
Lithuania	N	No	Yes	M-J-P	12 (3-3-6)	Yes	153 (115)	Rarely	15 000 (100%)
Luxembourg	N	Yes	Yes	M-J	32 (16-16)	Yes	2	No	50 000 (85%)
Netherlands	N	No	Yes	J-P	22 (10-12)	No	77 (22)	Rarely	75 000 (0%)]
Norway	N	Yes	Yes	M-J-P	7 (2-2-3)	Yes	208 (44)	Possibly	550 000 (0%)
Portugal [dead]	N	(M-J-P)							
Spain (Catalonia)	R	No	Yes	M-J-P	15 (1-5-9)	Yes	30 (25)	No	150 000 (0%)

(continues)

135

European Press Councils (2000) (cont.)

Country	Range[1]	Freed[2]	Broadcast[3]	Composition[4]	No. Members	Code[5]	Complaints[6]	Initiatives[7]	Budget (US $)[8]
Sweden	N	No	No	M-J-P	12 (6-6)9	Yes	438 (50)	Rarely	600 000 (0%)
Switzerland	N	Yes	Yes	J-P	21 (15-6)	Yes	40 (10)	Rarely	75 000 (0%)
Turkey	N	Yes	Yes	M-J-P	30 (12-6-12)	Yes	36 (34)	Often	75 000 (0%)

[1]National or Regional.

[2]Considers the defense of press freedom is one of its missions.

[3]Covers not only print media but also broadcasting.

[4]Composition: M: management (owners, editors) / J: journalists / P: public, non-media members / L: legislators

[5]The council uses a written code of ethics.

[6]Complaints received in 1998. Between brackets, complaints upheld.

[7]The council can take the initiative of judging some ethical misbehavior of the press.

[8]Between brackets, the proportion coming from the State.

[9]Six from the media including two appointed by the association of publishers, two by the union of journalists and two by an association common to publishers and journalists..

CHAPTER 8
Council into Commission
British Experience
of Press Accountability

Kenneth Morgan OBE

In the boardroom of Reuters news agency, in Fleet Street, London, surrounded by the offices of English newspapers, the General Council of the Press met for the first time on Tuesday, 21 July 1953. It was a voluntary body, established and paid for by the press itself—by newspaper journalists, editors, and owners. And it was neither imposed by, nor answerable to, government. It was Britain's answer to the problem of preserving the freedom of the press while trying to ensure its responsibility and of offering an inexpensive, informal way of resolving the grievances of those whom the press had wronged.

Thirty-seven years later, Fleet Street[1] was no more. The diaspora had taken place: the newspapers, scattered, were now edited and printed in Wapping, in Bermondsey, in Kensington and in the old London docklands. Fleet Street was a metaphorical expression; physically, just another street of lawyers, accountants, and banks. And on Friday, 28 December 1990 in the Council Chamber of the Newspaper Society in Bloomsbury, the Press Council met for the last time.

Its end came with the report of a Government appointed committee that recommended its abolition: The Committee on Privacy and Related Matters, chaired by a leading lawyer and academic, David Calcutt, QC.

---

[1]In the Renaissance, when the press began, it was a neighborhood of inns where coaches arrived with news from the Continent, and left with printed papers for the provinces. It came to symbolize the London (or national) press.

The report, instantly accepted by the Conservative government and by the Labour opposition, said the Press Council should be replaced by a Press Complaints Commission. This, too, should be voluntary, established and paid for by the newspapers themselves, but unlike the Press Council it should have no role in defending their freedom. It should deal solely with complaints against them. The new body, said the Calcutt Committee, would be the newspapers' final chance to prove that self-regulation could be made to work.

One might say: so far, so good. But if in someone's opinion (the report did not say whose) the last chance failed, the non-statutory complaints commission would be replaced by a statutory commission with new powers of law over the press. At worst, it would be replaced by a statutory complaints tribunal—a judge appointed by the Lord Chancellor sitting with two assessors appointed by the Home Secretary, ruling whether newspapers were in breach of a statutory code of practice to be "drafted by the Government in consultation with the press and other interested parties." The Committee recommended no new civil law to protect privacy, but it called for three new criminal offences of which for practical purposes only journalists could be guilty.

The story of how a freedom-cherishing democratic society moved from its position in 1953 to its position in 1990 is the story of the British Press Council. Press councils are not in fact a British invention. Long before 1953, recognizable ancestors had been founded, in Norway in 1912 and in Sweden in 1916. If the British Press Council is the father of press councils in Australia, New Zealand, Canada, and many less likely places, those councils have Scandinavian grandparents in Norway and Sweden, to say nothing of great aunts in Denmark and Finland.

In its international spread, however, the press council movement owes a great deal to the British example. To understand it, and its successes and failures, the differences between legal and cultural attitudes toward the press in Britain and in other countries must be remembered.

Britain has no First Amendment, no written constitution, no Bill of Rights. The European Convention on Human Rights, signed by the United Kingdom in November 1950 and ratified three months later, did not become enforceable in Britain's courts until half a century later, in 2000, under her Human Rights Act, 1998. Unlike most other European countries, she is a common-law country building up much of her law, sometimes untidily, by decisions of her judges; not laying it down neatly and logically in advance by way of a code.

Her press has no legal or constitutional guarantee of its freedom, but in practice it remains freer than newspapers in much of the rest of the world. Newspapers are unlicensed; journalists are unregistered; there is no body of special press law. Yet one cannot be complacent. One does well to remember that there is a great deal of ordinary British law that may not be aimed at the press, but nevertheless bears upon it very harshly. Significantly, Britain remained in 2000 a country that had an Official Secrets Act but no Freedom of Information Act.

Against this background, and with these traditions, Britain, after the Second World War, chose a voluntary Press Council instead of any piece of state machinery to try to resolve the conflict within a society that wants its newspapers to be free but expects them to be responsible.

As it developed, the Press Council ceased (in 1963) to be a body composed only of newspaper owners, editors, and journalists and later became a real, equal partnership of the press and the public, with an independent lawyer as chairman—though the press, mainly the owners, continued to pay the Council's bills.

The first independent chairman of the Council, Lord Devlin, a former Lord of Appeal (the highest tier of the British judiciary) spoke in the 1960s, identifying six pillars of a successful voluntary press council anywhere in any country:

- The press must accept that a press council is desirable.
- The government, whatever its form, must be responsive to public opinion and accept that the press has a constitutional part to play in forming and expressing opinion.
- The press must accept a corresponding obligation to conform to standards of conduct.
- Each newspaper must accept the obligation to publish adjudications by the council against itself.
- The public must be represented on the council.

and finally Lord Devlin emphasized :

- The council's function is to stand up for the freedom and rights of the press as well as to censure its misconduct.

He saw these things more clearly than some of his successors in British public life. One who saw main issues with equal clarity about ten years later, in 1978, was the chairman of the Third Royal Commission on the Press,[2] Lord McGregor of Durris, a professor of social institutions. He matched Lord Devlin's six pillars with three signposts. I believe they, too, are international.

- To maintain public confidence in the press, a press council must be wholly independent of government;
- The council must show its independence of the press;
- The public will not believe in a council dominated by journalists and other press people, but a press council must be expert and influential enough for its judgments to carry weight with the press.

---

[2]Set up by Parliament in 1974 to study the general condition of the British press, it presented its report in 1977.

Practically, in the British and in many other press councils, just as in the self-regulation of many other professions, fellow practitioners have often proved harsher critics of incompetent or unethical behavior than the laity.

The laity, the public members of the press council, were selected from the public at large. It was significant and important that in Britain neither the government nor Parliament played any part in the nomination or selection of the members of the council. There are different traditions, and press councils tend to inherit the characteristics of their countries, in the way that the British Press Council inherited the English tradition of common law rather than codified law. India inherited a substantial code of special press law. In that spirit, its press council (though otherwise very similar to Britain's) was established by law, not as a voluntary body. As a result, a proportion of its public members are appointed by Parliament to represent the political parties.

Similarly, from the restoration of democracy in 1974 until 1990, Portugal had a *Counselho de Imprensa* that was in its own phrase "inspired by Great Britain's Press Council." Yet the law provided that its members should include "four citizens with acknowledged merits elected by the Assembly of the Republic."

Change was on the march in both countries in 1990. In Portugal a new constitutional law abolished the old statutory Press Council in favor of a wider statutory media authority. Responding to the British Press Council's protest at this, supporting its old Portuguese ally, the Portuguese government said there were moves afoot there by publishers and newspaper unions to found "a truly voluntary press council which would be independent of the state" more similar, they said, to the Press Council in Great Britain.[3]

Meanwhile, however, the British government was accepting the Calcutt report, which proposed a Press Complaints Commission whose members would be chosen by an appointments commission selected "perhaps by the Lord Chancellor"—the only member of the British judiciary who is also a member of the Cabinet and a party political appointee. Happily, it has not come to that.

At the end of 1990, the Press Council was indeed disbanded as Calcutt proposed, and was succeeded by a voluntary Press Complaints Commission established by a new Press Standards Board of Finance that had, in its turn, been established swiftly by the principal organizations of newspaper and magazine publishers.

Government and Parliament still had (and ten years later continued to have) no role in the selection of members of the Complaints Commission. They were chosen by a small appointments body: the chairman of the Press Standards Board of Finance; the chairman of the Complaints Commission itself; and at first, in 1990, one independent, non-press member, a former politician. In 2000, the selection body had three independent members: a former Secretary of State

---

[3]Which, by 2002, had still not been done. See Mario Mesquita's presentation (p. 191).

for Northern Ireland, the Deputy Governor of the Bank of England, and the woman chief executive of the Association of British Insurers, sitting with the chairmen of the Commission and the Board of Finance.

The Press Council in Britain, like those elsewhere, judged complaints against the press on the basis of ethics, not law. Controversially, it asked complainants to waive a legal remedy if they wished the Council to adjudicate. It accepted complaints from anyone, whether they were or were not directly affected by the publication of which they complained. This is not the universal policy: in Sweden, for example, a complainant must have a direct interest in the matter of which he or she complains. In Britain, in 1990 about a third of the 1,871 complaints the Council handled came from parties unconnected with the matter. Third party complaints can be a time-consuming irritation to editors (and to the Council), but they can be extremely valuable in the setting of standards, when those directly involved have neither time, money, nor inclination to challenge a newspaper's conduct themselves.

The Press Council, too, dealt with complaints by the press about the conduct of people and organizations towards it, and the Council, sparingly, launched its own inquiries into particular issues of press conduct without necessarily reacting to a complaint. A major inquiry into the way British newspapers covered the serious riot at Strangeways Prison, Manchester, was the final example, in 1990. Earlier ones included general inquiries into press coverage of the "Yorkshire Ripper" murders[4] and the horrific Hillsborough football ground disaster.[5]

Always, as with every voluntary press council, there was concern and controversy about what sanctions the Council should have: whether it ought to have teeth and how sharp such teeth could be. The Press Council had none, except the single tooth, or rather tongue, of publicity. It released its judgments and expected their publication, especially by the wrong-doer concerned. In almost every case of a critical judgment in 37 years, it did get that publicity but the question remained: was this penalty enough? Should there be fines or publication bans, suspensions, and the paraphernalia of licensing? To pose the possibilities is to see their impracticability or undesirability. But the questions continued to arise—and indeed still do so in Britain and other countries that have chosen the voluntary non-statutory route.

They were asked with greater urgency and stridency in the 1980s as a mood of disenchantment with the excesses of intense competition at the rough end of the tabloid trade was reflected in Parliament. I say "reflected," but there is a paradox: the most severe and common criticism of these newspapers' conduct is that they intrude unjustifiably on people's privacy, invading private lives. Yet while the criticism came from the public, and still does, there was then, and still was in 2000, strong commercial evidence from daily sales figures running into many millions of a massive public appetite for just such intrusion and invasion.

---

[4]Thirteen women were sadistically killed between 1975 and 1981.

[5]96 people died in the crush following a panic at the soccer stadium in 1989.

Three elements of hypocrisy customarily mark discussion of press intrusion into the private lives of public figures: hypocrisy by public figures themselves, often politicians, who present one face in public but a conflicting one in private; hypocrisy by editors who almost invariably claim that stories and pictures about private lives have been published only in the serious public interest and never simply to titillate readers and boost circulation; and hypocrisy by readers themselves—the public—who condemn intrusion but rush to buy and read it.

It was strong parliamentary support in 1989 for Bills to provide a right of reply and a protection (the first in English law) for privacy, following in French footsteps, which led to the Calcutt Committee, and thus to the death of the Press Council and the birth of the Press Complaints Commission. They also led to a chilling phrase from the then Minister of State at the Home Office: "The Press is on probation." In fact, the press is on permanent probation but, from its birth in 1991, the Press Complaints Commission too was on probation, and still was in 2000. And so was the future of voluntary self-regulation of newspapers in Britain.

On the face of it, the differences between the old Press Council and the new Press Complaints Commission may not appear so great. In fact they are significant, and I am bound to say they cut two ways.

Unlike the Council, the Commission (I think, sadly) had no remit to defend or preserve press freedom. There are of course other organizations of journalists, of editors and of publishers, in Britain and internationally, who espouse that cause. Nevertheless, it is a pity that there should no longer be a body that is a partnership of press and public and cannot be written off as a newspaper special-interest group, but which is specifically charged to defend the press's freedom in the public's interest.

On an important practical point, it is agreed in its draft articles that when dealing with complaints, the Commission must have regard to generally established freedoms including freedom of expression and the public's right to know. In its first decade, it had come to recognize the need for newspapers to resist improper pressure from outside on their editorial independence.

Its prime role is to deal with complaints from people or bodies directly affected and it looked at first as if that might be the Commission's only role. But it has wisely reserved a discretion to accept complaints from third parties in appropriate cases. Regrettably, it makes very rare use of this discretion. It does not require complainants formally to waive their legal rights, though in practice it does not adjudicate on matters subject to legal action.

Its professed inability to launch a complaint or inquiry of its own, in the absence of a complaint from elsewhere, was an early weakness of the PCC. Later it modified this policy, though Lord Wakeham, its second chairman, made clear in 2000 that power to initiate action would be exercised only in "exceptional circumstances." I agree that a press council's (or complaints commission's) power to launch an inquiry itself should be exercised sparingly. Having power to do so, however, is vital.

The Commission is a smaller body than the Council was: 16 members instead of 37, and is more instantly recognizable as an apparatus of self-regulation. From the beginning, seven of its members have been currently serving editors. Since then the personnel have changed, of course, but the profile of the Commission's press members remains similar: editors of the *Daily Mail* and *News of the World* from the national tabloids; of the *Sunday Telegraph* from the national broadsheets,[6] and of a Newcastle evening paper, a Croydon (near London) suburban weekly, *Scotland on Sunday*, and the monthly magazine, the *Reader's Digest*. The range of experience is impressive, but there is still no representation of "working journalists"—rank-and-file reporters and sub-editors—as there was originally on the British Press Council, and as is still common in most countries' press councils and similar bodies.

Among the PCC's initial general (i.e., non-editor) members were three highly experienced and distinguished journalistic figures—a sort of half-way group between the press and public members. These were Sir Edward Pickering, the vice-chairman of *The Times* and *Sunday Times*, who had been editor, managing editor and editorial director of three other major national newspapers; Mr David Chipp, the former editor-in-chief of the Press Association, Britain's main home news agency; and Sir Richard Francis, former director of news and current affairs for the BBC. They sat with five other general members unconnected with the press.

In 2000, all nine public members, including the chairman, Lord Wakeham, emphasized the Commission's independence by being drawn from outside the press and without connection with it. Their backgrounds were varied: dental surgeon and former head of a hospital's trust; former chief officer of the Independent Schools Council; professor of social administration; former director of the Mental Health Council; chairman of Edinburgh Festival Fringe (and widow of a former Leader of the Labour Party); retired bishop; former Civil Service head of the Home Office; former Liberal-Democrat Chief Whip in the House of Lords; and Lord Wakeham, former Conservative minister and (at different times) Leader of both the House of Lords and the House of Commons. Their exceptional breadth of experience and of responsibility was impressive but, like in many English institutions, the membership might be thought to lack social variety—or blue-collar experience.

The Commission has a code of practice to enforce but it did not devise it itself. The National Union of Journalists and the Institute of Journalists have had codes of conduct for their members since before the Second World War but the Press Council for 36 years operated codeless after the manner of English common law. We British have all, even the most Euroskeptic of us, become more European in the last 20 years. In 1989, national newspaper editors appointed ombudsmen or readers' representatives and for the first time agreed on their own five point mini-code reflecting Press Council principles; and the

---

[6]Large-size quality newspapers.

Press Council published a 16 point code based on its earlier decisions. In 1990, the Calcutt Committee recommended its own code based on both.

In the light of these three codes, the newspapers and magazines have committed themselves, from January 1991, to a general code of practice covering the whole industry which it asked the Commission to enforce. Its sixteen points—from accuracy through privacy, misrepresentation, harassment, checkbook journalism to the important matter of protection of confidential sources—were not devised and imposed by the Calcutt Committee, but drafted and agreed by editors themselves, led by the then editor of the *News of the World*, who handed the code to the Commission and asked to be bound by it. On the face of it, that structure gave the new order a very strong claim to the title of self-regulation.

This code has a particular significance. The Commission interprets it in the spirit as well as in the letter, but the Commission does not step outside it. A complaint to be pursued must fall within the spirit of one or more of the code's articles. The intended result is a more sharply focused scrutiny of newspaper conduct than the view by the Press Council—but inescapably it is more restricted.

Even experienced editors, when framing a code, may not envisage all the improprieties which they, their colleagues and successors may come to commit. So either we would need to amend our view that the code be considered comprehensive, or the code itself would need much amendment and extension over the years. The intention was that it should be revised annually and so it has been. There are still 16 articles but their scope has been widened significantly.

The limitation of the Commission's adjudicatory role to those matters set out in the code means that the number of formal adjudications was likely to be smaller—at any rate in the early days—than under the old system. In its first year, 1991, the Commission received 1,392 complaints compared with 1588 received by the Press Council in its last, 1990. Eight years on, in 1999, the Commission received 2,427 complaints, but only 49 went to adjudication, of which 26 were upheld and 23 not upheld. In its first year, the Commission had adjudicated on 91 complaints, of which 46 were upheld, 48 not upheld. In its final year, the Press Council had given full adjudications to 174 complaints, upholding 85 in full, 7 in part, and not upholding 82. It is fair to bear in mind, however, that the Commission, as a matter of policy, lays much stress on and devotes much time to encouraging complainants and newspapers to settle their differences without going to the length of formal adjudication.

In fact, since the parliamentary debates at the end of the 1980s, and in face of the Calcutt threat, it is my impression that the behavior of British popular papers in the areas that caused concern has generally improved.

It cannot be said too often that society must recognize that part of the price of preserving a free press while demanding responsible newspapers is the toleration of some measure of irresponsibility. The press must recognize, however, that there is a limit to what measure of irresponsibility a public—or a parliament—will stand. At the time of the change from Council to Commission, there were signs, much clearer than before, that Britain was close to that line.

The question remains whether self-regulation by a voluntary press council or a voluntary press complaints commission (the name does not really matter) can satisfy the critics and survive in a recognizable form. So far the signs are that it can and it will. Strictly, the complaints commission has no more teeth than the old Press Council. The new strength it has is the expressed commitment of proprietors and editors, and the threat expressed by Government, in the late 1980s and early 1990s, that if self-regulation did not work, regulation by statute would follow.

The Calcutt Committee had recommended that the success of the new Commission should be judged after a trial period but did not say when or by whom. For the PCC's first twelve months, newspapers, predictably and sensibly, were rather obviously on their best behavior. Had their conduct and the voluntary commission's effectiveness been reviewed at that point, its success would have appeared obvious, but there was little enthusiasm by Government or press to renew the argument.

The press's "probation" dragged on. It was two years after his committee reported, and the PCC was established, before David Calcutt himself—this time alone—came to judge the experiment's success. The second year proved difficult: the old demon of competition for sales coincided with a spate of news stories and pictures about the private lives of public figures—members of the royal family, government ministers, and other politicians. Publication of some of them was clearly justifiable in the serious public interest; that of others was unconvincingly excused by editors on the grounds that they would interest the public.

Sir David (now knighted) concluded the new machinery had failed and recommended his worst case solution, a statutory press tribunal, but his advice was not followed. Several times, Government appeared on the point of producing legislative proposals on the press and privacy but deferred doing so. Cool consideration and appraisal of the adequacy of the voluntary self-control system were bedeviled by continuing disclosures, justifiable or unjustifiable, of the private lives of public figures.

The House of Commons all-party National Heritage Committee took evidence from editors, lawyers, politicians and experts (including me). It then made 43 recommendations of its own including the appointment of a super national press ombudsman—also to be voluntary—to oversee a new proposed press complaints body to be called the Press Commission. Coincidence struck again. Publication of the recommendations coincided with gross intrusion into the Princess of Wales's privacy by one tabloid paper printing covert pictures of her, dressed in a leotard, "working out" in a London gymnasium. The Commons committee instantly reconvened and called for its proposed super-ombudsman to be a statutory figure with legal powers, not a voluntary one. None of these suggestions, nor Sir David Calcutt's review recommendations, were implemented. The voluntary Press Complaints Commission has survived much in its original form.

The code has indeed been significantly and generally usefully amended, most often in response to the pressure of events. These included the death of

Diana, Princess of Wales, with her friend Dodi al Fayed, in a high speed Paris car crash. The crash was widely, but it later proved wrongly, attributed to their car being chased or harassed by paparazzi or journalists. Other significant extensions and changes of emphasis in the code about publication of pictures and stories of schoolchildren and adolescents followed the development of her son Prince William, second in line to the Throne, and complaints about press treatment or pictures of the children of Prime Minister Tony Blair.

The final years of Prime Minister John Major's Conservative premiership saw seventeen, mostly junior, members of his government leave office, jumping or pushed, following media disclosures about their private lives or commercial interests or conduct, but Mr Blair's New Labour Party's 1997 general election victory predictably brought something of a honeymoon period for the press with the government. There was therefore a relief from pressure for any more formal restraint on newspapers.

Such idylls never last; by the Millennium, the first rapture was clearly passing. By then, however, a wholly new factor, likely to impose or encourage restraint, and certain to affect the scope of Britain's machinery for dealing with disputes about press ethics, was on the scene. The European Convention on Human Rights was being written directly into British law and with it legal requirement to balance Article 10 of the Convention protecting freedom of expression with Article 8 protecting private lives and affairs. For the first time, by an unlikely route, there was emerging a remedy in the British courts for those who seek a defense against improper intrusion of their privacy by the press—but with the vital safeguard that freedom of expression must be preserved.

CHAPTER 9
Local Press Councils in the United States

The better known press councils are national or in Canada, regional councils. However, one of the earliest, the most simple, most flexible, least expensive type is the local press council. It may also be the least developed—though actually that kind of council may well exist and operate discreetly under many other names and even in a form different from those commonly known. Here are a few examples of what has existed in the United States (see Table 9.1 at the end of the chapter for a complete list).

In Illinois, there is a city, Peoria, which colloquially typifies the "provincial" United States. Traditionally, people attending an avant-garde show, movie, or novel would say, "Great for New York or Los Angeles, but how will it play in Peoria?" In that city, from 1970 to 1983, 21 housewives met once a month on the premises of the local daily, the *Journal-Star*. Each lived in one of the 21 distribution zones of the newspaper: she was expected to contact people at random in her neighborhood (mainly by phone) and find out what they thought of the newspaper. Then she reported the praises and criticisms of the readership to the management. A summary of those reports, about one-third of them negative, was printed in the paper. Although its circulation was only 110,000 copies, the *Journal-Star* spent $17,500 a year (in 1982) to cover the expenses of its Women's Advisory Board. The management thought that this was an inexpensive way of staying in constant contact with its customers and giving itself an image as a responsible public service.

This operation stopped when the owner changed. Admittedly, it had been managed by the sales manager of the newspaper. Some M*A*S (such as codes or ombudsmen) get accused of being nothing but PR gimmicks. Was not the Peoria council simply a successful promotion ploy? If so, why was it not imitated elsewhere in the United States? Who in France would be so out of touch with reality as to suggest such a council to a daily of similar size, such as *Le Midi Libre* (in Montpellier) or *Nice Matin*, newspapers devoid of substance and any sense of responsibility? If, in the view of the newspaper, such as a council is merely a way to polish its reputation, why haven't media everywhere followed in the footsteps of the *Peoria Journal-Star*? Maybe Peoria is very special. So let's have a look at a more ordinary little press council.

At about the same time, in Littleton, a suburb of Denver (Colorado), three times a year Garrett Ray, editor of two weeklies, the *Littleton Independent* and the *Arapahoe Herald*, together with semi-retired former editor Houstoun Warring, listened to the complaints and suggestions of 12 local personalities chosen by them to sit for three years on the Littleton Press Council. It had all started in 1946 when Warring had begun organizing an annual dinner during which the guests were expected to roast the newspaper. That practice had been abandoned in 1962. But it had been revived in 1967, at the time of the great protest movements, in the shape of a true press council, the minutes of whose meetings were regularly published.

That second type of local press council is more normal: a publisher aware of his/her responsibilities wishes to know how to improve his/her services to the community. The company cannot afford repeated full-scale readership surveys, so it regularly consults a few citizens. The Littleton council satisfied both the management of the newspapers and their readers. The former liked hearing about the grievances and desires of its customers. The latter liked to know that the two weeklies were open to readers opinions and willing to be held accountable.

Whereas in the 19th century a small town could have two or three newspapers, at the turn of the 21st century, even regional capitals rarely have more than one daily. Production costs and the competition of broadcasting and of new media are such that with the available advertising, only one daily per region and only one weekly per community can survive (say owners) or be highly profitable (say critics).

Is that important anyway? Isn't one newspaper enough? I believe it is, under two conditions: the first is that in the absence of aggressive rivals it does not fall into the blissful slumber of prosperous mediocrity; the second is that the owner does not turn it into a propaganda weapon to be used in his/her own interest or that of some group in the community. Actually, some observers judge that local monopoly may be politically and socially preferable to a multiplicity of partisan media. For one thing, it avoids the temptation of using sensationalism to dominate the market. Also, it gives the one survivor enough resources to obtain more news and present it better.

Lastly, if the newspaper, as it should, wishes to extend its sales to all parts of the population, it is led to publish a diversity of news stories and opinions that a reader would never be exposed to if he/she could choose a newspaper whose politics and intellectual level reflected his/hers. How many ordinary citizens buy several newspapers, when they exist, so as to have a full knowledge of the news?

An attractive argument, but how realistic is it? Many owners are moved only by intolerance or greed. Too many reporters suffer from laziness and incompetence. For either kind of media people, monopoly is a privilege to be exploited. On the other hand, there are many proprietors and journalists who, to some degree, feel the duty to serve the public better. And idealistic promptings can be reinforced by the call of personal interest when sales decline and the prestige of the profession remains at a low level.

Monopoly can become an opportunity for progress provided the newspaper or station enjoying it operates to the benefit and satisfaction of all the members of the community. To achieve that, it needs to know its various customers, to listen to their criticism, and, conversely, to be protected by them against its foes. A local press council can assume all three functions.

Whoever knows anything about national and regional press councils (see p. 109) has understood from the two examples just given that the U.S.-style *local* press council is something quite different. Fundamentally, its object is the same: improve news media by giving readers/listeners/viewers a possibility to express their views on the media. But almost always, a national council is (indirectly) forced upon media controllers by news professionals and, via the ominous rumblings of government, by militant citizens. In Sweden as in Britain, in Germany as in Israel, the press council was set up to avoid legislation that would have restricted press freedom.

On the contrary, a local council is always set up in close cooperation with the owners and often on their initiative. A local council aims above all at being a meeting place for news providers and news consumers—whereas a national council takes on the mission of using the power of public opinion both to defend freedom of speech against abuse by elected officials and bureaucrats and to defend the quality of information against abuse by media managers.

A true national press council consists of representatives of the associations of owners and of journalists, and a variable proportion of co-opted members of the public. It is an institution with recorded statutes, a permanent secretariat, an important budget. In contrast, a local press council is nothing but a group of concerned citizens who, at intervals, have conversations with some of the persons in charge of the media in their community.

Whereas a national council receives complaints, investigates, holds hearings, and passes judgments that are published by the media, a local press council offers the opportunity for a direct contact between producers and consumers, whose discussions quite often are not reported by the newspaper.

Apart from the one in Windsor (Ontario, 1971-1998), all known local press councils were born in the United States, between 1967 and 1973. Why? U.S. media structures offer one explanation. Contrary to the British press, the U.S. newspaper press is not primarily national, nor is it regional as in France—

but local. For a population four to five times bigger than the French, the U.S. has 20 times more dailies.

Another cause is historical. In the 1960s, U.S. news media suffered a serious crisis of credibility. Protesters accused them of serving a racist, war-mongering, nature-polluting, sexist plutocracy. On the other side, the conservative masses, led by the president and vice-president, accused the media of favoring subversion. Both sides demanded restrictions on the constitutional rights of the press. The former wanted laws to free the media from the stranglehold of financiers; the latter wanted laws that would muzzle a "mafia" of radical reporters.

To restore trust without restricting freedom of speech, some academic critics, militant journalists, and enlightened media owners considered adopting a solution that seemed to give satisfaction in Britain: the press council. The vastness of the land, the tradition of localism, hence the multiplicity of media, made it unlikely that any agreement could ever be reached at national level for the establishment of a single council. Moreover, the attachment to free enterprise and to press freedom is so passionate in the United States that even at the level of a state it did not seem easy to reach an agreement among professional associations.

The National News Council (1973-1984) was a private undertaking set up by a foundation: its reach was limited to media with national distribution. In two states only have professionals succeeded in creating a council.[1] In the very progressive state of Minnesota, newspaper proprietors in 1971 set up a regional press council which at the beginning of the third millennium kept giving satisfaction. And a similar one was set up in the State of Washington in early 1999. Besides, in Honolulu, on the island of Oahu, the local council covers in fact about 80% of the media in Hawaii and could be considered as a State council if it was not for its lack of means (see p. 159).

Apart from those four exceptions, the 20 known U.S. press councils were local: some were created by newspaper publishers; others were the joint achievement of a foundation and of journalism professors. Nearly all of them disappeared long ago. Were they merely an isolated phenomenon interesting only for historians of the U.S. press? No, for paradoxically, a majority of the dead councils did record some notable achievements. No, because a few seemed to have no trouble surviving and many others probably exist under a different name with no one paying attention to them except the enlightened citizens in their community.

The very first (known) local press council dates back to 1950. The publisher of the *Press Democrat* in Santa Rosa (California), at that time began inviting 15 eminent citizens to a monthly dinner to hear their grievances. "The council [. . .] outlived its usefulness after a period of about 18 months. After that

---

[1]As early as the 1930s, Chilton R. Bush, a pioneer journalism educator at Stanford University, suggested to California publishers that they form a council of citizens to offer suggestions and criticism on newspaper operations. His suggestion was in vain.

time the recommendations and comments became repetitious and it became more of a social gathering than a true critic of the newspaper."[2] When the daily changed hands in 1953, the council was suspended. Until 1967 no further local press councils were established, even though the first one had been praised by the major professional review, *Editor & Publisher*.

The notion of a local press council seems to have been publicized by Barry Bingham when he was publisher of the then remarkable *Courier Journal* in Louisville (Kentucky). The Bingham family was special in that it was content to make profits below the U.S. average so as to retain its independence from advertisers. That lasted until an heir demanded her part of the family wealth and the company was sold to the Gannett chain, the number one owner of newspapers in the United States.

In 1963, Bingham, addressing a SDX-SPG meeting of journalists, stated that local monopoly was dangerous for the press; that to keep the press healthy and vigorous there was a need for a committee of citizens that would criticize it and serve as a link between press and population. He was unable to set one up—but it was the *Courier Journal* that in 1967 appointed the first newspaper ombudsman. A few years later, it had three of them.[3]

In the following period, as protest swelled in the ghettoes and on the campuses, as the government's encroachments on press freedom increased, there was more and more talk of press councils. In the absence of any practical experience, the discussion did not lead anywhere.

A journalist by the name of Lowell Mellett had bequeathed to the journalists' union (The Newspaper Guild—TNG) funds to be used for stimulating the social responsibility of the press without threatening its freedom. The president of the Mellett Fund at the end of the 1960s was Ben Bagdikian, assistant managing editor, then second ombudsman of the *Washington Post*, later famous as one of the top media critics of the 1970s and 1980s,[4] who ended his career as dean of the Graduate School of Journalism at UC Berkeley: an exceptional life trajectory! On his initiative, in 1967-1968, the Mellett Fund subsidized a series of experimental press councils, local councils that were better adapted to U.S. reality than the British formula; a few academics were entrusted with the organization. They set up three very different pairs of quite different councils.

The Stanford professors opted to operate in Redwood City, a southern suburb of San Francisco, and in Bend, a town in Oregon. In Redwood City, the members of the council, chosen as representative of their community, were to evaluate the quality of the paper without any publicity being given to their meetings. After a few months, when the Mellett money had been spent and the

---

[2]Letter to me, dated July 8, 1976, by Arthur J. Volkerts, then editor of the newspaper.
[3]In charge of complaints concerning contents, advertising, and distribution.
[4]See his *The Media Monopoly*, Boston, Beacon, 1983 (6th ed., 2000).

organizer had to leave, the council vanished. The publisher, who was very jealous of his authority, had never liked it: a few years later, he judged the experiment totally fruitless.

In Bend, on the contrary, the council, made up of local VIPs, was given great publicity. Its function was to field complaints against the newspaper: its evaluation of them would be published in the daily. R. W. Chandler, the publisher of the *Bulletin,* gave the council his full support, as he felt it would help him know his customers better, his journalists would be less negligent, and his readers would have a higher opinion of the press. When the council came to an end, seven years later, the cause was the prolonged absence of Chandler and, mainly, the lack of grievances to examine.

The Southern Illinois University co-financed and organized the second pair of councils in two small towns in the state, Cairo and Sparta. The former was poor and the latter prosperous. In Cairo, the council was given the task of improving the relationship between the newspaper and the large (40%) black community. In Sparta, the object of the council was to evaluate the services of the newspaper on the basis of the criticisms that the inhabitants were invited to send in. The management of the newspaper showed little enthusiasm in Cairo, whereas they fully cooperated in Sparta. However, the result was the same: after nine meetings, when outside funding and organization ended, the members of the council decided to pursue their action—and never met again! In the case of Cairo, because the town was then rocked by violent racial riots; in Sparta, it was because the publisher refused to take over, considering it was not the job of a media owner—and anyway he could not spare the time.

In St. Louis (Missouri) and in Seattle (Washington), the desired goal was not reached either. In those two large cities, the Mellett councils limited their ambitions to establishing links between the media and the black community. The five meetings in St Louis were little more than shouting matches, whereas in Seattle representatives of the African-American population (which was far smaller than in St. Louis) and of the media debated specific problems with experts: the experiment went on for a year after the Fund stopped its financing. The press did start covering African-American affairs better—to the extent, some believe, that serious racial trouble was avoided. But there, too, when the academic assigned to the council left town, the council stopped its activities.

The council in Riverside (California) provides an excellent transition from the series of councils that originated locally. The publisher of the town's dailies took Bend as a model and received a grant from the Markle Foundation. That money was slated to hire a consultant. M. H. Hays, the publisher, wanted the Riverside council to be a model: council members were to be educated and guided by an expert in mass communication. Hays himself selected 11 very diverse representatives of his readership and gave the council daily publicity. But he insisted that it should be strictly independent. It is interesting to note that in the first two serious cases it had to deal with, the council sided once with the press against a local official and sided once with an official against the press.

The publisher highly appreciated the information he obtained via the council. But soon the money ran out as did the complaints and so the council disbanded. After that, the decision-makers at the newspaper were asked to keep regularly in touch with representative groups in the population so as to find out what they thought of the local press.

On the big island of Hawaii (not Oahu where Honolulu and Pearl Harbor are located), the publisher of the *Tribune Herald* had public relations in mind when he started a press council for his daily in 1971—but some time later a weekly, three radio stations, and a cable TV system joined the venture. The council gradually gained its independence to the extent that its founder became its opponent. Any individual or institution could become a member of the council for a small fee. News people could sit on the council but not vote. Actually, adjudication of complaints was rare. The main purpose of this council was bring together local officials, media, and citizens.

The town of Iowa Falls (Iowa) only had a twice-a-week newspaper. Its publisher created a press council to find out what its readers thought of it and also to explain to them what the newspaper intended and was able to do. Following the discussions in the council, many changes were brought to the *Citizen,* but after two-and-a-half years, the council started running out of steam and, at the age of four, it died peacefully: "It seems to have run its course," as the editor wrote to me.[5]

Greenville (Mississippi) had the same experience. The publisher of the *Delta Democrat-Times*, who used to feel very hostile to press councils, had been converted by the success in Bend. The council he set up with representatives of all parts of the population was given full independence to evaluate complaints, provided they were first presented to the media, not only the daily, but also two radio stations and a TV station. The plaintiff also had to waive the right to go to court. The few judgments the Greenville council expressed were published in print and on the air, but after two years, for lack of funds and cases, the council passed away.

So what conclusions can be drawn from this brief panorama?

First, it appears that over a period of ten years only some 20 local councils saw the light of day in a country which then had 1,700 dailies and 8,000 weekly newspapers, and that those councils vanished after a few months or a few years. Not impressive. The results of the experiment seem negative. On second thought, however, I believe one can make some more positive observations. News media showed they were prepared to cooperate with a press council consisting of lay people and some councils, of different types, succeeded quite well. So a breach was opened!

A survey done by the Associated Press Managing Editors association (APME) in 1969 showed that half the journalists were favorable to press councils, as well as three quarters of elected officials, civil servants, and leaders of civic

---

[5]Letter dated July 8, 1976.

groups. In 1974 researchers from Stanford University discovered that although 80% of publishers at U.S. dailies judged a press council useless, 70% of them were ready to publish its findings if there was a council in their community. Thus, the experiments and the publicity given them seemed to have born fruit.

A national press council is first and foremost a double-headed watch-dog, monitoring and protecting the media, and it benefits from standing outside the fray. In contrast, a local council is primarily a liaison committee that cannot function outside of small towns (average population: 50,000 inhabitants). It is not easy to find 10 to 15 members who are altogether representative, respected, devoted and imaginative. It is almost impossible to find a competent coach/leader. Except in times of crisis, the general public does not really care about the quality of media. Whether this is due to ignorance, apathy, or a feeling of helplessness, in small towns there are never enough militant citizens to keep a council alive—not to speak of setting one up.

So should that be left to publishers? Rare are those who are as enthusiastic as G. Ray and H. Waring were in Littleton or who are ready to pay what the *Journal-Star* spent in Peoria. Anyway, should the money and/or energy first come from media owners? In order to be efficient, a press council must acquire a moral authority that it can only obtain if it is independent. As Jim Richstad, who was both a university professor and a council founder wrote (see p. 162), a council should no more have the reputation of being the enemy of media as it should be viewed as too friendly with them.

Even if its creation, its funding, and its coordination were taken care of, a local council could die from lack of nourishment, having no cases to deal with. The fact is that many serious problems of the press cannot be solved at that level: could, for instance, the Cairo press council eliminate the legacy of centuries of racism? Other problems simply cannot be solved: can a weekly that sells 8,500 copies be as informative as the *New York Times*? Lastly, and principally, a publisher who sets up, or agrees to cooperate with, a press council, is a socially responsible media person to start with, who takes into account the criticisms and suggestions made by users. So after a couple of years a local council is doomed not to have any complaint to dig its teeth into.

Ideally, a local council should lead to more participation by the public in the management of media. Thanks to a council, citizens should start inciting the local media industry to fulfill its function as a public service and more fully assume its mission as a Fourth Estate in countries where political decentralization is in progress.

Practically, in the present environment, it seems that a local council will probably, in most cases, be only temporary. Its function would be to solve ongoing conflicts between the press and the public, as well as to inform one about the other. This could afterwards be entrusted to a part-time ombudsman, an employee of the newspaper who would receive complaints, give readers explanations, forward justified grievances to the editors, and be in charge of getting corrections and apologies published. When faced with a very serious problem, the ombudsman could ask the members of the council to meet again. Historically, except in Louisville where the publisher finally appointed an ombudsman because he found it impossible to set up a council, no ombudsman has ever been associated with a local council.

A national council is necessary—but not sufficient, even if it fulfilled all its missions (which is never the case): even if it did gather and distribute data on the structure, the functioning, the finances, and the evolution of the news media; even if it did encourage journalism training and research in mass communication. A press council located in the capital of the country cannot establish and maintain the constant link that must exist between press proprietors, producers and consumers at the level where they operate.

Because in today's circumstances the existence of a press council can hardly be justified in a community with only two or three media outlets, and because direct sponsoring by media owners remains indispensable, the solution might be to place a permanent press council at an intermediate, regional level. Three U.S. councils have shown the way.

The councils of Honolulu (1970) and of Minnesota (1971) are far from perfect. The one in Minnesota was originally accused of being too exclusively a tribunal, and of being too subservient to the publishers that set it up. Over the years, it has become far more educational and independent.[6] The one in Honolulu, on the other hand, as it is not officially recognized by the press, has suffered from lack of money and publicity. However, both can easily cover all the media in their area and do not have to fear any shortage of work. Both have gradually increased the range of their activities and their moral authority in the eyes of the profession and the public.

Those two councils owe their existence largely to the efforts of journalism professors Jim Richstad in Honolulu and J. Edward Gerald in Minneapolis. That fact points to a solution to a crucial problem, the independence of the regional press council. So that it is not made powerless because of either excessive control or insufficient support by media managers, why not place the council under the protective wing of a university? To the representatives of proprietors, reporters, and public, it would offer a no man's land in which to hold their private or public meetings. The university would also provide the council with experts (lawyers, sociologists, etc.) and, if it had a school of journalism, competent advisers and inexpensive researchers.

---

[6]Only about 25% of its budget comes from the media.

TABLE 9.1

Local Press Councils in the United States

City (population)	Created in/ Died in	Life Span	Created by	Media Involved	Composition
Littleton (CO) 26,000	1946-1962	6 years	publisher	*Independent* weekly, circ. 5,000	about 12 citizens
Littleton (CO) 26,000	1967-1985	18 years	publisher	id. + *Arapahoe Herald*, weekly, circ. 12,000	about 12 citizens
Santa Rosa (CA) 50,000	1950-1953	3 years	publisher	*Press Democrat* daily, 18,000	15 citizens
Redwood City (CA) 65,000	1967-1968	a few months	Mellett Fund	*Tribune* daily, 21,000	9 citizens
Bend (OR) 13,000	1967-1974	7 years	Mellett Fund	*Bulletin* daily 8,500	9 citizens
Cairo (IL) 9,000	1967-1968	9 months	Mellett Fund	*Evening Citizen* daily, 6,000	15 citizens (10 active) incl. 3 Blacks
Sparta (IL) 3,500	1968-1968	9 months	Mellett Fund	*News-Plaindealer* weekly, 5,300	15 citizens (12 active)
St Louis (MO) 622,000	1968-1968	a few months	Mellett Fund	2 daily, 1 weekly, 3 radio stations, 3 TV stations	14 black citizens 8 representatives of the media
Seattle (WA) 515,000	1968-1969	1 year, 7 months	Mellett Fund	2 daily, 1 radio, 4 TV	30 citizens and representatives of the media
Peoria (IL) 126,000	1970-1983	13 years	publisher	*Journal-Star* daily, 110,000	21 housewives

Hilo (HA) 80,000	1971- NA	NA	publisher	1 daily, 1 weekly, 3 radios, 1 cable system	about 40 citizens and representatives of associations
Iowa Falls 6,000	1972-1976	4 years	publisher	*Citizen* bi-weekly, 5,000	12 citizens
Greenville (MI) 39,000	1972-1974	2 years	publisher	*Delta Democrat-Times*, daily, 18,000, 2 radios, 1 TV	13 then 18 citizens
Riverside (CA) 140,000	1973-1976	3 years	publisher	*Press and Enterprise*, dailies 36,000 and 53,000	11 citizens

CHAPTER 10
The Honolulu Community-Media Council

Jim Richstad

A crisis in credibility struck the news media in the United States in the late 1960s, causing great media and public concern. This was the driving force in the late 1960s and early 1970s for establishment of local press councils in the United States.

In Honolulu, the trigger for the creation in 1969-1970 of a Community-Media Council (HCMC) was a conflict between Mayor Frank Fasi and the Honolulu *Star-Bulletin* newspaper; they were continuing a long and bitter confrontation, with the public being seen as the injured third party because of the restrictions on news reporting.

The mayor was unhappy over what he considered unfair reporting and comment, and asked for the removal of the *Star-Bulletin* city hall reporter. The newspaper refused, and the major declared the *Star-Bulletin* reporters persona non grata.

An activist community minister, the Rev. Claude F. DuTeil, didn't like what he saw—a mayor barring newspaper reporters from news about the city's official actions, and a newspaper being challenged about the fairness of its coverage.

Dr. DuTeil, considered the "father" of HCMC, said it was too important a community problem to be left to editors and politicians, and called on the mayor's office and the two Honolulu daily newspapers. He heard the same suggestion from all of them—perhaps a press council, such as those then starting on the U.S. mainland, could not only help resolve the immediate dispute but also take a wider look as well at improving the news flow to people in Honolulu. The two editors, as well as the mayor's aide who suggested a press council, became founding members of HCMC.

159

Dr. DuTeil, an ardent believer in grass-roots approaches to community problems, contacted the Journalism Program at the University of Hawaii for more information about press councils and perhaps some help in forming one. The call brought University President Harlan Cleveland, a former U.S. ambassador to NATO, and me, an assistant professor, into the picture.

A Community-News Media Conference was held January 13, 1970 to determine first if there was a community-felt need for a press council and, if so, what it would do.

To the first question, the answer was a resounding, almost unanimous, "yes" from the 150 or so community people at the workshops. To the second question, there was wide but not complete agreement. The council was formally initiated November 16, 1970.

OPERATIONAL PRINCIPLES

President Cleveland spearheaded organizational meetings, and soon several enduring principles emerged.

1. This was to be a grass-roots council, to meet the conditions of Honolulu. It was to develop its own rules and style, and not rely on mainland models. It operated on a limited budget, all of which was raised locally.
2. As a grass-roots council, its membership was to be based on community activity and representativeness. A labor leader might be selected for membership not because of his or her official position, but because of representation to an important part of the community and other active community interests not directly tied to labor.
3. The council would deal with all issues that affect the flow of news to the community, whether it involved action by the media, by public officials, or by anyone or anything else. The council was not just looking at the errors of the media but also trying to unblock news access to public information and officials and providing a forum for examination of broader issues on the role of media in the community.
4. The council restricted its activities to the island of Oahu, where Honolulu is located, given the costs of travel to other parts of the island state (the small daily newspaper in the city of Hilo on the island of Hawaii for a time sponsored a press council, although of a different type).
5. The council included members of the media. This was seen as necessary for a realistic look at the problems of news flow in the community. It also provided a direct channel of communication about council activities to operating heads of the newsroom in Honolulu. As time went on, it became clear that the council received the atten-

tion—if not always the admiration—of reporters because they knew their editors were there taking the heat for them.

6. The council neither sought nor wanted any authority or penalizing clout over the media—and it could not have any if it wanted—beyond generating publicity for its findings and providing a community-media forum for open discussions on news issues of concern. To avoid legal complications, the council only handled issues if the complainants agreed not to take the issue to court. The council felt it had one great asset—its credibility—and that would provide the persuasive power.

OPERATIONAL METHODS

The operational method was to take complaints, investigate them thoroughly, present findings, and make a judgment. There never were a lot of complaints. The council also looked at broader community issues and held educational forums. It preferred quiet mediation to public disputes—settling a news problem was the goal, not assessing blame. This modus operandi prevailed in 2001, with a few additions over the years.

A pro-active stance, for example, was developed after a few years. Led by Dr. DuTeil, the council started to reach out and investigate important issues, without specific complaints. This was dramatically shown when the council undertook a two-year study of "The State of Journalism in Honolulu," with a report in 1991 on newspapers and in 1992 on television news.

The development of community press (or media) councils and a national news council introduced a new and potentially highly effective element into press accountability in the United States. It generally has been a quiet movement, attracting little national attention; certainly the potential has always been more than the reality; and much of the enthusiasm of the 1970s is long gone, as are most of the councils. But the 30-year record of the Honolulu Community-Media Council proves the strong potential of press councils in the 21st century.

CONCERN WITH NEWS CONSUMER

Community press councils have significant characteristics as agencies of press accountability.

1. They are not special-interest groups. Council members should be fairly representative of the community so that they cannot be dismissed by the media as isolated or special-interest complainants.
2. Members know what's going on in the community, and what impact certain kinds of news coverage might have.   •

3. Over time, community councils develop certain understanding and expertise about the news media.
4. They can provide an effective buffer for unhealthy intrusions in the news process and freedom of the press by government and other public or special interests.

Although the demise of the national council in 1984 was a great loss to press accountability in the United States, local or community press councils were developed before the national council, whereas most countries in the world have only national councils.

The very localness of government in the United States places special importance on the community press. Many very basic questions of government are settled at the local level, and it is often only the local news media that report such events. With more federal responsibilities going to the states in the last few decades of the 20th century, community press councils could be of critical importance.

The localism is combined with the virtual disappearance of competitive newspapers in any but the very largest cities. Even Honolulu, which had two daily newspapers when the media council was formed, faced the possibility in 2002 that the Honolulu *Star-Bulletin* might close. The localism and local monopoly explain in part one of the most difficult and sensitive areas a press council contends with: relations between the news media and local governments.

Community press councils may lack full and detailed knowledge of how the press operates but often they have a knowledge of events and perspectives far beyond that possessed by reporters or editors handling the stories. The representative council knows what impact certain stories will have on the community or parts of the community.

The council can also apprise the media on what kinds of information and news are needed in the community. The call words of many U.S. editors today, facing static or declining circulation, is to find out what the community wants in news and, under the banner of "community journalism," how the newspaper can help promote community goals.

A representative council also is important for tempering criticism of the media, for making such criticism more specific and informed, and for deflecting irresponsible or misinformed or under-informed critics.

The only authority councils have rests with their reputation for fairness and objectivity. This reputation grows out of how well the council is run, how thoroughly and carefully it investigates the issues, how effectively it focuses on the important questions, and how clearly it establishes itself as objective and fair—not in the pocket of the media, not overwhelmed (however kindly) by the media, and it is clearly not anti-media.

Rather than duplicate or overlap with other critical accountability modes—such as university journalism departments, newspaper ombudsmen and local journalism reviews—the press council brings its own strengths to media criticism, elements that the others cannot provide and that enrich media criticism and accountability.

One of the strongest accountability functions is critical examination of the news media performance. This research could focus on bias, distortion, gaps in coverage and accuracy, as well as broad questions of how various parts of the community are being reported and the representativeness of coverage on certain topics.

The Honolulu council's "State of Journalism in Hawaii" reports in 1991 and 1992[1] evaluated newspaper performance, for example, on such points as the amount of space allotted to news, the amount of national and international news and ratio of news to advertising. A survey of 400 persons involved in community organizations rated the newspapers as "adequate" or better, "poor," or "bad" in eight categories. In television news, performance was based on "journalistic excellence and enterprise, balance and fairness, accuracy, objectivity, lack of errors, quality of filming, professionalism, significance and service to the viewer." In both newspapers and television, evaluators compared the Honolulu newscasts with similar programs in other parts of the United States.

Ethical questions can also become part of the agenda. Where can one go for answers to the questions implicitly raised by a minister at a media council meeting[2] that there was too little coverage of fundamentalist religious sects? How does the council find the answer to that kind of question?

Even after the usual explanation by the editor about news values and broad interest and significance requirements and the considered opinions of a representative group of fellow citizens, the minister may not be convinced. But at least there has been a forum, there has been a public challenge and response, and there has been some thinking on the balance of religious coverage that is suited to a particular community.

These are generally unanswerable questions, but they can be approached in a critical, caring sense by a community press council. No other press critics represent the community, or even speak with as much authority on community needs.

COMMUNITY JOURNALISM RESEARCH

Hand in hand with complaint adjudication and forums is the need for research on community journalism problems. Council members can handle many investigative functions, but certain complaints go far beyond the research or inves-

---

[1]Fletcher Knebel (ed.), "State of Journalism in Hawaii, Part 1: Honolulu's Daily Newspapers," Honolulu Community-Media Council, October 1991. Fletcher Knebel (ed.) and Jim Becker, "State of Journalism in Hawaii, Part 2: Honolulu's Daily Local TV. News Shows," September 1992.

[2]The examples in this chapter come from HCMC proceedings unless otherwise specified.

tigative resources of the council. If research resources are not adequate to the problem, the council faces having to drop the matter or settle for superficial research.

An example from Honolulu concerned allegations that many of the older movies being shown on television portrayed American Indians and other minorities in a derogatory manner, and the council was asked to seek ways to have the showings stopped. The first question was, "What are the facts?" Council debate came to a halt because the facts were not known and the difficulty of getting them seemed beyond the means of the council.

One method available to most councils is to interest university students and professors. This has resulted in some significant research that goes beyond council capabilities and can firm a bond with local academic institutions. The "State of Journalism in Hawaii" studies enlisted retired mainland newspaper editors and retired mainland TV news directors in evaluations, for example.

Anderson and Ghiglione make the point that media criticism is evolving or expanding from the essayist to a "more systematic, more complex and more institutionalized" base.[3] "The new media criticism costs big money" and requires "great quantities of research" and continuity of research.

Local press councils can provide a middle ground between the institutionalized and costly media studies and the often one-person operation of many journalism programs. The broadness and quality of community participation and knowledge can be used to make limited funds go further and provide a means of getting at performance and community-information-need questions that otherwise would go untouched.

COUNCIL METHODS OF OPERATIONS

Many critical functions have developed in press councils over the past several years. Community press councils by their nature are deeply involved in media criticism. Formation of a council is usually seen as a means of improving community understanding of the news media and its practices and improving the quality and extent of news service. These are two primary areas of press council critical functions—education and evaluation. A third related method is to provide a forum to enable community representatives and media operators to talk with each other.

Within these three broad areas, HCMC has used at least eight approaches, all of which can go on simultaneously, given the resources. They are:

---

[3]David L. Anderson and Loren Ghiglione, "The Critical Factor: Criticism of the News Media in Journalism Education," *Journalism Monographs*, 32, February 1974, pp. 23-32.

1. Hearing complaints brought by citizens, community leaders and government officials against the news media, usually for particular articles but also on broader questions of overall coverage, taste or relevance. This conciliatory approach gets parties in dispute together in a suitable forum for settling differences. This is the basic starting point for most councils, and some of them might not get beyond it. As a very important corollary, councils also investigate complaints by news media persons against news sources, often government or government-related sources. This is an important area of criticism. Councils that hear both sides of the news coverage situation are better able to balance often conflicting societal needs on news and opinion flow.

2. Study of broader problems, either related to complaints in specific situations or in matters of general community concern. Or it may be that there is a series of related complaints or situations that can be grouped and handled in a larger context: for example, coverage of an election campaign. Creation of dialogue is important here, involving community groups, students, the media, and others.

3. Development of codes or guidelines of professional conduct for the news media and news sources. A council can develop guidelines itself, or point to the need for them, or it can work through existing codes of particular groups. Examples here would be medical coverage, court-press relations, the ethical code of the American Society of Newspaper Editors, and so forth. Photographs are another area of particular concern to readers, especially when a tragedy is involved. HCMC helped develop codes for reporting public opinion polls, press conferences, covering demonstrations and other things. In the process of investigation of complaints the need for a code may emerge, or there already may be an informal code among journalists that can be formalized or improved.

4. Active roles in court cases dealing with the community news concerns. This can be as initiator or as an *amicus curiae* representing public interest as compared to news media interests or the other party's interest in the case. This type of activity lends itself to getting case law on the books and can have long-lasting impact. It is a costly and time-consuming approach, but one that at times may be the only effective means available to a council.

5. Initiation and support of, or opposition to, media-related legislation at local, state, and national levels. Press councils may develop their own legislative proposals and lobby for them, or they may study legislation dealing with the community news flow, take a position, and testify and lobby for or against legislation. This also uses precious and limited council resources, especially if expert opinion is needed and is not available *pro bono*. Honolulu examples include open gov-

ernment meetings and records bills, shield laws, newspaper preservation bills, and funding of public television.
6. Media councils can serve as organizing forces for other community groups concerned with the same media issues. In the mid-1980s the Honolulu council spearheaded a coalition of community groups interested in open meetings and records in government. The potential for action by uniting several strong community groups in this area into a "Sunshine Coalition" was impressive and led to other important exchanges of information and support.
7. Development of community-based journalism research to look specifically at the ongoing process of news service. The Honolulu council was unable to establish a community news research program, but found ways to bring in research through its own members and agreements with students and university faculty.
8. Outside evaluation of the local news media. HCMC's "State of Journalism in Hawaii" study used both Honolulu and mainland evaluators to assess newspaper and television news performance.

In practically every significant matter brought before HCMC there was great educational value in the discussions and reports. Although many of the matters were fairly specific complaints, there was a drive for the general principles. A complaint by a television news director about the availability of the Hawaii governor to the press, for example, was more broadly viewed as "What were the duties and obligations of government officials to meet the press, and under what conditions?"

The same government-press issue came up when the mayor's press aide excluded a Honolulu *Star-Bulletin* reporter from four news conferences because the mayor considered the reporter unfair. The newspaper sought an injunction, and the mayor banned the second newspaper reporter, from the *Honolulu Advertiser,* and that paper filed a suit. The mayor soon dropped the ban and the *Star-Bulletin* dropped its legal action. *The Advertiser* continued in federal district court in Honolulu.

The judge, Martin Pence, rejected HCMC's petition for *amicus curiae* standing, but suggested the council draft guidelines on press or news conferences for his consideration. Dr. William L. Rivers of Stanford University, a leader in the early press council movement, was in Honolulu at the time and joined council members and volunteer attorneys in writing guidelines.

Although the judge did not include the guidelines in his later decision, he commended them and suggested their adoption by the parties involved. The judge ruled that exclusion of newspaper reporters from a public official's news conference was a violation of the First and 14th Amendments to the U.S. Constitution. The council's attorney called it a significant ruling, and it serves as a powerful statement on a community's right to be informed about its government. The council prepared an article explaining its interest in the free flow of information and listed the guidelines. The article was published by the *Honolulu Advertiser* in its commentary section.

Getting national attention for the council's reports on serious matters has always been difficult. The press conference guidelines, for example, could be useful around the country wherever elected politicians bar access to the press. They represent an attempt to balance the needs of government, the press, and the community. A usual pattern in developing such guidelines is for the media to do it themselves, or with government input. This often leaves out the consumer, the community.

HCMC helped develop other guidelines—one involved election polling stories and another on television coverage of campus disturbances. Each illustrates a different mode.

The election polling example developed out of a complaint that the *Advertiser* and *Star-Bulletin* refused to publish a political poll that showed the mayor of Honolulu running strongly in a state gubernatorial campaign. The question soon focused on the quality of polling methods and, after investigation, the council asked two polling experts to meet with political party executives and council members to develop guidelines. The guidelines were acceptable to the political parties, the press, and the council, with the results published in one of the dailies.

Television guidelines on coverage of campus disturbances were codified by the council in its investigation of the potential of television coverage to incite or aggravate violence at the University of Hawaii. The council found the television stations were already operating, unknown to each other, under similar precautionary guidelines. The matter was dropped after the council found no evidence that television coverage had ever aggravated or incited violence on campus, and the guidelines have become part of the community standards for news coverage.

Election coverage complaints are a difficult area for press councils. Incidents often occur shortly before the actual election, and to have any impact on the campaign itself, speedy council action is required. The Honolulu council felt it couldn't use its usual committee investigation system and get a finding out before the election, so it vested quick-response power in its chairman and executive director.

A typical complaint is that news coverage of a candidate was distorted, and that other candidates received more favorable or less unfavorable press treatment. The council used its own resources to review such complaints, and in one the newspaper involved investigated on its own. A university student helped the council investigate coverage, in another example.

One of the early, far-reaching achievements of the council came from monitoring of the media by council members. A complaint was lodged by a council member and others that the local news media were consistently misidentifying the opposition forces in Vietnam, lumping all opposition under the terms "communist," "Red," or "enemy," when in fact there were quite different groups in opposition to the United States and South Vietnam. Many of the casualties labeled "communist" were not.

They contended that labeling all opposition or casualties as "communist" was careless journalism and tended to justify many of the acts of war. A council committee monitored the local media for a week, and concluded that the complainant was justified, that the media were using umbrella terms and thereby were inaccurately portraying the war.

Because most of the news reports of the war came from the news agencies, the results of the monitoring were sent to the Associated Press, United Press International, New York Times News Service, and the Washington Post-Los Angeles Times Service, as well as local media. UPI reproduced a large part of the report in its international newsletter, *UPI Reporter*, and the publisher of the *New York Times* wrote the council a letter in agreement. The council did not continue the monitoring, however, so the long-term impact is not clear.

Dr. Rivers, writing in *The Progressive* magazine, noted on the Vietnam report matter: "Seldom can a local council generate such impact. Not only do local councils focus almost exclusively on community concerns, commanding national attention to any of their deliberations is a matter of luck."[4]

The lessons here are that significant matters of national and international concern can be handled at the local media council level with limited resources, that findings of local councils should in some form reach the broader national audience, that local councils should include in their concerns how the great news gathering and distribution agencies function, and how that affects the quality and quantity of news about the outside world that flows into the community. Criticism and defense of the media cannot be segregated into "local" and "national" and "international": each community must examine the total news system that services it.

Another avenue for accountability is legislation. In 1975, HCMC was instrumental in the passage of effective "sunshine" or open meeting legislation for Hawaii, with the strong and coordinated backing of several other community groups. The *Star-Bulletin* higher-education reporter complained about closed sessions of the University of Hawaii Board of Regents. A council investigation found the regents (and many other public bodies) conducted discussions and took action in closed executive sessions and met in public only to vote, with little or no public discussion of issues.

The council, rebuffed by the regents, sought a law that would open meetings in which decisions and/or votes on public issues were taken. A council task force collected and studied existing laws from other states, and wrote newspaper editors and community groups in key states to see how their open meeting laws were working. The council developed a model law and had it introduced into the State House of Representatives. The effort was unsuccessful at that session, although the council and 18 other community groups and individuals testified in support.

---

[4]William L. Rivers, "Who Shall Guard the Guards," *The Progressive*, September 1971.

Between legislative sessions, the media council organized the Hawaii Task Force on Open Meetings with several other community groups, and a radio and television information program was started. Individual groups conducted their own campaigns as well.

These efforts paid off in the next Legislature with passage of sunshine legislation. The resulting law, far from perfect, led to continued community activity, and in 1982 resulted in a wide-ranging "Sunshine Coalition" that successfully worked to make the law better through legislative amendment. Efforts to weaken the law were opposed.

The undertaking showed the council had the staying power over a decade, and that it could organize a successful coalition of community groups. The council also testified in support of a "shield law" to protect or shield reporters from being forced by courts to disclose the sources of confidential information, and in support of public television funds. It opposed state legislation that would have established a Media Responsibility Commission to police the media and a bill requiring extensive financial disclosure by the two Honolulu newspapers.

ARE COUNCILS EFFECTIVE?

There are many examples to show how a local press council can hold the media accountable and open news channels in the community. The question remains, however: is the council effective? Does it make any difference? Are the newspapers better? Is television news better? With the wide access to news and information on the Internet, how can a council deal with those sources?

Usually such difficult questions are followed by silence. In Honolulu, there is a much greater awareness among the media concerning public evaluations of their performances. There seems to be an increased sensitivity and a willingness to engage in public discussion about performance that wasn't there 30 years ago. The council provides a forum for these community-media issues, and that is a value in itself. It also provides a channel through which other community groups, focused on other issues, can join in accountability in the media as it concerns them.

The "State of Journalism in Hawaii" study established performance and evaluation standards for newspapers and television news accountability. Fletcher Knebel, the driving force behind the study, was a veteran journalist and author. He was a strong force on the council and raised such basic questions as whether the media devote enough of their resources to news coverage.

Much of the work of a council is to bring understanding and conciliation, and that does not often lead to dramatic results. Warren Iwasa, the new HCMC president in 2000, said that often neither party is pleased with the results of mediation, but it "does bring about the very positive result" that the parties agree to accept the mediator's judgment and the grievance is not pursued further. A common observation is that councils are valuable just by their community presence as a third force between the press and public officials, and between the press and the public.

The Honolulu council urges complainants to first talk with the newspaper or television station involved, and sometimes that is enough. Even when council members see media changes for the better, it does not mean the changes were the result of council action.

Press councils provide a place where real complaints can be lodged, investigated, and brought to some kind of community, not legal, judgment. A strong, visible council can do much to focus public thinking on what the press should be doing and how well it is doing.

There are all kinds of questions on how best to organize and run a press council: membership, media's role, representativeness, types of complaints accepted, investigation procedures, ways of gaining public attention, organization of community-media forums, ways to lobby for legislation, how to be involved in court cases, financing, and research procedures.

These are important questions but the broader concerns are the overall value of press councils and how they can make a difference. Bagdikian's often quoted statement on press accountability is pertinent: "What we really need is something tangible and significant for the reader in his own locality [. . .] an assessment of his own newspaper as he sees it."

To be fully successful, press councils must go beyond debating groups, forums, and complaint bureaus. They must move to a new level of critical awareness of news media and their practices and impact on the social, political and economic context of the community. HCMC President Iwasa, for example, hopes to "encourage more people in the community to become active, vocal, and responsible grass-roots media critics."

Although the Honolulu council in its first 30 years has pioneered innovative methods in community media accountability, Iwasa said he was looking to revamp its complaint procedures, establish a web site and a weekly public radio program, bring in younger members and raise the council's profile in the community. The Honolulu council continues to play a vital role in the community in the new millennium.

ORGANIZATIONS IN THE U.S.

Honolulu Community-Media Council
Warren Iwasa, President, effective September 2000
P.O. Box 22415, Honolulu, Hawaii 96823-2415
Telephone: (808) 521-6323

Minnesota News Council
Gary Gilson, executive director
12 S. Sixth Street, Suite 1122, Minneapolis, MN 55402
Fax: 1 (612) 341 9358
E-mail: newscncl@mtn.org
Website: www.mtn.org/newscouncil

Washington News Council
Robert Utter, chair; John Hamer, executive director
PO Box 3672, Seattle, WA 98124.
Fax: (206) 938 6313.
E-mail: wnewsc@aol.com
Website: www.wanewscouncil.org

PART IV
Other M*A*S*

SECTION 1
Mediation: Ombudsmen

CHAPTER 11
The Newspaper Ombudsman and the Aim of Accountability in American Journalism

Theodore L. Glasser

Perhaps the most startling fact about American newspaper ombudsmen is their scarcity. Fewer than 2% of the daily newspapers in the United States employ one. Although no one has surveyed editors and publishers to find out their reasons for not hiring ombudsmen, the anecdotal evidence points to three popular explanations: (1) newsrooms cannot afford them, (2) they undercut the authority and responsibility of the editor, and (3) it hurts morale to have someone always second-guessing the quality and value of newsroom policies and performance.

Support for the idea of a newspaper ombudsman is neither widespread nor institutionalized by endorsements from press associations, trade unions or other prominent organizations of journalists. Imported from Sweden, where the term originally applied to a position created in the early 1800s to deal with citizens' complaints about decisions made by the executive branch of government,[1] the ombudsman concept applied to American journalism represents an effort by a few individual newspapers to accommodate disgruntled readers—and, significantly, to combat what is taken to be one of the enduring enemies of American press credibility: press arrogance.

---

[1]For a recent review, from an American perspective, of Sweden's press ombudsmanship, which began two years after the first American press ombudsman was appointed—see Steven Price, "Ombudsman To the Swedes," *American JR*, April 1998, pp. 46-48.

THE ORIGINS OF THE AMERICAN NEWSPAPER OMBUDSMAN

Two provocative magazine articles in 1967 provided the impetus for the press ombudsman movement in the United States. Writing in *Esquire* in March, Ben Bagdikian, then a reporter at the Providence (Rhode Island) *Journal-Bulletin,* expressed hope that some "brave owner will provide for a community ombudsman on his paper's board—maybe a non-voting one—to be present, to speak, to provide a symbol and, with luck, exert public interest in the ultimate fate of the American newspaper."[2] A few months later A. H. Raskin, at the time as assistant editor of the editorial page at the *New York Times,* offered a similar proposal.

In an essay in the paper's Sunday magazine, Raskin took editors and publishers to task for their "unshatterable smugness"; no other institution, Raskin observed, "is so addicted as the press to self-righteousness, self-satisfaction and self-congratulations." What is needed, Raskin wrote, is for every newspaper to create a "Department of Internal Criticism to put all of its standards under re-examination and to serve as a public protector in its day-to-day operation." And the head of this Department, Raskin suggested, "ought to be given enough independence in the paper to serve as an ombudsman for the readers, armed with authority to get something done about valid complaints and to propose methods for more effective performance of all the paper's services to the community, particularly the patrol it keeps on the frontiers of thought and action."[3]

Although neither Bagdikian's nor Raskin's superiors saw a need for an ombudsman, Norman Isaacs, then executive editor of the Louisville (Kentucky) *Courier-Journal,* accepted the idea with enthusiasm. In 1967 John Herchenroeder, a 62-year-old city editor with 40 years of experience at the *Courier-Journal,* became the nation's first newspaper ombudsman.[4]

Primarily responsible for dealing with reader complaints and questions, Herchenroeder's job in some ways resembled the "editorial secretary" position at the *Detroit News* in the mid-1920s or the even earlier Bureau of Accuracy and Fair Play at the New York *World* where readers with complaints could visit or call what Hohenberg remembered as the "genteel functionary in the small, little noticed outer office," who would "listen gravely, take notes, and give assurances that 'something would be done.'"[5] Herchenroeder, however, gave more than

---

[2]Reprinted as "What's Wrong with the American Press," pp. 3-17 in Ben H. Bagdikian, *The Effete Conspiracy and Other Crimes By the Press,* New York, Harper & Row, 1972, p. 17.

[3]A. H. Raskin, "What's Wrong with American Newspapers," *The New York Times Sunday Magazine,* June 11, 1967, pp. 28, 83.

[4]Isaacs recalls the appointment of Herchenroder in Norman E. Isaacs, *Untended Gates: The Mismanaged Press,* New York, Columbia UP, 1986, pp. 132-146.

[5]See Nelson A. Crawford, *The Ethics of Journalism,* New York, Alfred E. Knopf, 1923, p. 202; Les Brown, *The Reluctant Reformation,* New York, McKay, 1974, p. 66; and Cassandra Tate, "What Do Ombudsmen Do?" *Columbia JR,* May/June 1984, pp. 37-41.

assurances. From the complaints he received each day he prepared a written report, which he posted in the newsroom and distributed among top editors, and on occasion his reports brought about minor changes in newsroom policy.

Because Isaacs believed that Herchenroeder needed to devote all of his time to handling reader queries and complains, which increased from about 400 the first year to about 3,000 a decade later, the nation's first newspaper ombudsman did not engage in any *public* commentary on the press. Besides, Isaacs found the role of ombudsman and the role of press critic to be largely incompatible: "You can have a media critic or an ombudsman, but you can't have both in the same person."[6]

At the *Washington Post*, in contrast, which appointed the nation's second newspaper ombudsman in 1970, executive editor Benjamin C. Bradlee saw the two roles as essentially inseparable. "Going public," in Bradlee's view, is what gives the *Post*'s ombudsman the clout he needs: "It prevents editors from sweeping anything under the rug. You have a representative out there saying, 'Don't do that. You guys goofed. You fell short of your goals'."[7] Accordingly, Richard C. Harwood, who relinquished his responsibilities as an assistant managing editor and became the *Post*'s first ombudsman, not only dealt with reader complaints and prepared internal "oversight" memos addressed to "Bradlee et al." but contributed regularly to an editorial page feature entitled "The News Business," an occasional column intended to serve as "a vehicle for commentary by staff members and by outsiders on matters having to do with the workings and performance not only of the *Post* but of the rest of the news media."[8]

When in 1971 Bagdikian replaced Harwood as the *Post*'s ombudsman, the position moved further in the direction of press criticism. In principle, Bagdikian agreed with Isaacs that complaint-handling and press criticism ought to be kept separate: "a paper of any size wishing to do a complete job should have one person handling complaints, with the inevitable research that requires, and someone else to write the press criticism." Although Bagdikian was unable to achieve that separation, he was able to convince the *Post*'s management that it was inappropriate for the ombudsman to write confidential memos to the publisher and executive editor. "I don't see how I could be their agent," Bagdikian explained, "and a dispassionate critic at the same time."[9]

[6]Quoted in H. E. Goodwin, *Groping for Ethics in Journalism,* Ames, Iowa State UP, 1983, p. 27.

[7]Quoted in Tate, "What Do Ombudsmen Do?" p. 38.

[8]P. L. Geylin, *Introduction to Of the Press, By the Press, for the Press (and Others, Too),* L. Babbs, ed., Washington, DC, Washington Post Co., 1974, p. iv.

[9]Ben H. Bagdikian, "Confessions of an Ombudsman," *Nieman Reports,* Spring/Summer 1974, p. 16.

THE ROLE OF THE NEWSPAPER OMBUDSMAN

Although some of the best and biggest American newspapers employ ombudsmen, which means hundreds of thousands of readers have someone in the newsroom they know they can call or write when they have a complaint, comment or
question, the nature of the ombudsman's response varies considerably from one
newsroom to the next. Put a little differently, if a few dozen newspapers apparently agree on the importance of having an ombudsman, they generally do not
agree on what that job entails. As one commentator put it not too long ago,
"there are virtually as many definitions of the job as there are tenants of it."

> Some ombudsmen are drawn from the ranks of reporters and editors, others
> come from entirely outside the news organization. Some have indefinite
> and presumably long tenure, others are hired via non-renewable contracts.
> Some report to the editor, some to the publisher. Some are free to research
> and write whatever they please. Most endure in-house bargaining, if not an
> outright veto power from on high. . .
> Some are mandated simply to represent the general public, with specific
> emphasis on aggrieved targets of coverage. Some consider themselves in-
> house press critics and feel free to take on a topic whether or not there has
> been a consequential complaint from outside. Some are glorified public
> relations counselors whose primary duty is to placate complainants rather
> than to serve as an avenging angel on their behalf.[10]

Whether they are called "ombudsman," "reader's representative" or something else, they seldom play the role Raskin and Bagdikian had intended. None sits
on a newspaper's board, as Bagdikian wanted; and none really has the power "to get
something done about valid complaints," as Raskin proposed. To be sure, most
ombudsmen lack the independence and authority their position implies. They represent readers only in the sense that some bureaucrat at the local department store represents *customers*. They may try to serve the needs and interests of the larger community, but ultimately they must please management.[11]

---

[10]William A. Henry III, "Freedom and Accountability: A Search for Solutions," pp. 153-
177 in Everette E. Dennis, Donald M. Gillmor and Theodore L. Glasser (eds.), *Media
Freedom and Accountability,* New York, Greenwood Press, 1989, p. 171.

[11]In this sense ombudsmen typically serve a public relations function for their newspapers. See for example, James S. Ettema and Theodore L, Glasser, "Public Accountability
or Public Relations? Newspaper Ombudsmen Define Their Role," *Journalism Quarterly,*
64 (Spring 1987): 3-12. See also Lamar W. Bridges and Janet A. Bridges, "Newspaper
Ombudsman Role During Presidential Campaign," *Newspaper Research Journal,* 16
(Spring 1995): 76-90; and Neil Nemeth and Craig Sanders, "Ombudsmen's Interactions
with Public Through Columns," *Newspaper Research Journal,* 20 (Winter 1999): 29-42;
Neil Nemeth and Craig Sanders, "Meaningful Discussion of Perfomance Missing,"
Newspaper Research Journal, 22 (Winter 2001): 52-59.

How precarious a job it is becomes evident when an ombudsman truly offends, usually unwittingly, an editor or publisher. At the St. Petersburg (Florida) *Times* in 1980, for example, the ombudsman, Dorothy Smiljanich, publicly criticized the *Times* for assigning only white reporters to cover race riots in Miami. Executive editor Robert Haiman thought her criticism was unfair and demanded an apology. Smiljanich refused and quit. Haiman, in turn, decided not to reappoint an ombudsman.

A few years earlier, in another incident involving race and racism, Bagdikian, in his role as the *Post's* ombudsman, told a gathering of black members of Congress that boycotting a newspaper's advertisers was probably a more effective way to bring about newsroom changes than calling a publisher a racist. Bagdikian insisted that he was not *advocating* a boycott—only pointing out that the primary motivation of the American press is not to oppress blacks but to make money. An outraged Bradlee, Bagdikian's boss, nonetheless accused Bagdikian of being disloyal to management. Bagdikian resigned.

Retirement, however, is more likely than resignation. Ombudsmen tend to come up through the ranks of their own newspaper, often taking on the ombudsman job as their last newsroom assignment. In fact, ombudsmen are the oldest of any newsroom group—on average, older than publishers, editors, and reporters. Moreover, most ombudsmen find their jobs meaningful and satisfying. It should come as no surprise, then, that few ombudsmen end up in the predicament Smiljanich and Bagdikian found themselves in.

Individually, ombudsmen may have strong and consistent views of their role and responsibilities, but as group there is little consensus and considerable division. In a census of the members of Organization of Newspaper Ombudsmen (U. S. and Canadian newspaper ombudsmen), taken in 1985, ombudsmen were evenly split on whether, "in the final analysis, an ombudsman's loyalty is to the newspaper." Although most ombudsmen agreed that they ought to "lower the boom" when a newspaper makes a mistake, there was little agreement that they ought to provide "hard-hitting" critiques of reporters' and editors' work—and even less agreement that these critiques should focus on management's policies and decisions. Although most ombudsmen agreed that an "ombudsman must be a neutral mediator between a newspaper and its readers," most also agreed that, "in the final analysis, an ombudsman's loyalty is to the paper's readers." And notwithstanding their expressed loyalty to readers, a substantial portion of ombudsmen expressed reluctance to try to change the way their newspapers operate.[12]

Most ombudsmen believe it is an important part of their job to "see to it that corrections appear in the newspaper when necessary," but very few

[12]Theodore L. Glasser and James S. Ettema, *A Census of North American Newspaper Ombudsmen: Preliminary Findings*, Minneapolis, Silha Center for the Study of Media Ethics and Law, University of Minnesota, 1985, pp. 8-11.

ombudsmen are solely responsible for the publication of corrections. Indeed, half of the ombudsmen have no involvement whatsoever in the actual decision-making about corrections and their publication.[13]

THE LIMITS OF SELF-CRITICISM

As of the late 1990s, only about half of the members of the Organization of Newspaper Ombudsmen wrote a regular column.[14] Fewer than 12% of the ombudsmen regarded column writing as their most important duty; and, significantly, none of the editors to whom ombudsmen report regarded the ombudsman's column as the ombudsman's most important responsibility. *Public* accountability, it follows, does not appear to be a defining attribute of most of the members of the organization of newspaper ombudsmen.

Without a column as a venue for an open discussion of what the press does and how well it does it, ombudsmen can at best provide only a limited form of accountability, what Neil Nemeth in his recent study of the ombudsman at the *Louisville Courier-Journal* describes as "accountability to an individual complainant without attendant publicity."[15] Ombudsmen who write columns can provide a broader and more important kind of accountability, one that is, as Nemeth puts it, "both public and comprehensive." In practice, however, very few columns approximate that ideal.

The columns that do appear, with a few notable exceptions, serve a public relations function for their newspapers and do not provide a steady diet of local press commentary and criticism. As "insiders" with years—often decades—of newsroom experience, ombudsmen tend to explain and ultimately defend, rather than question and criticize, the traditions and values of mainstream journalism. Little has changed since the mid-1980s when a study, published in *Columbia Journalism Review*, found that most columns were predictably and interminably mundane:

> A reading of some 800 columns written by ombudsmen around the country shows that apologia is more the order of the day than incisive criticism. There are numerous explanations of how difficult the conditions are under which journalists work. Some ombudsmen specialize in eye-gumming discourses on lofty but irrelevant issues; others are preoccupied with trivia.

---

[13]Ettema and Glasser, "Public Accountability or Public Relations? Newspaper Ombudsmen Define Their Role," p. 7.

[14]Kenneth Starck and Julie Eisele, "Newspaper Ombudsmanship as Viewed by Ombudsmen and their Editors," *Newspaper Research Journal,* 20 (Fall 1999): 37-49.

[15]Neil Nemeth, "A News Ombudsman as an Agent of Accountability," pp. 55-67 in David Pritchard (ed.), *Holding the Media Accountable,* Bloomington, Indiana UP, 2000, p. 63.

Most are inclined to explain rather than examine, and often the explanations amount to something on the order of: we do it that way because that's the way we do it; it's our policy.[16]

Ombudsmen do, of course, use their columns to take their newspapers to task for violations of standards of professional performance. But their commentary usually focuses on an individual's lapse of judgment and seldom examines, though often assumes and describes, the institutional norms and newsroom values on which professional standards rest. Moreover, by using their columns as an opportunity to respond to readers' inquiries and complaints, ombudsmen further forfeit their critical distance and independence of perspective. Too many readers want to know why a newspaper dropped their favorite comic strip; not many, obviously, raise questions about the structure and control of the newsroom.

In short, ombudsmen's columns, though at times interesting and instructive, seldom provide what at a minimum the ideal of press accountability demands: a "tradition of sustained, systematic, and intellectually sound criticism of the press." By this Jim Carey, now on the journalism faculty at Columbia University, means criticism of the press, in the press—but decidedly not by the press: "We do not want the press educating us about the press any more than we want the State Department educating us about foreign affairs."[17] When the press looks inward, as it often does when its practices incite public indignation, the coverage and commentary—including the commentary ombudsmen provide—tend to restrict debate and curtail criticism by limiting the discussion to journalists and other knowledgeable insiders. This "narcissistic gaze," to use Barbie Zelizer's unkind but accurate phrase, insulates the press from outsiders whose critique might cast the controversy in very different terms: "In setting up a forum that is structurally immune to external criticism, journalism presents itself as one of the few institutions in our society that have both a right to self-correct and no obligation to engage other institutional voices in shaping that corrective."[18]

---

[16]Tate, "What Do Ombudsmen Do?", p. 39.

[17]James W. Carey, "Journalism and Criticism: The Case of an Undeveloped Profession," *Review of Politics*, 36 (1974): pp. 227, 239.

[18]Barbie Zelizer, "Journalism in the Mirror," *The Nation*, February 17, 1997, p. 10.

CHAPTER 12

The Newspaper Ombudsman
A Personal Memoir
of the Early Days

Alfred JaCoby

The first question for the new ombudsman back in the early days (the 1960s and 1970s) seemed to be universal: Just what did the word mean and what was the job about?

The dictionary wasn't much help. The general definition in a number or dictionaries, big and small, referred to a public official "assigned to investigate complaints against government." That concept had originated in Sweden. The enlightened Swedes, knowing that government and its bureaucracy were no respecter of freedom, had established this concept of a "watchdog" for citizen rights. The Swedish ombudsman was a government official. But we were journalists. We weren't public officials and didn't want to be. If we investigated complaints against government, we wrote about them.

And in many ways, we offended our readers. We committed errors and then made it hard to have the errors corrected. We were arrogant in our dealings with the public. We ignored some important stories and overplayed others. The public wasn't amused or charmed or, in too many cases, satisfied with the media. As for correcting errors, too many newspapers had a long history of not doing it.

This was the situation in 1976, when Gerald L. Warren was appointed editor-in-chief of *The San Diego Union* by owner and publisher Helen K. Copley. Warren had been deputy press secretary to President Richard M. Nixon during the Watergate years, then, after Nixon's resignation, he had served on President Gerald Ford's inner staff. He was one of the few close associates of Nixon to survive the Watergate fiasco with a reputation for honesty in the eyes of the White House press corps.

Warren had roots in San Diego. A former Navy pilot, he had entered journalism at the *San Diego Union* by registering for its training course in 1959. He had held a succession of jobs, including city editor and deputy managing editor. Then he had gone to Washington to join the Nixon administration. There he had seen the working of the ombudsman program at the *Washington Post.* When Helen Copley asked him to return to San Diego as editor of the flagship newspaper in her group, one of the acknowledged agreements in his pre-employment negotiations had been the establishment of such a program.

Walter MacArthur, a veteran city editor, was Warren's first appointee as "readers' representative." That name had been selected, rather than ombudsman, for the sake of clarity and to make it plain that his function was to serve the subscribers and not the producers of the newspaper.

The choice of MacArthur reflected the environment in which the first ombudsmen operated. Almost without exceptions, they were men (not women) who had worked for many years at the newspaper in top positions like news editor or city editor. That kind of choice had an advantage: those veteran journalists, as one editor confided to me once, "knew where the skeletons were hidden and would not be easy to fool." The drawback was that such appointments made it possible to shunt older journalists to the sidelines, in pre-retirement, and to hasten the rise of young people with new ideas. That option was attractive to publishers and editors who feared their staff was aging too much for the young audiences, a fashionable view then in newspapers whose circulations were declining.

MacArthur stayed in the position for about a year. He had to deal with all the teething problems. The function had not been clearly defined and he interpreted it as involving an improvement of the style of the *San Diego Union*, as determining a policy relative to sexism in contents (which in those days was revolutionary) and as increasing readers' feedback. To accomplish this last task, he undertook to have copies of stories mailed to the news sources and to ask them to evaluate their accuracy and fairness, a method now used by a number of U.S. newspapers. The record showed a high degree of accuracy in articles originating in the newsroom and a great satisfaction as regards their fairness.

After serving for a year as an ombudsman, MacArthur became an editorial writer— and I was appointed readers' representative, which I remained for the next seven years. Like MacArthur, I had worked at the newspaper for a quarter of a century, in various occupations. I had been a reporter, copy editor, editor of the special sections of the Sunday edition, head of the entertainment departments and, more recently, city editor. Over the years, I had also taken part in the planning and creation of several new sections, an experience I found useful when I undertook to develop and extend the function of readers' representative.

Thanks to the experience acquired over the first year, the mission Warren assigned to me was more precise than the one he had given MacArthur at the launch. He wanted errors to be quickly corrected. He wanted the ombudsman to have more contact with the public. He wanted the readers' representative to circulate memos within the newspaper to let the staff know the public's comments. The model for those notes was the *New York Times'* *"Winners and Sinners,"* the witty and penetrating bulletin written by Theodore Bernstein, a deputy managing editor, for distribution to the staff. Copies of *Winners and Sinners* were sent by the *Times* to many editors and publishers nationwide and it had become a model for internal comment.

Most of those missions were easy to fulfill. In those early days, before readers understood our motives, there were few requests for correction. As time went by, readers realized that their complaints would be dealt with fast and fairly. Many mistakes were easy to spot. Because of the long years I had spent at the paper, many factual errors about the local community would stand out like summer flowers in a meadow and they were easy to correct. We adopted a standing headline for corrections: "In All Fairness, We Erred. . . ." Later, we abandoned that rather awkward headline and decided to end every correction by stating that we would correct all errors and explaining how to contact the readers' representative. Whatever the manner of presenting corrections, we discovered the readers wanted us to show a little remorse, so the line "The Union regrets the error" was added to each correction.

Warren also wanted a weekly column addressed by the ombudsman to the readers. Some ombudsmen in the country wrote a column and some not. I hesitated at the start, for I wanted clear instructions as to what I could and could not write—and I wanted to know who would be entitled to revise or censor my prose. Although we never reached the stage of a written Statement of Principles, Warren and I did finally agree on a few informal concepts: I could write on any topic without being challenged; the column would not be changed without my permission; and only Warren, the editor, had the right to spike a column. I understood that circumstances might occur, unknown by me, that might require the column to be killed. On his side, Warren understood that I might decide not to continue the column if any one was censored. The only limit that I wanted was that my range not include the editorial page. Errors on that page could be corrected, but I did not want to have to comment on the opinions expressed in the editorials.

In practice, the agreement worked. My freedom to write was never, not once, restricted. No column was ever amended or censored. This didn't always please reporters or editors, but it quickly established the paper's commitment to making facts right, no matter whose feelings were hurt. The reader's representative could go anywhere in the newsroom and question any member of the staff in quest of information. This put a special pressure upon my own obligation to be free of errors. Opponents of the concept were always eager to gleefully point out the ombudsman's errors— and they always had to be corrected.

Warren's support never failed. Helen K. Copley, the owner-publisher, provided unfailing support. Staff members who protested against corrections or the column were advised to go and talk it over with me. When Mrs Copley received complaints about my writings from readers, she forwarded them to me without comment. Once, in my presence, a reader asked her: "Are you not upset when he writes a column saying the newspaper is wrong?" "Sure," she answered, "and sometimes it sets my teeth on edge." Then she turned to me and said: "But you must go on because it's good for the newspaper."

There were other ways of support. In an article in a national magazine, devoted to her career at the head of a major newspaper group, she said that having an ombudsman was one of the best things that had happened to the newspaper. In another interview, Warren said he would rather have an ombudsman than an extra reporter.

The support of Copley and Warren was not only verbal. To be well done, the job required a secretary and a separate office: they were given to me. A travel budget enabled me to go and spread the gospel of ombudsmanship all over California and even the whole West. I lectured on college campuses and at professional meetings. Later, when I became the first president of the international organization of news ombudsmen (ONO), the company largely financed our first annual conference which took place in San Diego.

With that kind of support, it was a great pleasure to write my weekly column on a wide variety of topics. Sometimes I would explain errors in much more detail than in the daily corrections box. Sometimes I would vigorously criticize the way the newspaper had covered some case, or the fact that news stories were tinged with bias or personal opinion. Sometimes the criticism was aimed at one particular story; at other times, at the whole coverage of some event. Once, after a long, confusing and bitter school board election, I excoriated the whole campaign coverage. Readers strongly reacted to the columns: letters and calls came pouring in day after day. To my surprise, however, the columns most appreciated were the didactic ones in which I tried to explain how a newspaper operated, or changes in production methods, or improvements in the presentation of the product.

It did not take me long to grasp that a job in which you are accountable only to the highest executive in the newsroom gives you a great power and takes away quite a few friendships. Often copy editors and reporters looked upon the ombudsman as a "dark angel of justice" (thus was I described by a reporter friend). Nobody really likes to be fingered as the one who made a mistake, or as the one who let it go through. And at the beginning nobody wanted to be identified as having provided the information that made a correction possible. The names of the culprits were rarely used in corrections in the *San Diego Union* and when they were, usually in the ombudsman's column, an opportunity was given them to defend themselves. In one case, I judged unfair the coverage of an election but, violating one of my own rules, I did not ask the involved reporter to present his viewpoint. Though he was not named in the column, he insisted on responding to the criticism in an article to be placed next to my column. That was refused but he was allowed to publish a reply in the "Letters to the Editor" page.

My rules of conduct at the *San Diego Union* established clearly my right to question a staff member about a possible error. In spite of that, it could happen that a reporter would refuse to talk about some case. My typical reaction to that was to point out that I was in a position to explain in my column that a reporter, who expected everybody in the public to answer his questions, had refused to answer mine about his accuracy and fairness.

A loss that all ombudsmen felt at the start was the collegial atmosphere of the newsroom. It becomes difficult to have casual conversations with reporters and editors when they know you may be seeking information for a correction. Few were the journalists who visit your office for a little exchange of gossip. Consequently, the long-distance telephone became our refuge. Newly appointed ombudsmen would call one another to ask "How did you manage this?" or "How about that?" and soon each ombudsman became the data bank of the system for new appointees. Later, with the improvement of communication technology, telephone conferences became part of our routine. Also, from the first years, annual symposia on media ethics at the Washington Journalism Center became the de facto yearly meeting of the ombudsmen.

So the concept grew. By the late 1970s, the newspaper ombudsman concept had solidified to the point that talk began about an organization. John Brown, ombudsman at the *Edmonton Journal* in Canada, proposed that the conference at the Washington Journalism Center be used to establish an organization of newspaper ombudsmen. Some opposition came in the argument that there weren't enough ombudsmen or that membership would hurt an ombudsman's independence. So the motion passed by a bare majority to establish an Organization of Newspaper Ombudsmen.[1] Brown was offered but declined the initial presidency—so it came to me and it fell to San Diego to organize the first ONO convention in May 1981.

Ombudsmanship is now in its second generation on most newspapers. None of the original ombudsmen is still working and several newspapers have had several persons in the post over the years: *The San Diego Union* has had four. Some papers have dropped their program. Many others have established one, to a total of about forty ombudsmen in the United States, not to speak of Canada, France, Great Britain, Spain, Brazil, Switzerland, among others. There is a strong international organization for media ombudsmen with an annual convention. Most practitioners of this new journalistic function report their feeling that, over the years, most newsrooms have become more conscious of accuracy and fairness. Time and again, I have pointed out that my colleagues in the newsroom are as anxious as I am that errors be made right and fairness be a watchword. Other ombudsmen give the same report.

Has it worked? For the most part, there is no way to measure such an impalpable reality as improvement in journalistic quality. A study, made in the early years, whose results were published in *Journalism Quarterly,* provides

---

[1]The name was changed to the Organization of News Ombudsmen when ombudsmen from other media were admitted.

some indication. In that study, those persons who had contacted *The San Diego Union*'s reader representative during a one-year period were surveyed. Other people, selected at random as a control group, were also contacted. Those in the first group generally reported a more positive feeling toward the newspaper as a result of their contact. Those in the second group, who had not contacted the reader's representative and were not aware of the program, generally had no changed feelings.

That was a subtle, but real, confirmation that seven years of my career had not been wasted.

CHAPTER 13
A Portuguese Ombudsman in the Daily Press

Mário Mesquita

In 1997, thirty years after the first U.S. experiment, two Portuguese newspapers (*Diário de Notícias* and *Público*) inaugurated the office of ombudsman. An interest in the press ombudsman had arisen in Portugal in the early 1990s. After the termination of the Press Council, the union of journalists recommended that news media companies provide themselves with mediators.

The Press Council had been created in 1975, after the Revolution,[1] following the British model, and had operated for some 15 years. It had been set up by government and was financed by it, but its composition was such as to guarantee a dominance of the representatives of the press and of the public (co-opted members). It was chaired by a judge appointed by the High Council for the Judiciary.[2]

The *Conselho de Imprensa* (press council) achieved a considerable feat in that it determined principles and norms in many fields: freedom of speech, the right of reply, power relationships within journalistic firms, the application of the "conscience clause,"[3] access to news sources, professional secrecy, governmental intrusion into the news process, limits to freedom of expression and plagiarism.[4]

---

[1]Which, with the help of the army, put an end to 49 years of fascist dictatorship.

[2]In charge of the appointment and promotion of judges.

[3]It provides that if a publication is sold, if it changes its nature or political orientation, a journalist may leave with all the severance allowances he/she would get if dismissed.

[4]See Alberto Arons De Carvalho, *A Liberdade de Informaçao Conselho de Imprensa* (1975-1985), Lisbon, General Directorate of Social Communication, 1986.

The political authorities decided to disband the council and to transfer part of its "ethical" functions to an independent administrative agency, the High Authority for Social Communication, which simultaneously functions as the regulatory agency of public broadcasting. The Press Council, abolished for the sake of (allegedly) liberal principles, thus expiated its original sin of having been set up by government. Several times since then, on the initiative of unions and of associations of press proprietors, there was talk of creating a new one, private this time, but to no avail.

The ombudsman appeared as an alternative. However, dependent as the ombudsman is on a media firm that appoints and on the personality of the person that is appointed, he/she cannot enjoy the same moral authority as a press council. Actually, those two M*A*S are not in competition with each other. The council covers a vast collection of media and can express an opinion on the major issues in social communication. The ombudsman is a local M*A*S, meant to deal with the problems that occur between a particular newspaper and its readers.

In Portugal, the ombudsman must coordinate his/her action with that of the "newsroom council" of the newspaper where he/she functions. The reason is that, according to the Law on the Press, in newspapers "with more than five journalists, newsroom councils shall be created which will consist of professionals elected by all the journalists working for the periodical, according to rules to be drawn up by them" (Art. 21). The newsroom council is expected, among other functions, to cooperate with the publisher and the editors in defining the line of the newspaper and giving its opinion on issues of an ethical nature and other matters (e.g. discipline) concerning journalists.

The text establishing the ombudsman of the *Diário de Notícias* contains several references to the possible cooperation of the ombudsman and the body elected by journalists. Besides, his/her appointment "requires the approval of the newsroom council, which must give its motivated judgment on the nominee, within ten days, failing which it is considered to have agreed." There are also references to the possibility that the ombudsman send "internal recommendations" to the newsroom council.

A POWER TO INFLUENCE AND PERSUADE

Within the journalistic enterprise, the ombudsman, in a way, plays the part of an "institutional traitor" for the sake of "complicity with the reader" and the defense of "a democratic quality of life."[5] As a columnist, he is free to criticize his own newspaper and, in some cases, the other media. Traditionally, the practice of the press consisted in hiding any mistake and admitting it only as a last

[5]Mário Mesquita, *O Jornalismo em Análise—A coluna do provedor dos leitores,* Coimbra, Minerva, 1998, p. 24.

possible resort. In recent times, an educational campaign has been waged vigorously in the profession to make it understood that in the interest of the firm it was better to recognize the error and, if possible, to correct it.

The mediator also stands as a major actor in press communication, whose purpose must be to optimize the relationship with the reader. At a time when media finally accept that they have a role to play in the public space, parallel to that of political, social, and cultural institutions, the ombudsman represents, for journalistic firms, a particularly interesting means of improving their public image.

The link that binds him/her to the company has a negative effect, of course, on the public's perception: he/she tends to be seen merely as "a cosmetic response to criticism." But it is indisputable that "the presence of ombudsmen can be an effective tool of corporate management to demonstrate to a skeptical public that they are serious about the idea of social responsibility."[6]

In the ombudsman's column, one finds a variety of topics dealt with, such as issues of rigor and accuracy; incorrect headlines or front-page summaries; the decision whether to publish certain stories, to set an event on the day's agenda; the relationship of journalists and their sources; the editing of "letters to the editor"; the use of photos; the confusion of journalism and advertising.

The role of the ombudsman is obviously limited by the institutional framework within which he operates. His major power consists in being able to criticize the newspaper in the newspaper's own pages. He/she does not act as an internal police enforcing an unwritten traditional "journalistic ethics," or some almighty code of ethics. Such ethical usage or charter establish general principles, but I believe that journalistic ethics is something to be developed day by day, case by case, within a debate to which journalists, media users, news sources, ombudsmen, and other interested parties must contribute.

In my opinion, the ombudsman is not an imitation magistrate, but rather a media critic, with the special mission of criticizing his own paper as if he/she were a common reader. And I include among the interesting aspects of the job a constant reflection on the circumstances, limits, and characteristics of ombudsmanship itself.

AN "INSIDER" WITH SOME AUTONOMY

As a general rule, observers consider the ombudsman to be an "insider," whatever his/her contract is, whatever his/her profile—because the ombudsman is selected and hired by the hierarchy, owners and editors. Indeed, the hiring of a personality from outside the newspaper, as is usually the case at the *Washington Post*, aims at giving the ombudsman a status as an outsider to the newspaper company.

---

[6]Louis A. Day, *Ethics in Media Communications: Cases and Controversies*, Belmont, CA, Wadsworth, 1990, p. 41.

In the case of the great Spanish daily *El País*, the concern to keep a distance from the company is less obvious, because the office of *"defensor de los lectores"* (defender of the readers) is filled by a mid-career journalist, but he enjoys a "status that protects his independence both as a worker and as a professional." The Portuguese experience at the *Diário de Notícias* was based on a choice of persons from outside the company who were given a limited duration non-renewable contract—yet the first appointees were former journalists from the newspaper.

The problem of autonomy exists not only in relation to the company but also to the profession. Even though one can imagine ombudsmen being retired judges, professors, or civil servants, actually the choice is usually of an experienced journalist. For his work to be efficient, "he/she needs to be respected by his/her peers and have nothing to expect or fear from the hierarchy."[7]

The fact that he is a journalist will make it easier for him/her to be accepted by his/her peers, who may see an ombudsman as "the least threatening" M*A*S because it usually is "a colleague quite familiar to the newsroom," and he/she can be looked upon as "an ethics coach operating within the team."[8]

Of course, some will suspect him/her of being nothing but a strategic weapon of the company, or even the advocate of the newspaper's editors and publishers. But others insist on the privileged location from where he expresses himself. The ombudsman-journalist is well aware of the processes of news production and of the mechanics of internal control; that enables him/her to analyze complex situations knowingly. Journalistic production takes place under many constraints, from a constant sense of urgency to pressure from sources. The likelihood of error is great, as is the degree of uncertainty in the process of news gathering.

That being said, there is no doubt that the ombudsman is a strategic instrument of the media company. The office constitutes a label of quality on the image projected by the newspaper, especially by a "newspaper of record" very much attached to its prestige and to the public's trust. The ombudsman contributes to developing a better, more sophisticated definition of the paper's ethos. Thanks to him/her, the newspaper appears to the reader as a complex entity, equipped with mechanisms of self-correction and criticism. So he/she adds to the credibility and to the integrity of the newspaper as an actor in the public sphere.

The ombudsman enriches the polyphonic blend of voices: the institutional one of the editorial page, the soft voice of the reporter, the anonymous voice of the news (at least where news and views are separated, U.S.-style). Among the other ingredients of the newspaper, what the ombudsman says stands out: it is critical and it is distant. He/she produces speech about speech.

[7]C-J. Bertrand, *Media Ethics and Accountability Systems,* Piscataway, NJ, Transition, 2000, p. 117.

[8]C-J. Bertrand, "The M*A*S—Media Accountability Systems," text distributed at the 1997 ONO conference in Barcelona (Spain).

There are quite a few ombudsmen who are pure PR agents, who operate with never a harsh word on the pages of the newspaper: that was the case with British national tabloids at the turn of the present century. But, as a general rule, the ombudsman adopts a critical stance, which inevitably generates tension in the newsroom. He/she thus operates as a kind of private regulator on behalf of the company and, in most cases, of the profession too.

THE FUNCTIONS OF THE OMBUDSMAN

Seven levels of action can be determined for the press ombudsman:

- He/she discusses the newspaper in its own pages, extending into the public space the debate on editorial decisions that traditionally was never heard outside newsrooms and the journalistic world (that is, the *critical and symbolic*[9] *function*);
- He/she throws a bridge to the readers, answering complaints and criticism (the *mediating function*);
- He/she is careful to correct inaccurate and incomplete data, calling on experts for assistance, if need be (the *corrective function*);
- He/she recommends to the hierarchy measures destined to repair whatever damage some newspaper acts have caused to readers[10] (the *persuasive function*);
- He/she explains to readers the mechanics of journalistic production, from the relationship with sources to the choice of the news to be published (the *pedagogical function*);
- He/she can, by his critique, influence possible decisions by editors and reporters (the *deterrent function*);
- He/she can encourage debate on political, economic, and social themes (the *civic function*).

His/her action takes place mainly afterwards, ex post facto, which guarantees his/her autonomy in relation to editorial decisions.[11] Nevertheless, the role of the ombudsman can only be fully played out if there is a minimum of agreement on ethics between him/her on the one hand and management and newsroom on the other.

---

[9]The ombudsman's action and his/her column symbolize the paper's desire for transparency and self-criticism.

[10]He can ask the executive editor to apologize for a mistake by a letter to a reader or, in a serious case, to publish a note in the newspaper.

[11]The ombudsman must not, I believe, participate in the editorial conference. If he/she did, he/she would be associated with decisions that might motivate complaints by readers. Some amount of autonomy would be lost.

The ombudsman has several means of action at his/her disposal in order to respond to the complaints of readers. He/she can use internal recommendations, or speak directly to the readers, or get corrections published, or transfer mail to the "Letters to the Editor" department. However, his/her main tool is the column he/she publishes every week.

"The most important thing the ombudsman does," says Carlos Chaparro,[12] "is to offer readers his weekly thoughts. [. . .] The ombudsman is a privileged observer and an analyst of journalistic achievements who has a huge educational potential. He upsets arrogant reporters, editors and publishers because he can teach readers a lot, by letting them participate in the criticism of the journalistic process."

A certain opacity characterizes the process by which the newspaper report of the news is elaborated and also the internal life of media firms. This contrasts with the constant demand for openness that journalists address to political, economic, social and cultural institutions. The explanation by the ombudsman of the process of production, besides its pedagogical value, contributes some transparency to the relationship of the media company with media consumers.

VARIOUS TYPES OF READERS

What kind of person is the reader who protests to the news ombudsman? That's a question I am quite often asked by journalists themselves. Four categories can be distinguished:

- the *average reader* who speaks for his own cause, because he/she has been part of a news story which he/she considers inaccurate or unfair;
- the *citizen reader* who wishes to talk about the paper because of a concern for the improvement of the public sphere;
- the *expert reader*: he/she belongs to a small group consisting of journalists (from other publications), professors, or personalities linked to the press world, who address the ombudsman after reading the press with the eye of the specialist;
- The *source-reader* who, as such, intervenes in the elaboration of the news.

We should pause a while to think about source-readers. At a certain period of my experience at the *Diário de Notícias*, a journalist criticized me for being not so much a mediator on behalf of readers as a mediator serving sources

[12]Journalism professor at the University of Sao Paulo (Brazil) in a personal interview.

of information. That was because several times I had judged that the protests of politicians or their advisers were justified.

The professionalization of political communication by specialized consultants over the last few decades has produced a fundamental change in the world of communication. Henceforth, it would be unimaginable for the ombudsman to go on receiving only letters from naive readers, ignorant of how journalism operates. On the contrary, he/she is more and more faced with criticisms from organizations set up to influence media and with professional "communicators" used to decoding newspapers.

Journalism increasingly consists in speech constructed from the speeches of organized "sources." Even events are often fabricated by communication strategists. So it is natural that the intervention of the ombudsman be requested by "sources" (members of the government, company heads, CEOs of associations, sports directors, press attachés, and many others) when they feel their unwritten "contracts" with journalists have been in some way breached.

Do sources aim at putting pressure on media, via the ombudsman? It's likely. But he/she normally enjoys enough autonomy to evaluate how justified a complaint is and whether to take action or not.

READERS AND CITIZENS

Most readers who get in touch with the ombudsman express themselves on topics that concern them directly: that corresponds to the obvious function of the mediator. The institution aims mainly at correcting the imbalance between an isolated individual, the reader, and the power of the media company, newspaper, and journalists.

However, the existence of readers who wish to participate actively in the debate over their newspaper constitutes, at least in my experience, the most gratifying aspect of the job. I mean those people who disapprove of the organization of a section of the newspaper or who question the reasons why a certain piece of news was, or was not, given special prominence.

The routines of journalistic production sometimes cause harm to citizens. Take a case that occurred at the *Diário de Notícias*. On the occasion of Women's Day, the President of the Republic awarded decorations to several women. The media focused on the tribute paid to the wives of two former presidents. Yet one of the most ancient and most prestigious medals was awarded to a mathematician—but she was unknown to the general public and the media kept almost totally silent about her.

If it had not been for a letter addressed to the ombudsman, the readers of this important newspaper would still not know the name of one of Portugal's most eminent researchers in the field of mathematics, Irene Fonseca.[13] The

---

[13]She is a professor at Carnegie Mellon University in Pittsburgh, Pennsylvania.

President wished to attract attention to the role of scientists, but the media concentrated their attention on known personalities and their rivalries, lowering politics, as they often do, to the level of "human interest stories," crime and accidents, celebrities and gossip.

Such an incident makes it easier to understand the impression of powerlessness that a citizen feels when he/she vainly tries to persuade the media to pay attention to some subject—even if that citizen happens to be the president of the Republic. Institutions and corporations organize to put pressure on media. Ordinary citizens cannot afford to.

I offer two thoughts by way of conclusion that can stand as a warning. The ombudsman is an instrument among others, one M*A*S among many. He/she can certainly be useful to improve the contents and the image of newspapers, but you can expect the function, because of its very nature, to be set up only in a few media companies, those that are especially concerned with their credibility.

Besides, the best defense of the press against its enemies, and against a dangerous distrust of the public, consists in giving up arrogance, in accepting criticism, and in stimulating debate. But if that behavior is not assumed by journalists as a whole, as a professional category, no ombudsman, however devoted and autonomous he may be, will be able to save journalism from its slow descent into propaganda and entertainment.

SECTION 2
Journalism Reviews

CHAPTER 14
A Short History
of U.S. Journalism Reviews

The day after the press was born, press criticism came to life, but until recent times, critics usually were either partisans or snobs. In the 19th century, the prostitution of the news media kindled the ire of advocates for social morality, but most of their criticisms were scattered and buried in small circulation magazines, books and reports. Then, around 1970, the concentration of discontent with the press reached such a point that journalism reviews (JRs) materialized all over the United States, devoted almost entirely to criticism of news media.[1] Eight of the ten largest cities had such a review. More than half the states had at least one, with a predictable concentration on the East Coast, in the upper Midwest, and in California.

Two-thirds of the reviews vanished in less than 18 months. Seemingly, the new genre was of an impermanent kind. This mattered little, insofar as the functions of the reviews appeared to be taken over by magazines and newspapers, or by professional and scholarly publications. The U.S. press from the 1970s onwards was scrutinized as no other free press in the world had ever been, by investigative reporters, columnists, ombudsmen, press councils, ethics committees and professors.

If journalism reviews had done no more than blast a breach in the ramparts of complacency, they would deserve a celebration, which they have not yet had: no book, few articles in academic journals, a few master's theses and

---

[1]For a list of 63 JRs from the 1960s to the early 1990s, see *St Louis JR,* July-August 1993, pp. 14-17. Also the list of Eleanor S. Block in *Serials Review,* Vol. 19(1), 1993.

doctoral dissertations, some pieces in trade publications, and a smattering of magazine stories have focused on these reviews—most of the attention going to the *Columbia Journalism Review*, the *Chicago Journalism Review*, and [MORE]. Actually, the JRs were both less than a dam-bursting flash flood—and more. At what could turn out to have been the takeoff point of a (very) slow revolution in the press, working journalists stepped out of the closet; they asked to be treated not as salaried scribblers, but as professionals, and they appealed to the public for support.

The JRs of the late 1960s and early 1970s were not so much a factor as an indicator of change. The need remains for independent, systematic, expert reviewing of journalism at the local, regional, and national levels. Neither the heterogeneous mass, nor the profit-obsessed media, nor, of course, the government, can provide the surveillance that a public-service-cum-political institution requires. Hence, what is called for is not just a laudatory post-mortem, but an examination of why and how a number of journalism reviews survive and why and how many more should be brought to life.

HOW THEY CAME TO BE

The leader of the troop appeared on the scene in October of 1968, when a group of Chicago journalists went public with their rage against the local press and established a model for about 25 JRs to be launched in the next five years (not to speak of those that never got off the drawing board in Albany, Boston, Buffalo, Cleveland, Detroit, Kansas City, and DC).

It was in 1961, seven years before, that for the first time a school of journalism assumed the "obligation that falls on a serious professional school [. . .] to help stimulate continuing improvement in its profession and to speak out for what it considers right, fair, and decent."[2] Taking its cue from a Harvard-based quarterly, the *Nieman Reports* (1947), it produced the *Columbia JR*, which not only set a precedent for eight campus JRs, but broke ground for all reviews, including the *Chicago JR.*

The birth of the pioneer JR, however, had occurred earlier still, on May 20, 1940, when veteran newsman George Seldes started *In Fact*, the first periodical to pick as its one and only target the sins of the press, both in omission and commission. With the support of big labor unions, the biweekly newsletter was to reach a top circulation of 176,000, higher than any later non-commercial JR, and to last 10 years, longer than all but three. But *In Fact* was "red-baited to death" and folded in October 1950. Seldes never was a communist, but libel and blacklisting act like a slow poison. Few newspeople nowadays have heard of the man. No JR (except the *St Louis JR*) carried a profile of the precursor, who died in 1995 at age 104.

---

[2]*Columbia JR*, pilot issue, Fall 1961.

Though the *Chicago JR* was not the first JR chronologically, it did mark the starting point of the phenomenon; it was a local review and it was created solely by working journalists. At that time, in the United States (and nowhere else) all factors coincided. The college-educated servants of conservative monopolistic media corporations had been pummeled into consciousness first by the civil rights movement, then by the anti-war movement, then by multi-directional protest. Not only did many reporters sympathize with the dissenters, but better than anyone else they realized that no such crisis would have taken place if the press had insured proper social communication. The journalists knew what a distorted picture the media painted of the protesters, and what a crucial weapon the media must be in any movement toward participatory democracy. To coordinate and lead their rebellion, news people could turn to no organization, but they had access to an inexpensive new technology that the "underground press" had already put to visible advantage against most institutions, including the media. However strongly they might resent the debasement of the press by private business, few American journalists would seek democratization of the news media by government intervention. The alternative was to do it themselves and the means came naturally—a counter press. The *Chicago JR* proved it could be done: it called a meeting of proselytes in April 1970 and sent evangelizers across the country.

In one vast concatenation, all JRs were related to previous criticism and to each other and to the most powerful movements in the American society of the 1960s. Let us take just one loop in the chain. As *Thorn* (*The Connecticut Valley JR*) perceptively remarked in its first issue (1971), the new "rash of journalism reviews" participated in "the spirit of blow-the-whistle Naderism." Now, Ralph Nader regards Seldes as one of the two early determinants of his vocation. A. J. Liebling, the famous press critic in *The New Yorker* from 1945 to 1963,[3] was another great reader of *In Fact*. He contributed to the first issue of the *Columbia JR*, from which the lineage is direct to the *Chicago JR*, then to [MORE], which created the Liebling Award. The first was bestowed to I.F. Stone, a self-confessed disciple of Seldes. Kinship, however, in no way implies total resemblance. It is not always realized how diverse JRs have been and can be.

TYPES OF JOURNALISM REVIEWS

Journalists being the individualistic creatures they are, it seems natural for the first type to have been the one-man JR. A distant forerunner was Arthur McEwen's *Letter*, a weekly published in 1894-95 by a former editorial writer of the San Francisco *Examiner*. Like him, in more recent times most critics have found it more judicious not to take on the press exclusively. In Washington, DC,

---

[3]See *The Wayward Pressman* (1947), *Mink and Red Herring* (1949).

I. F. Stone reviewed journalism only part time between 1962 and 1971, just as Cleveland's Roldo Bartimole has done since June 1968 in his biweekly *Point of View*.[4] Not that full-time newsletter JRs are unthinkable. In 1972, Robert Juran endeavored to cover the national media scene from San Diego. After six issues, he had only 300 subscribers and folded his monthly *Overset*, but then it was a magazine. And so was Joe La Rocca's *Countermedia* (Fairbanks, Alaska), which lasted two years (1972-74) but only as a part-time JR. Ron Dorfman, cofounder of the *Chicago JR*, which died with its October 1975 issue, considered the publication "could still be a thriving enterprise had I wished to produce it myself in newsletter format, on the model of *I. F. Stone's Weekly*." That is what Cary Stiff (formerly of *The Unsatisfied Man*, Denver) did in 1976 with his *Weekly*, which he wanted to be a JR for weeklies.

At the risk of offending those left-leaning mavericks, another newsletter needs to be slipped into this first category. The *AIM Report* takes the press to task for pro-liberal distortion: that it is only a secondary means of publicity for the little non-journalistic group called Accuracy in Media is, to a certain extent, irrelevant. Reed Irvine's periodical is to a large extent a one-man undertaking whose sole purpose has been to criticize the press. Probably also belonging here are an indefinite number of sheets mimeographed by media-oriented eccentrics. Such was *Gnats*, circulated within the San Francisco *Examiner* for two months in 1974 to try to lecture the paper into improving. Such has been the bizarre *Muckrackers* (1964), of which Ralph G. Morley, M.D., of Long Island, produced more than 80 issues.

News people do flock together periodically at favorite watering holes, and they can act together, provided their hackles have been sufficiently raised. That is where and how most reporter-JRs were born. In 1968, at a climax of the anti-war, anti-system agitation, the clubbing of journalists by the Chicago police during the Democratic Convention and the ensuing distortion of facts by media management under pressure from Mayor Richard Daley's machine bred enough furor for young local reporters to meet above Ricardo's Bar, form a militant group, and then bring out the *Chicago JR*. Within two years, two JRs appeared in the Bay Area, three in New York, one in Providence, one in St. Louis, and one in Denver. The two years after that were the peak period: in 1971-72, nearly a dozen reporter-JRs were launched, in Honolulu, Philadelphia, the Connecticut Valley, New York, the Twin Cities, Santa Barbara, Baltimore, Portland, San Francisco, and Houston. The end of the Vietnam War and the recession cooled the indignation in the press: then Watergate fired collective pride and selfish ambitions. Only two JRs appeared in 1973 (in Portland and Dallas), only one in 1974 (Anchorage), and one in 1975 (Spokane)—the latter two extremely short-lived.

Actually, the four reviews that followed in the tracks of the *Chicago JR* belonged not so much to the journalists' mutiny, as to the two movements that

---

[4]He was still at it in 1999.

created a propitious climate for it. The first was the Berkeley-based *Ball & Chain Review,* produced for nine months, beginning in October 1969, by six black reporters, including the famous Earl Caldwell.[5] The other three JRs were by-products of radical agitation about, but to some extent outside, the news media during the anti-war and women's liberation explosion of 1969-70. In New York, *Pac-O-Lies* (1969-70) came out four times, and the more moderate *Inside Media* put out one thick issue in March 1970. In January and April *Overload* was published by a Berkeley collective funded by Protestant churches.

From the spring of that year, JRs were started by news people, most of whom believed the press could be reformed if only its misdeeds were pilloried in the marketplace. Their staying power proved greater. *Thorn* went to press only twice in eight months, but Denver's *TUM* (*The Unsatisfied Man*), came out regularly for about four years (1970-75), and the *St. Louis JR* (1970) celebrated its 30th anniversary in 2000 (see p. 219).

What usually happened was that one day some 20 to 50 disgruntled news people met, set up an association, and sometime later took the plunge. In the Twin Cities, the spark came from the preemption of the press council idea by the Minnesota publishers; in Houston, from agitation about a Guild election. In many places, very simply, after months of griping and groping someone just said, "Let's do a review like those guys in Chicago." Each reporter would chip in a few dollars and the promise of a few stories. Then a smaller platoon of two to ten invested a great amount of time and toil to put together an inexpensive 4- to 24-page monthly (sometimes bimonthly) tabloid or (more often) magazine.

The makeup of the *Houston JR* was exceptionally attractive. Not all JRs could use artwork by Mauldin, like the *Chicago JR,* or by Prudim, like *TUM,* yet most looked decently professional. Few were mimeographed like the *AP Review* (1970) and the *Yellow JR* (Santa Barbara, 1972) or printed from typewritten copy like some issues of *TCJR* (*Twin Cities JR,* 1972). Money for the printing was not easy to find but usually was found. The *Chicago JR* obtained enough subsidies, subscribers, and street sales to keep its head more or less above water throughout its existence. The freely distributed *Hawaii JR* depended on donations, yet it died with money in the bank. Fund-raising parties, subscriptions, and forums kept *TCJR* in relatively good financial health until 1977. Most local JRs managed to hobble along from one issue to the next. Not all, though: The *San Francisco Bay Area JR* cost its founders over $2,000 before it was killed off.

There were at least three exceptions to that overall pattern. After J. Anthony Lukas, enraged by the coverage of the Chicago 7 trial, suggested to fellow newsman Richard Pollak that they start a New York JR, they obtained considerable financial backing and decided to put out a commercially viable tabloid that would take advertising (which most JRs shunned) and pay contributors (which no other local JR then did). And so, to cover the Big Apple, and to a

---

[5]*New York Times's* reporter who covered the civil rights movement.

lesser degree the national scene, [*MORE*] (1971-78) could use topflight talent. It quickly earned even greater visibility than the *Chicago JR* and gave impetus to the whole reporter-review movement.

The *Black JR*, started in 1976 by a former editor of *Muhammad Speaks*, the Black Muslim periodical, also aimed at a national audience but mainly that of black news people. After two issues, lack of funds put it in limbo. Quite different was the *Dallas JR* (1972-74). It was begun and financed, not by reporters, but by a church-based social action group. The Citizens for a Free Flow of Information hired a VISTA[6] worker with a little journalistic experience to edit a bimonthly critique of the local media with the help of some news people.

Most JRs were independent publications. A few, though, came out as parts of existing periodicals. Some of these were section-JRs that merely expanded the media columns or pages featured in newsmagazines and alternative papers: *Media & Consumer* (1972-1975) featured a 3- to 4-page "Journalism Review" section. In Sacramento, from September 1970 to at least the end of 1973, the mimeographed monthly *Guildsman* (later *Guild Journal*) often devoted more than half its pages to giving the JR treatment to the local daily, the *Bee;* and the *River City Review* (Omaha, 1975) was about one-third JR. Other reviews were piggyback JRs. The first issue of *Buncombe* (Baltimore) was inserted in *The Paper*, an alternative monthly. The only issue of the *Atlanta JR* (1971) had to be carried by the *Columbia JR*, and *Crossroads*, an alternative student publication on the Milwaukee campus of the University of Wisconsin, carried the four issues of *Add One* (1974). The latter review, however, which was done in close cooperation with the department of communication, belongs to the next category.

From 1971, JRs started flowering on campuses, some rooted in an SDX chapter and some in a school of journalism. The first was the quarterly *Review of Southern California Journalism* (1971-75): SDX students at Cal State in Long Beach and (mainly) two faculty advisors did what Los Angeles area journalists ceaselessly ranted about—and, with little support from the university or from the news people, kept it going. *The Lexington Media Review* (University of Kentucky, 1974) and *Monitor* (University of South Carolina, 1974) were annual SDX students' JRs, whereas the one-shot *Madison JR* (University of Wisconsin, 1973), the two-time *Texas JR* (University of Texas in Austin, 1974-75), and *Comment* (Seton Hall University, NJ; 1971) were non-SDX student undertakings. Such was also *The Pretentious Idea* (1972), an award-winning annual JR initiated by students and put out by them, but as part of the academic curriculum:[7] The journalism school of the University of Arizona in Tucson considered *TPI* a public service, just as its other productions, *The Epitaph* for the town of Tombstone and a Chicano monthly for a suburb of Tucson.

---

[6]Volunteers In Service To America (since 1965) fights urban and rural poverty.

[7]It died in 1986, because of lack of faculty interest. By the year 2000, one of the student promoters of the concept had become publisher of the Boston *Globe*.

Most of the annual JRs were woefully inadequate and got little attention from the local media, but they could develop, given more involvement of faculty and journalists, which is what the *Review* had—and also *feed/back.* The latter (1974), a quarterly, modeled itself not on the *Chicago JR,* as the *Review* did, but on the *Columbia JR.* The heir to a black, a radical, and a reporter JRs, indirectly subsidized by San Francisco State University, produced by the students of a Press Analysis class, with half of its material written by working journalists, the quarterly became one of the best JRs in the country.

Some news people tended to despise campus JRs; they took for granted the incompetence of their staffs and their submissiveness to the powers-that-be. The following category of part-time JRs would probably be excluded from the concept altogether by many journalists. In the late 1960s and early 1970s, all kinds of publications offered press criticism as a staple. Among them were some that dealt only with media matters. A few had always been censorious of the press; others became so. What they all had in common was that criticizing journalism was not their basic purpose. Older publications serve professional organizations, such as the *Bulletin* of the ASNE and the SPJ-SDX's *Quill,* both of which turned much more critical in those years—or the *Guild Reporter,* which, of course, has regularly thrashed the industry.

In 1968, the yearly journal of the j-school at the university in Missoula, *The Montana JR,* listed as the first of its goals "to report and evaluate the performance of the mass media, with emphasis on newspapers and radio-TV stations," but it was hamstrung by lack of resources.[8] The bimonthly *Grassroots Editor* (1960) long informed and anthologized local weeklies in a populist spirit that implied hostility toward the big over-commercialized media. Similarly, the *Alternative JR* (1966), being the bimonthly bulletin of the Alternative Press Syndicate, could not avoid attacking the straight press. *Seminar* (1966-1974) was launched as a house organ for the conservative Copley Press, then moved toward becoming an anti-radical-liberal JR. The monthly reports of the Freedom of Information Center at the University of Missouri inevitably monitored media performance, as they covered all issues pertaining to the free flow of information. *Media Report to Women* (1973) published news for and about a social group so under-represented and under-privileged in the media industry that it cannot but be critical of it (see p. 257). As the organ of the National Citizens Committee for Better Broadcasting, *Access* definitely read like a media review, but not a journalism review: its main concern lay in television's major products, not news.

JRs belong body and soul to print journalism. Any review anybody can cite out of hand was a printed publication, and a survey of JR contents shows that 90% is devoted to the magazine and newspaper press. Admittedly, some of the earlier JRs were broadcast, like D. Hollenbeck's CBS *Views the Press* on

---

[8]It died in 1980 and was resurrected in 1993, then put online.

radio after World War II and Charles Collingwood's *WCBS-TV Views the Press* in the early 1960s. Yet those belong on the margins of the phenomenon. One reason was that, whereas it took only a few dollars to get into print in the 1960s and 1970s, no one could get on the air without permission from the broadcasting barons. At least in the minds of radio-television executives, JRs were bound to express as much a desire to discredit a rival, and hostile, medium as to improve journalism—with some exceptions.

The 30-minute *Milwaukee Media Review* produced by the department of communication at the University of Wisconsin was an authentic JR aired by a CBS-TV affiliate twice a month from 1973 through 1975—at 8 a.m. on Sundays! The *Chicago JR* staffers in 1970 had a Saturday afternoon show on a small FM radio station; and *Thorn,* after stopping publication, was several times revived on WFCR-FM: those are rare cases of early multi-media JRs. Also in the 1970s, noncommercial broadcasting did some systematic media reviewing, like WNET's monthly *Behind the Lines* networked in prime time by PBS (1971-76); or, at the other extreme, *Media Under a Glass,* a little 30-minute weekly radio review done by students of Bowling Green University on WIOT-FM. There have been other broadcast JRs, such as the Pacifica stations' *feedback* (WBAI) or *The Wayward Press* (KPFK), and columns, such as Professor Roy Gibson's weekly two-minute review on KUTV in Salt Lake City.

Generally speaking, activist reporters, journalism school critics, and citizens' committees were kept off the air. Management alleged that because of government regulation, radio and television were very vulnerable; must shun controversy; and, as regards their own operations, stood under permanent multiform scrutiny. Actually, public affairs programming has always been minimized so as to maximize profits within the non-expandable airtime. As for broadcast journalists, high pay, short contracts, and little union protection make them very careful, and not too many of them have taken part even in print JRs.

OBSTACLES

Of the many reviews that appeared in the 1968-1975 era, most disappeared within two months to two years. A third of the JRs held out for only five issues or less and never had time to make an impact. Only a third of them endured for more than ten issues. By 1974 only four reporter-JRs remained. Was the whole eruption then "just a passing fad, a safety valve for one college generation affected with extraordinary irritability and impatience, and an ideological vogue," which was N. Hill's finale to his 1971 vilification of JRs in the *Saturday Review*? Is there something intrinsic or environmental that makes local JRs non-viable? They all encountered the same obstacles.

In their march toward journalistic professionalism, the rebellious mercenaries drew little encouragement from existing press-related institutions that should have supported the reform movement. Press clubs were usually not interested, though the public relations people who patronize them often eagerly subscribed to the reviews; and, exceptionally, the Honolulu Press Club funded one issue of the *Hawaii JR*. Although JR creators often were active Guild members, The Newspaper Guild limited its participation to exhorting locals to help financially. And in Cleveland, Denver, and Honolulu union membership voted *not* to give a JR any money. Nevertheless, it was at Guild newspapers that reviews usually appeared and survived. To quote Cary Stiff, "The Guild didn't support TUM, but we could criticize our bosses and get away with it without losing our jobs." Some local chapters of the SPJ-SDX did assist JRs. *The Review,* for instance, got bulk subscriptions from the four Southern California chapters. Those that actually founded JRs, though, were campus chapters, with the exception of Spokane.

As for national foundations, they fought shy, apart from the Fund for Investigative Journalism, which gave seven JRs sums ranging from $500 to $3,000. Big business, by the way, was more helpful: *TUM* obtained $1,000 from the Great Western Sugar Co. and the *Hawaii JR* was given grants by the Hawaiian Electric Co. and the Hawaiian Telephone Co. The Association for Education in Journalism (AEJ, now AEJMC) did not wish to get involved. As for universities, only 12 of the 60-odd accredited journalism schools ever seriously encouraged the movement. To end this pitiful list, let it be recalled that no Pulitzer Prize ever went to a JR, or to any press critic for that matter until 1991 when David Shaw, of the *LA Times*, was honored.

The major stumbling block in the path of JRs, however, was the small size of the journalistic community and the public's still very low level of interest in the media. In cities of 500,000 to 2 million inhabitants, most JRs could distribute only 500 to 2,000 copies. The *Chicago JR* was exceptional in reaching a top circulation of about 10,000, as on the national market [MORE] sold fewer than 30,000 and the *Columbia JR* fewer than 45,000. And those JRs had trouble keeping their lay subscribers: they stayed interested a couple of years and then felt they had their fill of media criticism. A small potential audience, and an even smaller actual readership, inevitably lead to a lack of revenue. Hence, after the first enthusiasm had waned, JRs had no funds to pay for good material and energetic staff. Only four of the reviews (including the three best) could afford a full-time editor. Declining quality and irregular publication soon lost the JRs what few readers they had to start with.

The second major hurdle for JRs is the arrogance and/or paranoia of publishers, editors, and (many) reporters. Their allergy to criticism is such that reviews were refused any kind of publicity and remained unknown to the general public. To sell 2,000 of its 5,000 print run, the *St. Louis JR* had to contend with the silence of the local dailies. In some cases, media executives screamed employee disloyalty and undertook to muzzle the reviews by threats, as in Chicago and Los Angeles, or by actual reprisals. Demotions and firings were used in Philadelphia and Houston. The would-be editors of *Thorn* and of *Atlanta JR* were bounced for merely planning a review. The Portland media killed the *Oregon JR* by vetoing any participation of their staff in it. All this, however, was relatively exceptional. Quite a few editors dialogued with the local JR in its "Letters" section, sent in their checks, and even wrote for it. Others were suspected of being in secret sympathy with the critics. As a consequence, all JRs carried bylines, except the first issues of the *Chicago JR*, the *AP Review, Pac-O-Lies,* and the *St. Louis JR*.

The worst resistance often came from the press proletariat. Not only were many reporters too satisfied, too cynical, or too scared to lend any assistance, but sometimes they clearly opposed the conceited "nest-foulers" and "biters-of-the-hand-that-feeds." JRs were variously stigmatized as mediocre exercises in futility, ego-trips, bitching bulletins, sly attacks on free enterprise, and even incitements to government intervention. The bimonthly *Buncombe* (Baltimore, 1972-73) offers a distressing example of JR unpopularity. It obtained so little response from working journalists that it had to return a $1,000 grant from the Fund for Investigative Journalism just before it quietly folded. As for the second major class of reviews, the campus JRs, universities, dependent as they were on the political and business establishment, usually were loath to antagonize the media. Journalism schools wanted grants for themselves and jobs for their graduates. Among their faculty, the "green eye-shades" tended to remain myopically loyal to the industry, and the scholarly "chi-squares" had little but scorn for day-to-day monitoring.

A third threat to the JRs derived from an internal flaw. Most reviews were a labor of love by an individual or a small group that had more idealism, more courage, more free time, or simply less to lose than their 70,000 colleagues. These people were individualistic reporters. They knew precious little about newspaper production, accounting, tax laws, and post office regulations; and getting a cooperative venture organized represented a terrible strain on their egos. Rather sooner than later, their ardor burnt out. The indifference their crusade met with was quickly debilitating, and the hostility it generated was hard to bear, especially in small communities. Add to that professional ambitions and family concerns, and at some point the leaders moved away from the JR, often away from the city, sometimes away from journalism. Usually no one had the zeal and skill to take over the burden; the JR then died or went into a quick decline. The staff of the radical reviews, like those of the *AP Review* and the *Ball & Chain Review*, drifted apart. *TUM* did not resist very long after Cary Stiff left his job on the Sunday edition of the *Denver Post* to start his own local weekly. The *Hawaii JR* folded not very long after the founding couple (both in television) stopped devoting their considerable free time to JR chores.

Quite a few reporter-JRs could have been saved by an alternative publication or by a journalism school, but they preferred to fold rather than compromise their independence. Working journalists had gone public with their criticism, but considered they alone were qualified to criticize. They often dismissed the *Columbia JR* for being academically dull and irrelevant. As for journalism school JRs, students were accused of not knowing what they were writing about. Reporter-JRs, however, showed just as serious a flaw. Rarely were journalists indicted as a class for vanity, submissiveness, greed, superficiality, incompetence, dislike of change, or lack of social consciousness. Reading them, one gets the idea that all the ills of the press originate with owners, advertisers, editors, politicians, and judges.

Self-righteous bias was not the only problem with media monitor contents. The material in the case of the *Yellow JR* (Santa Barbara, 1972) was so slight, it is no wonder only seven news people subscribed! But is there enough muck in any city (outside of New York and Washington, DC) to keep the rakers busy every month for years on end? A quarterly report-and-review covering all the media in a large area may have no difficulty filling 20 to 80 pages, but local JRs, most of them monthly, are open to the charge that they would print anything, mistaking rhetorical outbursts for investigative reporting, office gossip for useful revelations, private vendettas for legitimate grievances. Even the best JRs, such as the *Chicago JR* or *TUM,* published some badly researched, badly structured, badly written pieces. Rejecting, or merely editing, a free contribution can alienate one more member of the small journalistic community. Even good editing could not help non-stories.

Because almost all JRs originated within metropolitan newspapers (sometimes, as in Philadelphia, at one daily only), they got few stories from and about the other media. *TUM* was not the only review accused of neglecting the outstate press. Rare were the reviews that had broadcasters on their team such as the *Houston JR* and the *Hawaii JR*—so radio and television usually got short shrift.

Checking for accuracy, getting the opposing view, even good proofreading, rules that JRs vehemently advocated, they themselves violated for lack of volunteer labor. The staffs were not unaware of those failings; and some reviews, such as *TUM* and the *Houston JR,* printed critical evaluations of themselves. San Francisco's *feed/back* featured a one-page section by its own in-house critic in every one of its issues.

On balance, however, what strikes an unprejudiced reader is the excellence of so many articles that must have required long hours of investigation and writing, sometimes at considerable risk, and never for any reward. Judging from the later careers of many media monitors, it is obvious they were among the best local reporters, not soured mediocrities.

Even if material and manpower were abundant, a further problem would arise: how to tailor the product to the readership. Is a JR to be primarily an anti-house organ not meant for the public, as the *AP Review* was to the wire service and the *Journalists Newsletter* (1970-73) was to the Providence (R.I.) *Journal & Bulletin*? And then should it be directed at reporters or at editors and publishers? Or should the JR aim at a wider readership, the local decision-makers and opinion-leaders, or even the whole liberal constituency? And then should it focus on reviewing the media, reporting on them or supplementing them? A JR that undertakes to talk to both publics, as it ought to, must tread a narrow path between being an organizational bulletin, which bores outsiders to tears, and a popular magazine that news people would treat as junk mail.

A further pitfall, rarely mentioned, is political, in the wide sense of the word. If a JR's whole activity is not underpinned by some ideology, however vague, by some concept of what the press and society should be and how to progress toward that ideal, it is bound, sooner or later, to slump into monotonous sterility. The shocking revelation of journalistic offenses can be effective: a litany of sins cannot be—unless one or several paths to salvation are offered. After his survey of 20th century media criticism, one scholar was tempted to sweep it aside as useless, because most problems probably cannot be solved in a regime of private ownership of the press. Was there no difference between the press of the 1920s and that of the 1970s, no difference between the *Washington Post* and the *New York Post,* both privately owned? Has not the "social responsibility" doctrine of the press played some part, via criticism, in the improvement of the press? What is true is that the principles defended by JRs—such as accuracy, fairness, or minority employment—should be, and never were, rooted in a scientific theory and in a philosophy of social communication. Nor did reviews even express a strategy for public control of the mass media. "There's no journal that has a sophisticated left analysis of the media [. . .] understanding what the media are about, what they really represent, how they really function in society. There was, is, no public voice which translates that information into some language that is accessible to people who work in the media": such was the 1977 conclusion of Michael Singer, cofounder of *Pac-O-Lies.*

ACHIEVEMENTS

All those obstacles were too much for most local reviews, and they fell by the wayside. Even if they were a one-day wonder, if no second generation had been in the offing—on the Web—what did they reveal, expose, achieve that warrants them a niche in the history of the U.S. press? They revealed not so much the discontent among working journalists, which is endemic, as a quantum leap in that discontent. Groups of reporters walked out into the public squares to call attention to the press. This denoted a shift of loyalty from media capitalists to media consumers, from employers to clients—a sign of professionalization. No longer could JRs be dismissed as vehicles for mavericks to vent their spleen, as media lashing out at rivals, or as Ivy League journals lecturing the journalistic hoi polloi.

What JRs exposed were the sins and perils of the press, as seen from the inside. They provided hard media news and instant analysis. Whoever reads through them all gets an accurate picture of the American press in the 1960s and 1970s and an idea of its problems. The most common types of stories are the documented attack on a particular press misdeed (such as offering editorial puffery to buyers of advertising space or blindly supporting the local police) and the discussion of such general media issues as shield laws and gag orders. Most JRs also provide non-critical information on the media, both news and education. Many reviews, such as the *St. Louis JR* or the *Houston JR*, gave newsmakers space to express their views of the press. A few, such as the *Chicago JR*, published stories the media had spiked or ignored (e.g., the murder of Black Panthers or the regulation of cable television). Apart from major stories, all reviews had at least a few regular sections, including letters, typos-and-goofs, or book reviews. A number of JRs perceived that they had to be of practical use to reporters and kept them posted on the whereabouts of their colleagues in a "transitions" section. And just about all had a section for which they vied to find an original title—from [*MORE*]'s "Hellbox and Rosebuds" to *feed/back's* "etaoins and shrdlus"—an unpretentious list of "kudos and knocks" (*Hawaii JR*) that was the most popular, and perhaps the most immediately efficient part, of the reviews.

Discounting special issues such as the *Twin Cities JR*'s examination of business and labor coverage, all reviews dealt with a wide range of subjects, yet an examination of over 1,000 articles brings out a clear hierarchy of major themes. In first place come the dissatisfaction of news people and its many expressions: JRs, the alternative press, Newspaper Guild action, the Reporter Power movement, the general concern for ethics. Second in frequency is criticism of the mediocrity of the news, attributed sometimes to the sloth or crookedness of a particular reporter but much more often to the cowardliness, conformism, parochialism, or prejudices of editors and to the rapacity and avarice of media owners.

Three themes are almost equally represented in the third rank. First are complaints about the conservatism of press barons, their hostility to any kind of dissent, their staunch support of business interests and of incumbent politicians, their efforts to expand their wealth and power. Second are stories on the difficult relations of the press with government, the legislatures, the bureaucracy, the police, and the courts. And third are profiles of new or original press organs and practitioners. As a last major theme come attacks on sexism and racism in the news and in the newsrooms.

It is hard to measure what the JRs achieved, for other forces were pushing in the same direction, nationally and sometimes locally. In Honolulu and Philadelphia, for instance, a change in management so improved the environment at the better newspapers that some reviewers considered a JR was no longer required. Veterans of the durable *Chicago JR* can point to any number of local victories, and even the little *AP Review* seems to have provided *Newsweek* with a story. Admittedly, many JRs cannot document any significant achievement except surviving, but the longer-lived can list precedent-making changes of the kind that could snowball, such as hiring more women and blacks or putting an end to freebies and junkets. The readership of the JRs was undoubtedly small. The person-in-the-street had not heard about them, but they were known by higher officials, by politicians, and by businessmen, the country-club friends of publishers and station owners. They were scrutinized in the newsroom. Any self-respecting editor on a metropolitan daily read the *Columbia JR* and [*MORE*]. Who can doubt the impact when a mere allusion to his publication in a letter published by [*MORE*] prompted a top editor of the *Los Angeles Times* to send me a correction, all the way to Europe?

In the opinion of JR makers, the influence of the more durable reviews was threefold. A JR was a watchdog: "It made reporters aware that they had to be careful because their peers were watching over them" (J. Burris, *Hawaii JR*). It was a consciousness-raiser: "One thing we did was sensitize our audience to the problems of the media" (C. Stiff, *TUM*). And it was a forum: "What the review has done is to start some channels of communication among reporters. Before we never knew people across media lines" (C. Lacey, *TCJR*). To sum up, "Most of what the JRs accomplished is subconscious, it is intangible. It is in the atmosphere, in the relationship between editors and reporters" (D. Rottenberg, *Chicago JR*).

All reviews, consciously and more often unconsciously, were an expression of, and an encouragement to, a movement whose lonely champions were Ron Dorfman of the *Chicago JR* and Dick Pollak of [*MORE*]. Under the name "Reporter Power," it upset both media managers and realists, for they imagined that the lowly journalists dreamed of grabbing ownership. Whether militants called it "Voice in the Product," "Democracy in the Newsroom," or "Workers' Participation," what they actually wanted was no longer to be two-legged tape recorders for glorified shoppers. They wanted the news flow to be entrusted to them as expert professionals. They wanted it to be as free from control by dollar-hungry corporate executives as it should be from control by power-hungry politicians and bureaucrats. Few media companies have placed reporters on their boards of directors or even allowed them a say in selecting editors; but on the better papers, the autonomy of specialized staffers and the open-mindedness of management has improved. "In the past," Donald Drake (of the *Philadelphia JR*) said to me as early as 1977, "the total newspaper was determined by the people at the top. In the JR era, reporters started to say 'Hey wait a minute, we at the bottom want to have a say in the product because this is part of our life, and we are intelligent people.' So what happened was that the stories began to dictate what the newspaper would be like."

One way to achieve the distant goal of empowering journalists is to promote caste-consciousness. Another is to develop public support. All JRs did both as publications, but many went a step further. Most gave fund-raising parties that brought together news people from the various local media. Some organized conferences for the rank-and-file, and others included public relations people, journalism students, professors, and enlightened citizens. The best attended of these events were the Liebling counter-conventions organized every year by [*MORE*], after the first in 1972 attracted tremendous attention. *Ball & Chain Review* convened black journalists at Lincoln University (Jefferson City, MO). *TCJR*'s Midwest Forums were regarded as a major factor in its survival. *feed/back's* 1976 dinner was a disaster because 200 media people were expected and 400 came. Quite apart from the boozing and socializing, the popularity of all those meetings indicates how much reporters felt the need for them.

SINCE THE HEYDAY

The local reporter-JRs are long gone. The need for them may have seemed less obvious after the industry itself started indulging in media criticism. Alternative and community papers as well as city magazines bring out some stories that the newspapers had rather bury. Also, interested news people and lay people are too few, in any but the largest cities, to provide the topics and the work and the funds required to keep a JR alive.

Two solutions are available. One is to make the review only a part-time JR, like *Point of View* in Cleveland. Another is for the JR to ride piggyback, becoming an insert in another publication, which takes care of printing and distribution problems and widens the audience enormously. But this can deprive a JR of independence, make it too tame or too virulent, depending on the tone of the supporting publication. It has not been used much.

Only one local JR in the tradition of the 1960s has survived, the *St. Louis JR*, owing its durability to the devotion of an idealistic media freak; but in 1996 he finally handed the paper over to a university (see p. 229).

CAMPUS JRS

That is *the* solution for non-partisan JRs. The two oldest and best-known in the United States are based on campuses: the declining *Columbia JR* and the *American JR*. The latter, born *Washington JR*, was launched in September 1977 by Roger Krantz, a young non-journalist who soon had to sell it to a rich Texan family, the Cattos, who ten years later ceded it to the College of Journalism at the University of Maryland, which has made it into the JR most appreciated by journalists for its stress on current media issues and cases.

Universities tend to be conservative and j-schools themselves need all the criticism they can get—yet the advantages they offer outweigh the drawbacks. The *Columbia JR* and *feed/back* (until 1986)[9] were the first to demonstrate this, at the national and local levels. Association with a university does impose moderation; but this, after the wild squawks needed to attract attention, is more efficient. Such an association provides respectability, stability, protection, technical and administrative facilities, subsidies, and—most important, perhaps—expertise and manpower. Faculty can supervise the monitoring, content analysis, and surveys that the media themselves should do and that reporter-JRs could not afford. They can also free the review from the inevitably narrow vision of the news processors. Adjunct professors can insure permanent input and feedback from the press. Students can do the research and production and

---

[9]The team in charge folded it rather than lose control of it to a new department head.

thus acquire experience, ethical awareness, and credits. And the university is thus given an opportunity to exercise its vital function in the continuing adaptation and progress of society.

COMMERCIAL AND PARTISAN JRS

Between 1998 and 2001, *CJR*[10] and *AJR* had commercial competition. Back in the 1970s, largely through bad management, [*MORE*] had lost $450,000 in five years, was sold in 1976, turned into a magazine, and within a year was put to sleep. Quite different was *Brill's Content*, with a good businessman at the helm,[11] and a rumored $25 million to spend. It was a very thick slick monthly, selling 240,000 in 2000—which caused other JRs to wake up. But *Content* came under fire for a merchandising alliance with big firms (such as CBS and NBC) to sell media products on-line. Nevertheless, it found it impossible to survive the 2001 economic downturn.

Partisan JRs multiplied in the 1980s and 1990s, to serve what *CJR* calls "causist organizations right and left."[12] A majority are right-wing watchdogs, such as the productions of Accuracy In Media: the already mentioned *AIM Report* since 1972, "a twice-monthly newsletter geared to setting the record straight on important stories that the media have botched, bungled or ignored," a daily radio commentary on 150 radio stations, a weekly newspaper column—and a website.

On the left-wing, Fairness and Accuracy in Media (FAIR) started *Extra!* "offering well documented criticism of media bias and censorship since 1986 . . . [exposing] important news stories that are neglected and defend working journalists when they are muzzled." FAIR also produces a weekly radio program, manages a website and an e-mail "alert" system that reaches over 6,000 subscribers.

Even with foundation grants and prestige advertising, the *Columbia JR* has never balanced its budget. *feed/back* was built on the unpaid dedication of an exceptional trio: a department chairman, a star reporter, and a first-rate graduate student. Even annual campus JRs skipped a year from time to time for lack of funds. In the last issue of *TUM* (Winter 1975), Mort Stern, a former assistant publisher of the *Denver Post* and then dean of the University of Colorado journalism school, wrote that "critics are the media's best friends. The industry ought to be looking for ways to bankroll their critics, to permanently institutionalize criticism, out of self-interest." He added that universities should be involved in the undertaking. This is still true, but the industry has done very little. Fortunately, technology has come forward with a solution to many problems of the JRs.

---

[10]Whose circulation was down to 26,000 at the turn of the century from 35,000 in the early 1980s.

[11]Steven Brill, famous for his *American Lawyer* review and *Court TV* on cable.

[12]In a panorama of media criticism in the March/April 2000 issue.

THE CYBER JRS

JRs were a little slow at using the new technology. In 1987, "Paper Tiger TV " was launched on the New York cable using one of the "public access" channels. Then came the cyber-JRs delivered by e-mail on the web: one of the first was *BONG!* in 1988. The Internet solved the problems of printing and distribution. It also required a JR to keep watch on it: the *On-line JR* was created for that purpose by the Annenberg School of Journalism at the Southern California University.

All the print reviews, whether campus, commercial, or partisan, went on-line. Many new JRs were born on the web, national and local ones, general and single-issue, non-partisan and partisan. *Newswatch,* for instance, started early in 1999, whose mission, in its own words is "to watch the media watchdog on behalf of news consumers, and to give a voice to consumers who want to talk back to the media." Its goal was "not to make the job of the journalist more difficult but to hold them to their professional standards of fairness and accuracy." Unfortunately, it died in June 2000.

CONCLUSION

JRs remain a U.S. phenomenon. They have been extremely rare outside the United States—with remarkable exceptions like *Die Fackel* in Vienna (1899-1934)[13] or, nowadays, *The Seventh Eye* in Israel, a free magazine devoted to media ethics. The so-called *British JR* or *Australian JR* are simply journals, like the *Montana JR*. The JR function is, to a large extent, assumed by alternative publications, like the French satirical weekly *Le Canard Enchaîné* (see p. 352), much of whose material consists in exposing the abuses of media and in pub-lishing what they don't. The function is also assumed by the newsletters and websites of associations of media watchers and radical groups.

JRs are needed everywhere. Thirty years after the heyday of JRs, the press, in the United States and elsewhere, is still not doing an adequate job. They are needed at national and local levels. National JRs tend to limit their coverage to the best media, which are not what most people consume. JRs are needed because extremely few of the thousands of dailies and weeklies allow staff participation in editorial policy or use a battery of public accountability procedures. Only a minuscule percentage can or will salary a media beat reporter or an in-house critic or an ombudsman—and such employees are gener-ally not as tough-minded as an independent agent. In the United States, a tiny proportion of the news media benefit from a state or local press council. JRs are needed because news magazines, quality magazines and alternatives lash out at

---

[13]See "Radical Mass Media Criticism" by John Theobald in *Ethics and Media Culture,* D. Berry (ed.), Oxford, Focal Press, 2000, pp. 11-27.

the media only occasionally and avoid self-flagellation. The shell of smugness the press builds around itself was cracked in the 1960s and 1970s, not shattered. Also, journalists need a local rallying point of their own and must develop some kind of national solidarity.

For the role of elected bodies, tribunals, and regulatory agencies in the media sphere to be kept to a minimum, there has to be a democratization of media operations. That can be achieved through a wide informal network of M*A*S, operated by journalists, monitors, pollsters, researchers, critics, militants, and various mediators. Media reviews could become a major element of the system as watchdogs of the press, as reporters, promoters, and coordinators of all the other controlling curs, and as popularizers of research in the theory and practice of mass communication. All progress is predicated on the citizenry's awareness of how crucial the press is to them, how greatly its services could be improved, and how powerfully they can influence it.[14]

Some On-Line Reviews (November 2001)

www.cjr.org	Columbia JR	General—campus
www.ajr.org	American JR	General—campus
www.AmericanReview.net	American Review	General
www.poynter.org/medianews	Jim Romenesko	media news / links
www.webster.edu/~review	St. Louis JR	Local
www.bigmedia.org	Denver	Local
www.cursor.org	Minneapolis	Local—many links
ojr.usc.edu	On-Line JR	Covers web journalism
www.aim.org	Accuracy in Media	Rightwing
www.mediaresearch.org	Media Research Center	Rightwing
www.fair.org	Fairness & Accuracy in Media	Leftwing
www.journalism.org	Project for Excellence in Journalism	General
www.slipup.com	Media errors	
www.cmpa.com	Center for Media & Public Affairs	General—many links
www.mediawatch.com	MediaWatch	Anti-sexism, racism etc.
www.moralityinmedia.org	Morality in Media	Religious, anti-sex

[14]Many of the data in this chapter, especially from interviews, were gathered in 1977 and published as *FoI Report* 0019, University of Missouri, September 1978.

CHAPTER 15
The St. Louis
Journalism Review*t. Louis*
Journalism Review

Charles L. Klotzer

The birth of the modern journalism reviews produced in the United States by
working journalists, which flourished for a while during the late 1960s and
1970s, is capsuled in one paragraph by Ron Dorfman, co-organizer of the first,
the *Chicago Journalism Review*, now long defunct.

> The *Chicago Journalism Review* was a product of the local newspaper cov-
> erage of the Democratic national convention [1968] and the violence that
> attended it in the streets of Chicago. When the convention was over and the
> national press had left town, local editors proceeded, deliberately and
> shamelessly, to rewrite history in an effort to patch up Chicago's reputation
> as "the city that works."[1]

Dorfman recalls that Chicago newspapers told their readers that their
own reporters had lied. Outraged, scores of reporters met over several weeks,
raised funds from local sources, and published the first issue of the *Chicago
Journalism Review,* the prototype for nearly 30 others that cropped up in cities
and institutions around the United States.

It was a time of excitement, confidence, and rejuvenation. There was a
feeling that a better world was visible beyond the horizon or, at least, that
through commitment it could be created. For journalists, reforming the media
was an essential first step in that process.

---

[1]Ron Dorfman, "Present at the Creation," *Quill Magazine,* July/August 1988, p. 10.

THE CONCEPT

When I received the first issue of the *Chicago Journalism Review*, it immediately struck me: here was a means to influence and reform the media that control what we know about the world. Reporters are the final link in the publishing process. Thus, collaborating with reporters to establish a watchdog over the media would not only establish peer review of the print and broadcasting industry, but would also propel social consciousness and responsibility into the heart of decision-making.

The media are powerful. They define influence and often join forces with particular interests that may or may not serve the general public. But whereas politicians must always keep the electorate in mind, business leaders cannot forget their stockholders, and labor leaders their members, who calls the media to account for their treatment of news?

In retrospect, it is obvious that watching the media from a professional point of view was only one aspect of the media reform movement. The second and equally strong motivation was to reform the social process in which the media play such an influential role.

The first person I contacted was a young suburban reporter on the *St. Louis Post-Dispatch* (who later advanced to become an editorial page writer) at a meeting of a political reform movement, the now-defunct New Democratic Coalition, an outgrowth of the Democratic Party that appeared after the Eugene McCarthy debacle in the 1968 election. He and other reporters on both St. Louis dailies (then St. Louis still had two) strongly endorsed the idea. A string of planning meetings followed and in September 1970 the first issue was published.

ITS BACKGROUND

Actually, taking up the cause of media criticism in 1970 was not as impetuous as the above might sound. To understand why the *St. Louis Journalism Review* (*SJR*) could at the end of the century remain the sole survivor of the privately published journalism reviews, a brief synopsis of the decade preceding its birth is essential.

After I had worked for five years as a director of public relations and advertising for a large construction and engineering firm, my wife and I decided in 1960 that there must be more to involvement in good causes than belonging to the American Civil Liberties Union and other such organizations.

Thus in 1962, after forming a corporation and raising some funds, we started publishing a magazine called *FOCUS/Midwest* (*F/M*). The magazine, which lasted for 21 years until it was merged into the *St. Louis Journalism Review* in 1983, took on the whole range of social, political, economic, and cultural concerns that dominated the 1960s. More than 100 experts accepted to become editorial advisors in 13 different fields. These advisors came from—and the contents of *F/M* encompassed—the Chicago–St. Louis–Kansas City triangle. The hope that, once *F/M* was financially self-supporting in the Missouri-Illinois area, we could expand into adjacent midwestern states remained that, a hope. *F/M* never did expand.

Before commencing publication in 1962, I had consulted scores of publishers of smaller and other publications, alive and defunct, throughout the country. Having been a supporter of Adlai E. Stevenson for president, I also visited his colleagues in their Chicago law office, among whom were Newton Minow (later to become chairman of the Federal Communications Commission and coiner of the phrase "TV is a vast wasteland"); Willard Wirtz (who became secretary of labor); and McCormick Blair (who became ambassador to Denmark). They all pleaded with me not to publish *FOCUS/Midwest* because small magazines, they said, cannot economically survive.

The warning by these three lawyers was typical. They and many others agreed that in principle such a journal is needed, but it would not be supported with much advertising by the business community. Indeed, my research had shown that the amount of subscriptions and advertising would always be limited. What we could control, however, were the expenses.

We kept them to a minimum by operating out of our home for the next 15 years and hired only one part-time secretarial/clerical person. All columnists and other writers were either freelancers or experts in diverse areas who had a message to convey. Rather than pursue her social work career, my wife, Rose, worked along to keep *FOCUS /Midwest* afloat. We could not only see our three children grow up, but even be with them much of the time.

We had formed a corporation, sold non-voting (in order to retain editorial control) stock to like-minded supporters in St. Louis, Chicago and Kansas City. Without their support we would not have survived these initial years. Investors were told, "You have no vote, most likely your investment is lost, but you can frame the stock certificate and tell your kids you were an activist in the Sixties." These investments, however, were also limited and we operated consistently at an annual deficit.

After about six years, in 1968, we admitted that we did not have, nor could we obtain, the resources to promote *FOCUS/Midwest* adequately, nor were we willing to change its focus to gather more advertising. Technology came to the rescue. Up to then, typesetting was principally by Linotype slug-casting machines, originally an amazing invention by a German immigrant to America, but compared to contemporary methods, a monstrous contraption. In 1968, IBM produced the first cold typesetting system, looking deceptively like a sophisticated typewriter but capable of imitating the sizes, fonts, and spacing of regular typesetting. This system, we realized, would not only reduce our production costs, but would also open up the potential of a separate source of income, a typesetting business.

We formed Focus/Graphics, acquired first one and later four such systems. This equipment was succeeded by other innovations so that by the early 1990s, we employed 12 people at a full-service pre-press graphics company able to produce camera-ready pages or plate-ready negatives, in black and white, or four colors. By the end of the decade, we had gone fully digital. Changes in technology have been a constant. Today Focus/Graphics has advanced into book and catalog production and web development.

Its Organization

Thus, when in 1969 and 1970 we met with reporters to organize the *St. Louis Journalism Review* (*SJR*), we had already been operating the typesetting business for one year and, although we did not yet have any employees, we saw its growth potential and could not resist the temptation to publish a second periodical.

The space was available, we had the graphic capability to produce such a tabloid, and members of the local press volunteered to write. What was not covered was the cost of printing, postage, and miscellaneous circulation and clerical expenses. This responsibility we accepted and it is this separation of editorial from financial responsibility that kept the journal independent and afloat. In the 1980s, with the growth of the typesetting business, we even started paying contributors though modestly, and hired an assistant editor.

St. Louis journalists endorsed the concept that fairness is the major obligation of the media. Unless all segments of the public have access to the media, they stated, the newspapers and broadcast stations do not live up to the responsibilities that go along with the constitutionally guaranteed freedom of the press. Only the press can ensure an informed public, which is needed to make democracy work. And an informed public, declared the inaugural issue of the *St. Louis Journalism Review*, requires that every segment of society know about the needs and thoughts and fears of all others. The principal complaint of non-media people, *SJR* journalists felt, is the failure of the media to reflect contemporary forces and changing needs, irrespective of the powers that represent the status quo.

ITS POLICIES

To remain sensitive to changes, *SJR* decided to keep its own policies simple and flexible. In its first issue, *SJR* published operating procedures that have largely remained the same:

- Membership on the editorial board is essentially by self-appointment of working journalists to avoid dominance by an in-group. Later, Editorial Board was amended to Editorial Advisory Board and journalists, writers, and academics have also been invited and have joined the board.

- Board meetings, which are off the record, are open to all members of the working press who wish to support *SJR*.
- Listing of board members on the masthead is optional.
- Ideas and articles are solicited from all members of the working press as well as others not directly affiliated with the print or broadcast media.
- Subject matter should deal with the media and topics ignored by the media.
- Rebuttals will be published from persons or publications mentioned in *SJR*.
- The editor alone is ultimately responsible for the contents.

ITS APPLICATION IN ST. LOUIS

Local Media Economics

St. Louis, like many other cities, has become a one-newspaper town over the years. The metropolitan area is also served by five television stations affiliated with major networks, a public television station, and a couple of neighborhood stations. For years, radio has been dominated by a CBS station—now owned by Infinity Broadcasting—with all the others, about 45 AM and FM stations, sharing the rest of the listening pie.

In addition, the area also has a host of local publications, most of them free of charge; a slick city magazine; and an alternative weekly that for many years represented the major editorial competition to the *Post*. That weekly, the *Riverfront Times*, has now been bought by a chain of alternative weeklies and drastically changed its focus from traditional muckraking to in-depth reporting void of any social or political ideology.

The three black newspapers are ineffectual except for a limited readership within the African-American community. All these properties compete for the advertising dollar, a limited commodity. Daily news is provided primarily by the *Post*, the three television stations, and the CBS radio stations. Whoever attracts the most readers, viewers, or listeners, will gather most of the advertising dollars.

Forty years ago, Irving Dillard, former editor of the editorial page of the *St. Louis Post-Dispatch* warned: "The counting house runs far too much of American journalism today." Local television news directors publicly admit that broadcast news is tailored largely by what audiences want to hear rather than what they should hear. (This was particularly evident during the Gulf War.)

Unlike television and radio where every second counts, newspapers have space to offer a variety of news to attract a variety of readers. The usual description of such a metropolitan daily is a "shopping center": just as a shopper will only buy a few items although offered a huge selection, so readers of a daily paper can browse throughout but read only what interests them. Because tastes cover a wide spectrum, papers are forced to devote space to just about everything, from astrology and advice for the lovelorn to many pages of sports, and if that cuts into the news hole or analytical pieces, so be it.

Beyond Economics

The pressure of the balance sheet is only one factor that influences the scope and quality of coverage. Pre-dispositions by media management and the socio-political climate, have shaped what St. Louisans read and hear. A few typical examples (from *SJR*) of how the local media or their staffs have run afoul of their role follow. Although these examples date back many years, if not decades, they typify what ails the media.

- In many communities, the media are the cheerleaders for the local community not only at the expense of other communities, but also at the expense of accuracy. Many years ago, a key editor (of a now defunct daily) was actively engaged in collaring visiting out-of-town reporters for the purpose of giving them a "balanced" picture. The *St. Louis Post-Dispatch* has an ambivalent record. Although also a booster, it has not hesitated to voice strong criticism of local institutions and civic and business leadership.
- The *St. Louis Post-Dispatch* has devoted very little coverage to the many suburbs in this metropolitan area of nearly two million people. Suburban coverage has been taken over by the free newspapers that totally depend on advertising, where the balance sheet rules even more unabashedly than in the daily paid-subscription press. (Since this chapter was written, the *Post* has bought a chain of local, free suburban papers and some sources claim that some of the suburban coverage will be transferred from the chain to the *Post*.)
- Although dated, the following still represents one of the crassest breaches of journalistic ethics. At a time when fear of communism and subversion pervaded every branch of government, in the summer of 1971, one of the *St. Louis Post-Dispatch*'s investigative reporters became a paid informer for the St. Louis Police Department and testified before the now disbanded U.S. House Internal Security Committee. From September 1969 to August 1970, the reporter had been paid between $400 and $500, which, the reporter said, did not cover what he had spent and therefore he was not a paid informer. All the *Post* did was to pressure him to quit being an informer. He was kept on the staff. The incident was kept from the public until *SJR* broke the news.

- Similarly, for years the publisher of the best-known of the local black newspapers was an informer for the FBI during the discredited reign of J. Edgar Hoover and published items derogatory of leftist groups upon the instigation of government sources. This information was available to the *St. Louis Post-Dispatch* but was never published until one of the *Post* reporters turned over the material to *SJR*. However, the *Post* did publish that the FBI fed information to its competitor, the now discontinued *St. Louis Globe-Democrat.*
- Daily coverage and sustained investigative reporting is beyond the scope of all St. Louis media but the *St. Louis Post-Dispatch.* None of the television stations have investigative reporters who are permitted to pursue a story at length, for two or three months. Radio and television stations act like parasites on the news gathered by the *Post.* Typically, they have no reporters covering the police or crime, but monitor the city and county police broadcasts. If the happening is gory and violent enough, the cameras rush in. Otherwise, they read the early editions of the *Post* and clip the wire services. Whatever shortcomings or insights the *Post* and wire services provide are regurgitated by the broadcast media.
- Among the most censored reporting in any medium is its internal corporate and business deals and wherewithal. Typically, the *Post* has two specific reporters who cover the "beat." Their copy is read by key editors and probably by the business office as well. From the late 1980s media started covering the business of other media, but in the 1960s and 1970s even this was done rarely if ever (of course, that policy had to be changed when the owner, Pulitzer, Inc., became a public corporation).

SJR broke that taboo in its first (October 1970) issue, revealing that the *Post-Dispatch* and the *Globe-Democrat* had had a profit-splitting arrangement since 1959. The ignorance of at least one *Post* editor was underscored when he warned *SJR* that it was inviting a libel suit. Actually, *SJR* had merely reported on the testimony of Joseph Pulitzer, Jr.[2] before the U.S. Subcommittee of Antitrust and Monopoly on the Failing Newspaper Act (later renamed the Newspaper Preservation Act). Coverage by the local media of that arrangement and the later established Joint Operating Agency (JOA), which legally owned and published both the *Post-Dispatch* and the *Globe-Democrat,* always remained incomplete, sporadic and misleading.

---

[2]The various branches of the Pulitzer family own the *Post-Dispatch.* The two key stockholders are Emily Pulitzer, wife, and Michael E. Pulitzer, brother, of the late Joseph Pulitzer, Jr.

PROBLEMS AND SOLUTIONS

The above incidents and many others moved reporters into collaborating with the *SJR*. Traditionally, reporters do all their grumbling to each other—lamenting about the sins of their editors or colleagues. With *SJR*, they could express themselves publicly or, if necessary, anonymously, and know that their comments would be circulated and read not only by their peers but also by the public at large.

Acceptance by owners of the media and top management has been somewhat schizophrenic. In public, the media uphold our right to publish, but in the early years, they implied that journalists who collaborated with the *SJR* were guilty of biting the hand that fed them. Over the years, that attitude has been transformed into grudging acceptance, even respect. The short-lived *Post* editorship of Cole Campbell, a nationally known disciple of "public journalism," and his abrupt dismissal, has further boosted *SJR's* reputation. It was *SJR's* consistent criticism of public journalism and of Campbell's policies that heavily contributed to public rejection of the "new" *Post* and to Campbell's dismissal.

By March 2002, *SJR* had published 244 issues. It had done so with the help of about 40 to 50 journalists in the print and broadcast media, academics, and others who had some connection with communications or social concerns.

During the more than three decades of publishing, a number of problems arose that were resolved: they never threatened the existence of *SJR*. Indeed, the survival of *SJR* always depended primarily upon subsidizing the losses. What members of the advisory board and others added were credibility, information, and manuscripts—crucial in creating a quality product.

Editorial and Organizational Problems

Following are some of the major editorial and organizational problems that arose, particularly during the early years.

Editorial Control. Although initially I was just one member of the board, in effect I edited the copy as of the first issue. From known bad experiences of earlier alternative media, it was accepted by the board that the editorial operation cannot be conducted by a committee. Responsibility must rest with one person. After a while it was decided to list me as editor and publisher. This policy was retained in 1996, when *SJR* was given to Webster University in St. Louis. The assistant editor, Ed Bishop, was appointed editor and the founder became emeritus.

Bylines. Whether or not to use bylines has been repeatedly discussed by the board. Initially, it was decided not to use any bylines and accept collective responsibility for anything published. Editorial advisors always had the option not to be listed on the masthead if they disagreed with anything in an issue. Thus, those concerned had to attend and proof all of the copy. Few ever did. Actually, only two issues arose in 30 years where one reporter asked that his name be dropped for that issue.

From the start, some board members always felt uncomfortable with such a policy. Gradually, the policy evolved that articles were not bylined *unless* a writer insisted that his or her byline be published. That policy, too, went through further changes so that, today, *SJR* always uses bylines *unless* a writer specifically requests that it be not used. That also became necessary because of the greater use of freelancers.

Membership. Originally, the *SJR* board was composed exclusively of reporters from the print and broadcast media. Reporters, however, who write for a living day in and day out, sooner or later will find it too much of a burden to write in their free time. Over the years, therefore, the board was enlarged and became a loose coalition not only of reporters, but also of academics, retired journalists, and persons with specific expertise although not part of the media community. A classic example is *SJR's* former radio columnist, a follower of the airwaves for many years with contacts in the industry and access to news sources, but who actually is a dentist.

Great emphasis was always placed, however, on keeping journalists involved even if they merely attended our monthly brunch/discussion gatherings. Today, participation ranges from members attending all sessions, listed on the masthead and contributing regularly—to others who are not listed, do not attend meetings, rarely write, but will offer information when specifically solicited. Journalists in the print media have always participated in greater numbers than those working in broadcasting because their union, the St. Louis Newspaper Guild, is much stronger than the group representing TV and radio employees.

Activating Participants. Credibility with the media community was attained rapidly, especially among the local working force. Although some of the *SJR* board members have been active from the very beginning, new members must be attracted from the workforce on a continual basis. Because *SJR* can now count on the support of veteran reporters, their contact with new arrivals has been of considerable help. In the long run, however, new participants must have an opportunity to meet personally with the editor. Once the purpose of *SJR* is explained, their enthusiasm can be fanned into active participation.

Up to 1986, the level of participation varied greatly, When we changed our meeting to a Sunday morning brunch (paid for by *SJR*) at a well-known local café, attendance improved dramatically. It became a social affair where reporters could meet others and exchange news and views. Invitations to these brunches go out to about 45, with attendance ranging between 15 to 30.

Pay. For years, reporters wrote for *SJR* without pay. Obviously, submissions were frequently late and depended utterly on the good will of the participants. When it became possible to offer modest fees, submissions did become more regular. Indeed, work from freelancers can only be obtained on a paid basis. Pay means more than receiving a check; for most it means that they are professionals. Payment, even minimal, is therefore very important. Payments have remained modest, although *SJR* rates now rank nearly with the average freelance pay in this area. (Since the transfer of *SJR* to Webster University in 1996, pay for writers has substantially increased.)

News Blackout. The daily press has almost completely blacked out news of *SJR's* activities and reporting. Editors of the conservative *Globe-Democrat,* now defunct, would blacklist employees whom they thought cooperated with *SJR.* But for many years, even the liberal *Post* never mentioned *SJR.* Since the late 1980s, some mention of *SJR* has been made in some stories, but groundbreaking reports and news are consistently ignored. Television stations have been much more open to *SJR.* Whenever something affects the media—and St. Louis has been beset by newspaper closings and openings—*SJR* is interviewed.

When *SJR* celebrated its 30th anniversary in October 2000, which brought to St. Louis media personalities of national renown, the *Post-Dispatch* buried the item in a 7" notice at the bottom of an inside page next to a 3/4-page ad.

Circulation Promotion. In order to spread the word about *SJR,* we took advantage of fund-raising auctions by the local public radio and television stations by offering free subscriptions to contributors. The targeted audience are likely subscribers to *SJR* which benefited from free on-air publicity. Subscription solicitations never pay for themselves. The rate of return (between .5% and 2%) covers about half of the cost. Generally, publishers hope for a high rate of renewals to cover original expenses, which may permit an increase in advertising rates. In the case of *SJR,* the planning, production, and execution of a mailing is always too costly and time-consuming. Although a few such mailings have been undertaken, *SJR* has followed a different route.

We were continually on the lookout for mailing lists from organizations and other sources. They were added to our circulation as "gift subscriptions" for a six-month period and were so informed. After that period, they would be told that the gift had expired. The primary advantages of this approach was that it was less expensive, automatic, did not require any planning, and also circulated *SJR* to a larger audience. Readers had at opportunity to review the publication itself instead of deciding only on the basis of a promotional flyer.

Limited Resources. Promotion, reputation, acceptance and success depend largely upon the availability of resources. In the case of *SJR,* these were always extremely limited. Initially, for a number of years, *SJR* accepted no advertising, not because of fear that it would be co-opted by business interests, but simply because *SJR* could not afford to hire qualified salespeople, nor would its circulation warrant advertising. When in the late 1970s advertising was solicited, the income derived was always minimal. Acceptance by advertisers, up to this day, has been spotty.

WHAT KEEPS *SJR* GOING?

It would be misleading not to credit the publisher's continuous subsidy as the primary reason for *SJR's* survival. Since the first issue was published, none of the issues has broken even. But it would also be misleading to claim that the subsidy is the only reason for it to be still publishing. *SJR's* survival reflects community acceptance: it is recognized as being independent, credible, and concerned with ethics rather than economics.

SJR has a two-fold function: peer review and community involvement. That dual purpose is evident in *SJR's* circulation: one-third of its subscribers come from the media community and two-thirds are from the public at large. Peer review is a powerful tool. From time to time, it has been suggested that if we would publish just a few hundred copies and circulate them exclusively to media personnel the effect would be the same. Having a general circulation base offers more than just pressure on the media. It invites the public to share its reactions and its concerns with the media community.

Although it is much less known than *Columbia Journalism Review* (*CJR*) and *American Journalism Review* (*AJR*), *SJR* has won many awards. John Seigenthaler, former editorial director of *USA Today* and publisher of the *Nashville Tennessean,* when president of the American Society of Newspaper Editors wrote to its members:

> I am a regular *SJR* reader. The monthly has very interesting articles that are of great interest to me as a journalist, editor and publisher. That's why I take time, with every edition.
>
> One of the criticisms of the *Columbia Journalism Review* was that the articles were written sometimes by uninformed critics. You never get the feeling from reading *SJR* that there is any lack of knowledge on the part of the critic. Often there's clearly a slant, but, on the other hand, what is a review but opinion?
>
> There is too little criticism of newspapers in the United States.

In 1996, my wife and I decided that we had to disappoint all those who hoped that with my demise *SJR* would fade away. So we entrusted the future of *SJR* to Webster University in St. Louis, which has a dynamic journalism department. The university subsidizes the publication, but because it is bound by its incorporation statutes which we designed, *SJR's* editor and content remain completely independent.

In September 2000, number 229 of the review inaugurated the magazine format. Thus in appearance *SJR* was finally joining the exclusive club formed by *CJR* and *AJR*.

SECTION 3
Monitoring and Militancy

CHAPTER 16
Les Sociétés de rédacteurs
Newsroom Associations

Jean Schwoebel[1]

[The société de rédacteurs *seems to be the only French invention in the field of media accountability. The concept was born in 1961 when the journalists at* Le Monde *newspaper intervened to stop a take-over of the prestigious daily and restore the founder Hubert Beuve-Méry to the helm. Under the leadership of Jean Schwoebbel, they set up a "newsroom association" that obtained an important part of the capital. This insured that it would henceforth exercise veto power on major decisions.]*

When I first saw the short presentation of M*A*S written by Claude-Jean Bertrand, it caught my attention because it sets forth the considerations that I have ceaselessly advocated before the *sociétés de rédacteurs.* Let me remind you that I was the founder, and still am the honorary president, of the société des rédacteurs of *Le Monde*; and that I created the French Federation of Newsroom Associations of which I am also the honorary president. I have for many years fought for ideas and I was struck both by the similarity of our analyses and the difference in the conclusions drawn.

Those conclusions are typical of our friends the communicologists. I have had a long lasting feud with the schools of journalism and their "experts" because we live in two different worlds. They need to be much colder than we do; we are fighting the information battle, an extremely difficult, tough, and cruel battle.

---

[1]At the April 1991 Paris conference where the global notion of M*A*S was first presented, veteran journalist Jean Schwoebbel, from the most prestigious French daily *Le Monde*, improvised this address, which he later edited.

But that does not prevent us from sharing common features, and I wish to pay homage to the memory of a man who chaired the *Institut français de presse* (IFP),[2] Fernand Terrou: at the end of his life, he wrote me a letter in which he said: "I believe that you are right and I will join you in the fight you are waging." Alas, fate decided to put an end to his life shortly afterwards. So I think that in future battles academics will be by our side, a legion of competent combatants. I have only one criticism of them: when they talk of professional ethics and of "social responsibility," their speech is extremely sanitized, which is the more amazing as we live in a period of terrible cruelty.

Let me define the problem. How did those sociétés de rédacteurs, which I think are a French and very original species of M*A*S, originate? A simple observation: information is capital. It is capital because we come out of school with a sum of knowledge but, because of the speed of change, of progress, we must all constantly update our knowledge and opinions. It is through newspapers that you can update most easily. They provide you with texts that you read at your leisure, that you have time to think about. Information being capital, it is indispensable that we journalists enjoy independence, an independence guaranteed by the very structure of the company we work for, so that we can fulfill our tasks with the necessary accuracy and rigor.

At the end of that great cataclysm, the Second World War, with its massive slaughter of civilians as well as soldiers, after the Resistance and the Liberation of France—we found ourselves filled with the hope that those sacrifices would not have been in vain. That is why such international bodies as the United Nations were created.

As for the press, we hoped to make it truly independent, to give it the means of helping men avoid such catastrophes in the future. This thanks to a little more justice, a little more thought and, even maybe, I am not afraid to say, a little more realism, true realism—that which sees man not as just a soldier or a producer but also as a thinking creature. A creature with spiritual and intellectual needs which, if they are not fulfilled, will prevent him from experiencing happiness. We thought that we should take advantage of the tremendous changes caused by the Second World War. We were lucky in that legislation was then passed that enabled men with such ideas and concerns to come to the head of newspaper companies. Unfortunately, they proved mediocre managers and, after a time, had to hand over their rights and powers to other leaders.

But at *Le Monde,* by chance, we had a man for whom we all felt great admiration, a man whose competence, rigor, honesty, lucidity, whose sense of the needs of the future, were not commonly found at the head of a newspaper. So when [in 1951] Hubert Beuve-Méry judged it was impossible to continue and walked out, we journalists intervened and placed him back in power. And at

---

[2]The school of journalism within the University of Paris-2 is the oldest in France, yet not accredited by the journalistic profession, because it concentrates on teaching at MA and PhD levels, as well as on research. The concept of M*A*S was developed there.

that time we communicated to M. Beuve-Méry that in our opinion he was perfect—except that we did not find him democratic enough.

We wanted his experience to be useful to others. He believed that after him everything would fall to pieces. We told him that, in our view, things would have to go on after him; that we, nourished as we had been by his teachings, intended to pursue the work. And because of that, we asked to take part in the management of the paper—but not at the economic level as was claimed (we were accused of trying to set up a soviet). We simply wanted to participate in defining editorial policy and in defining the values the paper defended. Today, people talk a lot about traditional values, but they fail to translate them into concrete, present-day terms.

So in the midst of a vast external crisis, we took advantage of an internal crisis to create the first société de rédacteurs, which proved an immediate sensation in the world. And I was invited (though I never proselytized) everywhere: to Germany, to Italy, to Spain, even to England where I met, among others, the staff of *The Times*. I even went, at the request of Mrs. Indira Gandhi, to New Delhi, where a vast conference was being held of journalists from all over Asia: our formula seemed to them the most effective, as it seemed half way between the capitalist and the communist regimes.

Our project was realistic in the sense that the qualities of *Le Monde,* although they were partly due to M. Beuve-Méry, were also largely due to the collaboration that developed between director and journalists, on an equal footing. A sense of responsibility can only be acquired if one is given the opportunity to take responsibility. And we discovered that we could cooperate very well with a first-class director, especially if he believed that he was working with a first-class staff.

On a national level, we even managed to move politicians and, under the De Gaulle administration, we obtained that a commission be set up to study the possibility of some new legislation that would insure a balance between money and power. That is very important. Power, let me stress, is not always opposed to people. On the contrary, very often the mission of the state is to restore balance and to prevent abuse.

That is why we thought for a while that our formula would be adopted all over France and that it would serve as an example in other countries. But we then entered a new era, an era of prosperity in which money became more and more important because of the huge investments required by technological progress. Considerable funds were needed. News staffs found that their position grew weaker and weaker.

During the conference, a speaker, with diplomatic tact, suggested that the sociétés de rédacteurs could probably be called a failure. I hasten to retort that it is untrue . . . or rather, it was true then (1991), though there were still about twenty sociétés des rédacteurs that had not closed shop. Journalists have certainly put them on the back burner: they use them very rarely, on special occasions. But the sociétés exist, a score of them, half in the television sector.

We must now remind journalists that they suffer from a lack of solidarity. That is the obstacle we hit against.

At the present time, information is essential. We find ourselves again in a revolutionary period. Information is capital. People understood this—as do the government and the big corporations, and so there have been fierce fights to grab control of information. Those who had money could launch take-over bids with the result that today in France the big corporations are the masters of information. I admit that it is still possible to do one's job properly and many journalists do—but in conditions that are more and more difficult.

The Western world no longer has a clear idea of where it stands: its élites seem incapable of providing it with a great design that would correspond to the needs of our time. There is a great void. We are turning round in circles and all conflicts appear as fights between individuals. Now is the moment for us to remind the sociétés des rédacteurs that they have a part to play: at least they should offer an example of what can be done, they should help journalists respond to the needs of this era. What needs? To fight against the greed of men and their taste for power—that is what is fundamental.

In my view, more than rapacity, the taste for money, it is the taste for power that you find in every person, in those who possess the greatest power just as in those who hold a very little one. That appetite makes solidarity impossible, and impossible too, the indispensable sharing of power. There will be true authenticity, let me repeat, only on the day when people, whoever they are, will learn to share their power—when we news people will be able to cooperate, on an equal footing, with whom that we wish to inform.

On that point, I still have great hope for the sociétés de rédacteurs: present circumstances lead us all to think things over. Journalists, too, need to improve a lot. I have never ceased fighting for that—and that, actually, is why they abandoned me in the end: I was too demanding. I considered that we were not mandarins, that we had to accept that information was everybody's business. Certainly, we were professionals, but only in the sense that we knew the methods to question people and to report in the best possible way—but the press must remain a service rendered to media users. The tragedy today is that the press has become one among the powers-that-be and power is going to the head of the media stars. That is unacceptable and dangerous: it is a factor of injustice and inefficiency.

That is why—let me say it again—I think hard facts will force us to go beyond what we thought were our limits and to practice true realism. Right now we are witnessing the results of the so-called *realpolitik,* sinister results—disasters everywhere. Genuine realism consists in acknowledging the double nature of man, a creature of darkness, admittedly, but also a creature of light. That light must be used: it is a power, a treasure, vast wealth. I saw it in my own newsroom during the fall of the Soviet empire and the Gulf war, when I fought to get the staff to rise to the greatness of circumstances. I observed that the young were quite accessible: I had the extreme joy during a meeting to hear young journalists, usually intimidated in the presence of their elders, say to me that they could not understand the battles their elders were waging against each other—and that they recognized themselves in Jean Schwoebbel because of his book *La presse, le pouvoir et l'argent*.[3]

---

[3]Paris, Le Seuil, 1968.

CHAPTER 17
Monitoring Censorship

Carl Jensen

In early 1961, journalist Tad Szulc, of *The New York Times*, wrote an article that revealed the United States was about to launch an invasion of Cuba using CIA-trained Cuban exiles. The story was originally to be published by *The Times* under a four-column headline at the top of page one.[1]

But when word leaked out in Washington that *The Times* planned to run the Szulc story, President Kennedy called James Reston, *The Times'* Washington bureau chief, asking him to kill it. Reston told Orvil Dryfoos, the publisher of *The Times*, about Kennedy's call and suggested toning down the story and removing the references to the invasion. As a result, a heavily edited version of the story, with a one-column heading, appeared with no mention of the CIA's involvement or that the invasion was imminent.

Kennedy later told *New York Times* Managing Editor Turner Catledge, "If you had printed more about the operation, you could have saved us from a colossal mistake." It is generally agreed that if the media had widely publicized the coming invasion, Kennedy would have been forced to cancel it. *The New York Times* was not the only publication to censor the story. As David Halberstam pointed out in *The Powers That Be*, the media were "remarkably vulnerable to the seductive call of National Security." Television was equally lax in its coverage of the story.

It was not because the media did not know about the proposed invasion. The alternative press, led by *The Nation*, had already published informa-

---

[1]Updated and reprinted from *20 Years of Censored News* by courtesy of Carl Jensen and Seven Stories Press, New York.

tion that was censored by the mainstream media. On November 19, 1960, five months before the invasion, *The Nation* reported the Bay of Pigs invasion plan and urged "all U.S. news media" to check it out. It noted that if the report were true, "then public pressure should be brought to bear upon the Administration to abandon this dangerous and harebrained project." But the mainstream media ignored *The Nation's* plea and the United States suffered one of its worst foreign policy fiascoes.

Forty years have passed since the infamous Bay of Pigs invasion, years in which the issue of censorship, or self-censorship as the case may be, has not receded. And for the past 25 years, Project Censored, headquartered at Sonoma State University in Rohnert Park, California, has been monitoring the extent of such censorship.

I founded Project Censored as a seminar in the sociology of mass media in 1976 and it is now the oldest media research project on news censorship in the United States.[2] It is now directed by Peter Phillips, professor of sociology at Sonoma State University. Visit www.projectcensored.org for more information.

The primary objective of Project Censored is to explore and publicize the extent of news censorship in our society by locating stories about significant issues of which the public should be aware, but is not, for a variety of reasons.

Since its inception, the Project has hoped to stimulate journalists to provide more news coverage of under-reported issues and to encourage the general public to demand more coverage of those issues by the media and to seek information from alternative sources.

The essential issue raised by the Project is the failure of the mass media to provide people with all the information they need to make informed decisions concerning their own lives. Only an informed electorate can achieve a fair and just society. The public has a right to know about issues that affect it and the press has a responsibility to keep the public well informed about those issues.

THE MEDIA MYTH

We have all been brought up to believe in the power and value of the press—the great watchdog of society. It is the nation's ombudsman. It is the muckraking journalist with printer's ink in his blood who is willing to sacrifice all to expose evil. We were taught to believe *The New York Times* prints "all the news that's fit to print." We believed *The Chicago Times* when it said, "It is a newspaper's duty to print the news and raise hell."

I wanted to be a journalist from the time I was eight years old when I saw how important a newspaper, the *New York Daily News,* was to my father. He would bring it home each evening and sit at the kitchen table reading it from

[2]"Operation Spike," a conservative copy-cat version started by AIM, did not last more than a few years.

cover to cover before dinner. Later I came to believe that a journalist could make a difference and could even help to build a better world. I was in awe of the achievements of the early 20th-century muckrakers and seduced by the siren song of Horace Greeley, the 19th-century editor of the *New York Tribune*, who rhapsodized:

> Then hail to the Press! chosen guardian of freedom! Strong sword-arm of justice! bright sunbeam of truth.

Press apologists also like to quote Thomas Jefferson, our third president, who said in 1787,

> The basis of our government being the opinion of the people, the very first object should be to keep that right; and were it left to me to decide whether we should have a government without newspapers or newspapers without a government, I should not hesitate a moment to prefer the latter.

Those same apologists conveniently forget to mention what Jefferson had to say about the press in later times:

> The man who never looks into a newspaper is better informed than he who reads them, inasmuch as he who knows nothing is nearer to truth than he whose mind is filled with falsehoods and errors. (1799); nothing can now be believed which is seen in a newspaper. (1807); I read but one newspaper and that [. . .] more for its advertisements than its news. (1820)

Indeed the media-generated myth of the press as an aggressive, unbiased, honest watchdog of society, is just that—a myth. I fulfilled my childhood dream of becoming a journalist, but after witnessing first-hand the kind of reporting it took to be a "successful" journalist, I left that profession for another which, at least, wasn't hypocritical about what it really was—public relations and advertising.

My early disenchantment with journalism only grew through the years as I first witnessed how advertisers could influence the media, and later, as a university professor, when I created a national research project—Project Censored—that explored and exposed the media's failure to cover important issues.

Admittedly, not all media and all journalists are driven by the bottom line but many are, especially the large media corporations and the "brand name" journalists. The media are more concerned with their next quarterly profit than with the unique opportunity given them by the First Amendment. And most journalists are more concerned with keeping their jobs and increasing their income than with fighting for the public's right to know. This helps explain why millions of Americans turn to the alternative press for reliable information about what is really happening.

America's mainstream mass media basically serve three segments of society today: the wealthy, politicians, and the sports-minded. The news media have done an exceptional job of providing full and, on the whole, reliable information to those who are involved in or follow the stock market and to those who are involved in or follow politics and to those who are involved in or follow sports.

THE GOLDEN AGE OF MUCKRAKING

At the same time, the media have failed to inform, or protect the interests of, those less fortunate in our society. It was not always this way. For a brief ten-year period, at the turn of the century, a period sometimes referred to as the Golden Age of Muckraking, the media sought out, investigated, and published stories about the plight of all its citizens, including those at the bottom of the economic scale. The works of journalists and authors like Lincoln Steffens, Ida Tarbell, Upton Sinclair, and others, were widely read by many Americans and led to significant social change that benefited the general public.

Lincoln Steffens' *The Shame of the Cities* exposed and cleaned up municipal political corruption; Ida Tarbell's *The History of the Standard Oil Company* led to the dissolution of that giant monopoly; and Upton Sinclair's *The Jungle*, a powerful exposé of the meat packing industry, led to legislative changes and the first Pure Food and Drug Act.

Sadly, a century later, problems similar to these still exist. However, the muckrakers and the muckraking publications of yesteryear are not present today. Political bribes in government, earlier exposed by Steffens, are now often given in the acceptable form of PAC money and ignored by the press. The media not only fail to explain the negative impact of monopolies as Tarbell did, but instead act as cheerleaders for giant mergers; and instead of investigating and exposing the hazards and dangers of meat processing and packing as Sinclair did, the media are now content to sensationalize the deaths of children from e-coli rather than expose the conditions that create it.

Project Censored had its inception in the summer of 1976. I was then an assistant professor of sociology at Sonoma State University in Northern California and looking for a subject for a seminar in mass media that I taught each year. For some time I had been curious about how Richard Nixon could have won the 1972 election with a landslide vote nearly five months after the biggest political crime of the century—Watergate.

The break-in at the Democratic National Committee offices in the Watergate complex in Washington, D.C., by the Republican Committee to Re-elect the President (CREEP) in June 1972, sparked one of the biggest political cover-ups in modern history. And the press was an unwitting, if not willing, partner in the cover-up. The break-in, by CREEP employees known as the "plumbers," was described as a "two-bit burglary" not worthy of press attention.

The media's lack of interest in the Watergate story even prompted the *Washington Post's* Katharine Graham to wonder, in her 1997 autobiography, *Personal History*, "If this is such a hell of a story, then where is everybody else?" Fortunately, despite the skepticism on the part of their colleagues, Carl Bernstein and Bob Woodward, young reporters at the *Washington Post*, eventually made it a national news story. Bernstein later noted that out of some 2,000 full-time reporters in Washington for major news organizations, just 14 were assigned to the Watergate story on a full-time basis and only six of them on an investigative basis, even six months after the break-in. When Walter Cronkite, the legendary CBS-TV news anchor and America's most trusted man, tried to do a unique two-part series on Watergate on the *CBS-TV Evening News* before the election, a phone call from the Nixon White House to Bill Paley, chair of CBS, resulted in a scaled down version of Cronkite's scheduled program. Thus, it was not surprising that no one was even talking about Watergate on election eve, as Woodward told Larry King a few years ago (June 17, 1997).

Watergate taught us two important lessons about the press: first, the news media sometimes do fail to cover some important issues, and second, the news media sometimes indulge in self-censorship. It also led to the creation of Project Censored which has now become the longest running internationally recognized news media research project.

My 1997 book, entitled *20 Years of Censored News,* recalls, year by year from 1976 to 1995, the stories and issues the major media neglected to tell you about when they were timely and reveals what has happened with them since.

NEWS CENSORSHIP IS NOT A CONSPIRACY

It is important to understand that the 200 *Censored* stories in the book are not examples of some widespread media conspiracy to censor your news. News is too diverse, fast-breaking, and unpredictable to be controlled by some sinister conservative eastern establishment media cabal. However, there is a congruence of attitudes and interests on the part of the owners and managers of mass media organizations. That non-conspiracy conspiracy, when combined with a variety of other factors, leads to the systematic failure of the news media to fully inform the public. Although it is not an overt form of censorship, such as the kind we observe in some other societies, it is nonetheless real and often equally as dangerous to the public's well-being.

Other factors accounting for censorship include the following: sometimes a source for a story isn't considered reliable (an official government representative or corporate executive is reliable; a freelance journalist or eyewitness citizen is not); other times the story doesn't have an easily identifiable "beginning, middle, and end" (acid rain just seems to go on for ever and ever); some stories are considered to be "too complex" for the general public (nobody would understand the intricacies of the savings and loan debacle); on occasion stories are ignored because they haven't been "blessed" by *The New York Times* or the *Washington Post* (reporters and editors at most of the more than 1,500 daily newspapers in the United States know their news judgment isn't going to be challenged when they write and publish fashionable "follow-the-leader" stories, a practice that leads to the "pack" or "herd" phenomenon in journalism).

Another excuse the media sometimes give is that the story is too old, outdated, or that they've already covered the issue. Yet, just because a story was covered once doesn't mean the issue has been resolved. Sometimes updating an old story may not only serve the public well but could even result in a Pulitzer Prize for the journalist. One such story in 1986 focused on the issue of conducting radiation experiments on unsuspecting subjects dating back to the mid-1940s. But it wasn't until 1993 that an investigative reporter, Eileen Welsome of the *Albuquerque Tribune,* made it a national issue and won a Pulitzer Prize for her work.

One major factor contributing to media self-censorship is that some stories are considered potentially libelous. Long and costly jury trials, settlements out of court, and occasional multimillion-dollar judgments against the media, have produced a massive chilling effect on the press and replaced copy editors with copy attorneys. An equally ominous sign for freedom of the press was revealed in early 1997 when the Food Lion supermarket chain sued ABC-TV after it aired an exposé of its meat packing procedures. Food Lion sued on the basis of a false job application rather than libel, thereby circumventing libel laws designed to protect the press. Food Lion's argument was that the truth doesn't matter as much as the way the press goes after it.

The bottom-line explanation for much of the self-censorship that occurs in America's mainstream media is the media's own bottom line. Corporate media executives perceive their primary, and often sole, responsibility to be the need to maximize profits for the next quarterly statement, not, as some would have it, to inform the public. Many of the cited stories do not support the financial interests of media publishers, owners, stockholders, or advertisers.

Investigative journalism also is more expensive than the "public stenography" form of journalism practiced at many media outlets. And, of course, there is always the "don't rock the boat" mentality that pervades corporate media boardrooms and then filters down to the newsroom. The latter influence has only been exacerbated by the number of megamedia mergers in recent history. The need to play it safe is becoming pervasive as the stakes are becoming increasingly higher.

CENSORED SUBJECTS

A statistical analysis of the top 200 stories over a 20-year period reveals that although there are some variations from year to year, and from election to election, on the whole, there has been a systematic omission of a select number of issues. The subjects most often censored since 1976 are political, corporate, international, and military issues. Following are the number and percentage of all 200 *Censored* stories by subject matter—from 1976 to 1995:

Type of Story	No. of Stories	Percentage
Political	64	32.0%
Corporate	37	18.5%
International	30	15.0%
Military	28	14.0%
Environment	15	7.5%
Health	13	6.5%
Media	7	3.5%
Economy	5	2.5%
Education	1	.5%

It was interesting to explore whether there was a difference in the number of *Censored* stories by subject and by political administrations. And there was. There were significantly more political, international, and military stories exposed by the alternative media during the Reagan and Bush Administrations than during the Carter and Clinton Administrations. Conversely, there were significantly more corporate and environmental subjects exposed during the Carter and Clinton Administrations.

Although there is no fully reliable way to explain these differences, one could speculate that there may have been more reasons or opportunities to expose political, international, and military matters while Reagan and Bush presided over the nation. Or, perhaps Carter and Clinton were more effective in monitoring these sectors during their administrations. Or it could be that alternative news media, often used as our sources, were more interested in investigating political, international, and military issues during the Republican Administrations and similarly with corporate and environmental issues during the Democrats' incumbency.

However, the most disturbing result of this analysis is the number of issues that have still not been addressed by the major media since Project Censored first raised them.

Of the 200 *Censored* issues, more than three quarters can still be classified as overlooked or censored by the mainstream media. Just 46 of the original stories have since received significant attention by the press. Some of the issues from the late 1970s that have been addressed include: acid rain, the fight over who controls the oceans' resources, freezing the elderly to death for non-payment of utility bills and the commercialization of the Public Broadcasting System (PBS). Examples among the 150 issues that haven't been addressed include problems as near at hand as hazardous over-the-counter drugs and as far from home as the Indonesian repression in East Timor.

By ignoring many critical issues in the past twenty years, the main-stream media have lost the confidence of the American people. Newspapers and network television news programs have lost many thousands—perhaps millions—of readers and viewers as recorded by circulation figures and television ratings. So many that there is an industry term for the phenomenon: they call it "The Vanished."

However, it is still not too late to attempt to affect some change; we have an abiding faith in the will of the American people to want to know what is really happening in society and, when so informed, to pressure politicians to do something about it. Ironically, although Project Censored has achieved international recognition for its annual analysis of news media self censorship, one of America's leading journalism reviews has refused to cover the project. *The Columbia Journalism Review*, published by the school of journalism at Columbia University, has not reported on the project to this date.

The 20-year span of time represented by the 200 stories in this analysis also reminds us of the length of time it takes us, as a society, to recognize and deal with these problems, if indeed we ever do make the effort. Some examples include acid rain, a problem which we knew about in the early 1970s but are only now starting to take seriously; the preventable deaths, injuries, and illness suffered in the workplace, which we knew about in 1976, but have yet to even acknowledge as a major national problem; the threat of male sterility caused by chemical pollution, which first came to light in 1977 and yet even in the face of some startling research revelations about the worldwide drop in male sperm counts, it has yet to be put on the national agenda.

The single, most plausible, explanation for our failure to address these and other problems in a timely manner is found in our economic system. Capitalism dictates the need to make a profit—often regardless of the means necessary to achieve that profit. In the future, this era will be seen as one where we truly let significant problems get out of hand, a circumstance that led to the deterioration of much of our health and environment, a time when we permitted the robber barons to strip what was left of our earth's resources, a time when we allowed politicians to sell their souls to the highest bidder, and a time when we were distracted from the real issues of the day by media-hyped events such as the O.J. Simpson trial and the Clinton-Lewinsky affair. It is a time when the few got wealthy at the expense of the many and Mother Earth was left to suffer.

Author Matthew Josephson warned us of the robber barons of the late 19th century, in his aptly titled book, *Robber Barons,* in 1934. Leading the capitalist ruling class of that period, from 1861 to 1901, were Andrew Carnegie, Jay Gould, Pierpont Morgan, John D. Rockefeller, and "Commodore" Cornelius Vanderbilt. And they were the people who provided the fodder for the great exposés by the turn-of-the-century muckrakers. In some cases, most notably with Andrew Carnegie, who eventually founded America's public library system, the revelations of the muckrakers had a beneficial influence on the robber-barons themselves.

In our time, the one great hope we have for a just and fair society is a "watchdog" press to protect us from the present day robber barons. But, as we saw in the second half of the 20th century, the media, with rising profit margins, have joined the ruling capitalist class themselves, and are now part of the problem. Today they are little more than lapdogs.

It is impossible to fully measure the impact that the failure of the press has had on society. How many thousands, or perhaps millions, of lives would have been saved if the press had done its job instead of ignoring or covering up the problem. The lack of car safety features, the lax regulatory control of the airline industry, the link between tobacco and cancer, and the corporate greed of baby formula manufacturers that led to the deaths of thousands of Third World infants, are just a few examples of where the media could have made a difference. How many millions of taxpayer dollars would have been saved if the media had exposed the savings and loan scandal in its infancy? And how much of our nation's resources could have been saved if the media had told the public about the scandalous Mining Act of 1872 that continues to give away valuable minerals and metals from federal lands for a song? Perhaps more than any other single story, the tobacco issue reveals the impact of a flawed press.

CENSORSHIP

Some 3 million people in developed countries died from smoking cigarettes in 1997 (about one person every 10 seconds). The death toll is expected to reach 10 million annually by 2020. An estimated 60 million men and 10 million women died in the last half century from smoking worldwide. These frightening statistics come from a book, *Mortality from Smoking in Developed Countries 1950-2000,* published in 1994 by Britain's Imperial Cancer Research Fund, the World Health Organization, and the American Cancer Society. This 553-page report took a critical look at the worldwide death toll of smoking over the long term.

One has to wonder how tobacco came to be such a massive worldwide killer before some measures were taken to try to eliminate it. It wasn't until August 23, 1996, after significant and continuing, albeit belated, media coverage of the hazards of smoking, that the Food and Drug Administration (FDA) issued a regulation restricting the sale of cigarettes and smokeless tobacco to children and teenagers. Finally, in mid-1997, as a result of media exposure, tobacco company whistleblowers, 17 class action suits, and 40 state lawsuits brought by state attorneys general, the tobacco companies capitulated. They agreed to pay more than $368 billion to repay Medicaid and other health costs and to launch anti-smoking educational and advertising programs. More important, the industry agreed to submit to unprecedented new rules that aim to dramatically scale back tobacco's hold over people's lives.[3]

---

[3]*Los Angeles Times,* June 2, 1997.

It didn't have to take that long. After all, the link between smoking and cancer was known at least as early as 1938. George Seldes, a muckraking journalist, was the first media watchdog to criticize the press for censoring the connection between tobacco and cancer. In 1938, he tried, without success, to get the press to report the results of a critical five-year study, involving nearly 7,000 persons, by Dr. Raymond Pear of the Department of Biology at Johns Hopkins University. The study revealed that smoking decreased life expectancy. In 1940, when Seldes started his investigative newsletter *In fact* (see p. 202), he launched a ten-year crusade against tobacco, publishing some 100 items on the subject in the newsletter. The media continued to ignore the issue and few of his exposés were ever published in the mainstream press.

Project Censored cited the dangers of smoking tobacco as a Censored subject in 1979 (tobacco lobby fights self-extinguishing cigarette), 1980 (tobacco companies censor the truth about cigarettes and cancer), 1984 (cigarette advertising and *The New York Times*), 1985 (tobacco industry appeals to children and the Third World; National Institute of Health seeks stronger tobacco plants) and 1995 (ABC spikes new tobacco exposé). But it wasn't until the mid-1990s that the dangers of cigarette smoking were widely publicized in the mainstream media.

How could it be that a massive killer was identified more than half a century ago but was allowed to continue to kill millions of people? One has to ask why our watchdog media, who knew about the problem since 1938, failed to provide an earlier warning about this killer.

JUNK FOOD NEWS

Cynics say that the media give the public what it wants—that is, what I call "junk food news," because the people are not interested in reading about the issues raised by Project Censored. We contend that the public is not given the opportunity to read or hear those stories in the mainstream media and thus, unfortunately, will absorb only what the mass media offer. As author/poet T. S. Eliot warned presciently in 1923, "Those who say they give the public what it wants underestimate the public taste and end up debauching it."

The inclusion of personality news, featuring people like Patty Hearst, Elvis Presley, John Lennon, Jim Bakker, Jeffrey Dahmer, O.J. Simpson, Tonya Harding, and Monica Lewinsky among the top ten mainstream news stories in the United States, surely validates T.S. Eliot's warning.

The difference the press can make by doing the right thing is evident in the story of hunger in Africa. "Hunger in Africa" was consistently nominated as a "censored" subject during the early 1980s. When I would ask journalists why they did not cover the tragedy unfolding there, they would say, "It is not news" or "Everyone already knows about starving Africans" or "Nothing can be done about it anyway."

Early in 1984, an ABC-TV News correspondent in Rome came upon information that led him to believe that millions of lives were being threatened by drought and famine in Africa. He asked the ABC home office in New York for permission to take his crew to Africa to get the story. The answer was no.

Later, a BBC television crew, traveling through Ethiopia, captured the horrifying reality of children starving to death. When the world saw the bloated stomachs and bony limbs of the starving children on their television sets, it sparked a worldwide reaction, including an internationally televised rock-fest called Live Aid and the musical anthem "We Are The World," that reportedly saved the lives of 7 million Ethiopians.

Indeed, I believe the media can make a difference. To test this thesis, I researched and wrote a book, *Stories That Changed America: Muckrakers of the 20th Century,* published in late 2000. The book recounts the lives and stories of 21 remarkable individuals whose probing and influential work forever changed the United States during the 20th century. Included are Ida Mae Tarbell, Upton Sinclair, Margaret Sanger, Rachel Carson, I. F. Stone, Betty Friedan, Michael Harrington, and Ralph Nader.

It is the media's responsibility, as true watchdogs of society with the unique protection of the First Amendment, to explore, compile, and present information that people should be aware of in a way that will attract their attention and be relevant to their everyday lives. And, when the media do this, people will read and respond to the issues raised. And journalists need not be embarrassed when they cash their paychecks.

The press does have the power to stimulate people to clean up the environment; to prevent nuclear proliferation; to force corrupt politicians out of office; to reduce poverty; to provide quality health care for all people; to create a truly equitable, fair, and just society. The press had the power to save the lives of millions of smokers more than 50 years ago. Fortunately, it is still not too late for the media to save millions of lives in the future. This is why we must all look to, prod and support a free, open, and aggressive press.

We have a free press in the United States guaranteed by the First Amendment and we have the best communications technology in world history. Now let us seek a more responsible and responsive press—a press that earns its First Amendment rights the old fashioned way. Indeed, a press that is not afraid to do a little muckraking. Then, and only then, will we have the information we need to build a more enlightened and responsive society.

CHAPTER 18
MTT
A Media Consumers' Movement

Eric Favey[1]

AT THE START OF THE TELEVISION ERA

As soon as television appeared in France, the newness of the issues raised by the medium, together with the high cost, hence the rarity, of the first TV sets, gave rise to "TV clubs" within family-centered associations and popular education movements, which were numerous, diverse, and active in the 1950s. At the same time, the first specialized magazines were published that presented and commented upon the programs of the one-and-only channel.

In those days, except for a few privileged persons, watching television was a group activity, in the first locations to be equipped with a set: the premises of an association or a café. The many TV clubs transferred to the televised spectacle the aims and methods that had developed within the film-club[2] movement, then thriving, dynamic, influential.

Thus the first associations of television viewers were formed. They did not survive as the ownership of TV sets became common in homes and turned collective watching into family or individual consumption. Thus the conditions disappeared that had made it possible for people to think in common, and exchange and discuss ideas, without which any associative action will decline and fail.

---

[1]President of MTT and General Secretary of the *Ligue de l'enseignement.*
[2]Where film fans watched and discussed quality movies, often classics.

The parallel development of commercial periodicals specializing in TV listings led to the demise of reviews published by associations. What thought pieces were produced were doomed to appear in publications with a tiny readership.

As any other technological innovation that is massively adopted and generates a new type of consumption, television drew contrasting responses from the "experts": some forecast a new golden age for news and culture; others announced the apocalypse, the onset of a sub-culture for the masses, serving various imperialisms. But the great majority of viewers, truly delighted by the new home entertainment, ignored those forecasts. So the many different attempts to create and develop a TV viewers' movement, capable of defending their interests, met with failure, until the late 1980s.

FROM STATE MONOPOLY TO COMMERCIAL NETWORKS

At that time, the multiplication of channels, the increase of air-time, the appearance of commercial television (saddled with the demands of advertising), more precisely the abrupt privatization of TF1,[3] transformed the nature, the functions, the organization of the French TV networks as well as their contents and the quality of programs.

Great efforts were made to keep the public unaware of the shift that was about to change its status from that of "television viewers" (to be informed, educated, and entertained) into that of "target-audience" to be sold to advertisers, who then became the only true customers to please. Nevertheless, a certain number of abuses and ethical lapses occurred, some of which were publicized, even punished, by the state regulatory agency, then known as the *Haute Autorité*.[4] They generated misgivings in the population that grew more and more intense and widely shared. Angry viewers argued that their failure to get their protests heard was proof of the contempt that television decision-makers felt toward them. Only ratings and shares were taken into account.

Already audience statistics were interpreted, without justification, as a reflection of what viewers expected and appreciated, when actually they were, and still are, nothing but a measurement of people's reaction to the programs put on the air by the various networks.

"DAYS OF THE VIEWER"

In 1988, the malaise caused by the deadlock in the dialogue of the public with television (and other media) had become so perceptible that the Minister for

---

[3]TF1 was the original (state-controlled) French network. In 1987, it was unexpectedly privatized by the conservative government.

[4]The equivalent of the FCC in the U.S.—later known as the CNCL and since 1989 as the CSA (Higher Council for Audiovisual Media).

Communications, Catherine Tasca, attending the "Summer University"[5] of Carcans-Maubuisson, suggested that the *Ligue de l'Enseignement*, the promoter of the meeting, conduct a national survey by organizing "Days of the Viewer" to give those who wished to do so a chance to express themselves.

A planning committee was set up that brought together the Ministry, various government agencies, the television networks, the provincial daily press, organizations of media people, all the existing viewers' associations and, more generally, all French associations likely to be interested in the project. A series of eight "Days of the Viewer" were organized in the various regions, the last taking place in Paris in June 1989. From these, a number of lessons were drawn:

- Television and the other media were criticized, not because of what they were, by nature, but because of the negative influence they seemed to have on the environment in which each of us exercises his/her personal, family, educational, social, civil responsibilities.
- Considering the general malaise, people were amazed at the refusal of television to acknowledge its responsibilities in the fields of education and culture.
- Existing associations of viewers were not representative: none of them possessed a network of local chapters. As a result, most of the participants in the public meetings came either from family associations or from associations dedicated to youth, culture, or leisure activities.

Thus an opportunity was provided for local and regional leaders of the National Union of Family Associations (UNAF) and of the *Ligue de l'Enseignement*, to meet each other—often for the first time.[6]

In the course of frank debates, they realized that, despite their different philosophies and commitment, their analyses of the situation created by the evolution of media tended to converge. They shared the same determination to do something as media took more and more space in the daily life of people.

The conclusions from those "Days of the Viewer," drawn at the "University of Communication" in Carcans led the UNAF and the Ligue to publish a common declaration.

---

[5]"Summer Universities" is a name given to conferences held during the Summer usually by political parties. The one in Carcans-Maubuisson, later in Hourtin, brings together people interested in media: politicians, media professionals, citizens associations.

[6]A traditional opposition has long existed in rural France between the village priest (supposedly anti-Republican) and the schoolmaster (supposedly anti-clerical). Originally the Ligue was a creation of school teachers while l'UNAF gathered Catholic families. [Editor's note.]

THE CREATION OF MTT

On March 7, 1990, in Paris, the two institutions published a draft agreement: without in any way sacrificing their autonomy and with due respect for each other's specific interests, they had decided to combine their efforts to promote a movement of media users. Thus was the MTT[7] association born.

In applying the agreement, the regional units of both institutions were encouraged to meet and take whatever initiatives could be useful to the success of the project. The appeal was immediately and widely heard. At the level of the 90-odd French administrative entities called *départements,* MTT groups multiplied fast, both in mainland France and outlying territories, creating synergy between the two associative networks that were the most numerous and most deeply rooted in the nation, the most representative of French society. The *Ligue de l'Enseignement* gathers 34,000 associations and 2.5 million members; the UNAF, 950,000 families within 8,500 family associations.

Later, in November 1997, an amendment to the constitution of MTT made it possible for other associations and for individuals to join MTT, especially youth groups and students' associations.

MAJOR ORIENTATIONS

Since its creation, MTT has considered its mission is to gather, organize and compare observations and criticisms expressed by users of the media belonging to the two associative networks. To that end, MTT has multiplied, as close as possible to the media users, locales open to all those who want to act so that media will better assume their three basic missions: to inform, to educate, and to entertain. So, with them and for them, MTT is active:

- in defending media users and insuring their free choice—as well as promoting pluralism in opinions, needs, and cultures.
- in increasing the educational quality of all programs, of video games, and CD-ROMs, especially those aimed at young people.
- in encouraging the sense of responsibility of media professionals by vigorously supporting those that show respect for the public.
- in better informing the public, and improving its knowledge of media, which is indispensable to understanding the various existing systems.
- in supporting the specific missions of public service television companies and the policy of state support for media.

---

[7]An awkward name: Médias, Télévision et Téléspectateurs (Media, Television and TV viewers).

- in getting the representative character of viewers' associations recognized by government, by state institutions, and by the firms in the communication industry.
- in campaigning for tighter regulation of the distribution of game software, videocassettes and CD-ROMs.

METHODS OF ACTION

MTT's major activity has been encouraging the cooperation, throughout the country, between the members of local groups, whether they belong to the UNAF or to the *Ligue de l'enseignement*. The groups organize awareness sessions, information or training meetings, to improve people's knowledge of audiovisual languages, to help them integrate media in their daily life and to use the new communication technologies reasonably.

The next method consists of so-called "critical observatories," survey operations whose purpose is to collect the analyses, thoughts, aspirations, and suggestions of the basic media consumer. MTT's main mission is to make heard the views of media users who consider they have a right, even a duty, to raise their voices and who join together to that end. The critical observatory presents not just an opinion poll among many others, but the free expression of a voluntary movement by media users.

The collected data are processed by MTT activists in cooperation with specialized academics and communication professionals. The results[8] are published and distributed among the political authorities and public agencies, among media decision-makers and media professionals.

Every year, an MTT Prize rewards those who have best taken into account the public's desire for quality, its interests, its tastes, and the respect that it deserves. That operation, perceived as positive by media professionals, stimulates a true dialogue, even a collaboration, with the people in charge of audiovisual media.

The MTT newsletter "La lettre des téléspectateurs" aims at informing but also at offering a forum for exchanges: every issue triggers reactions on the part of political leaders, media professionals, researchers, and professors—as well as simple users.

Meetings at all levels reflect the activity of the association:

- International conferences: In Paris in 1992, MTT organized, jointly with the United Nations and Unesco, a meeting on the theme of

---

[8]"Critical Observatories" published as of 2000: "Game Shows," "What Children Learn from TV," "TV News in Question," "How Media Inform Us," "TV and Emotions—The Public's Reaction to a Campaign on AIDS," "Getting an Education from TV: The French Educational Channel," "Media and Violence," "New Media . . . Access for All."

"News Globalization: the Duties and Rights of Citizens." In 1996, a one-day international conference took place in the premises of the Conseil économique et social.[9] The topic was "Public Broadcasting and Viewers/Listeners in the Era of Globalization," with the participation of representatives of Unesco, of the World Radio and Television Council, and from media consumer associations in Germany, Belgium, Canada, Spain, the United Kingdom, Japan, Hungary, Portugal, and Switzerland. That first meeting was followed by conferences organized in April 1997 at the Unesco in Paris, and in May 1998 in Cologne (Germany).

- Meetings with major institutions: regular exchanges take place with the powers-that-be, ministries, and Parliamentary committees; with the regulatory agency for broadcasting (CSA) and media professionals—on the occasion of symposiums and consultations. On December 15, 1997, for instance, MTT was invited to take part in a round table organized by the CSA on the topic of "Media and the Protection of Children".
- The MTT breakfasts in Paris, during which some media expert lectures and answers questions, enable members of the association to learn about the research and opinions of specialists.

Thus, MTT has developed strong links with the media which were formerly extremely skeptical towards consumers' associations. Its services have come to be often requested. Beyond the old issue of representativeness, what distinguishes MTT from similar undertakings is:

- the concentration of its efforts on the monitoring of television, because it has gradually oriented and influenced the whole media system.
- the determination to shed a restrictive, sometimes nostalgic, view of television, and take into account present-day research on the actual uses made of audiovisual media.
- the insistence on the human rights of TV viewers, of media users in general, whose role no longer can merely be seen as that of passive receivers or observers. They feel a vital need to be offered quality news and entertainment programs: those messages are indispensable to the exercise by them of all their responsibilities in society.

MTT wishes to find the citizen inside the reader/listener/viewer. That is a crucial concern in an environment in which the development of audiovisual systems, of information technologies, is more and more governed by market logic.

---

[9]A consultative assembly of some 200 experts which assists the French government in matters economic and social.

SECTION 4
Training and Research

CHAPTER 19
Journalism Education and Research as M*A*S

Arnold H. Ismach

Ethics may be defined as rules or standards for moral conduct or practice in a profession. In the sense that such standards are expected to govern behavior, it cannot be said that the practice of journalism in the United States is bound by ethical rules. There are no universally accepted rules, nor is there a mechanism to enforce those rules that do exist.

The news media resist any restriction on their freedom, and that includes standards of performance that include sanctions. The only restraint on press behavior that exists overtly are state and federal laws that prohibit libel and limit the use of obscenity. Even these limits are under frequent attack by the press.

There are, nevertheless, an array of ways in which the news media in the United States are influenced toward ethical conduct and responsible performance. It may be too grand to call them "media accountability systems," but they have the effect of guiding the performance of journalists. These mechanisms include:

- Ethics codes adopted by some professional organization, such as the Society of Professional Journalists, the National Association of Broadcasters, and the American Society of Newspaper Editors. These codes are proclaimed but no sanctions are imposed for their enforcement.
- Professional periodicals and journalism reviews, which report on ethical failures and offer essays on the subject.
- Professional organizations, such as those named above, which include discussions of ethics at their annual meetings and discuss the subject in organizational publications.

- Press councils—there are only three remaining in the United States—which examine complaints about media performance.
- Ombudsmen, or reader's representatives, who deal with complaints directed toward their own publications.
- Coverage in the press itself of media transgressions, through news stories, analytical articles and letters from readers.
- Market forces, often revealed through research, which may influence the behavior of news media.
- Commercial influence, for example, from advertisers.
- Mid-career education of journalists, generally sponsored by media centers or institutes that are financed by industry.
- Workshops and short courses for journalists sponsored by state and regional press associations as well as by colleges and universities.
- Finally, journalism education programs in colleges and universities that lead to academic degrees in journalism or related fields.

Of this collection of forces that influence and mediate press behavior, none is a system in the scientific sense of producing observable and predictable outcomes. But each in its own way plays a role in shaping media performance, having a cumulative effect that leads to responsible journalism.

Several of these influences are relatively new. Discussions of ethics in trade journals and professional publications, for example, were not common 30 years ago. Similarly, only recently have we seen a willingness in the news media to examine publicly questions about press ethics and performance. Mid-career programs, workshops and conferences did not include sessions on ethics until the 1970s and 1980s.

But ethics and responsibility are a frequent theme when journalists gather these days. There is a widespread belief among reporters and editors that the press has improved greatly on these matters since World War II, although the public apparently doesn't share in that assessment. Public trust and confidence in the news media, as measured in opinion surveys, has declined substantially in the last 30 years.

I tend to agree with the assessment of most journalists. The degree of media responsibility and the level of ethical performance have improved significantly in the past generation. I would also argue that the improvements can be attributed largely to the influence of journalism education on the media work force. I will devote the remainder of this chapter to advancing that argument.

Journalism schools have become the principal developers of professional journalists, particularly for newspapers. This was not always true. Even though journalism schools were established at universities in the early part of this century, the American press did not significantly limit their hiring to graduates of such schools until after World War II. Only in the last quarter of a century have newspapers hired more than half of their news employees from journalism schools.

It is estimated that about 85% of newsroom employees hired by newspapers today are journalism graduates. This is up from 65% in the early 1980s. Because larger newspapers hire only those with prior experience, most of the new graduates go to the small- and medium-sized daily newspapers.

Because of the influx of journalism graduates, well above half of the total newsroom workforce is now in that category. In a recent survey of daily newspapers, more than half of the senior editors reported that they were journalism school graduates. The percentage is higher among their subordinates.

If the level of ethical sensitivity and responsibility has been rising among journalists since 1980, and if the number of journalists trained in professional schools has also risen during the same period, the correlation between the two is evident.

The graduates of journalism schools bring with them into the newsroom both the techniques and values that were learned in the classroom. Examining the textbooks used in journalism schools, it is clear that those values include a strong expectation that journalists, above all, provide balance in their stories. That they seek out opposing viewpoints on issues. That they be fair.

It is true that journalists are also strongly influenced by what they experience on the job. New reporters are resocialized by their employers and colleagues to behave in certain ways, and those ways may be counter to classroom learning. If that were the dominant influence on news practice, however, we would never see a change in that practice. And there is a consensus among press professionals today that ethics and responsibility have improved markedly. Therefore, the only apparent factor that would account for the change is the new workforce, trained in journalism school. The effect of their education is evidenced by a new climate that demands responsibility and ethical behavior. It is the rare editor or publisher today who would order clearly unethical behavior from employees. They know that it would be protested.

What is it about journalism education that would account for this new sensitivity to ethics and responsibility? There are a number of activities in journalism schools that lead to that result. Let's examine some of them:

- The classroom is the principal source of socialization. Most professional schools offer courses in news ethics, usually as an elective. But most other professional courses also include discussions of ethics as a component.
- An increasing number of journalism educators have taken a scholarly interest in the study of media ethics. Since the 1970s, the publication of books on ethics have increased from one or two a year to one almost every month or two.
- These same educators are speaking at conferences sponsored by professional associations and mid-career centers, taking their messages directly to the working press.

- Workshops and conferences are conducted by journalism schools for the working press. This occurs in all sections of the United States, with media ethics often an explicit topic.
- Some schools have established centers for the study of ethics and related concerns. One such program is at the University of Minnesota, where the Silha Center for the Study of Media Law and Ethics sponsors conferences and produces publications.
- Academic research and essays about ethics appears in the scholarly journals of the field, principally *Journalism & Mass Communication Quarterly*, the *Newspaper Research Journal, Journalism Educator* and *Mass Comm Review.*
- These same academic researchers will also write about these subjects in trade and professional publications, such as *Columbia JR*, *presstime*, and the *American JR*. (The two reviews, by the way, are published under the auspices of journalism schools, and are widely read by working journalists.)

There are two other ways in which journalism educators may influence the working press on the subject of ethics. One is by inviting professionals to campus as visiting lecturers or adjunct instructors, thus exposing them to academic thought on the subject. The other is the increasing use of journalism educators by news organizations as consultants or newsroom "coaches," thus bringing the academic perspectives directly into the workplace.

Of all of these activities, I believe that two are more influential sources of journalistic responsibility than the others. One is publishing in professional periodicals and the other is what occurs in the classroom. The working press read their own journals, and the classrooms are filled with tomorrow's working press.

Many of the other activities in journalism schools reach only limited audiences. My school, for example, annually presents a public lecture devoted to journalism ethics and responsibility. It is usually given by a nationally known figure, either academic or professional. The press is invited to attend, but rarely do we attract more than 15 or 20 from the immediate area.

At Oregon, we also present an annual seminar for working journalists. None of the two-day programs has been about ethics per se, but all have dealt with that question in the topics covered, which have ranged from reporting on AIDS to the use of political polls.

Also, conferences and workshops are few in number relative to the number of people at work in journalism. Although there is increasing interest in mid-career training among editors, it is doubtful that more than one in ten staff members attend such programs in any given year. This reality adds emphasis to the importance of college training as an influence in journalistic values.

Although specific programs vary somewhat in the approximately 125 four-year journalism programs at U.S. colleges and universities, most have common features. A typical program of study for a student preparing for a career in newspaper or magazine journalism would look something like this:

- Introduction to Mass Media (structure of media industries and current social issues involving the media)
- History of Journalism
- Mass Media Law
- Writing for the Media (an introductory course)
- Information Gathering (basic techniques, from interviewing to the use of electronic databases)
- Visual Communication (principles, theory, and practice, on an introductory level)
- Beginning Reporting
- Intermediate Reporting
- Advanced, or Specialized, Reporting—News Editing
- Journalism Ethics
- Public Opinion or Communication Theory (focusing on the effects of mass communication)

Typically, journalism majors take 10 to 12 courses. The remainder of their college programs usually consists of a wide variety of courses in the liberal arts and sciences. Journalism majors are often encouraged or required to take much of their college work in these fields: Literature, History, Economics, Political Science, Sociology, Psychology, a basic science such as Biology, and a foreign language.

In all, about one-fourth of a journalism major's total course work will be in journalism, the remaining three-fourths in the arts and sciences. In my school, we offer more than 40 journalism courses to undergraduates each year. These include courses in advertising, public relations, and radio/television news and well as in print journalism.

It is doubtful that any journalism student goes a week without a discussion of ethics and press responsibility in some class. Specialized courses in ethics have proliferated. By one count, approximately half of the schools of journalism and mass communication offered ethics courses in 1986.[1] In addition, courses on journalism history, law, and media issues—required courses in most journalism schools—regularly deal with ethics and responsibility. Naturally, questions of ethics arise in professional skills courses such as reporting and editing, with regularity.

Journalism education is a major enterprise in the United States. There are approximately 185 member schools and programs in the Association for Education in Journalism and Mass Communication (AEJMC), the principal academic organization. Of them, approximately half are accredited by a national council that examines, among other criteria, the adequacy of instruction in ethics. Journalism is also taught at perhaps 200 more institutions of higher education, but those programs are generally limited to a handful of courses.

---

[1]Lucinda Davenport, *Syracuse Scholar*, vol. 10, no. 1, p. 85.

Enrollments in journalism nationally have been about 80,000 during the 1990s, with perhaps a fifth of those enrolled in newspaper journalism. The remainder are in allied communication fields, such as broadcast journalism, advertising, and public relations.

From these numbers, it can be seen that the principal journalism programs may graduate as many as 4,000 young professionals each year, ready for jobs in the newsroom. All have been exposed to the prevailing values on campus dealing with journalism ethics.

Despite the evident influence of journalism schools on today's media workforce, many professional journalists are reluctant to attribute the current elevated state of press responsibility to the schools. There is, in fact, a great deal of tension between many professionals and the schools that feed their employment pipeline. Jack Hart, the newsroom training director of a large daily newspaper in Oregon, writes in the *Newspaper Research Journal* that "alienation between professionals and journalism schools has reached the stage of open hostilities in some parts of the country."[2]

Nevertheless, the principal professional organizations display at least a love-hate relationship with journalism education. The Newspaper Association of America, the American Society of Newspaper Editors and the Associated Press Managing Editors association, sponsor journalism education committees that each year produce reports that are distributed widely.

One such report, by the ASNE in 1990, grew out of a survey of editors. Ethics emerged as one of the dominant concerns of editors. Four of five editors said the study of media ethics was "very important" or "important" in the training of journalists. There was higher support for ethics instruction than for the study of media law, where fewer than half said it was very important or important. Nine of 10 editors said that ethics courses are useful in journalism programs—a higher percentage than for any subject area other than professional skills courses such as reporting.

Despite these beliefs, only about half the editors said they had a preference for journalism school graduates in their hiring decisions. The other half said they would be as likely to hire general liberal arts graduates for reporting jobs, despite the lower likelihood that the liberal arts graduates would have been exposed to the examination of journalistic ethics, let alone reporting and editing techniques.

Looking over the reports of the education committees of these professional organizations for a period of years, a pattern of criticism emerges. Editors complain that there is not enough study of the liberal arts in journalism programs, and in an apparent contradiction, complain also that there is not enough practical skills training in those same programs. The editors also argue that

---

[2]Jack Hart, "The Classroom and the Newsroom: Missed Opportunities for Journalism Education," *Newspaper Research Journal,* Fall 1990, vol. 11, no. 4, pp. 38-50.

more working professionals should be used as classroom teachers in preference to academics, and they complain that journalism programs place too much emphasis on communication theory. But beyond those generalizations, there is not much consensus among editors about what journalism schools should and should not be doing.

Of course, there is not much more agreement among journalism educators about what their programs should attempt. Like the press itself, educators reserve for themselves the right of autonomy.

Tension has always been present between academics and professionals in many fields—business, law, and medicine as well as journalism. It may always be thus. But on at least one subject, there seems to be agreement between journalists and journalism educators: the central importance of the study of ethics and press responsibility. That is what editors say they want to emphasize, and that is what journalism schools are emphasizing today.

CHAPTER 20
Journalistic Training and Professional Ethics in France

Michel Mathien

In France, thinking and debate over M*A*S is much less developed than in the United States. Clearly. But we may hope that a move in the right direction has started as a consequence of the crisis of confidence triggered by the Gulf War: at that time many questions were asked about the functions and the limits of the information provided by the mass media.

I have heard that during the 1980s about a book a month was published in the United States, dealing with media ethics. That clearly shows how much the two countries are out of sync; in France the interest in ethics only emerged in 1991. The only media that regularly cover ethics and questionable behavior in the various journalistic occupations are the union bulletins. The concern for making media, and journalists, responsible had long existed in professional circles but they had, until then, claimed exclusive rights to it. It was difficult for outsiders, be they media consumers or expert observers of the media, to be recognized as worthy of expressing an opinion on the subject .

That feature of the psychology of journalism needs to be taken into consideration—even though self-satisfaction, self-justification, and self-regulation have obviously never contributed to the solution of relational problems between a profession and the community in which it operates.

THE TRAINING OF JOURNALISTS IN FRANCE

Priority to "On the Job Training"

There is no doubt about the influence of the training of journalists. But its impact should not be exaggerated because of the importance given nowadays to media managers and marketing men, who are more concerned with PR than with information. Those people are rarely journalists, and too often they have no professional concerns but those they were taught in management institutes and business schools. Today, those decision makers take an ever larger part in deciding editorial contents. They tend to keep close watch on the production of media goods and to force their logic upon it: news for them is nothing but a commodity. Driven by commercial ambitions, growing ever more demanding as the environment gets more competitive, they are to be found in all media, and especially in specialized consumer magazines and in private broadcasting. Their approach to the news conflicts, to a large extent, with the training of journalists—which, it is fair to say, does not always pay enough attention to the economic reality of news and to the corporate need for sales.

In France, the Departments of Mass Communications and the vocational schools for journalists that are accredited by the unions and the associations of proprietors (i.e., only eight college/university level institutions in 2000) every year turn out about 15% of the total number of the new recipients of the professional ID card[1] as opposed to 50% in the United States. The number of young journalism graduates who every year enter the profession,[2] 12% in 1999, is very much lower than the total number of new entrants in the profession. Proportionately, the number of graduates has hardly increased over the last 20 years, whereas the number of holders of a professional ID card has more than doubled (from 12,500 in 1971 to 32,000 in 2000).

In other words, the profession is very open, especially in the print sector. That is a principle to which journalism remains faithful. It forms part of its status (as defined by the law of March 29, 1935):[3] there are no conditions of age, culture, degree, or training to enter it. That tradition does not seem about to be reassessed judging by the annual statistics of recruitment. It corresponds to a common wish of journalists and of their employers. So the social and professional consciousness of journalists depends upon the company acting as a domi-

---

[1]Whoever earns more than half his/her income from journalism is entitled to a professional ID card, which is delivered by a Commission consisting of representatives of publishers and journalists.

[2]Statistical surveys of journalists are rare. The latest to present a full picture was done by the IFP (Université de Paris-2) entitled *Les journalistes français en 1990: Profils et Parcours,* Paris, Editions Panthón Association, 2001.

[3]That law created the professional ID card, and granted journalists certain guarantees (minimum wage, vacation time, etc.).

nant training institution. I refer to "company" in the sense of a socio-technical complex with its culture, its history, its modes of action, with specific working conditions and a specific internal network of human relationships—which the non-graduate journalist will be able to discover during his internship.[4]

Media firms in general are not famous for organizing the initial reception of young professionals. With some exceptions, media do not schedule workshops or seminars for the "interns" who train on the job or who have just come from the schools. Only the Centre de perfectionnement des journalistes in Paris organizes some training sessions for working apprentices to facilitate their professional integration. Occasionally now, other schools follow suit. But not all future journalists can take advantage of it—far from it. The only area of real training is the workplace, to which may be added some collaboration with colleagues from other media while covering the news. The training is little more than technical and professional. Too often the apprenticeship is even limited to the few tasks associated with a particular work station. The role of chance is seldom compensated by measures that would promote contacts and the exchange of experiences or by the influence of a tutor or internship director. Admittedly, the intern is quite often encouraged to move around in the various departments, but it can happen that he/she will stay where he/she was first placed simply because he/she is needed there. That is true especially in the regional press and in local radio stations.

So the young journalist will begin his/her career in those circumstances and will then develop a view on the general philosophy of his/her chosen job. It is in the structured microcosm of the company, with its sociology and its psychology, in the structured microcosm also of the newsroom, that he/she will learn the principles and rules of media ethics, learn how to respect them or ignore them in the field, according to the instructions he/she will be given or to the overall policy that he/she will gradually perceive.

In that environment, the degree of unionization of the journalists in the company, or the presence of a *société de rédacteurs* (see p. 233), can also play a formative part and buttress his/her personal ethics. But let us not expect too much. Unionization is not doing well at all. And, with a few exceptions, the sociétés de rédacteurs, considering the high hopes they carried in the 1970s, have met with failure, which the profession (out of shame or nostalgia) is still reluctant to acknowledge.

Does not such training (a kind of shaping by the "company mold") induce a narrow vision of the profession, submissiveness on the job, and eventually an escape from the news media into corporate and institutional communication? This often occurs simply because the beginner does not have enough cultural baggage to do any more than report mechanically or hold up a mike.

---

[4]The rookie reporter must start as an intern. He/she will obtain his/her ID card after a trial period of one to two years depending on whether he graduated from one of the accredited schools.

The employer, the only judge of the satisfactory conclusion of the intern's train-ing, will finally ask the "Commission nationale de la carte d'identité des jour-nalistes professionnels" to grant the precious document that recognizes his/her status as a journalist. But these days, employers are increasingly reluctant to do that: they extend probation periods and short-term contracts.

For all that, one cannot pass a clear judgment on the personal qualities of journalists caught in such a program. They may have had, when they entered it, more of a college and university education than their colleagues who went through the schools. Actually, journalists are very good at boasting about their initial background, whichever it was, and flaunt superiority over a colleague by questioning the quality of the training he/she acquired.

Initial training on campus is no panacea, though it is supposed to enable journalists to distance themselves in relation to their employer, thanks to the abstract and practical knowledge they are supposed to have acquired. But quite often, the pedagogical project of the school is shaped in a strictly profes-sional, even utilitarian, perspective, to serve the industry. Rarely in those estab-lishments is the ultimate purpose of the profession debated or its place in soci-ety by the side of publishers.

Journalism Schools or Training Centers

Those centers prepare only a small proportion of the future full-time journalists. They grant 300 to 400 degrees every year to students who have had to pass an entrance examination, which is highly competitive because of the attractiveness of the field: only one tenth of candidates are admitted to the Centre universitaire d'enseignement du journalisme, CUEJ, in Strasbourg, for instance.

The schools do raise awareness of ethical issues in the media. Certainly, they are places where such issues are debated. However, it must be acknowledged that no specific teaching is devoted to "social responsibility," indispensable for a full grasp of a trade or profession—except from the view-point of media law. Ethical awareness is thus raised by way of the 29 July 1881 General Law on the Press, which deals with press misdemeanors and crimes, especially against public institutions and individual citizens (libel, insult, etc.). That legal knowledge, quite useful on the job, is usually imparted by some law school professor or by a practicing lawyer.

The various practical aspects of ethics in the daily journalistic routine are dealt with on the occasion of workshops, devoted, for instance, to making experimental newspapers. They are introduced by professional news people, full time or part time, who do most of the teaching in those schools. In that field, we find a process of acquiring know-how similar to that in other fields, similarly assumed by professionals. To a large extent, this is on-the-job training again. University professors hardly play any part.

Ethical thinking, which should be rooted in a global concept of journalism or of the role of information mediated by professionals, lacks any vigor. And yet enough questionable practices and serious crises appear on the news scene to justify some in-depth teaching. By analyzing how facts are treated and comparing the process with the values of the trade (or, more accurately, of the many jobs linked to journalism), such teaching could contribute to the development of an ethics of journalism and of media. Nor is material lacking in daily professional life: the growing influence of public relations services and of the directors of communication of institutions and corporations; the old usage of accepting freebies and small favors in return for publishing (or not publishing) a piece of information; the abuse of well-paid casual jobs, mainly by broadcasters but which is spreading to the print media.

The Association of Economic and Financial Journalists regularly expresses concern over the close links between journalists and companies. Similarly, journalists' unions, in their internal newsletters or in "white papers," denounce practices contrary to basic ethical principles (e.g., junkets offered by firms out to obtain favorable coverage). The 1918 French code of ethics (revised in 1938) stresses that a journalist accepts "the jurisdiction of his peers only, who are sovereign in matters of professional honor." Alas, in the face of the problems just mentioned, that jurisdiction has never made itself felt clearly and efficiently.[5] And at the start of the new century, the unions still would not hear about it.

The manipulation of news during the 1989 Romanian revolution (with the hoax of a mass slaughter in Timisoara) was later highlighted by Western media. But this did not prevent further manipulation during the Gulf crisis, then war (e.g., the case of incubators in Kuwait City that Iraqi soldiers were said to have unplugged). The fabricated "scoops," the frantic competition in which many journalists have gotten involved, whether they like it or not, because of choices made, of stages set, by businessmen or merchants of so-called *communication,* are topics that should be dealt with regularly.

What needs to be done is not constantly to add to the list of prohibitions in a code of ethics. What is necessary is to start trains of thought within the educational establishments and then extend them outside of the schools and beyond professional circles. Morality cannot be defined solely by one category of participants in mass communication. The whole of society must be involved in the continuation of the debate: thanks to spectacular scandals in the last few years, the ethics of social communication belongs in the public sphere.

---

[5]The Card Commission assumed that function for a few months after the Liberation of France in 1944. It attributed the card only to journalists who had not been involved with the enemy and the Vichy government. But the Commission has in fact no moral competence.

SOME ADVANTAGES FOR JOURNALISTS AND THEIR PUBLICS

To Face a Crisis of Confidence

The debate can only contribute to increasing the credibility of journalists, and hence improve the trust that the various publics place in journalism. An annual opinion poll[6] published since 1988 highlights the distrust media users feel towards journalistic contents.

Media Users That Distrust Media Contents

	1987	1988	1996	2000	2001
Television	37%	32%	49%	50%	47%
Newspapers	47%	38%	48%	45%	46%
Radio	37%	28%	33%	35%	36%

That disrepute, which has varied but rarely abated over more than 10 years, cannot but further stimulate thinking on media ethics and M*A*S, especially within journalism schools and media companies. Also, there are still a few institutions, here and there, that should try and recover their responsibilities in defining editorial policies. I mean the sociétés de rédacteurs.

ETHICS ASSOCIATED WITH GENERAL CULTURE

In a 1991 article published by the prestige daily *Le Monde*, the CEO of *l'Alsace*, a regional daily for which I worked for over ten years, acknowledged that when he took over the management of the company he had thought he could "produce a newspaper without journalists" and he admitted that he had been wrong ![7] Now, in the context of heightened competition, quality news is more and more expensive and still requires enlightened professionals to select and process it. Those professionals, contrary to what was believed in the schools in the 1980s, need a high level of culture, well adapted to their field of activity.

Today, training centers tend to return to "general culture" which they had forsaken in order to concentrate on technical and professional courses, which still fill three quarters of the available time. For that abandonment, which never was total, the justification claimed was, first, the "excessive" previous university training of students (3, 4 or 5 years), whereas the formal requirement to take the entrance exam was a degree given after two years of study. And, sec-

---

[6]Done by the SOFRES agency for the daily *La Croix* and the television guide *Télérama*.
[7]*Le Monde*, 10 April 1991.

ond, was the desire on the part of both employers and unions to increase the teaching of techniques; they wanted, and still want, beginning journalists who are operational immediately.

The Gulf crisis underlined the huge deficiencies of journalists in many fields, whether they were reporting from the battle field or were sitting in a TV studio: a poor knowledge of geo-strategic problems, of security issues, of military affairs, besides their ignorance of history, of Islam and other religions in that part of the planet, of the diversity of populations and cultures in the Arab world. Media are responsible for publicizing news that is accurate, honest, balanced, neither partisan nor ambiguous. So general culture must recover a major position in the syllabi of schools. Academics and researchers must play a more important part. The ethics of journalism and of media firms cannot be separated from an ever-renewed knowledge of things and beings.

The Kosovo crisis, with the NATO military intervention from March 24 to June 10, 1999, showed that the problems observed during the Gulf War were still there. Journalists were faced with propaganda, disinformation, and manipulation by Slobodan Milosevic's Serbian government, and also by NATO officials. The conflict in Afghanistan, following the events of September 11, 2001, intensified all those problems in the U.S. and the West in general. They rediscovered that reporting the news is quite different in an armed conflict and in time of peace; that, in the guise of informing, sources try to get a message through. So training in the handling of controversial and powerful sources, even within democratic societies, remains crucial.

The Strengthened Cohesion of a Profession

Lastly, a revival of ethical thinking would present another advantage: that of giving substance to a "profession" that, strictly speaking, is not one. There lies the whole problem of where journalists stand in society. They do not form a profession recognized by the community, a profession with rules endowed with the force of law, enforced by peers through well-defined channels. The statute that French journalists derived from the Act of 1935 is ambiguous, for it remains unfinished: the law makers intended to create a counterbalance to the power of publishers but never did. Publishers have in no way lost their prerogatives as CEOs, legally and practically. Nowadays, the employers, who never endorsed the code of ethics, and the journalists themselves, are not keen to create a regulatory body with an ethical mission whose pronouncements might challenge their manner of processing information.

In other words, M*A*S need to stake out, claim, and enlarge a domain in the public forum. Their questioning of media and journalists (the two cannot be separated) is bound to be dynamic, to stimulate progress. In a nutshell, the social regulation that media achieve through the mere dissemination of news should find in the M*A*S a counterweight to their excesses and errors, also based on the general interest.

The move towards accountability, which the M*A*S have inaugurated, is there to remind us that information, whatever the motives for its processing and distribution, must remain in the service of society. Unavoidably, all citizens must take part in the ethical debate on the future of society, locally and globally. Journalists cannot object to it without jeopardizing their profession, especially in the present environment, when means and networks of communication multiply, when new journalistic jobs and new ways of giving information are emerging.

CHAPTER 21
Research and the Improvement of Media

Michel Souchon

Can research be a means of improving the media? A vast question—to which I can merely suggest a few answers. I wish first to examine the research that is done within the media (or done directly to serve them), what in English is called "audience research." That type of applied, professional research is not supposed to improve media: quite the contrary—think of the repeated denunciations of the "dictatorship of ratings." I would like (a) to show that such studies can, on the contrary, contribute to making contents better. Taking an example, I will then maintain (b) that the notion of audience is far more complex than is often thought, and I will suggest different ways to count faithful viewers in order to measure the quality of programs. I will then make (c) a few observations on quality itself: it can be analyzed, and research can help reviewers to do their job in an intelligent and constructive way by providing them with criteria. Lastly, I will examine (d) the research done in places independent of the media: what is it and to what extent can researchers contribute to improving the service given by the media to the public?

A firm belief links those remarks, which may seem a little unconnected: there is not "good research" on the one side, which would be critical, accusatory and independent, and, on the other side "bad research," which, unconsciously or in its own interests, acts as an accomplice of the professionals in their efforts to make the public stupid.

Of course, I shall deal with those issues from my usual observation post—the study of television audiences—and will restrict myself to one category of actors: television viewers. I hope that although my scope is narrow, it will make understanding easier.

A. AUDIENCE RESEARCH AND QUALITY

The French use the phrase *étude d'audience*, which confines research, or might confine it, strictly to polling work aiming at counting newspaper readers, radio listeners, and television viewers. The word audience, in English, has a wider meaning: it refers to the public. So "audience research" covers all work aiming at a better knowledge of the public's behaviors, schedules, tastes, expectations—a far wider field than that of "downstream" studies of results obtained. It must be stressed, I believe, that audience research should not be—in fact is not—reduced to a mere analysis ex post facto of the success or failure of programs with the public. Hence, it cannot be limited to work after programs are put on the air. As important—maybe more important—is work done "upstream," studies made before production, scheduling, and broadcasting.

Any analysis of French society is useful to program executives, as 95% of French people live in a household with at least one TV set. They need to know the availability of the various groups in the population depending on the time of day, the day of the week, the season of the year; to know what interests the available people have—whether they read newspapers, magazines and books, what are the topics of their conversations, their leisure activities and cultural practices, and so forth.

It seems obvious to me that those audience research studies done upstream are means to improve service to the public by broadcasting programs that better correspond to its expectations. Far from me to try to persuade you that all the people in charge of our television channels are totally disinterested persons entirely devoted to the public welfare. But it is not possible to ignore that television is clearly meant to address the public, to help them in their lives by making them laugh or dream and by satisfying their curiosity, to broadening their horizons, giving them the information they need to understand the world and mankind. When you are in charge of audience research, you must show whoever commissioned the study that they quite often have an overly narrow view of what the public expects from television.

I believe that similar remarks can be made about "downstream" studies, those that aim at finding, after programs are aired, how they have been received.

Allow me here a short detour to point out that there is no contradiction between audience and quality. No legitimate marketing study has ever demonstrated a public preference for superficiality, entertainment and trivia," Philip Meyer writes (see p. 295). I fully endorse that statement. And yet a very common belief is that audience and quality vary in inverse proportion to each other. The two phrases "mediocrity of television" and "dictatorship of ratings" are equivalent—you can use them indifferently in conversation.

Two examples illustrate the phenomenon. A journalist, during the crisis at the end of 1990, the Gulf War being imminent, expressed what many in public broadcasting thought by saying that Hervé Bourges, then at the head of France-Télévision, the French equivalent of BBC-TV, would have to find his way out of a dilemma: "Must public service television aim at ratings and shares or should it show itself to be different?"[1] Similarly, *Le Débat*, a high-brow review, for its special issue on public television (September-October 1990) questioned various personalities in the following terms: "Do you think that public broadcasting should resign itself to a minority viewership by caring about quality before all—and should let big audiences go to private television networks? Do you believe, on the contrary that it should compete with the private networks?" Replies varied, but none of the people surveyed disputed the terms of the questionnaire.

Of course, it will argued that, although people never say to pollsters that they prefer what is mediocre, actually every evening their behavior, their choices in front of the TV set, prove that they do: they say they prefer documentaries to variety shows but three times as many of them watch the latter as the former. To that objection, there are two possible replies. The first, slightly provocative, is that variety shows are often better made, of a better "quality" than documentaries. The second is that documentaries very often are aired later, at a time when the total number of viewers is three times smaller. Let us combine the two replies: as documentaries are aired at 11 p.m., their producers believe they do not need to take the prime time "general" public into account. There begins a vicious circle: programs scheduled late are therefore not popular; being not popular they have to be scheduled late and so forth.

To apply to television an interpretation grid that suggests audience and quality are irreconcilable leads into a dead end. It locks television people into a "double bind," as described by the Palo Alto theoreticians: whatever you do, it will be wrong. If your programs show quality, you will be accused of lacking audience, of being incapable of interesting the general public. If your programs do attract a large audience, then they will be judged to be mediocre. The only proper reaction is to reject the dilemma and to state that quality does attract audiences and will attract them more and more.

The wager can be won: when two or three networks schedule fiction and variety shows, quite a considerable portion of the public can decide to watch a more demanding program, provided it is capable of interesting them, touching their emotions, widening their horizons. That fraction of the public is important: people who watch television a lot do it because they truly need television, because they do not have at their disposal many other means of entertainment, information, leisure. So their expectations are very varied. As Denis McQuail puts it, television for them is *"an all-purpose medium."*[2] Because for them television caters to many expectations, they pick very diverse programs.

---

[1] In the daily *Libération*, 21 December 1990.

[2] In Denis McQuail et al., *Sociology of Mass Communications*, London, Penguin, 1972.

Entertainment, comedy, and games, certainly, but also news, documentaries, works of fiction that are funny or moving or profound.

Ratings and shares do not have to be an instrument of content degradation. Analyzing the figures given by meters leads to a rediscovery of a simple truth: expectations are extremely numerous, far more diversified than demagogues think or elitists think, strangely united in the same belief: the public is mediocre; its expectations are vulgar; it can only be attracted by bad television.

B. THE TELEVISION AUDIENCE: BETWEEN TWO METAPHORS

I wish to develop an example here and show how, concerning audiences, a little science will carry you away from quality, whereas greater knowledge will bring you back to it—as Pascal said of faith. You often hear remarks like "My program had a 10% audience . . ." Did you say "audience"? What is the audience of a program? Using "audience surveys," you can define and evaluate the audience of a program in many ways. The reach or *cumulative audience* (*cume*) consists of all the persons who have seen at least a portion of a program. Let us call "audience for entire program (AEP)" all the persons who have watched a program from start to finish. The *rating* or *average audience* is the number of people watching, on average, at any given moment of the program. And so on. You can refine further and subdivide. Let us be content, for the while, with those three indicators. The most commonly used indicator, by the networks and in the press, is the *average audience rating*.

As often happens, the dominant indicator gradually replaces reality: its partial character is ignored. Then, confusedly, what is called the "metaphor of the movie theater" establishes itself: "My program got a 10% (average) audience" can be translated into "5 million people watched my program." It is known that the figures of cumulative audience are far higher than those of the average audience, but this is forgotten in the movie theater metaphor. Hence the interest in (the need for?) using another indicator: the AEP. Then you discover that the movie theater metaphor applies only to some of the people included in the average audience and has to be supplemented by the shopping mall or the waiting hall metaphor: people come and go, enter and exit.

The case must be made for the use of the figures of the AEP. That far too neglected indicator has deserved our interest since the zapping era started with the remote control. The risk is that we may move too fast from the movie theater metaphor to that of the shopping mall. Maybe there are still some old-fashioned people who, secretly, almost ashamedly, do not watch television but do watch particular programs—just like in the film *Fahrenheit 451*, there were a few stubborn, clandestine, readers of books.

As that example shows, the audience that programs obtain is a phenomenon far less simple and one-dimensional than is often said. Studying the figures, trying better to understand what viewers think and say about programs, how they behave, how they live their relationship with television, analyzing what they do with what it gives them—all that can contribute to the improvement of television and enable those who produce the programs to find new avenues of communication.

C. QUALITY CAN BE STUDIED

Standing on the border-line between the applied research done by professionals and that done outside the media (by universities, research centers, think tanks etc.), let us say a few words on studies made of program quality. In after-dinner polite conversation about television, one cliché is that no one knows what quality is in television; that to talk about it is no less futile than (as the French say) "to discuss colors and tastes." I am opposed to the idea of grading programs for quality (from the Q grade used in the distribution of the fee money among networks after the French 1974 Broadcasting Act to repeated attempts more recently to devise quality ratings), but I do believe that there can be an agreement on criteria and the dimensions of television quality. It's somewhat like objectivity in journalism: some say it does not exist and yet it is clear that one report is more honest than another, because the reporter checked his/her sources, dug deeper in the archives, gives diverse opinions, and so on.

As regards television, it is possible, I believe, to agree, after analysis and debate, on the fact that one program is better than several others: best stage direction, best scenario, best dialogues, best scenery, as they say at awards ceremonies. Professionals are capable of evaluating their own work and that of their peers. Star reporters can tell when one of them has put in a lot of work at getting striking original pictures and when he/she has just dipped into the archives of photo agencies. Similarly, scheduling can be intelligent and inventive or dull and conventional (more or less inventive, of course, or more or less conventional—never totally one or the other). It is only in after-dinner conversations, among people who do not watch television, that all programs become all the same and uninteresting, that any series is worth any other and all are worthless. That's not true, of course: programs are not equivalent and some are much better than others. And because there is a difference, taste comes into play, which influences the understanding of the quality of television.

There, it seems to me, is a field that has not yet been explored enough. Television criticism in the print media has not yet come to maturity (with a few exceptions): it is too often written by people who do not like television enough, who do not know it well and have little esteem for those who watch it. Research on the theme of quality in its many dimensions would help critics play their part better: they would then have an indispensable function in the correlated improvement of programs and of viewers' choices.

D. ACADEMIC RESEARCH

In France, contacts between professionals and university researchers are neither frequent nor good, when they exist at all. What researchers in academe expect of the media is sponsorship, funding for their work. They find it hard to accept that they are not greeted with open arms. As for the professionals, they criticize the researchers for the unbearable slowness of their studies, ill adapted to the rhythm of media production, and also the very limited practical interest of their work. Also, professionals often echo R. K. Morton's remark (loosely quoted) on the difference between empirical and critical sociologists. The former say: what we come up with might not be interesting but it is true. The latter say: what we come up with might not be true but at least it's interesting!

Moreover, media professionals are sometimes under the impression that university research is still holding to the old mechanistic models according to which media tell us what to think and make us think what they say we should think. Funding such an archaic denunciation of media manipulation would be like welcoming people who hold a begging-bowl in one hand and a grenade in the other.

Clearly there is a misunderstanding: research on media effects has long been far more sophisticated. It has established that, although media do tell us what to think, they are not able to make us think that, because the reception of media messages is variable and selective; that, when you seek media influence, you find personal influence; and that when you seek evidence of change, you mainly find re-enforcement and so forth.

By analyzing the role and effect of media in our society in a more discriminating, more subtle manner, research could provide professionals with some enlightenment regarding how media operate and how their messages are received, which would help them to communicate better.

And even when research turns more critical, it is a useful, even a necessary, goad. Let's take a few examples among the objects of recent research. Some studies tend to show that the impact of media is important: the strong effects of media, it is stated, can only be discovered when an analysis is made of their re-enforcing role in the service of the status quo. That re-enforcement is the powerful effect of media (this idea is a re-appearance of the theories of "critical sociology" expounded years ago by the Frankfurt School and revived more recently by various authors such as Todd Gitlin).

Other researchers have shown that media, far from reducing cultural or informative gaps, make them even worse, by a cumulative process: knowledge goes to knowledge like money goes to money.

Studies have described how media act within our societies, stating that they have had a major importance and a strong impact because they "set the agenda" for us: they establish what we shall discuss, when and in what order of priority; they tell us what to think about, what to talk about. They all set what we are not to think about, or talk about, and thus lead us into a "spiral of silence"[3] that excludes some topics and personalities from the democratic debate.

Professionals can, of course, reply that it is easy to criticize and treat as negligible such research of the kind that I fleetingly mention here. But I believe it is wiser to take it into account. Although the results of university research are not all as valuable, some should trigger self-examination and some reassessments in the media world. There professionals could find useful food for thought in their ethical cogitation.

In short, it would be excellent if the two research production locales—the "on" and the "off," as they say in the famous theater festival of Avignon in Southern France, moved closer to each other and cross-fertilized. I said at the beginning that there was not "good research" on one side—research that is academic, critical, and radical—and, on the other side "bad research"—professional, well-integrated, an accomplice of media. Both can produce important or meaningless, useful or interesting conclusions. Collaboration, competition, exchange of services between the two sectors would certainly advance research and might contribute to improving the media.

---

[3]A concept developed in Germany by Elisabeth Noelle-Neumann in the 1970s.

CHAPTER 22
Research as a M*A*S
The Case of Newspapers
in the United States

Philip Meyer

In a free society, the marketplace is the ultimate accountability system. The efficiency of the marketplace depends on two factors: a non-monopolistic structure that guarantees consumers a choice and a two-way flow of information between prospective buyers and sellers. Market research is a useful, although perhaps not necessary, component of the information process.

For more than a century, newspaper owners benefited from an inefficient market. Production technology was capital intensive, discouraging competition. Advertiser support tended to cluster at the dominant newspaper in any given market, leaving the others to slowly die. By the end of the 20th century, only a few major U.S. markets had more than one traditional, central-city newspaper claiming its entire metropolitan area, and in those the process of consolidation through attrition of the weaker papers was continuing.

That situation left the dominant papers free of many of the constraints of the marketplace. Drawing 70 to 80% of their revenue from advertisers rather than readers, publishers had a market-driven motivation to provide a credible, prestigious environment for the advertising but there was not a strong linkage between reader preferences and newspaper content. The typical newspaper was too economically secure for that. Retail advertisers typically spend 1 to 2% of their gross revenues on advertising and newspapers remained the most efficient vehicle for retail and classified advertising—even after the development of broadcast media. Given those conditions, ownership of a newspaper was very much like having the power to levy a retail sales tax. Running a newspaper did not take much talent, and the economic incentives yielded publishers whose

energies were directed toward production efficiency: getting the product out of
the plant and on the customer's doorstep as regularly and cheaply as possible.

Publishers' meetings were dominated by speeches decrying the cost of
raw materials and sharing tips on cost cutting. It is therefore not surprising that
the market ethic never became fully developed during most of the life span of
the newspaper industry in the United States. Instead, a service ethic prevailed.
Responsible editors realized the importance of their function in a democratic
society and fought to give their readers the information they needed as citizens.
Whether or not the readers wanted this information or shared the editor's evaluation of what was important was of little or no concern. Editors took a paternal-
istic view in choosing the information to impart and believed that their responsibility ended once the choice was made. If the public did not know what was
good for it and did not spend the time or the energy to comprehend what the
editor was telling it, that was not considered the editor's fault. The editor was
more concerned with what his peers in publishing thought of the product than
with the opinions of the customers.

DECLINE OF THE SERVICE ETHIC

Cracks in the traditional service ethic began to appear in the 1970s. At the start of
that decade, market researchers—whose mission was primarily to produce evidence of newspaper readership for advertisers—began to notice that readership
was declining. The first bits of evidence were inconclusive—losses of a percentage
point or two from year to year, well within the margin of expected sampling error.
But when losses of the same magnitude began to appear consistently, year after
year, it became clear that a major transformation was under way. The marketplace
was sending a message. The customers were voting with their feet, that is walking
away from the product. In 1967, 73% of adult Americans read a newspaper every
day. By 2000, that number had dwindled to 36%.[1]

The industry response was tempered by the fact that newspapers maintained their prosperity despite the loss in readership. Market researchers demonstrated that most people continued to read newspapers at least once or twice
during the week, making multiple ad placements effective. And the readers
were upscale economically, making them the most desirable customers.

Nevertheless, publishers, worried about the long-term trend, began a
gradual shift to a marketing orientation. The International Newspaper
Promotion Association and the American Newspaper Publisher's Association
began a periodic seminar on marketing taught by faculty members of the

---

[1]These data come from the National Opinion Research Center, University of Chicago,
which has asked about newspaper readership in most years from 1972 to the present. The
1967 data is from the study on "Participation in America" by Sidney Verba and Norman
Nie with data collection also by NORC.

Harvard Graduate School of Business Administration. Market researchers such as Joe Belden and Ruth Clark were recruited to apply their expertise to the task of persuading the public to read newspapers. As a Washington correspondent specializing in public opinion research, I found my own efforts being directed by my employer, Knight Ridder Inc., toward marketing problems. And the Newspaper Advertising Bureau, a New York-based trade association, launched an ambitious study called The Newspaper Readership Project to create a pool of basic knowledge on which newspaper marketing programs could be built.

These efforts came to very little. The decline in newspaper readership slowed briefly in the early 1980s and then resumed its linear course. Publishers so far were only interested in low-cost attempts to solve the problem: typographical changes, incremental shifts in content, new strategic mixes of existing resources. But at least a mechanism for research as a Media Accountability System had been created.

LESSONS OF THE 1970s

The lessons of the market research efforts of the 1970s were summed in my *Newspaper Survival Book*.[2] There were eight of them:

1. *Make television work for you.* Newspaper editors had been very slow to recognize that television created a common experience that could bind an audience and carry over into print. Newspapers, I argued, should keep track of television content, criticize it, help the audience organize its viewing, and fill in gaps by going after unanswered questions raised by TV in the minds of the audience.
2. *Emphasize specialized content.* Editorial intuition tended to favor material with the broadest appeal. But a newspaper audience, the research had revealed, was a mosaic of many different specialized interests, and a print medium could reflect that.
3. *Exploit print's power as an information retrieval device.* Newspapers had traditionally been edited on the theory that the typical reader starts on page one and progresses dutifully from front to back, reading or at least scanning, everything on every page. In fact, patterns are quite individualized, with each reader navigating through the paper according to his or her idiosyncratic tastes. To make this navigation easier, newspapers should anchor their material, label it, and index it so that the content can be accessed in any order—just like a computerized database.
4. *Provide material for children.* Television socializes its audience early in life. Newspapers should try to do the same.

---

[2]Bloomington, Indiana UP, 1985.

5. *Do not fear media overkill.* When a story is prominent in other media, an editor may conclude that readers have heard enough about it. Usually, the reverse is true. Because the editor pays more attention than the general public, he or she may be too quick to estimate the saturation point. What seems like a surfeit of information may just be an appetizer.

6. *Do not underestimate the importance of national and international news.* Editors have a bias in favor of local news, perhaps because it is under their control. But readers really do care about national and international events and are quick to see the potential effect of those events on their own lives.

7. *Design the paper to sell itself in the home.* Advertisers are more interested in the number of people who read the paper than in the number who buy it. The 1970s research showed a surprising number of people who had the paper available in the home but did not pick it up on an average day. The same kind of attention given to the graphic presentation of street-sale editions needs to be applied to editions for home delivery.

8. *The hard-core non-reader can be safely ignored.* In a typical U.S. market, only 10% of the audience never sees the paper. An editor should ignore that group and concentrate on increasing the frequency of reading among the other 90%. The pure non-readers are at the bottom of the scale educationally and economically and quite unlikely to respond to improvements in the newspaper. Converting casual readers to committed ones promises to be much more fruitful.

LEARNING FROM *USA TODAY*

Some of this advice was counterintuitive from the perspective of editors. And some of it was expensive. Knight Ridder experimented briefly with a children's feature and then abandoned it when advertising support failed to materialize. Gradually, in the 1980s, newspapers began to format their content more precisely. In this they were inspired more by the success of *USA Today* than by what their market researchers were telling them. But many editors continued to cling to the old service ethic, charging that the market ethic would drive them toward superficiality, entertainment, and trivia. The fact that no legitimate marketing study has ever demonstrated a public preference for superficiality, entertainment, and trivia did not dislodge them from this conviction.

At the end of the decade of the 1980s, several things happened to make publishers once again sensitive to the marketplace. A restructuring of the retail industry replaced large downtown department stores, traditionally a major source of retail advertising, with specialized stores away from downtown. A cyclical downturn in retail sales reduced the amount of money available for newspaper advertising. New, technology-driven forms of advertising media, competed with newspapers. And suburban papers continued to gain at the expense of central city papers. A new generation of editors began to consider the marketing approach.

THE BOCA RATON CASE

The most spectacular example of marketing research serving as a M*A*S came in 1990 with the refurbishment of the *Boca Raton News*. A new generation of managers was in charge at Knight Ridder, and CEO James K. Batten, along with President Anthony Ridder, began emphasizing accountability to the customer. In March 1989, they launched their 25/43 project, so named because that was the age range of the baby boomers, a group so influential in American society that its tastes and readership habits were spreading to both older and younger people. The project began with a review of the research literature, including the largely neglected material from the 1970s. Prototypes were produced and tested in focus groups. Then a decision was made to make Boca Raton the "weapons laboratory" for the company and create a virtually new newspaper. It was launched in October 1990.

The *Boca Raton News* borrowed many ideas from *USA Today* and went farther. It was designed to be read on two levels, quick or leisurely. The quick reader could scan headlines and news summaries for a fast overview. The leisurely reader would navigate toward more detail on most topics. Everything in the paper was anchored, meaning that the similar materials were always found in the same location. The continuation of stories from a section front to the inside was done so that both the start and the continuation was a self-contained unit. The reader could enter at either point and never had to feel guilty for not reading it all.

RANDOM ACCESS ADS

Classified ads in the *Boca Raton News* were arranged in tabular format rather than rolling gray blocks of small type. A reader looking for an apartment to rent could scan the table by price, location, and size by choosing the appropriate column. International news was accompanied by a world map keyed to the stories so that the reader received a geography lesson along with the news. Another map accompanied the domestic news summary. Yet another map section, called "News Near You," showed readers the relationship of local happenings to the places where they lived, worked, and drove. Standing features such as advice columns, comics, and TV schedules were packaged together in a tabloid section.

Even the editorial page could be read on two levels. Each editorial began with a simple statement, in distinctive type, of the issue being discussed and a simple declarative sentence summarizing the newspaper's stand. The body of the editorial followed. At the end, also in a distinctive type face, was the mobilizing information, specification of things the reader could do to act on the issue if he or she agreed with the newspaper's stand.

Like *USA Today,* the *Boca Raton News* when it was in its "weapons lab" mode, was designed to fulfill the surveillance function. In an age of information overload, the reader needs a first look around to use in deciding what events are worth the cost, mainly in time, of further inquiry. The second look may be provided elsewhere in the newspaper or the reader may have to go to other sources, but at least he or she knows what to look for.

USA Today in its earlier years and the *Boca Raton News* in its temporary experimental phase (Knight Ridder sold the paper in 1997), were examples of a sophisticated application of marketing research in that they used research to identify customer needs and then worked backward from the need to the product. The more common practice in the newspaper industry has been to treat the research as a referendum, asking potential readers to define the product directly. But that approach puts too great a burden on the readers, expecting them to articulate needs and visualize a product to fulfill them. They can't do it. You have to see a *USA Today* to know that you want it. Traditional market research efforts could only make incremental, quantitative changes in content. *USA Today* and the *Boca Raton News* were qualitatively different in structure as well as content.

THIRD-PARTY ACCOUNTING

In market research, a media organization creates its own Media Accountability System. Research techniques can also be used for third party evaluation of a product. A basic theory for public accountability of private business grew out of the social protest movements for peace, civil rights, and the environment in the 1960s and 1970s. This period also saw the first application of computer-enhanced quantitative research methods in the social sciences, and some social scientists thought they saw a way to use these tools to audit the social responsibility of private corporations.[3] Business firms were suddenly being held accountable for consequences of their actions that went well beyond their traditionally defined responsibilities: effects of pollution, advancement of women and minorities, energy conservation, and product quality were among the new issues. If impacts in these areas could be quantified, the social scientists interested in this area reasoned, then good and bad behavior would be made more visible. Businesses could be subjected to a social and ethical audit as well as profit and loss accounting.

---

[3]Robert W. Ackerman and Raymond A. Bauer, *Corporate Social Responsiveness: The Modern Dilemma,* Reston, VA, Prentice-Hall, 1976.

The social audit movement faded in the 1980s, partly because the ambitions of the quantifiers went too far beyond the narrow range actually subject to quantification. However, in the newspaper business, there are several interesting opportunities within that narrow range.

ACCURACY MEASUREMENT

One obvious measure of media performance is accuracy. Researchers in the United States have been interested in the topic since 1936.[4] Their method has been to send randomly chosen articles to persons mentioned in the articles and ask them to point out any factual errors. Such persons are not always disinterested judges, of course. Later efforts have allowed reporters to challenge claims of inaccuracy. In an experiment at the *Charlotte Observer*, independent judges weighed conflicting claims on accuracy whenever news sources and reporters disagreed.[5]

The advent of computerized newspaper databases that permit whole text searches opens some other opportunities for third-party M*A*S. Another basic measure of media performance is correctness in use of language. A newspaper's care in spelling and grammar can easily be checked by searching the electronic database for common misspellings and errors of grammar. Thus a search of the *New York Times* for the first half of 1989 revealed that it misspelled the word minuscule as "miniscule" 11% of the time. Some smaller newspapers misspelled the word more often than they got it right.[6]

Less trivial applications of content analysis have been proposed. One scholar has proposed a four-point test of editorial vigor to be made by reading newspaper editorials for the following qualities. A vigorous editorial is one that:

1. Takes sides
2. Deals with local matters
3. Selects controversial topics
4. Provides "mobilizing" information,

that is, suggests specific ways in which the reader can act on the editorial's exhortation.[7]

---

[4]Mitchell V. Charnley, "Preliminary Notes on a Study of Newspaper Accuracy," *Journalism Quarterly,* December 1936, pp. 394-401.

[5]Philip Meyer, "A Workable Measure of Auditing Accuracy in Newspapers," *Newspaper Research Journal,* Fall 1988.

[6]Philip Meyer and David Arant, "Use of an Electronic Database to Evaluate Newspaper Editorial Quality," *Journalism Quarterly,* Summer 1992.

[7]Ralph R. Thrift Jr., "How Chain Ownership Affects Editorial Vigor of Newspapers," *Journalism Quarterly,* Summer 1977, pp. 327-321.

Another possibility for a third-party auditor would be a market-basket test of news content. By tracking the events in a given time period from a variety of media an investigator or a panel of judges could list those specific bits of information that are important to the typical reader and perhaps even weigh them according to their relative importance. These events would form the market basket of information to use as a standard for judging what any given news medium actually provided. Such an evaluation could easily be done retroactively by computerized content analysis.

APPOINTING THE AUDITOR

Who should do the third party audits? Interest groups pursuing their own political agendas might be a source of support. For example, organizations that look after the interests of the physically disabled sometimes criticize insensitive treatment of their clientele as evidenced by the use of certain words or phrases. They would rather, for example, see the phrase "uses a wheel chair" than "is confined to a wheel chair" because the latter phrase leaps to a conclusion about a person's limitations. A simple search of a sample of newspapers in electronic databases to see how often they use the less sensitive phrase would provide a provocative comparison.

Academic researchers, supported by journalism-related foundations, began to play a more active role toward the end of the century. The Knight Foundation backed the efforts of Jay Rosen and W. Davis Merritt[8] to develop a theoretical foundation for a more self-conscious involvement by news media in community affairs. The development and evaluation of their output, called "public journalism," formed a new research stream.

As the century turned, a reaction began to develop to the primitive evaluation tools used by investors in media companies who tended to focus narrowly on quarter-to-quarter changes in earnings. Journalism educators and media-interested NGOs began to seek ways to measure quality in journalism and track its effects down to the bottom line.

These third-party efforts held more promise than the industry's own self-evaluation programs. Seeking to make investor decision making more efficient through better information, these programs promised to provide the ultimate test of the market as an accountability system.

---

[8]Jay Rosen, *What Are Journalists For?*, New Haven, Yale Univesity Press, 1999; Davis "Buzz" Merritt, *Public Journalism and Public Life: Why Telling the News is Not Enough,* 2nd ed., Mahwah, NJ, Erlbaum, 1998.

PART V
M*A*S in the World

CHAPTER 23
M*A*S in Japan
A Battle to Open the Media World

Takeshi Maezawa

Fist of all, it should be stressed that since the end of World War II the Japanese media have enjoyed total press freedom: the Allied Forces[1] and the new Constitution prohibited any restriction on free speech. So all there is are a few laws, criminal and civil, that provide for compensation in case of an infringement of human rights by media, such as libel or invasion of privacy. The Broadcasting Act does authorize the government to cancel a station's license, but that has never been done.

At the turn of the present century, however, the media were being severely criticized by citizens because of their unacceptable behavior. The media show too little reluctance about being intimate with the government— and their newsgathering is often tainted by unethical conduct. Clearly, the people's demand for the creation of self-regulation and accountability systems in the media world is fast increasing.

Now, allow me to start by presenting two subjects that may help you understand the background of media accountability in Japan. One is the traditional behavior of Japanese media people and the other is a controversy over the origin of ombudsmanship.

---

[1]Which, however, never permitted criticism of the atomic bombing and of military occupation.

THE MORALITY AND BEHAVIOR OF MEDIA PROFESSIONALS

Dentsu Inc., Japan's largest media company, an advertising agency to be precise, admitted on June 23, 2000, its liability in the suicide of a worker due to overwork.[2] Dentsu and the parents of Ichiro Oshima, who killed himself at the age of 24 in August 1991, 16 months after joining the company, agreed on an out-of-court settlement following a recommendation of the Tokyo High Court that some 168 million yen (US $1.25 million) be paid in compensation to the parents.

This was a typical case of *karoshi,* or death by overwork. If you ask Japanese employees why and for whom they work so hard that they can die, some will say that they prefer to work than to enjoy their lives. Actually, they feel obliged to be the dedicated workers that will do all they can to benefit their company till they reach mandatory retirement age. They pledge loyalty to their company as a samurai did to a daimyo, or feudal lord.

Such stories reflect contemporary Japan. Japan is said to be a modern nation industrially and economically, a most prosperous nation. But intellectually Japan is not modern or open. The Japanese are concerned for their community, in which they live and work, in other words for their company, for their native country, and not for the rest of the planet.

The media world is no exception to the general trend. Most media professionals have a narrow outlook and are far more interested in their company's or country's interest than in justice and fairness to the readers, listeners, and viewers.

In one of his books,[3] Ivan P. Hall, an expert in Japanese studies and a journalist who has been living in the country for more than 30 years, named Japan an "intellectual closed shop." This significant feature of Japanese society seems protected by two barriers against outside aggressors: geographical isolation as an island and linguistic isolation thanks to the Japanese language. As a matter of fact, this industrially very modern nation has been maintaining its exclusionism, refusing to import global standards to this day.

Isolation from the rest of the world and a close attachment to the domestic tradition have served many Japanese companies and institutions well, but one institution has certainly suffered from them: journalism. Journalists in Japan are not seen as independent professionals working in the public interest; instead, they are seen as, first and foremost, employees of a company. This allegiance has the effect of keeping Japanese journalism from reporting on important issues and from being accountable to readers.

---

[2]*Kyodo News,* June 23, 2000.
[3]Ivan P. Hall, *Cartels of The Mind: Japan's Intellectual Closed Shop,* New York, Norton, 1997.

According to the 2000 survey of the World Association of Newspapers, Japan stands first in global circulation on a list of 64 countries with 72 million copies sold every day. And it is second in market penetration with 574 copies sold per 1,000 inhabitants.[4]

Japanese newspapers enjoy the most prosperous and profitable business circumstances in the world under protective laws and regulations that include "retail price maintenance," which permits newspaper companies and home-delivery services to sell each newspaper at a price that can be arbitrarily fixed by the newspaper companies—an exemption to the Antitrust Law.

Because their businesses are thriving, newspaper professionals and companies are not seriously concerned about independence and accountability to readers—contrary to journalists and newspapers in other democratic countries with a liberal economic regime. At the International Press Institute's conference held in Kyoto in April 1991, the organization's director praised Japan for its "free and democratic press," whereas, on the contrary, Dutch journalist Karel van Wolferen, one of the guest speakers, was unreservedly critical of the Japanese press, saying: "I do not think I exaggerate when I say that nowhere else in the industrialized world is self-censorship so systematic." The fact that he was quoted only in the English-language newspapers published in Japan provided evidence of the truth of his speech.[5]

The situation at the beginning of the 21st century is not different from what it was then. On October 13, 2000, Dr. Ivan P. Hall told me, at the Foreign Correspondents' Club of Japan, that most newspapers would not touch his book with a ten-foot pole, nor would NSK (*Nihon Shinbun Kyokai*), the association of newspaper publishers and editors. They refused to publish reviews of the book arguably on account of his frank and penetrating criticism of Japanese society—and of its media.

Japanese media are never curious to hear about journalism in other democracies. According to Tsuneo Watanabe, chairman of NSK,[6] "Japan is the only country in the world to have developed high-quality popular newspapers and we have nothing to learn from countries in Europe and America."[7] What some foreign journalists have said to me is "I wonder whether Japanese journalists really know what journalism is all about." Foreign correspondents discover, and Japanese reporters don't realize, that in Japan there are so many taboos on newsgathering that reflect Japanese society. Here are a few examples of them.

---

[4]*2000 World Press Trends*, Paris, World Association of Newspapers, 2000.

[5]Takeshi Maezawa, *Watchdog—A Japanese Newspaper Ombudsman at Work*, Tokyo, Cosmohills, 1994.

[6]He is also President of the *Yomiuri Shinbun* newspaper, which has the largest circulation in the world (14.5 million copies a day).

[7]In *NSK Weekly Newspaper*, June 26, 1999.

THE PRESS CLUB SYSTEM

No one knows exactly how many press clubs actually exist because almost every main office of a political, administrative, and corporate organization, in Tokyo and other cities, has a press club in it. "Estimates can be found ranging from the 440 identified in 1993 by the semi-governmental Foreign Press Center to perhaps as many as 1,000, including local branches, throughout the country," Hall wrote in his book.

The club system excludes any reporter who is not a member from freely gathering news at that source and it generates an extraordinarily close relationship between reporters and decision-makers. A story will demonstrate the evil of the press club system.

The day before then Prime Minister Yoshiro Mori's scheduled news conference on May 26, 2000, in which he was to defend his "divine nation" statement,[8] a copy of an elaborate memo was found in the press club room at the PM's office that contained advice on how he should defend himself against questioning by reporters—as well as secret information about media companies and journalists. An unidentified NHK (public broadcasting) reporter, assigned to the Cabinet, had reportedly written the memo. Some magazines and newspapers reported the incident a couple of weeks later, attaching a copy of the memo—but most dailies, including the *Yomiuri,* have never mentioned the incident. No one was accused of any violation of journalistic ethics and no media company ever seriously tried to find and fire a suspect. NHK and the press club published short comments saying they had nothing to add. There was no further reaction except from some media watching organizations.

THE COVERAGE OF THE ROYAL FAMILY

The Imperial family is the most difficult beat for a reporter, because he/she must learn a mass of traditions and special customs, and must also obey strict regulations to the letter.

When Korean President Kim Dae Jung visited Japan in October 1998, according to the English-language newspapers,[9] Emperor Akihito and the President "talked" or "spoke" to each other at their meeting. But in Japanese language newspapers, whereas the President "talked" or "said" things, the Emperor had never "talked" or "spoken" with anyone. Instead, the word was *noberareta,* which is one of the special words used in any story about the most eminent persons, which hark back to the days of feudalism. Only a very few reporters assigned to the Palace Press Club can master such a special etiquette.

---

[8]The PM had been quoted on May 16 as declaring at a meeting of the Federation of Diet Members Supporting Shinto, "Japan is truly a divine nation with the Emperor at the center."
[9]They are published by the major Japanese newspaper companies.

When Emperor Showa passed away on January 7, 1989, many readers wondered why the media had so many stories portraying only the good side of the Emperor and the imperial system, instead of also mentioning more negative aspects, such as the Emperor's responsibility in the war—or the so-called "chrysanthemum curtain," the barrier put up by servants of the court who isolate the royal family from media and the public. Critics in magazines[10] questioned such an editorial policy—but no newspapers.

CONTROVERSY OVER THE ORIGIN OF OMBUDSMAN

There's another point that I wish to consider: the debate among members of the Organization of News Ombudsmen (ONO) over the origin of the concept. Media scholars, of course, know that "ombudsman" is the Swedish name for a defender of the public against institutions, that there are many ombudsmen in Sweden including, since 1969, a Press Ombudsman attached to the Press Council (see p. 361). Also they know that the quite different in-house ombudsman appointed by newspapers to listen to readers' complaints is an earlier (1967) U.S. invention.

The latter is the one I wish to deal with. First question: Where did that M*A*S originate, North America or Japan? In the late 1990s, U.S. ombudsmen acknowledged that it was invented in Japan. Second question: Does the Japanese system, in fact, deserve the name of ombudsmanship?

The controversy arose from differences between two versions of the ONO brochure.[11] One was released in July 1993 and the other in September 1999. The chapter "Is This a New Idea?" in the first brochure states:

> Relatively speaking, yes. The first newspaper ombudsman was appointed in June 1967, in Louisville, Kentucky, to act for readers of *The Courier-Journal* and *The Louisville Times*. The Canadian appointment, at the *Toronto Star*, was in 1972.

The new edition of the brochure added different data:

> [But] the general concept stems from a "Bureau of Accuracy and Fair Play" established in 1913 at *The New York World*. Nine years later, *The Asahi Shinbun* in Tokyo established a committee to receive and investigate reader complaints.[12] It was modeled after the *World's* bureau.

---

[10]The magazine press in Japan is relatively under-developed and far more independent.

[11]"Editors for the Public: What are News Ombudsmen and Why Should the Media Have Them," Sacramento, CA, *ONO*, 1999.

[12]The Tokyo *Asahi Shinbun*, October 21, 1922.

Another mass circulation Tokyo paper, *The Yomiuri Shinbun,* set up a staff committee in 1938 to monitor the paper's quality. In 1951, this group became a 28-member ombudsmen committee which today hears reader complaints about the paper and which meets daily with editors.

Soon after releasing that new version, Linda Raymond, ombudsman for *The Courier-Journal,* in Louisville, wrote a column entitled "We Were Wrong":[13]

> For 32 years, *The Courier-Journal* has taken pride in the belief that it appointed the first newspaper ombudsman and launched the international newspaper ombudsman movement. We were wrong.
>
> We didn't know that the concept had already been operating for many years in Japan when, in 1967, *Courier-Journal* editor and publisher Barry Bingham Sr. established the post here and John Herchenroeder became the first to fill it.

Arthur C. Nauman, then treasurer of ONO, noted in his message to ONO members that journalists, scholars, MA candidates and ombudsmen had all assumed over the years that the movement had started in the United States. "So we all violated a cardinal rule of journalism: don't assume anything." However, in spite of Linda's candid admission, the question, "What is the origin of ombudsmanship?" has never actually been answered. We are faced with another difficult question, "Can we consider newspaper-contents checking systems in Japan as an ombudsmanship equivalent to that in America?"

THE COMMON SYSTEM FOR CONTENTS EVALUATION

Now, I would like to come to the main topic of this chapter, media accountability systems in Japan. The characteristic features of Japanese society and journalism are reflected in the structures and operations of M*A*S in the Japanese media.

The most common system for enforcing ethical standards in the Japanese press is *Kijishinsa-iinkai* or *Kijishinsa-shitsu,* that is to say, an "internal committee for newspaper contents evaluation." This system plays a major part within newspapers by guaranteeing good quality contents and by insuring the ethical education of employees. Scholars of media ethics would, of course, say that its main function has little directly to do with accountability to readers.

In his book,[14] Claude-Jean Bertrand has listed 14 types of M*A*S consisting in individuals or groups. Among them he includes the in-house critic sometimes found in the United States and he refers to the Japanese system as follows:

---

[13]"Forum," *The Courier-Journal*, September 5, 1999.

[14]C-J. Bertrand, *Media Ethics & Accountability Systems*, Piscataway, NJ, Transaction, 2000, p. 117.

The Japanese have had *shinsashitsu* since 1922: those "commissions for the evaluation of contents" are to be found in every major daily as also in news agencies and at the HQ of the NSK. . . . There, in the press sector, you find the "quality control" that has given Japanese products their worldwide reputation.

The main function of *shinsa-shitsu* in each newspaper has been "quality control" for a long time. This kind of commission has guaranteed the comparatively high quality of newspapers, in particular since the end of World War II, when the press was given its freedom. Most newspapers did not give their *shinsa-shitsu* any accountability function—yet, inevitably, some of the *shinsa-shitsus* have been gradually increasing their accountability function.

The *shinsa-shitsu* with the largest staff is the one at the *Yomiuri Shinbun*. The system there was reformed in 1951, changed from a small team to the present committee of 27 members. If literally translated, the Japanese name of the committee would be "The Committee of Newspaper Contents Inspectors." But the word "inspection" in Japanese implies "censorship," so it was nicknamed the "Ombudsmen Committee." Since 1985, in fact, it has endeavored to fulfill the usual functions of newspaper ombudsmen in the United States and other countries—mainly a consequence of my attending a conference organized by ONO in 1980, as a senior member of the committee.[15]

CHARACTERISTICS OF IN-HOUSE CHECKING SYSTEMS

Let's have a closer look at the internal newspaper contents evaluation system in Japan. The history of contents checking in the Japanese media goes back to the 1920s. Most newspapers have operated such a program for more than 35 years, and a few newspapers started it before World War II.

The major reason why they don't, and shouldn't, name their checking M*A*S an ombudsman system is their lack of openness towards readers and their lack of independence from their superiors. "The news media are the most exclusive society," says Professor Seiya Ikari.[16] "They refuse to disclose information, which they must if readers are to trust them [. . .] No bylines, no responses to readers: that all shows their lack of accountability."

Also, of course, it would be next to impossible for the members of this system independently to investigate their colleagues, critically to evaluate the contents of articles by them and to submit a candid opinion to their superiors. It is far from easy in any journalistic environment, but remember that these people are average employees in a Japanese company—as I mentioned before.

---

[15]I was senior member from 1981 to 1991, and ombudsman for the English language *Daily Yomiuri* from 1987 to 1993.

[16]Of Tokyo Keizai University, in a private conversation.

A NSK committee composed of seven representatives of *shinsa-shitsu* did a research tour of the United States in 1987 to gather information that could help Japanese newspapers develop better M*A*S. One document that they found most interesting was the "Guidelines for Ombudsmen,"[17] which states:

> The ombudsman must be independent, and that independence must be real. He should be answerable only to the person with the highest authority over the news department.
>
> The objectives of a newspaper ombudsman shall be:
> 1. To improve the fairness, accuracy and accountability of the newspaper.
> 2. To enhance its credibility.
> 3. To make the newspaper aware of the concerns of and the issues in, the communities served by it.

In contrast, the people operating "newspaper contents checking systems" are reluctant to disclose information about themselves and to invite readers to a discussion meant to raise ethical awareness. These systems are not made to be responsive and they have no tradition of dealing with readers who have complaints, suggestions, or questions. These M*A*S have been functioning as quality control bureaus for products (printed newspapers), but they have seldom disclosed the full information necessary for their credibility because of their lack of full independence from the newsroom. What information? For example, information on why so often newspapers don't identify public officials in news stories or attribute documents to anonymous sources. If a reader asks a journalist a question about a news story, he/she will seldom receive a clear explanation or correction of it. The media world is one of the most self-contained uncommunicative communities.

When in 1984 I wrote to Arthur Nauman, by then president of ONO and ombudsman at the *Sacramento Bee*, in California, suggesting that we stay in touch, he answered," Obviously, you and we have common goals." ONO permitted me to join as an associate member, then as a member the following year, and since then members of the *Yomiuri* committee have taken turns at attending its annual conferences and other meetings. They strive to promote the newspaper's openness to readers and their independence of the newsroom.

THE SURVEY OF NEWSPAPER CONTENTS CHECKING PROGRAMS

As of April 1997, according to a survey by *Nihon Shinbun Kyokai* (NSK), 56 of 94 daily newspapers responding had their own department for a *shinsa-shitsu*

---

[17]Adopted by the ONO on May 12, 1982, at a meeting in Washington, DC.

mission. The total number of daily newspapers in NSK is 116, so about half have such a department.

In the same way as the Japanese names for the *kijishinsa-shitsu* of newspapers are various, their systems and roles differ from one newspaper to another. However, the NSK survey disclosed that 40 out of 56 of those systems are composed of several members. All the Japanese, including journalists, are reluctant to act independently and will always prefer to do things in a committee.

The number of staff assigned to newspaper checking duties is 481 in all and averages nine per newspaper. That may seem a lot, but 80% of them hold other jobs on the newspaper. As for supervision, one fourth of these groups are directed by a managing editor and one third directly by a president or publisher of the company. The M*A*S is accountable only to the top person in the company. Thus it is guaranteed complete independence from the newsroom. Such commissions have spread from nine companies in 1989 to 15 in 1997.

The functions of the M*A*S are various, from spotting errors (including the use a wrong term or the omission of a word) to educating reporters and writers about media ethics by releasing a report or a memo, or sponsoring a meeting. Most conclusions of the checking and evaluation of newspaper quality are released in the newsroom through oral and printed statements to reporters and editors.

Once every several years, the NSK survey task force asks newspapers to rate five of 10 functions. In the surveys of the 1980s, most newspapers ranked accuracy of contents first and the adequacy of editing and page layout second. In recent ones, they were relatively more concerned with "human rights and decency."

Categories of Functions	Number of Newspapers		
	1997	1989	1982
Accuracy of contents of news stories	54 (1)*	50 (1)	59 (1)
Soundness of news value judgments	50 (2)	46 (2)	51 (2)
Protection of human rights and decency	44 (3)	37 (4)	37 (6)
Makeup skill (headlines and layout)	40 (4)	38 (3)	50 (3)
Comparison with competitors' reporting	33 (5)	34 (6)	40 (5)
Accuracy of words and figures	27 (6)	35 (5)	41 (4)

*Figures in parentheses are the ranking.

At the *Yomiuri,* 17 of the 27 regular members are chiefly occupied with checking stories and articles on various pages of the paper. The rest, called "readers' advisers," deal with questions and complaints sent by readers via mail or phone. They receive more than 100 telephone calls a day from readers, but most of the calls are to ask for information about current events—and not usually to complain.

The main objectives of the committee are supposed to be the improvement of the accuracy and fairness of the newspaper; and the improvement of the reporters' understanding of the rights of the citizens.

Its activities of the committee include:

- Daily conferences with editors to evaluate articles.
- Twice-weekly in-house reports.
- Columns and reports in the paper—though not since the mid-1990s because successive executive editors and chairmen of the committee have shown no interest in dialogue with readers and in the publication of articles on media ethics.
- Examining applications for awards and prizes.

In order to reach those goals, in 1982 the committee published a guidebook for reporters and editors on media law and ethics, called *"The Reader's Viewpoint, The Writer's Viewpoint."* This was Japan's first publication in this field.

THE COMPLAINT COUNCIL FOR BROADCASTING

Voluntarily, in June 1997, NHK, the public broadcaster, and the National Association of 190 commercial Broadcasters (NAB) jointly founded the "Broadcast Freedom and Other Human Rights Organization" (BRO) as a non-governmental, non-bureaucratic body, independent from all but the media. BRO announced:[19]

> The purpose of this creation is to be actively committed to the accomplishment of the social responsibilities incurred by broadcasters and to deal promptly and effectively with complaints made about broadcast programs, from the standpoint of viewers or listeners so as to ensure freedom of speech and expression in broadcasting and protect the basic human rights of viewers or listeners, thereby contributing to ensuring accurate broadcasting and raising broadcasting ethics.

In fact, BRO was established largely under pressure by government, in order to avoid restrictive political action following a series of unethical acts and scandals involving TV staff. And after the majority party made an extremely strong recommendation to regulate television by law.

BRC, composed of eight members, including people with academic experience and understanding, is a subordinate branch of BRO.[18] Its only func-

---

[18]Literally translated, these names mean "Organization (BRO) and Council (BRC) for Freedom of Speech in Broadcasting and Other Human Rights of the Audience."

[19]See www.bro.gr.jp.

tion is to consider the contents of complaints submitted by individuals[20] and to present the results of its investigation and discussion as its "opinion" or "recommendations." In 1997, the committee received 925 complaints, 1,984 in 1998, 2,640 in 1999, and 2,244 in 2000—and issued five opinions and three recommendations in its first four years. The opinions just requested broadcasters to be more careful in the future.

On October 6, 2000, the committee issued its first recommendation that strongly demanded that a TV station broadcast a special segment as a correction to an unfair piece of information in a criminal report, plus an apology to a complainant who had suffered seriously because of it.

OTHER M*A*S

Once or twice a year, a national meeting of the representatives of *kijishinsa* sections from all member newspapers takes place. The meeting is funded and organized by NSK to try to harmonize guidelines for the Japanese media. Local meetings for the same purpose are held separately once every month in major locations, like Tokyo and Osaka.

NSK has its own section for checking newspaper contents called *shinsa-shitsu,* or The Newspaper Ethical Standards Monitoring Chamber. The chamber examines every copy of its member dailies to check whether or not their contents conform to the Canon of Journalism.

The Japanese media also have a significant national organization named "The National Council to Promote Media Ethics." The national council was formed in 1958, after a first local council was established in Tokyo in 1955, with the aim of evaluating ethics and promoting freedom of the press. The council is composed of the representatives of major media associations and companies including newspapers, TV stations, book and magazine publishers, advertising agencies, and movie producers. It holds an annual conference and a monthly seminar, and also possesses research committees working in defense of press freedom.

As early as 1976, in the English version of the NSK annual report, the head of the *shinsa-shitsu* for the *Asahi Shinbun* was quoted as saying, "In addition to being newspapermen, we believe we are the representatives of our readers."

Unfortunately, *Asahi* staff came to be accused of one of the most serious ethical lapses committed by journalists in Japan. On April 20, 1989, the evening edition of the *Asahi Shinbun* carried a photograph of a coral reef on which the initials "K.Y" had been carved. The caption of the photograph asked "Who is this K.Y who damaged a coral reef?" However, it turned out that the newspaper's photographer himself had defaced the coral. He was fired—and the President of the *Asahi Shinbun* resigned. A few months later, the *Asahi*

---

[20]Complaints by organizations are unacceptable.

announced in the NSK's English language *News Bulletin,* "Our newspaper has established an Advisory Press Council composed of five prominent persons including a former chief justice of the Supreme Court. It is generally hoped that it will perform as an ombudsman for the newspaper."

The idea of this council was excellent. The council is meant to provide opinions and recommendations to the president of the *Asahi* with a view to improving the standards of journalism from the viewpoint of readers. But its aims and activities are too different from those of a regular press council or of a normal ombudsman. None of the council members ever investigates a controversial case or writes a report as a representative of readers: they just submit their comments to the president and other top executives.

The *Mainichi Shinbun* newspaper, the third largest newspaper in Japan, announced on October 13, 2000 that the newspaper was establishing a "Council for an Open Newspaper." The council is composed of five members, including a lawyer, a professor, and a journalism critic. The council is to consider complaints from readers and citizens covered in news stories, and the newspaper will publish the results. The notice also said: "The newspaper expects that the council will perform like an ombudsman." There again, the idea is excellent.

As of January 2002, 23 newspapers and news agencies had similar councils.

THE NEW CANON OF NSK

One of the problems about respecting media ethics is that Japanese media companies and organizations are reluctant to draft a code or practical guidelines that could serve as a basis for evaluating ethical violations. Actually, judging from past cases, it would be impossible for media persons to keep within such practical guidelines. That is why media codes in Japan have few precise or concrete provisions.

On June 21, 2000, NSK formulated a new Canon of Journalism (see p. 80) not only for journalists but for everyone engaged in newspaper work. NSK said, "Over half a century has elapsed since the adoption of the Canon of Journalism on July 23, 1946." And Chairman Tsuneo Watanabe issued a statement saying, "Under circumstances marked by dramatic changes in the surrounding society and media, NSK has instituted a new code of ethics that shall be suitable for the 21st century."

Few media people find it reasonable to revise a canon unless it provides more specific and concrete guidelines than the previous one. Also, many journalists found that the real aim of the revision was not to make the canon better but, as we say, to "oil the government's hand" and insure that the "retail price maintenance" policy be maintained for newspapers. As a result, the new canon provided neither specific nor concrete guidelines. Nevertheless, it is of great interest to Japanese journalists that the notion of "independence," and the definition of it, were added to the new canon. The article including it says:

Member newspapers uphold their independence in the interests of fair comment and free speech. They must reject interference by any outside forces, and resolve to remain vigilant against those who may wish to use the newspapers for their own purposes.

The most questionable point is the absence in the new Canon of any provision regarding "conflict of interest." If the practical guidelines regarding "conflict of interest" and "the appearance of conflict of interest" were provided, the new canon would have been found excellent and meaningful. Newspapers in Japan too easily admit the fact that many of their executives and employees are appointed by the government as members of political and administrative advisory committees; how can they avoid conflict of interest?[21]

A TREND DANGEROUS FOR FREEDOM OF THE PRESS

At the turn of the present century, the Japanese media faced a most difficult situation: freedom of the press was threatened. On the one hand, it was obvious that both print and electronic media had often violated the rights of people in the process of covering the news and had even victimized quite a few of them by invading their privacy. On the other hand, however, there existed a far more dangerous trend: the ruling parties, the administrative authorities, and some civil organizations have been eager to contrive legal restrictions for the mass media.

An example: the existing Act for the Protection of Personal Data in Computer Processing applied to the various bureaucracies. But in October 2000, the government's Committee on the Protection of Personal Data submitted the draft of legislation that would authorize the government to regulate newsgathering and reporting.

In November 2000, the Council for the Promotion of Civil Liberties at the Ministry of Justice released an interim report including a recommendation that an independent organization be established to deal with human rights violations and that restriction of the press might be needed to stop such violations. The recommendation proposed that administrative authorities be entitled to investigate and to fine media companies and professionals, and also to suppress a publication without a court order, if the press proved unable to establish an effective system for preventing violation of the human rights of people covered by news media.

---

[21]Kiyofuku Chuma, chairman of the NSK subcommittee on the study of the Canon of journalism, responded thus to my question at a seminar of the Institute of Mass Communication Studies, October 23, 2000: "It is very difficult for NSK to agree on whether or not a newspaper person should participate in the government advisory committee. Some newspaper executives would argue that newspaper professionals should aggressively express their opinions at the government committees because a journalist, as a member of the Fourth Estate, has a special responsibility to do it for the public."

The Japanese Federation of Bar Associations, at its 1999 conference on the protection of human rights, adopted a resolution that requested that the media provide fair news reporting and respect human rights. It also suggested the establishment of an independent news (press) council by the media as well as the adoption of ombudsman systems by newspapers as soon as possible.

Surprisingly, the federation's conference the next year adopted a contrary resolution that abandoned the idea of a news council and instead recommended that the government pass a law that would substantially include those same provisions drafted by the council of the Ministry of Justice.

I wish to insist that the media companies and journalists in Japan should read again the Constitution of Japan, which became operational on May 3, 1947, which states in its Article 21:

> Freedom of assembly and association as well as of speech and all other forms of expression are guaranteed. No censorship shall be exercised, nor shall the secrecy of any means of communication be violated.

And yet freedom of speech will hardly be able to survive in 21st century Japan if ever any one of those media-regulating measures comes to be adopted. I wish to conclude by saying that Japanese media should promptly "improve their checking mechanisms and their system for responding to readers' inquiries" —thus echoing the official view of the NSK presented on December 14, 1999, in a hearing session conducted by the Council for the Promotion of Civil Liberties at the Ministry of Justice.

CHAPTER 24
M*A*S in the United Kingdom
Between Complaint and Compliance: Groping for Media Accountability

Michael Bromley

In an edition of the most widely accessible annual guide to (and for) the media in the United Kingdom, several dozen non-governmental organizations were listed in 18 categories of "Pressure and Advice Groups." Elsewhere, in the same directory there was a section for "Consumer Watchdogs." The media were directly represented in neither. Whereas there was a single page devoted to "Complaints to the Media," for the most part the various media accountability systems (M*A*S) in Britain were included in two listings of "support groups."[1] This is not a matter of mere semantics. Media accountability in the United Kingdom is not yet routinely accepted as an everyday form of dialogue engaged in (equitably or otherwise) by the media and their practitioners, on the one hand, and interested publics on the other. Perhaps nowhere in advanced mediated societies is it more true that "ordinary people have fairly limited opportunities to participate in the generation of mass media content, not to mention to discuss it with the journalistic and political élites."[2] Media accountability, whether rooted in models of citizenship or consumerism, is more commonly considered as a set of polarized activities—either oppositional and adversarial (and overly configured around a notion of "complaint") or defensive, supportive, and compliant.

---

[1]Steve Peak and Paul Fisher (eds.) *The Media Guide 1998*, London, Fourth Estate, 1997, pp. 137, 247, 272, 373-374, 392-400.

[2]Tanjev Schultz, "Mass Media and the Concept of Interactivity: An Exploratory Study of Online Forums and Reader Email," *Media, Culture and Society*, 22(2), 2000, p. 206.

In the United Kingdom, as elsewhere, it is widely acknowledged that the relationship between the "free" media and the need for those same media to be accountable—the nature of the media as "the servant of the public"—is necessarily complex and problematical, and the dilemma of reconciling "the public interest" with what interests the public became even more apparent after the death of Diana, Princess of Wales, in 1997. Yet, in circumventing broader public concerns, media accountability has been limited in practice to direct, often personal, negotiation—for example, pressuring or persuading a publisher or editor to acknowledge an error or print a letter—and the often protracted and expensive processes of litigation and formal complaint to a statutory or voluntary body. This denotes a situation in which "accountability" has tended to be regarded less as a form of public answerability than as a question of corporate or individual liability.

Publics and the media not only intersect unequally, but the relationship is framed by a transparent and unapologetic dominant ideology situating the media as entities of broad cultural importance derived primarily from their status as "industries." This also incorporates the "professionalism" of journalists. As a result, publics are viewed as more subservient and passive "audiences." The paradoxical effect is that "There are few remedies open to ordinary citizens who know that [. . .] justice has not been done or the truth has not been told, and desperately seek vindication by calling upon the defenders of the public conscience to come to their aid."[3] To a large extent, consideration of M*A*S has been reduced to deliberation of the need to "cut back the political and economic power of huge media organizations" as a prerequisite for establishing a "popular" dialogical ethos and revitalizing the public sphere.

Certainly, over the longer term, consumer pressure has been ineffectual. For example, a widespread boycott of *The Sun* newspaper in and around Liverpool in response to its (mis)reporting of the Hillsborough football stadium disaster in 1989 seems to have had no lasting impact. At the same time, the evidence from the courts and the proceedings of the Press Complaints Commission (PCC), a voluntary body in the print sector, suggests that these routes to remedy are productive, if at all, for only the rich and famous who have lately resorted to them in growing numbers. Nevertheless, at the core of the debate there remains a preoccupation with the relative merits of voluntarism and its supposed superiority over compulsion—most specifically that self-regulation is more effectual than the law. The death of Diana refueled arguments about the erosion of an approach based more on top-down direction, and the greater reliance placed on popular opinion (or consumption) as a mechanism of accountability, and refocused attention on the systems of "lighter touch" regulation that had been instituted in the 1990s.

---

[3]Clive Soley, "Complaints Against the Media: Legal or Administrative Remedies," speech delivered in London, 15 October 1992.

VOLUNTARISM IN ACTION

Notable successes were claimed for this approach, particularly by the PCC, which in 1998 began to emphasize the extent to which it acted "to protect the most vulnerable in our society—children, victims of crime, people suffering at time of grief, hospital patients and many others" and served "ordinary members of the public who could never afford to use the law to conciliate a dispute with a newspaper or magazine."[4] The BBC asserted its "commitment to accountability" through "a two-way process" founded on "listening to audiences." The Independent Television Commission (ITC), a statutory body, held eight public consultations in 1999 and six in the first half of 2000. The Broadcasting Standards Commission (BSC), also a statutory creation, argued for "empowering the digital citizen." In a submission to the Government, it said

> A successful communications content ecology in Britain in the twenty-first century will have three characteristics: empowered users, able to make informed choices and contribute to the public debate; more accountable content providers who take responsibility for articulating and measuring up to their own values; and residual regulatory powers to ensure compliance with essential minimum standards.

All this, it was contended, was compatible with "the lightest regulatory touch appropriate and possible."[5] Others, however, noted a failure to "put the public at the center," and the demise of the long-established, if flawed, formal forums for extending the grounds of, and participation in, debate, such as Royal Commissions and other forms of State-sponsored public inquiry.

There has been growing evidence of public dissatisfaction with, a declining faith in, and mounting criticisms of, the formal M*A*S. Consistently, around two-thirds of all complaints made to the PCC concern not the invasions of privacy that animate celebrities and politicians, but inaccurate reporting. Although not truly comparable, complaints of inaccuracy and general "unfairness" made to the ITC accounted for 42% of all complaints about news and factual programming on the main Independent Television (ITV) Channel 3, Channel 4, Channel 5, and cable and satellite stations in 1997, and nearly 30% in 1998. The number of complaints about fairness made to the BSC rose in 1999-2000.[6] Nevertheless, the PCC, which already has a dedicated privacy

---

[4]Press Complaints Commission (1998), *Annual Review* 1997 at www.pcc.org.uk/annual/97/default.htm: accessed 31 Aug. 2000; Press Complaints Commission (1999), *Annual Review* 1998 at www.pcc.org.uk/annual/98/default.htm: accessed 31 Aug. 2000.

[5]Broadcasting Standards Commission, *Empowering the Digital Citizen: A Submission for the Communications Reform Review*, London, BSC, n.d., p. 15.

[6]Chris Frost, *Media Ethics and Self-Regulation*, Harlow, Longman, 2000, p. 215; Broadcasting Standards Commission *Review 2000*, London, BSC, 2000, pp. 16-19.

commissioner, reaffirmed that "the protection of personal privacy—balanced by the public's right to know—is central to the PCC's work. The Commission therefore continues to be especially vigilant in this area"—even though such cases make up less than one in eight of complaints received. In matters of broader public interest, the PCC often appears powerless, however. For example, more than 10% of complaints in 1996 (306 out of 3,023) were made about crude, xenophobic tabloid newspaper coverage of the European soccer championships, Euro '96, held in England. After an investigation, the Commission found that the code of practice had not been breached and, in adding to the widespread condemnation of the coverage, was restricted to lamely criticizing the "editorial judgment" of some newspapers.

Similarly, the ill-defined "public interest" defense permissible under the code allowed the Commission to dismiss all complaints made in 1998 about a number of "high profile" cases where payments for stories were made to criminals, including two convicted of killing children. In October 1996, Lord Wakeham, the chair of the PCC, warned editors that there was a danger of the over-use of the public interest defense, and "injudicious reporting of the private lives of individuals 'backed up only by the flimsiest of public interest defences'." Moreover, what stirred the public did not always move the Commission: on average, a quarter of cases brought to the PCC were ruled as falling outside its remit: 819 in 1996, 593 in 1997, and 689 in 1998.[7] The figures for the Broadcasting Standards Council were similar: 21% (591 out of 2,838 in 1994-1995), and for the Broadcasting Complaints Commission overall an enormous 83% in 1995 (945 out of 1,135) and close to 85% in 1996 (926 of 1,093).[8]

TABLOID JOURNALISM

It is perhaps not surprising that instances of excessive tabloid journalism continue to be evident, despite a number of revisions of the PCC code, and the Commission's insistence that over the past five years there have been "significant and dramatic changes in press behaviour."[9] For example, one tabloid newspaper secured secretly filmed footage of a Member of Parliament in bed with his mistress and published an exposé based on the evidence. When the MP resigned, a cable television associate broadcast parts of the video. Two months

---

[7]Quotes and figures taken from PCC annual reviews for 1996, 1997 and 1998. See also: Piers Morgan "Innocents in a Hell-hole," *The Guardian Media*, 25 May 1998, p. 9; Nick Hopkins, "Woodward Selling Her Story," *The Guardian*, 30 May 1998, p. 2.

[8]Frost *op. cit.*, pp. 218, 220. The Broadcasting Standards Council and the Broadcasting Complaints Commission were merged to form the Broadcasting Standards Commission in 1997.

[9]Lord Wakeham in PCC *Annual Review* 1998.

later, a different paper in the same media group entrapped the son of the Home Secretary into selling two of its reporters a small amount of cannabis, and most of the rest of the press joined a campaign of innuendo and threats until the courts waived the legal prohibition on publishing the boy's name. In neither case did the PCC intervene, although prima facie its code had been broken in both instances. Despite a concerted effort being made after Diana's death to protect her two sons, press infringements occurred. Noteworthy complainants to the PCC have recently included not only the Prince of Wales, but also the Prime Minister and Mrs Blair, Elton John, and Paul McCartney.

The scale and scope of tabloid journalism techniques used in the United Kingdom were indicated when a private investigator was convicted of 12 offences of procuring from the main telecommunications company the unlisted numbers and itemized telephone accounts of celebrities, and selling the information to, among others, four Sunday newspapers. It was "a lucrative celebrity-snooping business," *The Guardian* argued, with no attempt being made to propose a public interest justification.[10]

One of the bigger tabloid scandals was not celebrity-based, however. In March 2000, after a public encounter with its rival *The Sun, The Mirror* was adjudged to have been guilty of "numerous and flagrant breaches of the code" in the work of its financial "City Slickers" feature, implicating both the editor and the deputy editor, and causing the PCC to approach the paper's owner, Trinity Mirror, directly.[11] There were feelings that broadcasting was not immune from "tabloidism" of this sort either. Such fears seemed to be most conspicuously borne out by a £2 million fine imposed on Carlton Television for faking evidence in a documentary program on drug trafficking; faking in another program made for the same company; the presentation of a staged event as authentic in a Channel 4 documentary: and the alleged concocting of crimes for an investigative reporter to "solve" on air.[12] These cases reflected a rising public concern with television documentary practices: in 1999-2000 the number of complaints to the BSC about documentaries rose by almost 250%.[13] More of a furor was created by the disclosure that guests on a day-time television chat show were bogus. This led the editor of *The Mirror* to argue:

---

[10]"A Private Sector," *The Guardian*, 6 Dec 1997, p. 24.

[11]Press Complaints Commission, "Code was Breached, Rules the Commission, as it Refers the Adjudication to the Publisher," 15 March 2000 at www.pcc.org. uk/adjud/press/pr150410.htm: accessed August 31,. 2000.

[12]Independent Television Commission (1998), "ITC Impose £2M Financial Penalty for "The Connection'" at www.itc.org.uk/news/news_releases/worddocs/upl_198.doc: accessed September 7, 2000; Independent Television Commisssion, *ITC Annual Report for 1998*, London, ITC, 1999; Janine Gibson "Carlton investigates Cook Report 'set ups'", *The Guardian*, 14 Feb. 2000 at www.guardianunlimited.co.uk: accessed September 8, 2000.

[13]Broadcasting Standards Commission (2000), *loc. cit.*

CHAPTER 24

After years of denouncing tabloids like *The Mirror* for our supposedly unethical, devious, deceptive and dishonest journalism, the world of television has been made to look a right hypocritical Charlie. It turns out that nothing the tabloids have done even comes close to the disgraceful farrago of daytime chat shows.[. .]. we've caught you all with your high moral trousers firmly round your ankles.[14]

It should be acknowledged, however, that these infringements in large part came to light and were dealt with by elements of the United Kingdom M*A*S—through newspaper reporting and investigation leading to inquiries and actions by regulators. As the M*A*S most regularly confronting the commercial tabloid culture, the PCC has demonstrated an ongoing concern with "Raising Standards of Reporting. Sorting out Disputes. Serving the Public."[15]

Without doubt, the death of Diana and the public response associated with it represented some kind of turning-point in ways that prior incidents leading to political attempts to introduce statutory controls hadn't. National newspaper editors in particular were divided between a minority with feelings of guilt (the editor of *The Guardian* argued that the press had been "out of control") and the majority who felt that any blame lay with public taste. The concerted response, which did not really resolve the question, was to incrementally strengthen voluntary self-regulation and the exercise of self-restraint (less checkbook journalism, fewer kiss-and-tell stories, a moderation of harassment). Changes were implemented in broadcasting, too. Failures of the project were dismissed as mere "hiccups." In symbolic, as well as practical terms, success was counted in terms of the (quite literal) disappearance of paparazzi.[16] At the same time, while newspaper reading in general has been in long-term decline since the late 1950s, the losses of readers among tabloids, and most especially Sunday papers, has recently been proportionately greater.

Although it would appear premature to conclude that the worst excesses of "tabloidism" have been taped, let alone tamed, nevertheless, in the later 1990s, and especially since 1997, the formal M*A*S embarked on considerable reforms designed to a large extent to tackle the broad issue. Many of the processes are in place, and it has been demonstrated that they are capable of generating relevant actions. The critical third dimension necessary to facilitate the full panoply of M*A*S (monitoring, criticism, access, and greater awareness) is less secure, however; this is the active participation of publics, and their open interaction with the media and its professionals. Measured by crude aggregate numbers alone, it is clear that the regulatory M*A*S have stimulated greater public involvement. The total numbers of complaints received by the PCC rose by 65%

footnote[14]"Can We Trust Anything We See on Television?" *The Guardian*, 20 February 1999 at www.guardianunlimited.co.uk: accessed 8 Sept. 2000.

[15]Lord Wakeham (2000), *loc. cit.*

[16]Lord Wakeham (2000), *loc. cit.*

between 1991 and 1998. Complaints to the Broadcasting Standards Council and the Broadcasting Complaints Commission taken together increased at more than twice that rate (136%) between 1990-1991 and 1994-1995; and by 1999-2000 the figure for their successor body, the BSC, showed a further 30% growth. Whether this amounts to (inter)active participation is doubtful. Nevertheless, some advances were made in this area, too. In 1991 fewer than 5% of complaints received by the PCC were resolved through direct conciliation between members of the public and the press, resulting in apologies, the publication of corrections or the granting of the right to reply; in 1998 the figure was more than 22%. In 2000, the BSC introduced a similar category of procedure.[17]

OPENNESS OF THE MEDIA

Traditionally, however, wringing even small apologies and corrections from the British press has always been difficult. Broadcasting is not significantly better off in this respect, despite its statutory obligations and the right-to-reply guarantee contained in the European Union Broadcasting Directive. One well-established forum for dialogue between the press and the wider public, the letters-to-the-editor page, is more often than not skillfully manipulated to sidestep criticism of press performance.[18] Attempts to get the press to set up mechanisms for responding more openly to public criticism have mostly failed. For example, a press freedom and responsibility proposal that would have established the right to corrections through an Independent Press Authority was vigorously opposed by the overwhelming majority of newspapers and journalists. Both the ITC and the Radio Authority (a statutory body) can require the broadcasting of apologies and corrections (although their powers derive principally from their roles as licensing regulators), and the BBC's Programme Complaints Unit (PCU) (with appeals to the Governors' Programme Complaints Appeals Committee) does so as part of its remit to "recommend appropriate redress." The BSC, on the other hand, has no authority to order errant broadcasters to issue apologies or corrections, and the PCC relies on voluntary compliance, although it claims that, "Throughout the eight years of the PCC, every critical adjudication against a newspaper or magazine by the Commission has been printed in full and with due prominence."[19] This has not always been the case.

---

[17]Frost, *op. cit.*, pp. 4, 209. Broadcasting Standards Commission (2000), p. 4.

[18]Michael Bromley, "'Watching the Watchdogs?' The Role of Readers' Letters in Calling the Press to Account," *Sex, Lies and Democracy: The Press and the Public*, H. Stephenson and M. Bromley (eds.), Harlow, Longman, 1998, pp. 147-162.

[19]Press Complaints Commission (2000) "Key Benefits of the System of Self-Regulation" at www.pcc.org.uk/about/default.htm: accessed 8 Sept. 2000.

Broadcasters do have a legal duty, however, to make a formal record of all complaints and telephone calls; for example, the BBC does so via its Viewer and Listener Correspondence section which undertakes that "they are seen daily by top managers and programme makers throughout the BBC."[20] The PCU also generally pursues complaints with "the program-makers and editorial executives directly responsible." The Channel 4 program *Right to Reply* and the BBC Radio 4 show *Feedback* adopt similar approaches, and the ensuing discussions are broadcast. Other programs have perhaps been less effective: the BBC 1 television viewers' feedback show, *Points of View*, was described by one of its former presenters as a kind of meaningless, if entertaining, exercise in trading off claims and denials.

The press has so assiduously operated its peculiar form of editorial protectionism that the appearance of fissures in the façade seem genuinely remarkable. For example, in the month following the death of Diana the printing of an apology (albeit only two paragraphs on page 23) by the *Mail on Sunday* for publishing a photograph in contravention of the PCC code was regarded as significant enough to be referred to during a TV news program the following day. Although Wakeham claims that "most" inaccuracies are corrected,[21] the only national newspaper to have instituted any visible structural change in practice has been *The Guardian*, which appointed a readers' editor to "ventilate and respond to readers' concerns . . . [and] To seek to ensure the maintenance of high standards of accuracy, fairness and balance" in the paper. These objectives are met by publishing both a daily column of corrections and clarifications and a weekly commentary, as well as acting as a kind of internal ombudsman and an ethics coach to the paper's journalists.[22]

One shibboleth that has been abandoned is that of refusing to report and comment on the media themselves—the so-called principle that "dog doesn't bite dog." Specialist media sections appear in broadsheet newspapers (*The Guardian, Times,* and *Independent*) and weekly magazines (*New Statesman, Spectator,* and *Private Eye*). Programs covering the media come and go, although *What the Papers Say*, a weekly review of the press, has been on air (first on ITV, now with the BBC) for three decades. Coverage of the media is commonplace and most "serious" papers and broadcasters employ correspondents and even editors in the field and, as we have seen, the reporting is often investigative and critical. All the same, this interest may be driven at least as much by the expanding economic importance of the media industries than a commitment to openness. As a whole, what are called the creative industries generate revenues of £112 billion a year (equivalent to more than 4% of gross

---

[20]BBC Online, "Feedback" at www.bbc.co.uk/talk/index.

[21]Lord Wakeham (2000), *op. cit.*

[22]Michael Bromley and Hugh Stephenson "Digging Journalists Out of Holes," *British Journalism Review*, 9(1), 1998, pp. 59-66.

domestic product) and provide employment to about 1.4 million people. So-called content producers employ around half-a-million people, among whom 63,400 work in television and radio and 80,000 in the press. The media sector overall is estimated to be about twice the size of the automobile industry. This situation means not only that the media are often "big news" or that coverage has spilled over more consistently and prominently into the financial and business pages of newspapers and segments of broadcast news, but also that specialist media sections draw in lucrative "help wanted" advertising.

Much media self-appraisal is still essentially defensive. There is a large number of annual awards, many sponsored by industry and commerce, which are usually year-on-year self-congratulatory exercises, and which attempt to impose no absolute standards. The longevity of a sometimes, but not always, critical review of the press like *What the Papers Say* should be compared to the brief run enjoyed by a far more uncompromising show, *Hard News*, which specialized in exposing "the miscreants of Fleet Street" and drew the wrath of much of the national newspaper industry.[23] There is also a significant trade press and a number of guides and directories. However, there is little space for authentic public participation. The most common defense for this is that the situation at present provides the valuable "informed opinion" of those in the know in preference to the ignorant "rhubarb" of the popular voice.[24] The assumption of the media is that almost any significant levels of public participation, and particularly in editorial matters, will amount to a trespass on press freedom, not least in opening the way to prior restraint. The preferred alternative is "tough," post facto (self)regulation, and a market research-informed "professionalism."

THE DECLINING CONFIDENCE IN JOURNALISM

This approach is predicated on assumptions about editorial independence; that journalists are relatively free to report, analyze, and comment based on "professional" values, such as objectivity, accuracy, and fairness, which are designed first and foremost to serve the public interest. The commercialization of the media, however, has acted at least to severely distort this ideal. It is widely accepted that, above all, the media are influenced to an inordinate degree by "proprietorial pressure . . . [and] the profit motive."[25] This raises questions inter

---

[23]Raymond Snoddy, *The Good, the Bad and the Unacceptable: The Hard News about the British Press,* London, Faber, 1992, pp. xiii ff.

[24]Sue Arnold, "Spellbound by the Children's Serial, Irritated by Jim from Slough," *Observer Review,* 22 March 1998, p. 11; Maggie Brown, "BBC2 Goes for Fantasy," *The Times,* 20 March 1998, p. 45.

[25]Soley (1992), *loc. cit.*

alia about the ways in which the media report themselves. For example, might *The Guardian* have had covert motives for investigating documentary-making for one television company when the paper's owner, the Guardian Media Group, itself had interests elsewhere in TV? Similarly, to what degree was *The Times*'s media editor constrained in covering stories involving his own newspaper, his editor and his proprietor, Rupert Murdoch? Such questions are not hypothetical: Murdoch's company, News International, has used its newspapers, *The Sun*, *The Times*, the *News of the World*, and *Sunday Times,* both to support its satellite broadcasting arm, BSkyB, and to attack the BBC. When the issue of such conflicts of interest surfaced with the decision of the publishing house, HarperCollins, to cancel its agreement in 1998 to publish the memoirs of the former Governor of Hong Kong, Chris Patten, because of its supposed impact on Murdoch's wider media interests in the Peoples' Republic of China, more than one author or journalist called for "a common code, a strong shared ethos of editors and writers which says that beyond a certain line you do not go."[26]

In the absence of an editor's code, the ability of media owners and senior managers to expand their sphere of influence into the newsroom seems unstoppable. The extent to which the emergence of so-called market-driven journalism has contributed to a declining public trust of journalists remains largely a matter for conjecture. In 1997 a poll suggested that only 7% of people had a "great deal" of confidence in the press (compared to more than 55% for the police).[27] The collective confidence of journalists has certainly taken a downturn. The proportion of practitioners in membership of the National Union of Journalists' (NUJ) has fallen by at least a third, from more than 90% to less than 60%. Part of the consequence is that the NUJ code of conduct (which dates from 1936) and the union's ethics council have little, if any, practical application. The council's work effectively stalled over the objections from some rank-and-file members to self-policing. Ethics is marginalized in journalism training, which places greater value on the acquisition of basic technical skills and the development of personal traits; and the academic critical research tradition is dismissed as irrelevant to media practice. No journalism school in the United Kingdom publishes a review. Two new academic journals addressing journalism have British editors, but none is located in a J-school.

Enough concern has been expressed over the state of journalism for the quarterly *British Journalism Review* to have been established in 1989. A major self-declared objective was to redress a "lack of reflective and analytical culture" among UK journalists.[28] Its circulation remains small, however, with fewer than 450 copies in 1995. There is a large number of professional organizations with a variety of aims

---

[26]Timothy Garton Ash, "A Culture of Cowardice," *The Independent*, 1 March 1998, p. 17.

[27]Henley Centre, *Planning for Social Change 1997/8,* cited in Jamie Wilson, "Companies Cashing in on Trust," *The Guardian*, 14 October 1998, p. 11.

[28]"Why We Are Here," *British Journalism Review* 1(1), 1989, pp. 2-6.

and objectives, ranging from improving standards in specific areas to lobbying on behalf of general (media-related) interests. Several publish newsletters and journals; many are cross-media; most are introvert. Some media workers participate in specialist interest groups (Amnesty International Journalists' Network, Article 19, Campaign for Freedom of Information).

A small number of individual journalists, such as John Pilger and Paul Foot, publicly critique the structure and performance of the media, and the former BBC correspondent Martin Bell left journalism to stand for election to parliament in 1997 after promulgating his notion of a "journalism of attachment," which challenged the usefulness of the kind of "impartial" reporting that characterizes the BBC. For the most part, the memoirs and autobiographies of media figures do not problematize the media, although a few journalists have published supposedly tell-all accounts of working for the tabloids.[29] Those who do speak out tend to do so at considerable risk. The East Asia editor of *The Times* claimed he was forced to leave his job after commenting at a Freedom Forum meeting on the influence of Murdoch on the paper's coverage of China, and the television journalist and presenter Martyn Lewis was largely held up to ridicule over his suggestions for a "good news" agenda.[30] Perhaps as a result of fearing the further commercialization of the media, and its association with a decline in status, journalists have become increasingly self-protective.[31] In the 1990s more journalists than at any previous time believed in professionalizing the occupation.[32] Recent court decisions, the government's hesitant moves towards freedom of information, and the partial exemption granted the press after concerted lobbying from the privacy provisions of the European Convention on Human Rights may unintentionally offer the media additional scope to defend journalism that is newsworthy in the public interest but only on the grounds of professional judgment: acting merely on commercial interests may have the opposite effect.[33] All the same, the commercial "instinct" of the press (and, by extension, broadcasting) still prevails over its editorial independence.

---

[29]Sally Bailey and Granville Williams, "Memoirs are Made of This: Journalists' Memoirs in the United Kingdom, 1945-95," *A Journalism Reader*, M. Bromley and T. O'Malley (eds.), London, Routledge, 1997, pp. 351-377.

[30]Michael Bromley, "The Manufacture of News—Fast Moving Consumer Good or Public Service?" *Ethics and Media Culture: Practices and Representations,* David Berry (ed.), Oxford, Focal Press, 2000, pp. 111-131.

[31]See "The Media May Change But the Journos Will Stay," *UK Press Gazette* (12 June 1995), p. 19.

[32]Anthony Delano and John Henningham, *The News Breed: British Journalists in the 1990s*, London, The London Institute, 1996, pp. 9-10.

[33]Louis Blom-Cooper, "Press Self-regulation at Law," *PressWise Bulletin* 1, 15 Nov. 1999 at www.presswise.org.uk/bulletinarchive.htm: accessed 11 Sept. 2000.

PEOPLING M*A*S

One alternative explanation for any detectable growth in public disaffection with journalism is that general critical awareness and understanding of the media have grown considerably. The number of places on university media studies courses rose from 6,000 to 32,000 between 1990 and 1997 with an associated veritable explosion in textbook publishing. By 1999 journalism was an element in around 200 college and university courses: in 1989 there were just six journalism schools in the United Kingdom.[34] About a half of arts graduates reputedly aspire to work in the media, and nearly 10% of all graduates want to enter journalism. At the same time, by most measures the UK is the largest user of personal computing in Europe. An expansion in the 1980s in desktop publishing (community newsletters, fanzines), which rapidly grew to outnumber the newspapers published in the United Kingdom, has been followed in the 1990s by an explosion in web sites run by ordinary citizens and groups, indicating a significant do-it-yourself media sector. Even so, it is often argued that the public still does not have the skills for (nor, perhaps, the interest in) debating complex media issues.[35]

Lay intervention has been more usual in the narrower field of program and press content, epitomized by the "Clean Up TV" campaign associated with Mary Whitehouse from the 1960s. The National Viewers' and Listeners' Association formed and mobilized public opinion on matters of taste and decency, notably nudity, sex, violence, blasphemy, and swearing. However, when the Conservative government of Margaret Thatcher appeared to threaten the public service tradition in British broadcasting in the late 1980s, "ordinary" listeners and viewers were less visible in the group organized to campaign against the supposed dismantling of the BBC and for "quality television," which was comprised predominantly of celebrities and television and radio executives. The major overseeing bodies claim to consult the public regularly through seminars, forums, online interaction, open meetings, and so forth. The ITC maintains 12 viewer consultative councils, and the BBC has national broadcasting councils for Wales, Scotland, and Northern Ireland, and an English national forum representing regional and local advisory councils. Both organizations sponsor research into public opinion on broadcasting.

The primary concerns of lay organizations such as PressWise, the Voice of the Listener and Viewer (VoL), and the Campaign for Press and Broadcasting Freedom (CPBF) have been to articulate the views of "ordinary people" (PressWise) and "the citizen"s voice" (VoL) across a wider range of

---

[34]Figures taken from a survey conducted for the Centre for Journalism Studies at Cardiff University.

[35]Emily Bell, "Over the Hills and Far Away, Regulators Run Off and Play," *Observer Business*, 22 March 1998, p. 5.

issues of policy, ownership, freedom of information, journalism practices, and citizens' rights. A concern is that public consultations on policy are less open than they may seem, and that at a time of considerable change in the media they have failed to "generate the wide-ranging public responses [. . . for] shaping media policy.[36] One criticism of the formal M*A*S bodies themselves is that their memberships are highly circumscribed by a priori social and political determinations.[37]

Tulloch's argument that at this level M*A*S have been absorbed into the system of state patronage, acting primarily as conduits between the media and politics, and providing only virtual representation of broader publics through "the great and the good," seems to be borne out by an exploratory analysis of their memberships. Of the 58 members of the main M*A*S bodies[38] (12 BBC Governors, 12 Broadcasting Standards Commissioners, 11 Independent Television Commissioners, 8 Members of the Radio Authority, and 15 Press Complaints Commissioners) in place in September 2000, nearly 27.5% were titled, and another 14% were holders of other state honors. About half had connections with either business in general, the media businesses, or media management (including the six named editors on the PCC). Almost half were drawn from public service and politics. This last category, although probably underestimated in this analysis, still made up about a fifth of all appointments. Only a handful of the 58 did not appear to have any obvious links with business, politics, the media, or public service. Crude aggregates obscure considerable variations in the compositions of individual bodies. For example, none of the members of the Radio Authority, seven out eight of whom were appointed since 1997 by the Labour government, had titles, whereas seven of the 12 BBC Governors were titled or the holders of other State-awarded honors.

Nevertheless, as publics become more media aware, more critical of media performance, and more capable of calling them to account; as the media move more into the economic mainstream, have become more powerful and exert greater influence—factors that have been reflected in a new prominence of political and public debate about the media—and as the state professes to reduce its direct control over the media, there has been no corresponding popularization of the highest levels of formal M*A*S. Simultaneously, there has been a growing public disenchantment with both politics and the media, and the relationships between them, as the expansion of public relations and particularly "spin doctoring" threatens to supplant the Fourth Estate with the Fifth Estate. The absence of popular delegation may be viewed as a critical flaw.

---

[36]Campaign for Press and Broadcasting Freedom (2000), "Response to ITC Consultation on Public Service Broadcasting" at www.cpbf.demon.co.uk/itc.htm: accessed 31 Aug. 2000.

[37]See John Tulloch, "Managing the Press in a Medium-sized European Power," *Sex, Lies and Democracy: The Press and the Public,* M. Bromley and H. Stephenson (eds.), Harlow, Longman, 1998, pp. 63-83.

[38]M*A*S are not normally statutory—for exceptions see p. 21 [Editor's note].

THE IMPACT OF BEING DIGITAL

Governmental rhetoric surrounding what the Department for Culture Media and Sport (DCMS) refers to as the digital "revolution" is pretty unambiguous. Attention is to be paid to "the needs and demands of *consumers*" rather than publics.[39] It was within this overall frame that the department established a viewers' panel to monitor the progression towards the full digitalization of television (expected to be completed between 2006 and 2010). A wide-ranging review of communications reform, which began in 1998, was driven by the perceived "convergence" of broadcasting and telecommunications and rapidly became engulfed in existing debates about the state of the media. The review included a one-and-a-half month consultation process that drew more than 150 submissions, but these were funneled through a panel of so-called experts. Indeed, the proliferation and convergence of outlets contingent on digitalization may actually render collective views (particularly on content) less relevant. Content could be classified electronically at source, and the same computerization would permit automatic access at the point of consumption to encoded classifications. This would seem to signal the diminution of public debate and attempts to negotiate forms of consensus over taste. What may well take their place are an enhanced reliance on professional decision-making in media production and greater individual choice in consumption—judgments made more in private than in public. As two of the government's so-called experts put it, "The constant reminder of the global anarchy of the Net is an excellent check to bureaucratic nannying." It might be prudent, therefore, to be somewhat cautious about hopes that digitalization will serve through the sheer force of its characteristics inevitably to reinvigorate the popularity of M*A*S by facilitating interactive participation.

Although both the government and many media are committed in principle to "electronic openness," the record of the latter in practice is not always impressive. All the major, and many of the smaller, U.K. media maintain online presences (usually sites on the worldwide web).[40] Some, including the BBC, encourage forms of public involvement through the provision of multiple links to sections and individuals in their organizations, explanations of corporate structures and policies, data and information; for example, the Welsh language Sianel Pedwar Cymru (S4C) site posts the updated list of interests declared by members of the S4C Authority. *The Guardian* newspaper's Guardian Unlimited site posts editorial and other staff e-mail addresses, and *Guardian* journalists contribute to chat rooms. Overall, however, there is little evidence that any initial momentum towards greater openness has been consis-

---

[39]Department for Culture Media and Sport (2000), "Communications Reform White Paper" at www.culture.gov.uk/creative/index.html.

[40]Michael Bromley and Howard Tumber, "The First Cyberspace Election," *British Journalism Review* 8(2), 1997, pp. 68-74.

tently maintained. The range of the conversations in Channel 4's on-line chat-room "T 4" appeared to be more limited, and more focused on television programming and celebrity, in 2000 than an earlier version, "Reach 4" in 1997. Other media have used the web as simple extensions of their principal analog activities. Granada Television's <g-wizz.net> is designed for fans of the company's TV soap operas, and the *Daily Star*'s <megastar.co.uk> specializes in a kind of quasi soft porn. It is tempting to conclude that the media have so far utilized digital forms of communication not to engage with publics but as marketing extensions of their analog output, and have merely transferred their traditional closed-ness to the web. Interactivity, as Schulz observes, has become "a dull buzzword" with little real meaning behind it yet for M*A*S.[41]

CONCLUSION

The media are accorded no specific constitutional role in the United Kingdom, and there is no comprehensive media statute. Freedom of expression relies on the assertion of what in the 18th century were called the "rights of free-born Englishmen," most of which have been significantly eroded since. At the same time, restrictions on the media have been imposed piecemeal through either statute or case law. More than 250 statutory instruments curtail the disclosure of information and the work of journalists. Yet, with the exception of a relatively modest amount of broadcasting law and the special provisions in the application of the European Convention on Human Rights (mentioned above), legislation does not treat the media as a special case. The market has been mobilized over time as the chief regulatory mechanism. This has always been the case with the press, and has become increasingly so in regard to broadcasting since the late 1970s. Yet this has been coincidental to a marked decline in levels of public confidence. More than a decade ago, the editor of an influential trade paper urged that it was time that newspapers acquaint their readers with their editorial philosophy, and to regard "honesty and accuracy as marketable assets."[42]

Many other U.K. institutions and authorities have recently embarked on processes of self-examination. Social sustainability, it is argued, will be achieved only if "substantial opportunities for public interests and public concerns [are] to be taken into account in the course of policy formation." Such "cautious experimentation" in public participation might include consensus conferences, citizens' juries, and deliberative opinion polls, and is likely to focus on areas where ethics and social sensitivity are foregrounded.[43] There seem to be

---

[41]Schulz (2000), pp. 205, 217.

[42]Anon., cited Soley (1992), *op. cit.*

[43]John Durrant, "Do Not be Afraid of Democracy," *Research Fortnight*, 4(9), February 25, 1998, pp. 14-15.

striking parallels with the media here. As has been observed elsewhere of the arrangements for advisory committees to the government on science and technology, existing processes, however admirable, may need to be replaced with "new ways of taking account of the public interest."

The government's response was to propose the replacement of all five statutory regulators with one Office of Communications (Ofcom) which would bring the media and telecommunications under a single regime. Ofcom was not expected to begin work until at least 2003 on the completion of a broader package of communications reforms. In the meantime, the voluntary PCC entered something of a crisis when Lord Wakeham resigned because of his (unrelated) business involvement in the collapsed U.S. firm Enron. Almost immediately, a number of national newspaper editors began questioning the PCC's role and performance. The chief practical concern was the relationship among the PCC's director, its former director and later deputy private secretary to the Prince of Wales, and the editor of the *News of the World*. Various critics complained that the PCC was overly reliant on striking informal, behind-the-scene deals; had too close relationships with some newspaper editors; was too disposed toward "the rich and powerful"; was too inaccessible; and lacked transparency. Whether such developments would lead to greater public involvement in these M*A*S remained a moot point.

The analysis presented here suggests that such a change of attitude has not taken place in the media principally because of one particular internal factor—the imbalance of power between corporate media ownership and management, and journalism, which has led to serious erosions of editorial independence but at the same time has underpinned editorial protectionism. To some extent, that situation is reflected in the compositions of external M*A*S that overly reflect the relationships between the media and politics, rather than journalists and their publics, and thus restrict their effectiveness. This alone does not completely explain the lack of public participation in M*A*S, however. If it is allied to a broader lack of consumerism, which comes about perhaps because of a strong residual public service media ethos and a historically patrician skew to voluntarism, then it becomes more apparent why M*A*S have found it difficult to engage positively with ordinary people, whether as consumers, audiences, or publics. In many respects, the United Kingdom has the M*A*S it requires: the task at hand is to "let the people in."

CHAPTER 25
M*A*S in Germany
Some Gaps in the System

Barbara Thomass

Since the beginning of the 1980s experts in communicology in Germany have discussed media ethics. Since some deplorable media scandals like the publication in 1987 on the cover of the best-selling magazine *Stern* of a photo of the dead cabinet minister Barschel in a bathtub, or like journalists doing interviews with criminals who were holding hostages, media accountability has been a subject in Germany both for professionals or for social scientists. Progress in discussing media accountability and in organizing it have been made, but there are still gaps in the system and improvement is sorely needed. Here an overview will be presented of the major elements of a structure insuring quality standards in Germany—together with an assessment of it.

INDIVIDUALS OR GROUPS

The oldest and most traditional institution for media accountability or self-regulation in the print area in Germany is the German Press Council. It consists of ten journalists, appointed by the two German journalists' unions and ten representatives from the associations of newspaper and of magazine publishers. Founded in 1956 under pressure from politicians, it underwent a serious crisis at the beginning of the 1980s. It was called a "toothless tiger," which was deserved if one considers that the most severe sanctions it can impose is the obligation to publish a reprimand pronounced by the adjudicating body of the Press Council. And as more and more newspapers did not even respect this obligation, the representatives of the journalists doubted that there was any sense in collaborating with their employers in this institution and withdrew. But the reorganization of the German Press Council in 1985 and a written agreement that the adhering publishing houses would print reprimands led to a improved image for the council and more effectiveness.

The German Press Council applies its press code (see p. 82), consisting of 16 articles. When there are any new developments in society or the press, these articles are supplemented by "guidelines," which give more specific instructions as to proper journalistic behavior. Thus after the above mentioned interview of a hostage-taker, the Press Council added to article 11 on the sensationalization of violence and brutality a guideline: no interviews should be made of persons who are in the process of committing a crime. Another means the Press Council has of enriching the debate on journalistic standards is to comment on issues that emerge in professional practice, for example, reporting on business and markets. As an increasing number of journalists own stock themselves, conflicts of interests may occur. As a consequence of this debate, in May 2000 the Press Council changed one of its articles prohibiting journalists from letting their personal interests interfere with the coverage of such issues (Article 7).

This continuing updating of the code requires a close monitoring of social developments and changes. Thus the xenophobia and violence of neonazi groups towards non-German citizens caused the Press Council to set up a commission to develop more precise guidelines to article 12 on the protection of minorities. Hence the decision that mentioning the ethnic or religious background of a suspect is only acceptable if it is needed for the understanding of the reported event, and the journalist must take into account that such mention may worsen prejudice against minorities.

Everyone is entitled to complain to the Press Council and the Council itself can initiate grievance proceedings. Complaints, which have to be in written form, are submitted to a Complaints Committee. This will examine whether there has been a violation of the code and, in case of a justified complaint, will issue an advice notice (which can be considered as an internal comment of the Press Council on the event) or a notice of censure or a reprimand, the latter being distinguished from the former by the greater moral weight it is supposed to have, and which has to be published. But it is still a common practice that newspapers or magazines, even though they belong to an association which is part of the Press Council, will refuse to publish the reprimand. In addition, the Council cannot exert any influence on the form of the publication.

In 1999, the number of complaints lodged reached 534, which again showed an increase after years of constant increase. Most of them were about lack of truthfulness, accuracy, and thoroughness. Only 185 complaints were examined because they seemed to be relevant. Ten were finally considered to concern violations of the press code and were sanctioned by a reprimand. For more details, see the council's website: www.presserat.de/statistik.htm.

Those data reflect that the *Presserat* is not very well known in Germany, and its executive director admits that they should intensify their public relations. Although the Council's reprimands stimulate thinking and debate within the newsrooms, better efficiency and visibility could be achieved if it held its sessions publicly, if it worked faster (some procedures take too long because of stalemate resulting from the equal representation of journalists and publishers), and if the prestige of its members was greater.

In 1997, the Press Council declared itself to have jurisdiction over the Internet publications of the publishers, too. Then a self-regulatory body similar to the Press Council was founded in 1998 to deal with any publication of newspapers or magazines on the Internet (Freiwillige Selbstkontrolle Multimedia, FSM). The Associations of newspaper and magazine publishers, the association of on-line providers, the German Telecom, T-Online, Microsoft, the Association of Private Broadcasters, and others agreed to examine complaints concerning Internet contents, but not to exert any prior censorship, as some Internet pioneers feared they might. When the FSM deems that a complaint is justified, the only possible sanctions are the demand that the object of the complaint be deleted, that a disapproval or a reprimand be published by the publisher himself. If the reprimand was not published, the firm concerned could be excluded from the FSM. As international providers are not covered by this self-control body, the limits of enforcing accountability on a national level are obvious.

Traditionally, self-regulation and media accountability in the audiovisual media world were included in the constitution of public service broadcasting itself. The broadcasting corporation in each of the states (Länder) of the federal republic, and the nation-wide ZDF, are governed by independent Broadcasting Councils (Rundfunkrat), whose representatives are supposed (according to the Federal Constitutional Court) to reflect the "socially relevant groups" of society. These delegates are either elected within legislatures or they are selected by the said groups, including political parties, business and labor organizations, churches, farmers' or women's or sports or cultural associations, and so forth. Even though in theory few or none have been sent directly from the major political parties, the councils are heavily influenced by party interests. So monitoring political independence in the different Länder and fighting against political pressure on broadcasting are not on the agenda of the broadcasting councils.

Nowadays, commercial broadcasting dominates the market. In accordance with the federal broadcasting structure in Germany, its supervising bodies (Landesmedienanstalten) also operate at the level of the Länder. They are not strong enough, by far, to fulfill their function of monitoring and criticizing commercial broadcasting stations, especially as they are only entitled to perform an ex post facto control. So, commercial audiovisual media have not been covered from the beginning of their existence in 1984 and for nearly ten years by any body that could force them into accountability.

Due to increasing criticism about the presentation of sex and violence on commercial television, the industry in 1993 founded a self-regulatory body (Freiwillige Selbstkontrolle Fernsehen, FSF), which is mainly concerned with recommending adjustments of time slots for fiction films that could harm the taste and morality of children. "Commissioners for the protection of youth" in the commercial channels, which fund this body, submit such films to the FSF in advance for it to decide when they should be scheduled or whether some cuts are needed before showing the film in prime time. Thus, responsibility is entrusted to the networks themselves and the amount of work for the controlling committee, consisting of independent experts, is not too heavy. As public attention to this area intensified at the turn of the millennium, the channels realized it was important for them not to violate adjudications by the FSF, and in general they do what they are asked. In addition, the FSF publishes a quarterly magazine called *tv diskurs* about issues of media accountability.

Discussion of the effectiveness of these self-regulatory bodies is not complete so long as other elements of the media accountability system are not taken into account. A unique media supervising group consisted of the commission established by the President of the Federal Republic, Richard von Weizsäcker, in 1993. This group of renowned experts studied and discussed developments of ethical standards in television and one year later published the "Report on the Situation of Television" focused mainly on commercial TV. It expressed concern over the decline of the credibility of media. It listed plenty of failures in the performance of media and demanded that structures be set up that would improve the accountability of media.[1] Re-enforcing the responsibility of the newsrooms and establishing a media council were two of its recommendations.

There have been special events involving media accountability, such as the annual meeting of the Bavarian supervising body for commercial broadcasting which was devoted in 1993 to the subject of responsibility in television. Or a public discussion to which the *Frankfurter Rundschau*, a quality daily, invited professionals and scholars on the occasion of the book fair in Frankfurt in 1994. Or round tables of experts on media responsibility, which were organized by the Bertelsmann company. Such meetings have been held mainly when media scandals triggered a public debate, but did not become established as a permanent process.

An important group working for higher standards in newspapers is the so-called "Initiative Dailies," which is connected to the state-financed Bundeszentrale für politische Bildung, an organization dedicated to supporting political education in various fields. They have organized a series of workshops and seminars, for example, on professional local journalism or adjusting dailies to new demands of the audience. They sometimes deal with media ethics. Their regular publications, on reporting elections, press freedom, covering ethnic minorities or economic issues, help direct the newsroom to sound and accurate journalism in a particular field.

Although in-house criticism—as during a regular meeting of the staff for reviewing what has been done—is a common feature in most of the print

---

[1]Jo Groebel et al. *Bericht zur Lage des Fernsehens.* Gütersloh, Bertelsmann, 1994, p. 129.

and audiovisual media, this is focused on the general appearance of the paper or the programs: the aim is not to scrutinize the medium for possible violations of ethics. Nor are ombudsmen to be found in German newsrooms. In both cases, the absence may be because peer group criticism is not highly appreciated within German journalism. However, with the development of special media sections a small but qualified group of media reporters has grown in Germany from the middle of the 1990s (see below).

Quality control is also provided by groups within the professional organizations, on an occasional basis, when there have been clear violations of professional ethics. It can happen that the German journalists' association (Deutscher Journalistenverband) or the journalists' group within the general services trade union Ver.di react with press releases or articles in their internal publications. They try to avoid blaming any particular journalist, but rather concentrate on the general context in which media failures occur—such as accelerated speed in processing the news, media concentration trends, and growing competitiveness on the media markets.

There are hardly any mainstream media in Germany that are owned by the newspeople themselves. Within the famous newsmagazine *Spiegel,* the representatives of the employees, who own 50% of the shares, are mostly interested in defending their material interests. Editorial co-partnership is restricted, as could be seen when a new editor-in-chief was appointed against the votes of the newsroom.[2] In some leftist newspapers, such as the nationwide daily *Tageszeitung* or the weekly *Freitag,* readers hold shares in the company, but their influence on editorial policy is small.

Media watch groups do not have any noticeable influence in Germany. Some come from leftist organizations such as the Heinrich Böll Foundation, which is supported by the Green Party and concentrates on the issues of reporting on developing countries and on ethnic minorities in Germany.[3] Consumer associations such as the Verbraucherzentrale deal with media issues only very rarely.

TEXTS OR BROADCAST PROGRAMS

The press code of the German Press Council is the most important text on professional ethics in Germany. Although the responsibility of the Council is only for print media, the text is regarded as a guide for every journalist.

---

[2] Günther Frech, Mythos Spiegel?—Spiegel Mythos! *M Menschen machen Medien* No. 2, 1995, pp. 24-25.

[3] Media Watch. *Rassismus und Südberichterstattung. Kriterien für Medienkritik und Berichterstattung.* edited by Heinrich-Böll-Stiftung e.V., Dritte-Welt-Journalisten-Netz e.V., Cologne, 1994.

Besides this, another text is of great importance, as it deals with the very problematic relationship between journalists and police, especially when reporting protest marches that are controlled (or blocked) by policemen or other police actions. Under pressure from journalists' organizations, the Home Secretaries of the various *Länder* agreed on "principles of behavior for press and police" that should guarantee good working conditions to both professional groups, so each can fulfill its tasks without restrictions or curtailments by the other.

Another sort of text is the so-called "statutes of the newsroom" (*Redaktionsstatute*). They were the achievement of journalists' associations which secured for the staff of a newspaper or magazine certain rights when facing their editors and publishers. It was supposed that more editorial independence, hence a higher standard of quality, could thus be achieved. But they did not fulfill expectations, especially in the case of a serious conflict: for example, the *Spiegel* had a *Redaktionsstatut* which gave the editors a right to participate in the choice of the editor-in-chief, but when the publisher preferred another candidate, he just ignored it.

It is almost unknown for media to be open-minded about criticism or to organize it for themselves. The law provides for a right to reply, so when media make corrections on their own initiative, they bury them shamefully in some small obscure corner. Correction boxes as a visible ingredient of the newspaper are not to be found. Similarly, "letters to the editor" are mostly limited to some eulogizing comments on some ongoing political or social issues. Comments on the medium's performance are not considered. On-line message boards have been introduced since newspapers became available on the Web, but their use for purposes of media criticism is rare.

In contrast with this, since the beginning of the 1990s regular media sections are to be found in many newspapers and newsmagazines. Two new weeklies, *Focus* and *Die Woche*, started it and many dailies followed suit. Some quality newspapers such as the *Frankfurter Rundschau*, *Die Zeit*, or *Süddeutsche Zeitung* monitor the performance of media, whereas in most other papers such departments concentrate on media markets, products and personalities—features, however, which also help provide the audience with some knowledge of the industry. In recent times, there have been instances when monitoring and criticism also came within the range of these pages. The publication of faked interviews with Hollywood stars in the *Süddeutsche Zeitung Magazin* and the debate about the TV show *Big Brother*[4] seem to indicate the emergence of a more attentive attitude towards media contents. But it raises a big problem, because media reporters are dependent on the general editorial

---

[4]This show started in March 2000. Ten candidates were cut off from the outside world for 100 days within premises where they were observed by cameras. Every evening, the audience was presented with a daily summary of their activities and was to decide to exclude one person. The last remaining participant got about $115,000. This format was developed in the Netherlands and then adapted in Germany, Spain, and so forth.

policies of their publishers. They often face obvious limits, for example, when they wish to cover the activities of their employer on the media market. Reporting on media thus runs the constant risk of turning into public relations for the media involved.

Media sections in broadcasting also grew in the 1980s and even more in the 1990s, mostly on public broadcasting channels. But aside from some exceptions such as *Parlazzo,* on the Third Channel[4] of the public broadcaster *Westdeutscher Rundfunk,* which used its forum for a critical discussion of new program developments such as reality TV, daily talk shows, and so forth, by media reporters and producers, covering media was increasingly integrated into entertainment shows, where analytical quality is sacrificed to giving entertaining information on how television is made or exaggerations in the style of satirical parodies. Formats like "The worst of. . . ." or "Zapping" illustrate existing quality standards and their violations.

There are some "journalism reviews," such as the two periodicals of the trade unions—*journalist* and *M Menschen machen Medien*—and also independent ones such as *Medium Magazin* and *Message,* which have been on the market since 1998 and are published in cooperation with the *British Journalism Review* and the Italian *Problemi dell'informatione.* Their general tendency is to support the profession and report on media developments in general. Yet, they do contain elements that can be described as monitoring and criticizing, such as a regular column in *Medium Magazin,* the editorial letter to the reader in the trade union publications, or many essays in *Message.*

The range of books by professionals and experts that expose media failings and recommend improvements is rather wide. Since Günter Wallraff, who revealed the working methods of the tabloid *Bild,*[5] many other journalists have contributed a large number of critical descriptions and thoughts on media performance that have sensitized an interested public on media quality.

PROCESSES

The education of journalists is an ongoing process that, over the last three decades or so, has had a perceptible influence on media accountability. For a long time, a two-year apprenticeship was the normal access to journalism, but it is more and more frequently supplemented by higher education, most often not journalism stud-

---

[4]There are 15 regional corporations that cooperate in the ARD and contribute according to their size to the first public TV channel, called *ARD.* In addition, they produce a Third Program, which offers regional news and more culturally oriented programs.

[5]Günther Wallraff, *Der Aufmacher. Der Mann der bei Bild Hans Esser war.* Cologne, Kiepenheuer & Witsch, 1997.

ies. The quality of the two-year internship, which is done mostly at a regional news-paper, has for more than 20 years been a point of intense controversy between, on the one hand, journalists' organizations which wanted to include in it some intellec-tual content and ethical concerns and, on the other, employers' associations which were more interested in a purely practical education. An agreement at the beginning of the 1990s and offerings by various journalism schools of short seminars (from two days to a maximum of a week) have clearly improved the situation. But contin-uing education is still not a big issue in German newsrooms.

In the first half of the 1990s, 11% of practicing journalists had had no formal education in journalism. Sixty percent had done the two-year apprentice-ship, 64% had been to university, either in journalism and mass communication or in some other faculty.[6] A combined education (two-year apprenticeship and journalism studies, two-year apprenticeship and communication studies) is fre-quent. Nearly 10% had been to a journalism school outside the university. So, the education of journalists has obviously improved over the last 20 years, as a steadily growing number of journalists have obtained university degrees—although the quality of journalism education is still very variable from one insti-tution to the next. Also the evidence suggests that questions relating to profes-sional conduct and journalism ethics are increasingly entering the syllabi of journalism programs.

A strong element in the German media accountability system is non-commercial (media and journalism) research. At the beginning of the 1990s, two typical investigations of journalism provided insight into the moral attitudes and alleged behaviors of journalists. Both agree that journalists in Germany have generally high standards when investigating stories and that the image of the reporter is of one who presents facts and remains neutral—but not one who takes on the role of social critic or controller.

Communication research has dealt intensively with the issues of media ethics since the beginning of the 1980s.[7] But the main aim of research activities is the systematic structuring of the field and the development of media ethics theory. Empirical analysis of the contents, or of the absence of contents, in media, which makes it possible clearly to assess media performance and accountability, is not prominently represented. Research on the perception of media messages, however, is an important activity as well as research on the effects of media. The results: media have great impact and are powerful, but their effects are achieved through complicated processes, which have to be dis-

---

[6] Siegfried Weischenberg, "Die Ausbildung der Journalisten: Akademisierte Praktiker." In *Sage und Schreibe special April 1994: Journalisten in Deutschland. Was sie denken—wie sie arbeiten*, 1994, p. 26.
[7] Barbara Thomass, *Journalistische Ethik. Ein Vergleich der Diskurse in Franreich, Grobbritannien und Deutschland*, Opladen, Westdeutscher, 1988.

tinguished precisely.[8] Links between the scientific community and journalism are gradually being established, as, for example, through conferences organized by university institutes that invite practicing journalists, or on the initiative of newspapers that want to obtain the opinion of scholars from journalism studies about their product.

Considering what I have just said of the media accountability systems in Germany, it is not surprising that discussions have taken place as to the desirability of a general media monitoring institution. This suggestion was brought into discussion in the sphere of communication science as well as in journalism and was made clearer by the above-mentioned commission that published the "Report on the Situation of Television." The fundamental idea is that the media audience can be more and more regarded as made up of consumers, addressed as such by commercial media. Like any other consumers, they need protection and advice. So the suggested institution should assume the functions of testing, archiving, and informing on any programs put on the air. It should provide a permanent monitoring service and publish the results. The institution should also act as a forum for media professionals and as an ombudsman for complaints from the audience.[9] This is a debate in which differing factors (mainly, the fear that existing organizations have of losing their influence) prevent a quick solution and so the discussion faded away.

Lastly, it may also be regarded as an accountability process when the relationship between politics and journalism is more and more discussed within the profession. The end of the era of chancellor Helmut Kohl, who treated the press and its representatives with some contempt, made it possible that journalists question themselves about their relationships to power. With the move of the German capital from Bonn to Berlin, a framing factor in this relationship had been changed as well. As professional activity and the media landscape became far more competitive in the metropolis, the styles of relations between politicians and journalists changed and triggered a discussion about power and the press, which appears in the columns of some quality papers.

Singular events, publications, and public discussions on media accountability are widespread in Germany and can be regarded as important elements in a media accountability system. They tend to be reactive and depend on the heat of public debate, following not only single media scandals or failures,

---

[8]For an overview of German communication research, see Hans-Bernd Brosius and Christina Holtz-Bacha (eds.), *German Communication Yearbook,* Cresskill, NJ, Hampton Press.

[9]Friedrich Krotz, "Verbraucherkompetenz und Medienkompetenz. Die Stiftung Medientest als Antwort auf strukturelle Probleme der Medienentwicklung" in Wessler et al. (eds.), *Perspektiven der Medienkritik. Die gesellschaftliche Auseinandersetzung mit öffentlicher Kommunikation in der Mediengesellschaft,* Opladen, Westdeutscher, 1997, p. 259.

but also accompanying long-term developments. The repeated errors and failings in conflicts, crises and war reporting have justified such discussion about journalistic behavior and performance. Systematic M*A*S that allow continuous monitoring and supervision are still to be developed. But the ongoing discussion of media ethics has augmented the general awareness of a need for adequate structures. Thus, the idea of a media council or a media testing institution has a decent chance of being established. It could be considered as a great achievement within the M*A*S system in Germany.

CHAPTER 26
M*A*S in France
Much to Do and Little Done

After major scandals such as the Timisoara massacre hoax (in Romania, 1989) and the reporting of the Gulf War (1990-1991), there were many debates, in France as elsewhere—a lot of breast-beating and finger-pointing. What is left of it? It now seems agreed that the three means of improving media must be used together: the Law, the market, and ethics. And there is more acceptance that ethical rules must be enforced with no recourse to government.

But what has been decided? What has been achieved? What French M*A*S were there at the beginning of the third millennium?

First, a few words on the situation of journalism in France. French magazines are doing well,[1] but dailies are not. They do not get much advertising,[2] and also seem unable to attract a large readership. Their financial resources are small and so is their credibility. As an annual survey[3] has shown since 1987, the public does not trust journalists. And the decline of sales is one clear sign of this. According to Serge July, an eminent journalist and director of the daily *Libération,* "The first explanation is that newspapers offered for sale in France are bad."[4] (Starting with his own, some would add.)

---

[1]The French read about twice as many magazines as the British or the Germans. The news magazines are remarkable by their number and quality.

[2]The proportion of the GDP invested in advertising is lower in France than in most of Europe. In the mid-1990s, the press obtained 44% of its revenues from advertising, as opposed to 63% in Britain and 65% in Germany.

[3]Commissioned by the TV magazine *Télérama* and the Catholic daily *La Croix.*

[4]In *La Tribune de la vente* (NMPP), November 1986, p. 27.

Experts will accuse the media, be they national or provincial, left-wing or right-wing, of not having paid much attention over the years to serious phenomena likely to upset various powers-that-be, such as alcoholism, the abuse of drugs in sports, the underhanded financing of electoral campaigns, graft at the several levels of government—or the defense of consumers[5] or the protection of the environment.

But what strikes the general public are the dramatic transgressions. There have been more than a few in France in the 1990s: doctored photos, manipulated interviews,[6] staged documentaries. "L'Affaire Botton" put corruption in the limelight: it involved several top-level journalists who accepted gifts from a crooked millionaire who happened to be the son-in-law of an ambitious politician. Media inventions were exposed, such as a television program about the corneas of Latin-American children supposedly stolen to be implanted in the eyes of wealthy Westerners. Also exposed were invasions of privacy and denunciations that had lethal effects, such as the suicide of Prime Minister Bérégovoy or (so it was believed) the death of Princess Diana. Highly visible also was the long-standing intimacy between media and government: is there another democracy where the President (François Mitterrand in 1992) would be interviewed on television by journalists who happened to be the wives of two of his ministers?

All these cases, far from being isolated accidents, derive from old traditions, made worse by regrettable new trends. The experienced observer is hardly surprised by the excessive abuse poured by foreign correspondents in Paris on their French colleagues: "All corrupt and moronic . . . actually, they're all in advertising . . . working for a daily consists in taking stories from the wire service AFP and embellishing them . . . they write without having anything to say . . . a catastrophe especially concerning the economy . . . they think they are very important, indispensable . . . they are in the service of the government . . . the exposé of a major scandal is impossible in France."[7] When abroad, one is inclined to slanderous arrogance. These correspondents, who come from a different journalistic culture, interpreted as journalistic flaws behaviors that belong to another tradition. However they are also largely right.

Ethical problems in France are the same as in other countries, only more serious than in some, because so little is done to solve them. For information about what is being done, three surveys conducted in 1998 are available, two of them done under the aegis of the *Fédération nationale de la presse*

---

[5]With few exceptions, major media never echo test results published in *Que Choisir*, the review of the consumers' union.

[6]The best-known TV anchorman in the country, unable to interview the Cuban dictator, took the tape of a Castro press conference and slipped in views of himself asking questions to make it look as a one-on-one conversation.

[7]During interviews done in 1991 by an MA student of the Institut français de presse.

française (FNPF);[8] the third, which I did on regional dailies, openly aimed at discovering what "media accountability systems" were in operation.[9]

The first survey, of some 200 dailies and news weeklies, was triggered by concern about the growing number of legal actions (which remain relatively few, however, an annual average of five per publication). In half the cases, they are libel suits, due to inaccuracies. Quite often the reader first tried to obtain redress by means of a letter to the editor or by using his/her legal right of reply. In one case out of five, the cause is invasion of privacy or unauthorized use of his/her picture.

Considering the whole of the printed press, 38% of conflicts were settled amiably, 60% of them in the case of regional dailies. In other words, about two thirds do go to court, 40% for regional dailies. So a sentence in the report is worth quoting: "When the amiable approach leads to a positive outcome, it's always through the publication of a correction or the granting of a right of reply, i.e. by publicizing parts of a dialogue with the reader." A crucial remark.

The second survey, like the first, was motivated by the decline in the public's trust. A former editor of *Ouest France* (the largest-selling daily in the country) interviewed 28 publishers. The topic: "How to reconcile press freedom with respect for the dignity of every individual." Media managers appear in general to be very favorable to "editorial charters [= codes] and similar devices, because of a desire to show the responsibility of the publisher." This is great news for someone like me, who in the late 1980s presented media ethics and M*A*S to an assembly of regional publishers and met with Siberian indifference. They now have a positive view of ethics but, they say, its operation must not "lead to an appearance before some institution likely [. . .] to publish opinions that might be used in court against newspapers." That is a old objection to codes and to a M*A*S such as a press council, though its validity has never been proven.

Media managers suggest three means to promote ethics. First, training, both on the job and on campus: the teaching of media law should be developed in journalism schools, and also the raising of an awareness of ethical issues. Second, charters, which are useful both as pedagogical tools while they are being drafted and later as internal rules of conduct. Third, the vigilance of all editors in the newsroom. A majority of the publishers expect the FNPF to stimulate a reflection on media ethics. It should define basic values and keep an "ethical watch." They even considered an "observatory of the ethical practices of the press"—in which lessons would be drawn from the daily experience of newspapers. All that sounds excellent—even though, several years later, it remained an unrealized project.

---

[8]See the reports of F-X. Alix and F. Devevey, in the review *MédiasPouvoirs*, Fall 1998.
[9]See C-J. Bertrand, *Media Ethics and Accountability Systems*, Piscataway, NJ, Transaction, 2000, pp. 133-136.

The best way to learn how to serve the public well is to enable the public to express its opinion about what is done, is not done, and could be done. Rare nowadays are the people in the industry who dare claim that it is enough for the public to express its opinion by not buying a paper or by zapping to some other channel. M*A*S are the needed means of criticism, suggestion, and dialogue.

THE PRESENCE OF M*A*S

The Usual Ones

Codes. The code of the SNJ, adopted by that journalists' union in 1918, was one of the first in Europe—but, just like unions in other nations, the SNJ never cared much about enforcing discipline. Most of the other codes date from the 1990s. The so-called "ethical reference" of the Provincial Daily Press Association (SPQR) was published in 1995. Of the prestigious Paris dailies, the left-wing *Libération* has a code as does the Catholic *La Croix*. In January 2002, fifty-seven years after its founding, the No. 1 quality daily *Le Monde* published a style book that had been many years in the making. It includes a three-page code (the word is not used) containing "principles" and "the rules and usages" of the newspaper.

Two thirds of the major provincial dailies claim to have codes, drafted by management, a few in cooperation with newsroom rank and file. But in the rest of the press, hardly more than half the titles have a "code," often just a few rules concerning freebies and junkets. A few newspapers have documents that deal with media ethics; others claim to have or to be preparing one. For *La Voix du nord* (in the city of Lille), it's a practical guide for the newsroom drafted in 1993 by the management and the 70 journalists working in teams. For *La Nouvelle République* (in the city of Tours), it's a "compendium of customs that have gradually become established in the newsroom." At *L'Union* in Reims, a style book was inspired by studies made of readers' expectations and discussed in workshops; about a quarter of it deals with ethics. *Ouest-France* has a code limited to the coverage of "human interest stories" and court reporting, which is regularly amended at biannual seminars.[10] *L'Alsace* has a similar one.

According to the FNPF survey, over four out of five codeless media firms have set up a "think tank" in which management and journalists cooperate—and also a few readers in one tenth of cases: this could be the sign of a slow but very positive evolution within the industry.

Criticism. There is no U.S.-style journalism review like the *American JR*. "Media" pages in dailies and newsmagazines are far more numerous than they used to be, but seldom critical. Among television and film guides, only one, the high-brow *Télérama,* publishes strong opinions, pro-and-con views of movies, and parallel studies of comparable TV shows.

---

[10]See the text in Bertrand (2000), pp. 101-104.

In the early 1990s, you could find a few columns devoted to ethics in trade reviews. I did one in the bulletin of *Reporters sans frontières* (1989-1990), which was terminated abruptly, and another in *Journalistes Infos* (1994-1995), which was interrupted by the demise of the publication!

More common have been reports and special issues of reviews: a *White Paper on the Ethics of Journalists* was published by the SNJ union in 1993. The journal *MédiasPouvoirs* devoted two issues to that topic, in 1989 and 1998.[11] And, during the crisis following the Gulf War, a few other publications did the same, some cultural such as *Esprit*[12] and *Le Débat*,[13] others trade-oriented such as *Les Dossiers de l'Audiovisuel*.[14]

Fortunately, books abound: book publishers show far more courage than media about attacking media. And the volumes come in great diversity, from statistical to radical, from scholarly to journalistic. For instance, *Chiffres en folie*[15] documents the wild use of figures and statistics by the press, and *Comment manipuler les médias*[16] consists of 101 recipes for subverting the media. *Mauvaise presse*[17] contains Cyril Lemieux's critical research in the sociology of the reporter's work, and *L'Omerta française*[18] exposes what news the media omit and why.

Some of the books are written by journalists, retired like F-X. Alix or A. Woodrow,[19] or working like Daniel Cornu and Serge Halimi, whose *Les Nouveaux chiens de garde* became a huge best-seller (250,000 copies sold) with little help from the media. Intellectuals and academics also contribute criticism, such as Pierre Bourdieu, Régis Debray or Dominique Wolton. Yet it is interesting to note that in its *Que Sais-Je* encyclopedic series (with now several thousand titles in print), the Presses Universitaires de France published *The History of Gibraltar, Emperor Hadrian* or *The Tango* in the 1950s—but its first book on media ethics only in 1997.[20]

What about broadcasting? At the turn of the century, the (educational) channel "La 5ème" aired *Arrêt sur image*, a one-hour program produced by a journalist from *Le Monde*, which investigated cricisms made of various media.[21] The indictment can be tough, but the accused are always given a chance to clear

---

[11]Spring 1989, Fall 1998.

[12]"Mais où va le journalisme?," December 1990 issue.

[13]Nos. 60 and 61, July-August and September-October 1990.

[14]No. 36, March-April 1991.

[15]By an association of magistrates and journalists, Paris, La Découverte, 2000.

[16]By Patrick Farbiaz, Paris, Denoël, 1999.

[17]Paris, Métailié, 2000.

[18]By S. Coignard and A. Wickham, Paris, Albin Michel, 1999.

[19]See the bibliography.

[20]But then three of them: *Ethique de l'information* by D. Cornu; my *La Déontologie des médias* and *Médias et déontologie* by H. Pigeat.

[21]First at 8.45 p.m. on Wednesdays, later at 12.30 a.m. on Sundays.

themselves. The top TV channel TF1 did nothing, but other commercial networks were bolder: for several years, Canal Plus presented Marc-Olivier
Fogiel's abrasive interview program *TV Plus*, on Saturdays from 7 to 8 p.m.—
but it came to an end in mid-2000. And in a related field, M6 had for many
years broadcast its excellent *Culture Pub*, which provided a weekly critical coverage of the world advertising scene.

Media Users' Associations.   Very regrettable, and hard to explain, is
the fact that the two major consumer defense organizations, one State and one
private, both ignore media. Their magazines, *Que Choisir?* and *60 Millions de
consommateurs,* report on comparative analysis of television sets and the services of banks, but never on the quality of women's magazines or TV news.
They seem stuck in a pre-media world.

As for dedicated citizen groups, too often they only last as long as the
founder's enthusiasm. Woodrow found[22] seven of them in 1990: ten years later,
two of those had vanished and four had merged into two. MTT, which was
founded by national federations with far wider purposes (see p. 251), survived a
little better because it could (at least in theory) rely on many local chapters: this
made it possible to do vast surveys and to lobby both government and media
corporations. In Belgium, the militant Association des Téléspectateurs Actifs
(1993) strove to put pressure on institutions by various actions, such as putting
out a bulletin called *Comment télez-vous?*

Three other associations, with more modest ambitions, had occupied a
few niches. The left-wing ACRIMED (1996) gathered academics and journalists once a month for a presentation and debate, mainly critical, on the performance of news media—and it kept a website alive. APTE (1986) aimed at
teaching citizens how to handle images—especially teaching children how to
use media. Thucydide (1997), inspired by the Gulf War, strove to improve
media services through more input by historians and other social scientists.

User Access.   Generally speaking, media show little interest in establishing regular contacts with their audiences, either by means of press councils,
liaison committee, call-in sessions, or even Letters to the editor. Not that the
French public keeps quiet: the non-commercial TV network France 3 receives
2,500 to 3,000 letters a week. The people do want to be heard, but the French
press refuses to listen. Dailies started publishing letters to the editor only after
1968—reluctantly. By 2000, *Libération,* which had initiated the change, had
dropped its own letters column. *Le Monde* published only a small page once a
week plus a few scattered items. But the little *La Croix* had a full (tabloid) page
daily; the Catholic press is in general more inclined to accountability. No more
than a third of provincial newspapers had such a letters section.

---

[22]In his *Information Manipulation*, Paris, Editions du Félin, 1991.

Broadcasting did even less. The public network France 3 had cancelled its 25-minute program *On se dit tout* [Let's tell one another everything] on Sundays at 1 p.m., by which it gave access to viewers. As for France 2, on Saturdays since 1998, its ombudsman had a program called *l'Hebdo du média-teur,* just after the midday newscast.

Ombudsmen. The French call them "mediators," arbitrators rather than "reader's advocates," not quite the same. In 2000, there were about half a dozen in all. Since 1998, there have been some in public broadcasting: two for news shows, at France 2 and France 3, and one for non-news programs aired by the holding company France Télévision. An ombudsman also worked for international public radio RFI. At Radio-France there were long discussions about having an ombuds-man but the news directors opposed the project. Yet, the least one can say is that the existing referees rarely side with the plaintiffs. As for contact between top executives and media users, it was to be found in just one monthly program, *Je veux parler au directeur* [I want to speak to the boss] in which the president of national radio station RTL fielded questions from listeners.

Only two *médiateurs* function in the daily press. *Le Monde* had appointed one in 1992, but some observers wondered whether he was much more than a letters editor,[23] in charge of public relations. The other *médiateur* had been appointed in 1995 to serve the group of *Le Progrés* newspapers in the Lyon region: he did not write a column and was meant to stay out of the limelight, but to keep in touch with the potential readership and to report to the newsrooms. By 2001, he was not opera-tive any longer.

Research. That last and important M*A*S is often ignored. Research on what media do and do not do, on their long-term effects and so forth, is done within the National Center for Science Research (CNRS); in observatories/think tanks, more numerous now; and mainly in the universities where the informa-tion-communication field has finally, belatedly, been given official recognition as a bona fide discipline. Alas, it is typical that the Institut français de presse (IFP),[24] the oldest of the university institutions, is not accredited as a school of journalism by the profession. That is where the largest number of students are working on PhDs.

ORIGINAL M*A*S

Some of the M*A*S that are special to France are exceptional, such as the fea-ture-length documentary that Pierre Carles pieced together with bits of audio

---

[23]A few magazines have claimed to have an ombudsman, who in fact simply handled the letters to the editor.

[24]Université de Paris-2.

and video tapes that revealed the over-close relationship of bigwigs in the TV business with the authorities—and quite a few limitations to their freedom. Carles showed it in festivals or within networks of citizens' associations; an ad hoc association was even formed aimed at showing the film in theaters. Although some aspects of the movie might be questionable (even illegal), the major media were not justified in ignoring it.

Some M*A*S function away from the limelight. At one point, the relatively new cable and satellite channel Régions equipped a dozen of its viewers with video-cameras so they could take part in some live programs, five minutes a day. Another channel posted on the screen a questionnaire about its programs which viewers could fill out by pressing buttons on the remote.

On the other hand, some M*A*S are permanent and well-known, mainly the weekly *Canard Enchaîné* (500,000 copies). It was born during WW I to debunk official propaganda. It now belongs to its staff and takes no advertising, and so enjoys more independence than other periodicals. One of its main activities is to criticize the media and to publish what others dare not print—which is exactly the double mission which most U.S. JRs assumed in the late 1960s and early 1970s (see p. 201). *Le Canard* is the French newspaper that foreign correspondents in Paris most appreciate. In a similar style, TF1 once aired a program called *Droit de réponse* [Right of Reply] by Michel Polak (1981-1987), but it was abruptly ended when he turned its guns on TF1's new owner, a construction conglomerate. In 1998, Canal Plus showed *Le Vrai Journal* by Karl Zéro, a parody of a newscast (Sunday, 1 p.m.) that boasted that it exposed what the regular media omitted.

As far as citizens' action is concerned, "TV Carton Jaune"[25] was set up (in 1992) by two lawyers: they wanted to take class actions to court on behalf of media users whom they wished to mobilize into pressure groups—but they met with little success. As for *sociétés de lecteurs*, there is only one in existence, at *Le Monde*.

Le Monde was also the birthplace of the first *société de rédacteurs*, following a dramatic internal crisis in 1951 (see p. 233). That has also been the only successful one, according to the 1973 Lindon Report which evaluated the *sociétés*. Maybe this is because most do not own enough shares in the company to be able to block major decisions. In the early 1990s, they were to be found at the newsmagazines *Le Point, l'Evénement, l'Express, Courrier International*, and at dailies such as *Le Figaro, Libération, le Parisien, Sud Ouest*. In Paris as in the provinces, at the AFP wire service, at the Europe 1 national radio station and Radio France, they have shown little efficiency and gone into hibernation. They only wake up in critical periods, such as when a publication is being sold. The major TV network TF1 has one and also France 2. Radio station France Culture has one and also France Inter, but it is inactive.

---

[25]With a "Yellow Card," a soccer referee punishes a player for a serious violation of the rules. A Red Card means expulsion from the field.

NOTABLE ABSENCES

Indisputably, some progress took place over the last 20 years of the 20th century. For instance, audience measurements started being published, whereas they used to be treated as corporate secrets. Newspapers started publishing correction boxes and commissioned readership surveys. However, it all adds up to little, very little. What is achieved in one place is not imitated elsewhere. By 2000, *Le Monde* had signed on its third ombudsman, but no other daily had followed in its footsteps.

So there you have France, one of the ten wealthiest nations in the world, well provided with media and other resources; a country proud of having been the birthplace of the 1789 Revolution and cradle of human rights. And yet, the "social responsibility" of media, and the M*A*S, are less developed there than in any similar nation. France is one of the only countries in Europe, together with Ireland and Greece (not the most developed nations in the European Union), not to have, never to have had, never even to have seriously considered having, a Press Council, the best symbol of media accountability, the most spectacular M*A*S—and potentially the most efficient because it gathers owners, professionals, and citizens (see p. 109).

What does an eminent historian of the French press, Pierre Albert, think about it?[26]

> It had been hoped that the decisions of the "arbitration commission," provided for by the 1935 Act defining the status of journalists, would gradually generate the substance of a code of professional ethics—but it was quickly forgotten. The Deschizeaux Bill which, in November 1936, aimed at creating a seven-member Order, a "Conseil de l'ordre de la presse," never was even debated.
>
> In the effervescent renewal of the Liberation (1944), nobody mentioned the creation of such a body: the notion of an "Order of Journalists" was even more unpopular then because of those created in Italy, Germany, Spain and Portugal by fascist governments to muzzle the press.
>
> A proposal was made in 1964 by the Federation of Journalists' Professional Associations to set up an "Superior News Council." A proposal was made in 1970 by the Lindon Commission report on *"sociétés de redaction"* to endow the press with "a moral magistracy" modeled on the British press council. And the same proposal was made by the Federation of *sociétés de journalistes* in April 1971. All have met with the overt hostility of owners' associations and the indifference of the authorities.
>
> In 1986 the Commission for Press Transparency and Pluralism was disbanded; it had been set up by an Act of November 1982 on the suggestion

---

[26]From his presentation at the symposium "Forum sur les M*A*R*S," 19-20 April 1991 in the Palais du Luxembourg.

of the 1979 Vedel Report for a Commission on Press Operations.[27] That suppression too can be interpreted as a process of rejection by our institutional system of any independent regulatory body meant to stand between the Law and the media.

According to the FNPF survey, in the late 1990s some publishers were in favor of creating an ethics committee, which could give opinions, or even be asked to adjudicate on cases presented by aggrieved readers. That small minority might one day be tempted by a press council.

One may regret that news media never took their cue from advertising. The *Bureau de Vérification de la Publicité* (BVP, 1935) is sponsored by advertisers, ad agencies and representatives of all advertising vehicles, and organizes joint meetings with consumers. Its rules were inspired by a precise international code that posits the existence of an enforcement body. Newspapers and magazines endorse the BVP voluntarily. Because it enforces the rules strictly, it can claim to be a buffer between the profession and the state, whose restrictive laws also exist.

There is another fundamental M*A*S: education. On a long-term basis, it might be the one with the best chance of improving media. However, the media industry has shown little regard for it: at the turn of the century, it let the two most renowned schools totter for years on the brink of bankruptcy. Those two schools, by the way, do not belong to a university, which in the United States would be unthinkable. Indifference, misunderstanding, or even contempt are still rife between journalists and academics. Interesting also is the fact that, in the schools accredited by the profession, the teaching of ethics, when it exists, is very limited, even more than the teaching of media law—no semester or annual course.

The media industry, which rarely finances university research directly, even that which could lead to higher profits, has not set up any of those U.S.-style foundations that use their funds to promote journalism research and teaching. Nor has it created centers for media studies and for the improvement of professionals, such as the Nieman Center at Harvard University or the Knight Fellowships at Stanford. Never in France have millions of dollars been granted by media corporations to j-schools for buildings or equipment, for libraries and endowed professorships. Even industry grants to students or researchers are very rare.

CAUSES OF NON-DEVELOPMENT

General Causes

Three groups take part in social communication, other than as sources of news or income: press proprietors, journalists, and members of the public. As in other

---

[27]A parallel to the "Commission des Opérations en Bourse," the French equivalent of the US Securities and Exchange Commission (SEC).

countries, the problem with much of the public in France is that it is not interested. Because it has few means to express itself, it thinks it is powerless: tradition has taught it cynicism. Few users are ready to campaign for the improvement of media.

As for press proprietors and journalists, they have the same reactions to M*A*S as in all democracies. M*A*S use one or several among four methods. First, criticism: that is unbearable to thin-skinned professionals with a fragile ego. Second, monitoring: that is too expensive and too threatening. Third, feedback from users: why should those contemptible creatures be given a voice in the product? Fourth, training: there again, too expensive—and also too slow, useless, and maybe dangerous.

Journalists do not object to talk about ethics, about the sins of others (especially the stars of the profession) on the occasion of symposia, of regular summertime conferences,[28] and special issues of reviews. But they never consider actually doing anything. Thus at the daily *Libération,* they lengthily debated having an ombudsman but ten years later they still did not have one.

When M*A*S are mentioned, media "watchdogs" howl that freedom is in danger—not their freedom from advertisers or shareholders or newsmakers (whose existence is not obvious to all) but their freedom from media users. They do not wish to be accountable to them—in any way. Wondrous it is to see how the stars of journalism and lowly reporters, media executives and union leaders, all drape themselves in a freedom that belongs to the public.[29]

M*A*S face stubborn and irrational opposition. It causes a strange feeling to hear the former head of a French wire service address an international conference on the topic of codes and press councils in such terms that it seemed that his intelligence had suddenly deserted him. And his words were quoted by an editor from *Le Monde* invited to the conference:[30] a worldwide media ethics was impossible, unacceptable, dangerous; every journalist had a moral conscience and that was enough; any notion of a social responsibility was but a mask of the totalitarian state. No wonder that when, in one of his columns, the "mediator" at *Le Monde* dared to mention the name of an editor, there was talk of "Stalinian censorship" in the newsroom and two journalists offered to resign.

Another source of hostility is professional solidarity. Dog does not eat dog. We're all in the same boat. The arrogance of the stars pushes in the same direction as the fears of the rank-and-file. The former harp on their independence while they socialize with the powerful. The latter claim they do as best they can to stay independent, but need to obey orders so as to preserve their

---

[28]Such as the "Université d'été de la communication" in SW France. See p. 253, note 5.

[29]Similarly, authors write books on media ethics, but pay little attention to M*A*S or dismiss them out of hand, with a few exceptions (Alix, Cayrol).

[30]See "Le retour du 'Nouvel Ordre Mondial de l'Information'?" in *Le Monde*, 24 September 1998.

income. Black sheep do not exist—with a few exceptions, such as an immediate rival or a publication of an opposite ideological hue. A nice illustration of cronyism was provided by Serge Halimi's pamphlet (1997), which blasted only a clique of greedy media celebrities—but met with the silence of most big media—until the sales went over 100,000 copies. A major target of the book is the exchange of favors within the clique: it is interesting to compare the reviews of even mediocre books by journalists with those (if any) of books by external observers, even superbly gifted, like Régis Debray.

It is also interesting to witness what venom pours from the pen of a columnist at a quality daily reacting to criticism by one of its competitors:[31] "Are we to believe that there now exists an unofficial Order of Journalists? That now a disciplinary commission meets, which is entitled to deal out condemnations and compliments, reprimands and (self-attributed) good grades, to decide what is right and wrong in journalism, to judge others without questioning one's own behavior . . ." and so on. Yet a few years before, two directors of that newspaper had stressed that "criticizing journalists, challenging their methods and making them clear, pointing out their sins, informing about the news business, is no crime of *lese-majesty*."[32]

In the eyes of the media user, such a notion is almost too obvious for words—but it might come as a shock to professionals trained in the European tradition reflected in the 1918 SNJ code of ethics. There—and in the 1954 Declaration by the International Federation of Journalists, restated in Munich in 1971—journalists claim not to be accountable to the news consumer: "the journalist recognizes, in professional matters, the jurisdiction of his colleagues only; he excludes every kind of interference by governments *or others*" [my emphasis].

If one sends a critical remark even to a quality publication, such as *Le Monde* or *Télérama,* the television-and-movie guide, one usually meets with silence or anger. Many journalists do not seem aware of what they do wrong (or don't do at all). Those who do don't see why they should render accounts. Quite a few profess to scorn whatever comes from outside the profession, from citizens or academics—an attitude that may originate in a feeling of inferiority.

Gallic Causes

Some sources of the hostility towards M*A*S are more specifically French. Journalistic traditions in France do not harmonize well with the "social responsibility" concept, with the duty of being accountable to the public. Two traditions seem stronger in France than in Anglo-Saxon nations: subordination to economic power and subordination to political power.

---

[31]*Le Monde*, 19 May 1998, p. 33—aiming at *Libération.*

[32]J. Lesourne and B. Frappat, "Médias et déontologie," *Le Monde,* 12 February 1993, a long presentation of ethical principles and intentions.

While French broadcast journalism became infamous for its submissiveness to the authorities after 1944 (and until 1982),[33] the Paris press was already disgraced by its venality between the two world wars, when it was, far more than now, a national press. Corruption used to be open, almost insolent:[34] now it is more subtle. As in Italy, close links exist between media and other major industries: construction, armaments, insurance, water distribution. At a lower echelon, a provincial businessman will tell you what he likes about newspapers in his region: they publish all his press releases.

Some top-rung journalists prostitute themselves in their spare time emceeing conferences for IBM, or Moulinex, or political parties—not to forget junkets to exotic locations and superb Christmas presents. As for the underlings, their dependence is made worse by job insecurity. One out of five journalists (holders of the official press card)[35] is a freelancer—and the proportion, which is especially high in the magazine and broadcast sectors—is rising. The predicament is made worse by the weakness of unions: too few journalists join and the unions are too numerous. Beginners find themselves so vulnerable that they tend to accept any assignment, use any method, to safeguard their job.

"M*A*S," says Pierre Albert, "were born in countries with a Protestant culture where the central government is weak and the State is decentralized, where they did not need the law to protect press freedom,[36] where the citizen is wary of the authorities, where journalism finds that its mission is to reveal the facts rather than to express opinions, where the citizen expects the news media to provide, not an evaluation of life in the world, but information on society." Alas, it is not just for news that media in France have gotten into the habit of relying on the State. It gives them subsidies[37] and protection of various kinds;[38] it provides the schools to train their staffs; it stands ready to shield them with its laws and courts—all of which seems rather unhealthy for democracy.

Press freedom came to France late—in 1881 for print media and 1982 for broadcasting. Freedom of speech is not as respected as it is claimed to be.[39]

---

[33]Where else than France could a conference of a Press and Freedom Foundation be chaired by a former minister of information of the 1960s, infamous for his stranglehold on French broadcasting—and president of the foundation?

[34]See the excellent book by Marc Martin, *Trois siécles de publicité en France,* Paris, Odile Jacob, 1992—a critical history of advertising in France.

[35]Only delivered to one who gets more than half his/her income from journalistic activities.

[36]Actually, Sweden established press freedom by law in 1766. And the United Kingdom is very much centralized. That is a common myth in France.

[37]Basic to the survival of the French world agency, the Agence France Presse.

[38]E.g., protection against new media; or the prohibition of advertising for certain types of products on TV.

[39]See Pascal Ory, *La censure en France à l'ère démocratique,* Brussels, Complexes, 1997 [Censorship in France in the Democratic Era].

During the Algerian War (1954-1962) whole print-runs of some periodicals were regularly seized. Later, the display, though not the sale, of other periodicals was forbidden. At the beginning of the third millennium, the country still had no Freedom of Information Act. A legal taboo weighed on certain topics (e.g., amnestied crimes). Little respect was shown for freedom of expression as soon as it disturbed—especially if it upset the Establishment. In January 1999, the European Court of Human Rights issued a spectacular condemnation of France (not the first, not the last) in the case of revelations by the weekly *Canard Enchaîné*.[40] Seemingly, journalists defend their independence with all the more vigor as they enjoy it less. Especially, they defend freedom so intensely that they forget how closely linked it is to responsibility, in which they are not much interested.

Some customs derive from the tradition of subjection to the government or to a party[41]—rather than of devotion to the interest of citizens. Those customs consist, for many journalists, of an indifference to the pursuit of data, to the accuracy of news, to the quality of sources; they consist of a concern for literary elegance but a scorn for expertise and preparation; of the habit of mixing personal opinion with news, comments that are often insignificant because of the incompetence of the reporter. Professionalism is too often missing.

As Emmanuel Derieux[42] observes, "the official explanation for the 'union to reject' the M*A*S is that in France, a nation of Roman tradition, we possess written codes of statute laws. [. . .] and that is considered quite enough [. . .] People do not realize that, contrary to the Law, ethics finds it not enough just to avoid social unrest or damage to individuals. What ethics is concerned with is the good, or better, performance of a profession." Recourse to the law is a French tradition. The French tend to be cynical: they do not believe in self-regulation. In their eyes, only the courts are capable of maintaining order. Public institutions are there to protect everyone's rights and settle conflicts.

Yet the 1881 law is not much enforced in the media sphere. Take the right of reply, which is sometimes used as an argument against the M*A*S. Quite often in fact, media, when they judge that an applicant does not wish (or cannot afford) to go to court about it, will spike his request for a correction. In the last decade of the 20th century, more people have been suing, which cost the media a lot for their defense but they rarely lost. In 1997, out of 240 press cases processed by one of the two (more or less specialized) courts in the Paris region,

[40]Which in 1993 had used tax returns to document the revelation that the president of the Peugeot-Citroën company had given himself huge pay increases while opposing little ones for employees.
[41]Not so long ago, political polarization was such that any critic of a right-wing medium would be automatically labeled as left-wing—and vice versa.
[42]In his intervention at the "Forum sur les M*A*R*S" conference, 19-20 April 1991.

200 involved the gossip magazines[43] and only five concerned broadcasting; the figures were about the same at the other court. Politicians do not wish to give new vigor to the old statute for fear of media reactions.

CONCLUSION

Considering the ugly sequence that took place in the United States in the 1990s (Simpson/Ramsey[44]/Lewinsky), it may not be clear to everyone that a concern for ethics produces any practical effect. Considering the almost general decline of the British newspaper press, quality and popularity, over the last decades of the 20th century, we may wonder whether an interest in M*A*S, such as a press council, makes the slightest difference. A closer look is called for: actually, the United States and the United Kingdom are nations where M*A*S never multiplied.

In continental Europe, a sense of public service survives, a respect for Republican institutions and for the rights of the individual, whatever his/her rank in society. That tradition generates a restraint, a kind of self-regulation on the part of media and of individual journalists. Media voyeurism, for instance, is generally limited to exhibitionists, princesses, fashion models, and movie stars.

Whatever criticisms their news media deserve, the French are at least as well informed about their country and on the world as the U.S. public—and they have kept a far superior interest in political life, judging from the proportion—two thirds—that normally votes at major elections. And speaking of criticism, no other profession in France (law or medicine, for instance—not to speak of higher education) has accepted criticism and practiced self-criticism as much as journalism has, in the 1990s.

It is not impossible that both the profession and the public may in the near future become fully aware of the need for accountability. The interest in media ethics is slowly increasing on both sides. At the turn of the century, according to respected editor Noël Copin, French journalists accepted that non-professionals talk about the profession—whereas in the late 1980s when the Catholic daily *La Croix* and the TV magazine *Télérama* started their annual survey of public opinion on the media, the reactions of journalists had been fiercely hostile, especially in the older generation.

---

[43]Rarely sentenced to pay more than 15,000 euros to a show biz personality.

[44]A six-year-old beauty queen murdered in Boulder (CO) in December 1996.

CHAPTER 27
M*A*S in Sweden
Stability and Change

Lennart Weibull
Britt Börjesson

On November 30, 1999, four leading Swedish newspapers published an identical news report concerning the spread of neo-nazism in Sweden, covering several pages in each paper. The common effort between fiercely competing papers was extraordinary, but also from an ethics point of view the story attracted a lot of attention and criticism. What caused the critical reactions were not the articles per se, but that they identified 62 alleged neo-nazis, almost all of them men in their twenties, by name and photograph. The question was raised if it was really ethically acceptable to identify these individuals, especially those who had not committed any crimes or ever been sentenced by a court. The Press Ombudsman (PO) commented on the story and said that it might be compared to a modern pillory. He also added that the story seemed to indicate a change in Swedish press ethics.

The ethical debate did not concern the aim and content of the story, which was strongly applauded, but the identifications of the individuals. The reactions can only be understood within the tradition of Swedish press ethics, one of whose main pillars has been a very restrictive policy in terms of naming individuals suspected of crimes. Such a practice developed over a long period and is based on the code of conduct of journalists and anchored in decisions taken by the Swedish Press Council. However, already in the late 1980s a slight change in attitude was observed, partly affected by the investigation into the assassination of prime minister Olof Palme in 1986, where naming of suspects did occur. Looking back on Swedish media ethics in the last decades, it is quite clear that the debate on "anonymous reporting" in the late 1980s was of significant importance. It both proved the strength of the Swedish code of conduct, and in a way it changed the system. What is the situation of the Swedish media accountability system today?

It is important to stress that this presentation is made not from the viewpoint of professional journalists: it is based on extensive research into Swedish media ethics, especially the code of conduct and the Press Council. This research is being conducted at the Department of Journalism and Mass Communication of Göteborg University. It started in 1988 and has analyzed the development of the ethical system, of media performance, of actual decisions by the Press Council over time and the anchoring of the system among journalists, news sources and the media audience.[1]

THE SWEDISH MEDIA SCENE

By tradition newspapers play a very important role in Sweden. The newspaper circulation per inhabitant is one of the highest in the world. Even though there was a decline in newspaper circulation at the beginning of the 1990s, almost three out of four Swedes are daily readers of a morning paper: one out of three reads a tabloid regularly. The newspapers are also strong in business terms. Of 15,000 Swedish journalists almost 60% work in the daily press, compared to about 15% in radio and television.

Swedish newspapers are mainly local or regional. Only two tabloid newspapers can be regarded as national. By tradition, the press is affiliated to political parties; almost all newspapers state that they have a partisan orientation (four-fifths with a non-socialist and one-fifth with a socialist outlook) on their editorial page. Until the mid 1970s this was also true of the news pages, but since then a modern professional journalism has taken over.

As in most European countries radio and television in Sweden were introduced as public service media. Radio was granted a monopoly of broadcasting in 1925 and in 1955 TV was organized as a part of the new Swedish Broadcasting Corporation. In 1969, a second television channel was added, also part of the public service company. Then, in the late 1970s, voluntary organizations were allowed to establish the so-called neighborhood radio. This new system, like the existing one at the time, was noncommercial.

During the 1980s there was a rapid increase in radio broadcasting. Public service radio launched a system of regional and local radio stations. The only change in television was the introduction of Swedish-owned, commercial TV channels broadcasting to Sweden via satellite. Then, at the beginning of the 1990s, the system changed. In 1991, a national commercial television channel was introduced, and in 1993 commercial radio stations started.

---

[1]Lennart Weibull and Britt Börjesson, 1995, *Publicistiska seder*, Stockholm, Tiden-SJF.

In terms of legislation the Swedish print media are strongly protected. The Freedom of the Press Act is a constitutional law. It dates back to 1766 and has been regularly extended. The right to publish and to disseminate information is protected as well as the rights of sources to be anonymous. Only one responsible editor can be charged for any offence resulting from what has been published. Further, to guarantee an open society, the press law states the principle of public access to all official records.

There are, of course, some restrictions in the press law, regarding among other things slander and military secrets. However, libel cases are very rare in Swedish courts. An analysis made in the 1970s showed that only one out of four of the suits resulted in a jury verdict of guilty (this is the only area where the Swedish judicial system requires a jury). This was even clearer in cases involving people in high political positions. Another Swedish feature is that cases including personal offence almost never involve large amounts of money.

The foundation for the freedom of all other media than the written press is the Freedom of Expression Act, enacted in 1991. In principle it grants radio, television, and mass-distributed electronic media the same protection and the same duties as those of print media. It also contains the same principles concerning the one responsible editor. The main difference in comparison with the freedom of the press act is that the Freedom of Expression Act contains some regulation, for example, general principles of programming. Such content obligations are further specified in the Radio Law, which regulates both radio and TV.

THE SWEDISH SYSTEM OF MEDIA ETHICS

Within that very liberal tradition, a system of voluntary media ethics has developed. The roots of the system date back to the last decades of the 19th century and it has expanded over time.

The Swedish media accountability system is based on the three main organizations in the field: The Swedish Association of Newspaper Publishers,[2] The Swedish Union of Journalists, and The Publicists' Club. The latter is an organization of publishers and journalists interested in the ethical conduct of Swedish media. As early as 1916, these organizations signed a document stating the vital importance of a media accountability system and agreed on forming a press council. In the beginning of the 1970s they also formed a special council for cooperation in the field of media accountability. This council is responsible for the administration of, and information about, the media accountability system. The system as a whole is presented in Figure 27.1.

---

[2]Svenska Tidningsutgivareföreningen, TU; Svenska Journalistförbundet, SJF; Publicistklubben, PK.

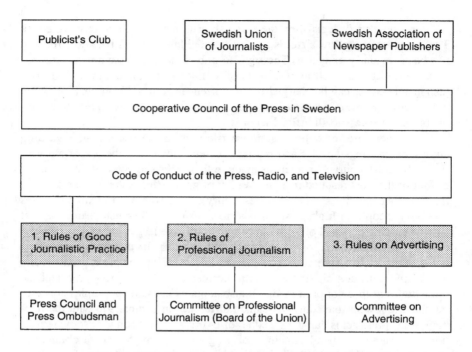

Figure 27.1. The Swedish system of media ethics.

The three sets of rules, which form the basis of the system and represent the Swedish code of conduct, are the following:

1. **The Rules of Good Journalistic Practice** (The Publicity Rules): they regulate the fairness of reporting, respect of privacy, the rights of interviewees, the right to reply, the treatment of pictures, and so forth. These rules, established by the PK, are the oldest part of the code of conduct, and date back to 1900.
2. **The Rules of Professional Journalism:** these rules deal chiefly with the journalist's conduct and concern the integrity of journalists, humiliating assignments, acquisition of material, relation to news sources, and so forth. These rules were originally the internal code of conduct of the SJF, dating from 1968.
3. **The Rules of Editorial Advertising:** these rules cover the relation between advertising and editorial content. They state that news should be judged by news value, not by advertising value. Advertising must not look like editorial pages. These rules were initiated by the TU in 1970.

Each set of rules has its own supervising institution. The rules of good journalistic practice, which are regarded as the most central, are supervised by the Press Council and the Press Ombudsman (PO). The rules of editorial advertising are supervised by a committee with the same name and the rules of professional journalism by a special committee appointed by the board of SJF.

The rules of good journalistic practice originated as a code of conduct for newspapers and magazines, but in 1976 some relevant paragraphs were included in the so-called radio agreements, the documents regulating the conduct of radio and television. The conduct of radio and TV, however, are supervised, not by the Press Council, but by the Investigative Council for Radio and Television, a government agency responsible for all broadcasting regulation. Because of the fact that the rules of professional journalism cover all members of the SJF, they concern both print and broadcast media as a whole.

In terms of accountability, the most interesting part of the system is "good journalistic practice" supervised by the Press Council and the Press Ombudsman.

THE ORIGIN OF THE CODE OF ETHICS

The principles of good journalism practice originate from intense discussions on the character of crime reporting in the late 19th century. The Publicists' Club (PK), established in 1874, was the main forum for the debates. In 1900, the board of the PK sent out a memorandum to all its members to be distributed to all newspapers. It contained a proposal to avoid publication of news on young crime suspects and on criminals only sentenced to light punishment.

This early request for more responsible reporting does not seem to have had a great impact on actual reporting. Then, in 1916, on the initiative of the PK, the three press organizations established a so-called honorary court of justice—the Press Council—to deal with the supervision of good journalistic practice. In 1923, the PK decided on a first written, general code of conduct. The code was mostly concerned with the publication of names. It stated that if news on minor crimes were to be published, at least the name of the suspect should not be given.

In the following decades the code of ethics was gradually extended. In 1933, the rules were made more concrete, among other things banning the reporting of names of persons sentenced for minor crimes or crimes where a suspended sentence was the rule. Further, it was stressed that other possible identifiers, such as titles or party affiliation, should also be avoided. Suicides, sex crimes, and so forth should be treated with great caution.

In 1953, a new era started for the code of ethics. The background of the revision was the fact that the press law had been changed as a result of experiences during World War II. The revised code differed a lot from the old one. Whereas the old code stressed what should be avoided, the new one laid out

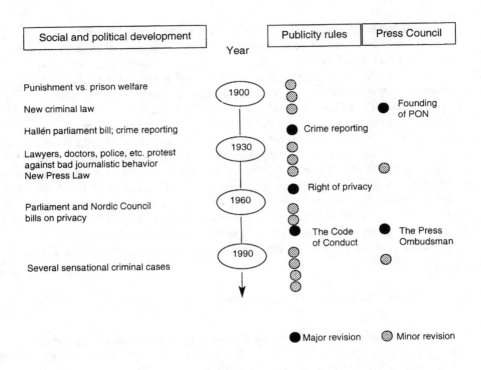

Figure 27.2.

some general guidelines for reporting, for example the importance of accurate information, respect of individuals' privacy, as well as caution in reporting names and publishing news pictures.

In the next major revision (1967) some of these principles were strengthened and the right to privacy of public persons was added. Two years later the institution of the Press Ombudsman was established. In 1970 the rules of good journalistic practice were integrated into a general media accountability system, the Code of Conduct for Press, Radio, and TV, and formally called Publication Rules (or Publicity Rules). The latest revision of the rules has sorted out the ethical principles under the following six heads (as translated by Nordenstreng and Topuz, 1988):[3]

- To give accurate news
- To give space for rejoinders
- To respect personal integrity
- To apply caution in the use of pictures

---

[3]Kaarle Nordenstreng and Hifzi Topuz, 1989, "Journalists: Status, Rights and Responsibilities." Prague, International Organisation of Journalists.

- To judge no one unheard
- To apply caution in the use of names

The code has gradually developed. It started with a few formulations about what kinds of crime reporting should be avoided and it is now a concrete set of rules of what to do and not to do in journalism (see p. 93). But the focus has always been on personal integrity, defined differently at different periods. And new principles have been added, for example, the stress on the accuracy of news reporting.

How can this development be explained? If we look into the preparatory work or the rules, we find that most of them had their origin in a strong feeling about the social responsibility of the press. Because the press has an important mission in society, it must be trustworthy and therefore it needs to self-regulate. At the same time, it is clear that the strengthening of the rules in 1923, 1953 and 1967 coincided with Parliamentary bills proposing government regulation of media ethics. The establishment of the PO in 1969 was directly connected with a proposal for legislation on the right to reply. With the revision of the system, the press showed the critics that it had a social responsibility. At the same time, it was a successful way of protecting the freedom of the press: By giving up some of the freedom, you can save it for use when it is really needed.

THE CODE IN PRACTICE: THE PRESS COUNCIL

The Press Council (1916) is older than the written code of ethics (1923). It was originally set up more as a sort of forum for solving conflicts between publishers and journalists, sometimes even conflicts concerning salary contracts, and was not related to the code of conduct. Its main aim, however, was to solve conflicts relative to news presentation, thereby protecting "the requirements of honor" and the "standing of the press."

Although it was not originally regulated, the Press Council gradually developed a procedure for treating public complaints. Individuals, organizations, and private companies could, if affected by newspaper publicity, ask the council for its judgment on the case. There was, however, a severe restriction: an "expense fee." This was at a level that made it impossible for ordinary people to make complaints. During the 1950s and 1960s, the Press Council was widely criticized: the number of complaints increased, partly as a consequence of changing journalistic practice, but the Council did not cope with the situation and was regarded as inefficient.

The administrative problems of the Council were hardly surprising. Its organization was not meant to deal with a large number of complaints. The work of its few members was voluntary; only the chairman and the secretary received a (symbolic) remuneration. The Council could not meet the needs of the new situation. It had to be reformed.

The 1969 revision of the Press Council represented a profound change in the media accountability system as such. The aim of the new organization was to make it easier for the general public to make complaints. The expense fee disappeared and information about the Press Council was increased. The introduction of the PO was vital. The PO was meant both to help in this process and to take initiatives in cases of unethical conduct.

To show that the Press Council was to be taken seriously, its composition was changed. Now the press interests lost their dominance and representatives of public interests were appointed. The three press organizations received one seat each, two seats were for the representatives of the public, and the chairperson should be an experienced lawyer. Although the Press Council was strengthened, it still operated rather like a court of honor. If a newspaper is found guilty of violating the rules of publication, the paper is obliged to publish the council's decision and to pay a small fee to cover the costs of the council. The court has no power to enforce this, but only in few cases have papers ever refused.

Even in practice the new organization meant a real change. The number of complaints increased dramatically (Fig. 27.3). In the 1980s, there were about 350 complaints a year. At the start of the 21st century, the number is approximately 400. About one out of five complaints has been judged to be justified. This proportion seems remarkably stable over the years.

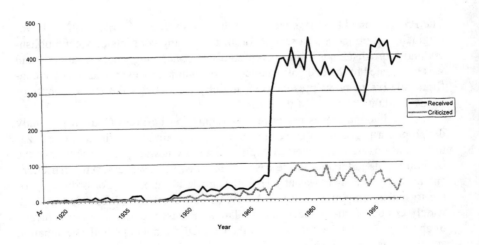

Figure 27.3. Complaints received by the Press Council (including those initiated by the ombudsman), 1916-2001, and percentage of those upheld, wholly or partly

One important feature of the new situation in the early 1970s was that a large majority of the increased number of complaints came from private persons (Fig. 27.4). However, although a majority of the complaints stem from the general public, the Press Council and Press Ombudsman are not as well known as could be expected. Only about 40% of Swedes (aged between 15 and 79) could, with or without help, identify the role of the Press Council or Press Ombudsman, when asked in a telephone survey (Fig. 27.5). There are considerable differences in knowledge depending on age and stated interest in politics: among people with higher education the portion with knowledge of the PC and PO is almost 65%.

The cause of a complaint to the Press Council or the PO is usually an issue of personal integrity. The single most common reason is that a person has been accused of, or associated with, some crime or immoral conduct. Almost 60% of all complaints from 1916 to 1987 fall within this category. The second biggest category is inaccuracy in reporting (about 50%).

There has been a change over time. The percentage of complaints resulting from personal offence dropped after 1970, whereas complaints resulting from inaccuracy or bias have increased. Most of the persons mentioned in the articles under complaint are non-elite. During the 1980s, 79% could be classified as non-elite; in the period before World War II the figure had been about 60%. The four evening tabloids are relatively more often criticized by the Press Council. During the 1980s and 1990s, about 20% of the complaints concerned

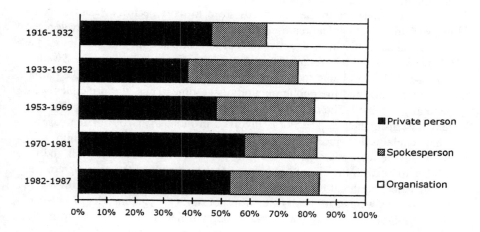

Figure 27.4. Proportion of private individuals, spokespersons, and organizations appearing in articles leading to complaints, 1916-1987.

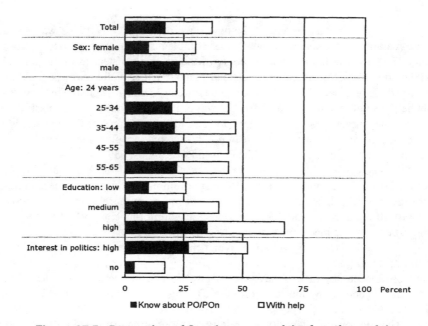

**Figure 27.5. Proportion of Swedes aware of the functions of the
ombudsman and of the Press Council.**

this group, whose share of the total circulation is less than 5%. But its share of
complaints was even higher in the 1970s.

The changes in the late 1960s seem to have been the result of some
pressure from the political representatives of the Swedish people to develop and
extend the code of ethics. The revisions of the code and the introduction of the
PO were preceded by proposals or debates by parliamentarians in the Swedish
Riksdag. It is reasonable to believe that the criticism expressed by the parliamentarians reflected the public opinion of the time. Thus, the principles were
generally accepted. The introduction of the PO in particular meant that the system was strengthened. The PO is involved in more than 70% of the cases—
which explains that since 1980 there has been an Assistant PO to help him.

One main reason for the strong position of the Press Council and the
PO has to do with the climate of opinion at the time when the new system was
introduced. The threat of legislation on the right to reply meant that the press
organizations were eager to show their responsibility by giving a lot of independence to the PO, stressing that it was an ombudsman in reality, if not formally,
having the same function as the other Swedish ombudsmen. At the same time
the sanctions granted to the Press Council were not too powerful, meaning that
the system was not a threat to the routines of newspaper reporting.

1990s: Criticism and Revisions

However, the situation did change in the late 1980s. There again, the cause can be found in the climate of opinion of the time. The arguments against a restrictive ethical framework of the media were similar to the criticism often made of many huge institutions in the Swedish society, for example, government agencies, trade unions, and big corporations. It is also typical that this criticism was mostly heard from journalists of the younger generation, criticizing the collective character of press ethics—and from publishers of some major newspapers. Further, the role of the PO was increasingly criticized. Here also the criticism originated from both publishers and journalists, who argued that the PO had often been more active than necessary in trying to formalize press ethics. Actually, his initiatives were relatively few—only some ten cases per year.

The criticism was also reflected within the main organizations responsible for Swedish press ethics. However, the criticism did not violate the basic principles of press ethics, but focused on the responsibilities of individual journalists and newspapers, which were said to have been neglected within the formal framework of the publication rules. After a number of debates, a first step in altering the system was a general, introductory amendment added in 1990 to the code of conduct: "Ethics do not mean a formal application of a set of given rules, but responsible behavior in the task of journalism."

Through this introductory paragraph the system could both function as an institution and leave room for continuous renewal. On the other hand, this formulation, although elegant, did not remove the institutional profile of the system, and some liberal groups continued to criticize the institutional character of it. The criticism focused on the Press Council as the best example of a rigid body, functioning almost like a legal court, but the PO was also regarded more as a critic of the press than a defender of press ethics, making journalists' decisions understood by the general public.

The second line of criticism has been the conservative character of the Council's decisions. For example, the tradition of anonymous presentation of people suspected of crime was regarded as too cautious. This criticism came mainly from Stockholm newspapers, meaning that Swedish journalism generally is too careful in the reporting of crimes and the like. It is well in line with the differences between journalists in the capital and the countryside found in our research. More as a matter of principle, it was stressed that a paragraph in the code was formulated in negative terms: 'Do not publish the names . . .' So the wording was changed to "Consider carefully the publication of names." This was regarded to be a more positive formulation, making an active journalism possible.

The 1991 changes answered some of the criticisms by the liberal groups. But it was very clear that the critics wanted more profound changes, mostly a change in the practice of the Press Council and Ombudsman, making them more active in the field. However, this activity also meant conflicts.

When, in 1992, the newly appointed Press Ombudsman resigned unexpectedly after less than a year into the job, after a conflict with the Press Council, it was a clear illustration of the issue. So the main task of the committee appointed as a result of the PO resignation was to investigate the organization of Swedish press ethics and to propose a revised model.

Its solution was to weaken somewhat the position of the PO in a formal way, meaning that his main role would be to prepare complaints for decisions by the Press Council, rather than make his own statements. On the other hand, the PO would not be integrated in the Press Council, meaning that he was not supposed to be present at its meetings. Instead, the function of the PO as a direct mediator between persons complaining and newspaper editors was stressed: it was presented as "immediate press ethics." This opened a new role for the PO as an active proponent of press ethics also in the general debate. In line with these principles, the new PO, appointed in 1992, was the first in the job who was not a judge or a lawyer, but a newspaper editor, interested in discussing ethical problems.

The Anchoring of the Code

The code of ethics developed as the mainstream media organizations responded to the ideas of the time. The result was a complex system of written principles. In the 1950s and 1960s the code of ethics and the Press Council were repeatedly criticized. Media ethics meant nothing, it was argued. Publishers and journalists did not care and the general public did not know. As we have seen, there was a change after the reorganization of 1969.

Given this debate, it is important to look more closely into the perceived legitimacy of this system in terms of anchoring. In our research on Swedish media ethics, we have asked both journalists and the public questions on media performance, on media credibility, and on the role of the organizational framework of media ethics to find out more about the anchoring of the code: how do the journalists and the public regard the system of press ethics of today—in theory and practice?

The first question concerns the importance of each of the main areas covered by the code of ethics. In a survey of Swedish journalists, conducted at the end of 1989, we studied both general attitudes and opinions on concrete cases, and in 1994 and 1999 follow-up studies were made.[4] Regarding the areas

---

[4]Britt Börjesson and Lennart Weibull, 1991, *Views on Press Ethics—Do Readers and Journalists Agree?* Department of Journalism and Mass Communication, Göteborg University. Britt Börjesson and Lennart Weibull, 1995, "Namnpublicering i medierna," in S. Holmberg and L. Weibull (eds.), *Det gamla riket,* Göteborg, SOM-Instituet. Britt Börjesson and Lennart Weibull, 2000, "Pressetik i förändring," in S. Holmberg and L. Weibull (eds.), *Det nya samhället.* Göteborg, SOM-Institutet.

covered by the rules of press ethics we asked how important they felt these areas to be (see Figure 27.6).

As can be seen in Figure 27.6 the index of balance goes from +99 (accuracy of news) to +72 (caution in the use of pictures). There are only minor differences between journalists of different age, education, or experience. The figure shows there is an unanimous view that the areas covered by the rules are very important. There were only slight differences over the ten-year period.

In 1989 and 1994, a question with the same wording was also put to the general public, more than 90% of whom are regular newspaper readers. In 1989, the general public and the journalists differed slightly in their views on personal integrity and identification of individuals by name: the public rated the principles of respect for personal integrity and caution in the publication of names somewhat higher than journalists did, thus being somewhat more restrictive than the journalists. In 1994 those differences had faded: the acceptance especially of the publication of names is now higher among the public. It is reasonable to see this as an indication that the changes of the press ethics system in the early 1990s were generally accepted. The overall view of the areas covered by the rules is very positive and the differences in judgments are almost the same as among journalists.

The general conclusion based on these surveys is that the anchoring of the ethical principles is very strong among journalists as well as among the general public. At times, the need for a written code has been questioned by critics inside the media. It has been argued that written rules may be dangerous, because they might cause individual journalists not to reflect on ethical problems in their work, and to apply the rules mechanically. However, such a criticism does not seem to raise much echo in the typical Swedish journalist. A majority believe that written rules are important.

Older journalists generally tend to stress the importance of written rules more than do the younger journalists. For example, among the latter only a minority regard written rules of accuracy as important. One interpretation is that some rules concern such obviously important issues that they are of little help and might even seem absurd. The fact that older journalists generally view written rules as more important than do younger ones might mean either that they have more experience of ethical problems or that they are more socialized within the existing system. Another interpretation is that there is a generational difference and that the young generation reflect a sort of neo-liberal view that all types of regulation are an obstacle.

The debate on press ethics seldom concerned the importance of ethical rules per se, but rather how the rules of ethics actually were applied by the media. Surveys of the opinion on the ethical conduct of news media have clearly shown that the morning press,[5] together with public radio and television, are rated quite

---

[5]The regional and local newspapers to which people subscribe (as opposed to tabloids, bought in the street) dominate the newspaper scene.

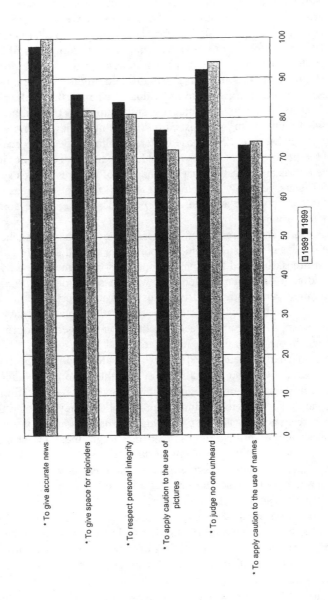

Figure 27.6. How important is it to respect the publicity rules when reporting news? Swedish journalists, 1989 and 1999, index of balance.

high, whereas the tabloids have much lower ratings. It is interesting to see that these ratings are very similar for the journalists and for the public. The perception also seems to be quite stable over time. Concerning the tabloids, ratings do not necessarily reflect their actual performance, but express what people expect of them.

The general public was also asked to what extent they thought that media in general behave ethically. Their evaluation of media conduct can here be directly compared with that of journalists. We found that the public rates the ethical performance of the media much lower. For morning newspapers, the biggest discrepancy is found for "respect of personal integrity," but there is also an evident difference for "judge no one unheard" and "apply caution to publication of names." In other words, the criticism of the public in terms of ethical conduct concerns mostly issues of how people are treated by the media and less accuracy in itself.

The key to the interpretation is the judgment of how individual persons are treated in the news. For the general public, there is only a thin line between investigative reporting and sensationalism—and the public feels very strongly when this line is crossed. In condemning sensationalism, the public is almost unanimous.

ISSUES OF PERSONAL INTEGRITY

Even though the general public stresses the importance of protecting personal integrity in newspaper reporting, the issue is of course more complex. What is regarded as acceptable reporting has to do both with the type of event and the position of the individual concerned. To understand how people in general (including journalists) reason in concrete cases we asked respondents whether certain possible events should be reported or not, and whether the individuals involved should be identified or not. Examples of events: "Adults and children killed in a severe bus accident," "Politician prosecuted for tax evasion," and "A company director prosecuted for drunken driving." Figure 27.7 shows the journalists' judgment of how these events should be reported.

If we compare the judgments among journalists with those of the public overall, there is striking similarity. Both the public and the journalists are in favor of publication, except in the civil custody case. However, there is also an important difference: the general public is less inclined to identify the victims of the bus accident, but more inclined when it comes to the murder suspect and drug peddler as well as the tax-evading politician.

The interpretation of these attitudinal differences from the 1990s is of great importance to understand the anchoring of Swedish press ethics, because they denote the traditional distinction between public and private. The figure concerning publication clearly indicates what is perceived as a public interest. The public is less inclined than journalists to accept the identification of non-public persons: private citizens have a right not to be exposed in the news, even if they appear in the public sphere. But it is also obvious that a politician seems

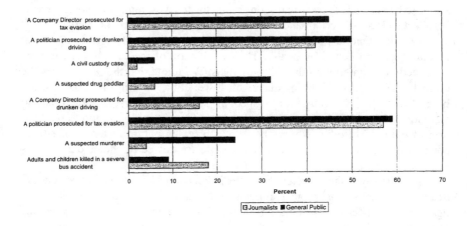

Figure 27.7. Should mass media publish such news—and how should the identity of the people involved be treated? Journalists and citizens of Sweden, 1999: Percentage who find it reasonable to give full identity of the people involved.

to be more of a public interest than a company director; or that tax evasion seems to be more related to the public interest than drunken driving. In other words, the definition of the public interest depends on who you are as well as what you have done. So there are two basic dimensions of public interest: one concerning the person and the other the sphere. A public person can be found both in the public and the private sphere just as a non-public person can.

On the basis of this reasoning a simple typology has been constructed (Figure 27.8). It demonstrates that there are at least four possibilities when we try to determine the public interest. The upper left square (1) is obviously the most private one and the lower right the most public (4). According to the results presented it seems to be an almost unanimous feeling that events covering square 1 should be restrictively reported and made anonymous. For square 4 the situation is the other way round. This is the typical arena for traditional political news reporting.

The remaining two squares cover areas where there have been disputes concerning personal integrity in news reporting. Square 2 covers events where non-public persons appear in the public arena, and square 3 events when public persons are in the private sphere. Of course, it is very difficult to draw clear lines between public and private spheres. However, our fictitious events can help us with some illustrations. For example, the victims of a bus accident belong mainly in square 2 and the politician prosecuted for drunken driving is close to square 3.

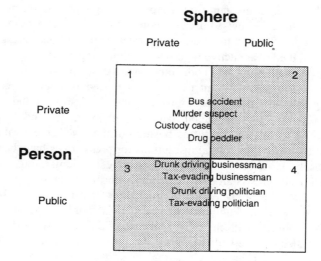

Figure 27.8. Matrix of private and public spheres.

If we use these examples, there is an interesting way to interpret the observed differences in judgment between journalists and the general public in terms of personal integrity. It is clear that the main problem for journalists is where to draw the line between squares 4 and 3. They tend to be more restrictive in this than the general public. On the other hand, when the general public perceives problems of personal integrity in the news reporting it mostly concerns square 2. Therefore the public is less inclined to accept the identification non-public persons; private citizens have a right not to be exposed in the news, even if they appear in the public sphere.

SWEDEN: A STRONG SYSTEM OF PRESS ETHICS

Back in 1986, very few Swedish media published the name of the man suspected of the assassination of the Prime Minister until he was sentenced in court. In 1999, however, it was accepted that the names and pictures of persons suspected of Nazism be published. This could be expected, considering the development of the rules of good journalism practice. The debate initiated in the late 1980s, which reflected the climate of opinion of the time, meant a change in the system of Swedish press ethics. The revision of the code stressed the importance of the individual journalists and their personal responsibility.

In actual reporting, however, there was only a minor increase in the willingness to publish names. Few names of suspects are still published, if they are not perceived as public persons—and the ethical principles still have great weight. The rules of the game are accepted among journalists as well as among the public. Thus, the revised organization of the Press Council and the PO has not profoundly changed the working routines of institutional press ethics. The Council and the PO are active in terms of stimulating complaints and their decisions are generally respected both among journalists and the general public. The new role of a Press ombudsman with a background as a newspaper editor, participating in editorial discussions in individual newsrooms and in the public debate, seems to be strongly appreciated by both journalists and the public.

The reason for this strong position of the Swedish ethical system is to be found in the fact the formal institutions for press ethics have been—and still are—closely associated with the two strongest organizations on the media scene. They encompass all relevant media: almost all newspapers are members of the TU and almost all journalists, including freelance writers, belong to the SJF. Furthermore, the Publicists' Club acts as a forum for media ethics and is itself closely linked with the other two institutions: almost all the members of the PK are also members of one of the other two. With such a strong backing of the organizations it is not surprising that the system is respected.

But another reason for the strength of the system has to do with its development. Our studies of actual media performance in crime reporting have clearly shown that when new rules were introduced they were very much in accordance with existing practice. The changes were handled with care by the organizations. This made the acceptance of the rules very easy. The long period of development has meant that the system today has a very strong tradition, which, in itself, is important for the maintenance of the system. Thus, it is not unexpected that this strong system, based on two main pillars—the Code of Conduct on the one hand and the Press Council and PO on the other—only slowly changes its character. Even if the tradition of collective handling of ethical issues is weakened, the system based on individual responsibility is dependent on collective decisions.

The debate during the changes of the 1990s illustrated the two poles between which Swedish press ethics oscillate: on the one hand the idea of formal rules enforced by strong institutions and on the other responsible behavior on the part of individual journalists. The common denominator between the two is a fear that press ethics might develop into some sort of legal procedure. How the balance between those two poles will develop, however, depends to a large extent on the climate of opinion. At the turn of the century, it was important that the discussion had created an interest in ethical issues. The discussion had forced everyone in journalism to think about what is right or wrong, and why it is so. And such a process, we believe, is what makes a journalist a responsible journalist.

CHAPTER 28
M*A*S in Israel
"You'll Never Know It's There"

Yehiel Limor[1]

A racy advertisement, popular in Israel during the late 1970s, promoted sales of a new kind of brassiere with the slogan "You'll never know it's there." The product was thus presented as an appurtenance that emphasizes what it ought to, conceals what it ought to, and—above all—lets the wearer feel free and unfettered.

Israel's media accountability systems largely resemble that intimate item of feminine apparel. They emphasize the presence of ethics and self-regulation yet conceal the weaknesses of the means of enforcement and the holes in the safety net designed to ease the public's mind, assuring the general population that the media act out of dedication to professional principles and honesty while allowing media personnel to feel unbound by restrictive chains.

Since its inception, Israeli society has adopted principles of Western democracy. The Declaration of Independence of the fledgling state, born in 1948, is replete with human and democratic values, even though the term "democracy" is not stipulated explicitly therein. The media, most of which began operation before independence was declared, also adopted the democratic ethos, but in a manner slightly different from standard practice in other democratic countries. Security threats from neighboring Arab countries, wars, and acts of terror rendered the media amenable to military censorship, accepted willingly rather than by coercion. Furthermore, social problems resulting from successive waves of mass immigration led to the adoption of several characteristics typical of "devel-

[1] I express my gratitude to my colleagues Dr. Hillel Nossek and Dr. Amit Schejter for their helpful comments.

oping media."[2] The more established the young state became and the less imminent the threats to security, the more media liberated themselves from commitments unacceptable in well-established democracies. One inevitable by-product of this new reality was the persistent recurrence of the accountability issue on the public agenda, in the political system, and among the media themselves.

Demands for media accountability largely stem from the media's quest for unique status. The media constitute part of the overall social system and are bound by the common norms and reciprocal supervision systems that regulate relations among the various institutions in society and state. Nevertheless, they seek freedom from supervision because of their role as "watchdogs of democracy." This dual reality, in which the media function as "in/outsiders"[3] is fertile soil for tensions between the media institution and other institutions in society, especially the political. Time after time, these tensions arouse demands for external supervision of the media or, alternatively, for effective, substantive self-monitoring and self-regulation by the media themselves. Such demands have always been voiced in Israel, as in other Western democracies. However, they intensified greatly in the 1990s for two principal reasons: changes in the structure of the Israeli media map and criminal activities involving several key Israeli media figures.

The accelerated structural processes that affected the Israeli media map in the late 1980s and early 1990s—specifically, increasing concentration of ownership and cross-ownership—led to the rise of "media barons" who accumulated mighty communications and economic power.[4] The new baronies, whose wide-branching activities extend beyond the boundaries of the media, aroused concern both within and outside the media institution that such power might be abused and therefore ought to be controlled somehow.

Furthermore, the Israeli police conducted, in the late 1990s, a series of complex investigations, following suspicions that two Israeli media barons, along with journalists and other senior employees of their respective newspapers, were involved in commissioning illegal wiretaps and listening to illegally obtained telephone-call recordings, primarily for purposes of industrial espionage or leak prevention. Following the police investigation, the editor-in-chief of Israel's most popular daily newspaper, *Yediot Aharonot,* and the owner/editor-in-chief of its closest competitor, *Maariv,* were put on trial.

---

[2]See D. McQuail, *Mass Communication Theory*, 3rd ed., London, Sage, 1994.

[3]D. Caspi and Y. Limor, *The In/Outsiders: The Media in Israel*, Cresskill, NJ, Hampton Press, 1999.

[4]Y. Limor, "The 'Little Prince' and the 'Big Brother': Mass Media in Israel in an Era of Changes," in D. Caspi (ed.), *Communication and Democracy in Israel* (pp. 29-46), Tel-Aviv, The Van-Leer Institute & Hakibutz Hameuchad, 1997 [in Hebrew]. Y. Limor, "The Media Barons is Israel," *Yearbook of the Association of Tel-Aviv Journalists* (pp. 97-111), Tel-Aviv, The Association of Tel-Aviv Journalists, 1998.

These two factors—the first common to other democracies and the second unique to Israel—intensified the accountability issue and openly placed the question of "Who'll watch the watchdogs?" on the public and media agendas. This question, that plunged the Israeli media institution into turmoil and even threatened to bring down the central pillars of media accountability, will remain a key issue of concern to the Israeli public and media throughout the early 21st century.

LEVELS OF MEDIA ACCOUNTABILITY

This analysis begins with the identification, differentiation, and characterization of Israel's media accountability systems. Research literature focuses primarily on the three most familiar and common systems (press councils, codes of ethics, and ombudsmen), usually addressing them in a general sense only. Consequently, a more precise structural differentiation of the various media accountability systems would appear to be in order. Accordingly, these systems will be examined in terms of their role in overall relations between the media institution and other institutions in society, as well as within the media institution itself.

Practically speaking, one may identify five levels of media account-ability—two statutory and three voluntary[5]—some or all of which are in force in most democratic countries.

Basic Laws

The first and highest level of media accountability is statutory, wherein the internal supervision systems of the media institution, and especially its code of ethics, are derived from basic laws and draw their power from them. Various free professions, especially medicine, law, psychology, social work, and others, operate within a statutory framework, according them not only social legitimacy but also legal recognition. One characteristic of such professions is a code of ethics, with internal systems to supervise adherence to the code, punish viola-tors, and in extreme cases even ban offenders from the profession. Examples of countries with such media legislation are India, in which the Press Council operates by virtue of the 1965 Press Council Act, and Denmark, in which the Code of Conduct is part of the 1992 Media Liability Act.

Secondary Legislation

Media accountability systems of this type are not anchored directly in legisla-tion. Nevertheless, the law authorizes (and sometimes even compels) certain

---

[5]The term M*A*S is rarely used in this chapter as the author also considers governmen-tal systems [Editor's note].

bodies to institute codes of ethics that are granted statutory validity. Examples prevailing in the United Kingdom include the *Code of Practice* of the Broadcasting Standards Council and the regulations determined by the Independent Television Commission and the Radio Authority.

The first two types of accountability systems are anchored directly or indirectly in law or are operated by bodies with statutory status, whereas the three remaining ones relate to voluntary systems, whether implemented by bodies that themselves have statutory status (such as the Israel Broadcasting Authority) or those that do not.

The Institutional Level

These systems address the media institution as a whole. The most salient example is the press council common to all media, printed and electronic. Such councils are active in various countries, such as Catalonia, Chile, Estonia, the Netherlands, Quebec, Tanzania—as well as in the U.S. state of Minnesota.

The Single Medium Level

Such systems are operated by some or all of the organizations or employees of a single medium. Outstanding examples include the British Press Complaints Commission, which covers only the printed press, as well as the Press Councils of Sweden, Norway, and Germany. Other examples would be the *Statement of Principles* of the Association of Newspaper Editors (ASNE), the Codes of Ethics of the Society of Professional Journalists and of the National Press Photographers Association—all in the United States.

The Organizational Level

Organizational accountability systems apply to two types of organizations: Those operating by force of law (primarily public broadcasting systems) and privately owned media organizations. Examples include the BBC *Producers' Guidelines* and the *Journalistic Standards and Practices* of the Canadian Broadcasting Corporation, internal guidelines by individual newspapers (such as the *New York Times Manual of Style and Usage*), or news agencies (such as *Reuters' Handbook for Journalists* or the *Associated Press Stylebook and Libel Manual*). Ombudsmen, maintained by newspapers in the United States, Canada, Brazil, Japan, or Spain belong to this category as well.

MEDIA ACCOUNTABILITY SYSTEMS IN ISRAEL

Four of the five systems mentioned above are active in Israel, two statutory and two voluntary.

Statutory—Basic Laws

There are two systems in Israel at this level,[6] both consisting of ombudsmen employed by the electronic broadcasting media. All broadcasting media in Israel are subject to stringent regulations that prohibit the operation of an unlicensed broadcasting station and strictly limit the number of licenses granted.

One such system is operated by the State-run Israel Broadcasting Authority (IBA), which includes the First Television Network and Israel's State Radio (Kol Israel), consisting of eight channels. An ombudsman was introduced voluntarily by the IBA in the 1980s, but the position only acquired legal status in 1994, several years after the establishment of the Second Authority, when the Broadcasting Authority Act was enacted. The IBA ombudsman's annual report for 1999 indicated that he had received 427 complaints that year (as compared with 248 in 1998 and 350 in 1997), 29% of which concerned the content of broadcasts. Other complaints concerned personal offense (1.4%), rudeness and crude language (3.9%), advertising content (2%), and reminders to pay the IBA television license fee (31.4%).

The second system is operated by the Second Broadcasting Authority which supervises Israel's Second (commercial) Television Network and 14 franchised regional radio stations. The ombudsman's role is anchored in law: Article 114 of the Second Authority Act stipulates that the ombudsman is charged with "examining complaints received from the public regarding broadcasting." The Second Authority ombudsman's annual report for 1999 indicated that he had received 392 complaints (compared to 369 in 1998 and 272 the previous year), 12% of which were found to be unjustified. The largest share of complaints (about 27%) concerned the content of broadcasts and more than 8% addressed the amount and content of advertising.

Statutory—Secondary Laws (Regulations)

Israel has three statutory systems of this type, all applying to the electronic media. Two of them, the respective codes of ethics of the Second Authority and

---

[6]In 1997, a special public committee appointed by the Ministers of Justice and of the Interior recommended anchoring in law the Israel Press Council (established in 1963 as a voluntary body). However, the committee, headed by a former Minister of Justice and including jurists and journalists, did not recommend any binding legal status.

of the Cable and Satellite Television Broadcasting Council (which supervises cable and satellite television services), have adopted many of the standard ethical principles of Western media, including objectivity and balance in broadcasting, right of reply, rules for reporting on arrests and suspects, mandatory broadcasting of "information whose transmission is in the public interest," non-disclosure of sources of information, and the like. These principles bind operators of the Second Television Channel, regional radio stations and cable television stations, all of which operate under limited-term franchises.

The third such system consists of the *Israel Broadcasting Authority Regulations,* which include the following stipulation (in the Section entitled "Offended Party's Right of Response"):

> If the Authority is about to broadcast a program that is prima facie liable to offend someone, the Authority will take reasonable steps, according to circumstance, to ascertain the said person's reaction before broadcasting the program. [The Authority] will air the reaction together with the program in a manner and format that it deems fit, unless it perceives that the said reaction is unfit for broadcasting or that untoward use was made of the said response option.

The regulations defining the IBA ombudsman's role should be included as well. As indicated above, the position itself is mandated by the Broadcasting Authority Law. These regulations, anchored in a statute as of 1996, declare that "anyone may appeal to the ombudsman to protest or complain about any matter concerning the Authority's broadcasts or the manner in which the Authority operates."

Voluntary—Institutional Level

The Israel Press Council (IPC), often perceived as the supreme body of the Israeli media institution, belongs to this category, although its authority over the media is highly limited, as clarified below.

The British Press Council model, according to which similar councils were set up in many countries, served as a source of inspiration in Israel as well. The IPC, established in 1963, comprises representatives of three sectors: the National Federation of Israeli Journalists (30% of the IPC's membership), newspaper owners and editors (30%), and the general public (40%).[7] Consequently, one may categorize it as a "genuine council" (see p. 113), as it comprises representatives of the public as well as of the media.

---

[7]The President of the IPC in 2000, Mordechai Kremnitzer, is a law professor at the Hebrew University in Jerusalem. His predecessors included a former minister of justice, a former president of the Supreme Court and a former state attorney-general.

The IPC, like other press councils throughout the world, fulfills a dual central role, as defined in its Regulations, most recently amended in 1996: "To uphold freedom of the press and the public's right to know" (section 2a), and "to maintain journalistic ethics, ensure their fulfillment and handle complaints regarding their violation" (section 2c). In other words, the Council serves as a check against external attempts to control the press and to limit its activity while also instituting an internal supervisory mechanism. The latter not only aims at achieving appropriate professional standards but also at proving that the media institution is capable of regulating itself and therefore requires no externally imposed supervision. To these two main roles were added several others, in harmony with the objectives of the original British Press Council, turning the Council into a kind of combination trade union (journalist training), research institute (trend monitoring), and tribunal (complaint handling).

The IPC's most important output is its regularly amended *Professional Code of Ethics*, intended as a binding guide for the entire media institution. Newspapers and journalists accused of ethical violations appear before a special ethics court, which includes a public representative as chairperson. The IPC received about 2,200 complaints of violations between 1963 (when IPC was established) and 1999.[8]

Since its founding, the IPC has been striving to block external restriction on the media, especially attempts at legislation that might limit the activities of the press, either directly or indirectly, or affect its functioning adversely. For example, a proposed law was shelved that was intended to prohibit publication of the name of a suspect before he/she was brought before a judge to extend detention. It was withdrawn after the IPC included an explicit directive to the same effect in its code of ethics. Other proposed legislation concerned expansion of the Libel Law. Such attempts are not unique to Israel, of course.

Voluntary—Single Medium Level

Formally speaking, Israel has no such accountability system. On a practical level, however, one might consider the IPC a single medium level mechanism rather than institutional. Although the IPC is supposed to represent all the media and all their member organizations, not all broadcasting organizations are among its members. The IBA does not belong to the IPC because it is bound by the Broadcasting Authority Act and therefore cannot subject itself to the authority of a voluntary body as well. The same is true of Israel Educational Television (which is part of the Ministry of Education) and the Second Authority. Only the Israel Defense Forces radio station (Galey Zahal) is a member of IPC since 1999.

---

[8]As of 2002, no research had been conducted on the activities of the IPC. A comprehensive study by me on that issue was forthcoming.

Actually, many of the employees of these organizations, as well as those of the IBA, are subject to the Press Council's authority by virtue of their membership in the National Federation of Israeli Journalists, one of the Council's founding bodies. Yet, there have been cases in which the IBA barred its employees from appearing before the IPC's ethics courts even when complaints had been lodged against them. The reason given was that IBA employees are legally subject to the IBA's own disciplinary court, which enjoys the same legal authority as civil service disciplinary courts. Consequently, they are not to be exposed to double jeopardy.

Voluntary—Organizational Level

Israel has two systems at this level. The first consists of the ombudsmen employed by several newspapers (and by the IBA). The second is the IBA *Guidelines for Broadcasting News and Current Affairs*, written by veteran IBA official Nakdimon "Nakdi" Rogel and commonly known as the *Nakdi Guide*, which closely resembles the BBC's *Producers' Guidelines.*

The first newspaper to appoint an ombudsman was the daily *Maariv.* Its readers' advocate published regular reports in the paper itself, criticizing professional malfunctioning and ethical violations by reporters and editors, even without waiting for complaints (in many cases without mentioning them by name). Intensified financial competition between the dailies led in the mid 1980s to cessation of public self-flagellation, relegating their respective ombudsmen's activities to a position behind the scenes.

The *Nakdi Guide,* combining professional guidelines and a code of ethics, is aimed at IBA television and radio employees, especially those involved in news and current events. In fact, many of the ethical principles determined by the IPC were adopted post facto by the IBA and included in the *Nakdi Guide.*[9] First issued in 1972, the *Guide* has since undergone many changes and emendations, as reflected in the increase in number of sections from an original 42 to 169 in the latest edition (1998). The first three editions were mimeographed and distributed only among IBA employees, whereas the fourth edition was hardbound and even offered for sale to the general public

The High Court of Justice rejected an appeal demanding that the IBA render the *Nakdi Guide* obligatory, with legal status resembling that of the Second Authority and Cable Television Council codes of ethics. In its decision, the Court concurred with the IBA, declaring that it was not obliged to transform the document's status from non-statutory to statutory.

---

[9]Y. Limor and I. Gabel, Five Versions of One Code of Ethics: The Case Study of the Israel Broadcasting Authority, *Journal of Mass Media Ethics,* 17(2), 2002.

THE FUNCTIONING OF MEDIA ACCOUNTABILITY SYSTEMS

None of Israel's numerous media accountability systems functions as well as it should. Each suffers from various functional flaws and defects characteristic of similar systems in other countries.

The oldest and most significant system is the Israel Press Council. The public recognition it enjoys is reflected in Supreme Court decisions. In one case, the IPC *Code of Ethics* was cited as an appropriate legal reference (Sept. 1977); in another, the Court determined that a decision of the IPC Ethics Court, which found a journalist guilty of a serious ethical violation, was to be submitted to the panel that recommended the journalist for the Israel Prize, highest award in the country (May 1997): the man did not get the prize. In a third instance, the Jerusalem District Court adopted the IPC *Code of Ethics* as a standard attesting to good faith for purposes of defense against a libel suit (1989).

On the other hand, the IPC suffers from the same disorders that plague its counterparts in the rest of the world: tense relations among component members, lack of resources, ineffective means of enforcement, poor public awareness of its existence and much skepticism regarding its effectiveness.

The IPC's most outstanding weakness is its incomplete representation of the media industry in Israel. The Israel Broadcasting Authority, the largest and most important broadcasting body in the country, is not represented on the Council, nor are hundreds of local newspapers and periodicals. As early as 1968, the IPC decided that it also possessed authority to handle complaints against non-member publications. Nevertheless, the practical—and maybe even moral—validity of its decisions in such instances remains limited at best. Moreover, the National Federation of Israeli Journalists, one of its component bodies, does not represent all individuals involved in press activity in Israel. Many of the journalists employed by periodicals and local newspapers do not belong to any of the three component associations that constitute the federation—and, as such, are also not subject to the IPC's authority or code of ethics. In practice, there's a paradox: the broader the public recognition gained [by the Council], the fewer the media officially represented. One may even go so far as to say that the number of media professionals that the Council officially represents has declined as well. The situation became even more severe in the early 1990s as several daily papers that belonged to the IPC closed down and numerous local papers and periodicals that were not IPC members were added to the media map.

An examination of IPC activity over the years shows that media organizations and their owners and employees generally accept the Council's authority and agree to cooperate with it, depending on time and circumstances. The greater the external pressures on the media institution and the greater the threats of restrictive legislation, the more tightly the IPC's membership closes ranks, forming a protective rampart to repel any attempts at coercion from without.

In normal times, however, when the situation is not perceived as threatening, the breaches in the IPC wall become evident. Ill will among representatives of journalists, of editors, and of owners have often paralyzed IPC activity—and even threatened its very existence. Such unstable relations effectively reflect an ambivalent attitude towards the Council and its work. Newspaper owners are reluctant to reinforce the IPC's status and power, fearing restriction of their commercial freedom. Editors are similarly unenthusiastic about a strong and active Council; some even believe that there is no need for the IPC at all, whereas others maintain that its principal function is to guard freedom of the press and not "freedom *from* the press." Journalists, too, fear that as individuals they would be adversely affected by enforcement of the code of ethics without appropriate backing from the newspaper owners.

The IPC has two sources of financing: newspaper owners and journalists. Although these two groups do seek to maintain the Council as a protective armor against external pressure and threats of legislation, they are not interested in having it become too strong or financially sound. In 1998, the IPC's activities nearly ground to a halt because of budgetary problems. In this as well, the Israel Press Council resembles most of its counterparts worldwide.

The IPC, like most other press councils, lacks the "teeth" required for enforcement in the ethical sphere. The only punishment that its ethics court may mete out is publication of its decisions, that is, public censure of those found guilty of ethical transgressions. Officially, the newspapers that belong to the Council are obligated to publish decisions concerning themselves, but not all observe this rule scrupulously. Failure to publish these decisions weakens the IPC's power, blunts its moral authority and ipso facto adversely affects its very existence.

Although we possess no empirical data concerning public awareness of the IPC's existence and effectiveness, we may posit that throughout its 35 years of activity, the Council has not succeeded in gaining recognition among the general public—while, on the other hand, it has acquired such status among major establishment groups. The relatively small number of appeals to the IPC each year may well reflect the small extent of the public's awareness of the Council and its roles and functions. Alternatively, it may indicate skepticism regarding the Council's efficacy as a media supervisor and self-regulation mechanism, reflecting the media's poor credibility as well.

A comprehensive study revealed, for example, that 22% of the Israeli public believes that the media "harm" or "greatly harm" the state, and another 37% indicated that they "contribute" or "contribute greatly" to the state. The media are viewed in a far less positive light than other institutions in Israeli society, such as the Supreme Court, the Israel Defense Forces, the Police, the State Comptroller, and even the Cabinet and Parliament (Knesset). Only political parties are ranked as more harmful and less contributory.[10]

---

[10]G. Barzilai, E. Yuchman-Yaar, and Z. Segal, *The Israeli Supreme Court and the Israeli Public*, Tel Aviv, Papyrus, Tel Aviv University, 1994. (In Hebrew).

Other systems in Israel have similarly failed to achieve public recognition. The *Nakdi Guide*, vaunted as the IBA's ethical touchstone, is unfamiliar not only to the general public but also to many IBA employees. Moreover, its length and complexity render it difficult to study and internalize. Speaking off the record, senior IBA employees admit that they do not always adhere scrupulously to this code because "it does not always suit dynamic realities." The two other codes of ethics in the broadcasting sphere—those of the Second Network and of the Cable Television Council—are limited by their very nature, primarily because they are phrased in general terms and because their statutory status has not yet been tested in court.

The public also appears to be unaware of the ombudsmen functioning at two of the three major dailies, because the papers do not publicize their existence or the details of their activities. Generally, ombudsmen are only familiar to the reporters and editors of their respective newspapers. The IBA and the Second Authority ombudsmen are slightly better known, especially because both organizations periodically remind the public of their existence and function. The limited role played by ombudsmen in the various media organizations in Israel repeatedly raises a question already asked about their U.S. counterparts: is this public accountability or only public relations?

PRESSURE AND COERCION AFFECTING M*A*S

Many journalists in Israel, as in other Western countries, believe that media accountability systems are vital not only to guarantee media independence but also to maintain professional and moral standards. Such systems help increase the media's credibility among the public, opening the two-way channels of communication that are an essential component of "public journalism."[11]

On the other hand, some journalists express reservations about setting up such systems and are particularly reluctant about giving them "teeth," believing that their only commitment should be to professional norms. They claim that professional journalists must obey the law and accept comprehensive social responsibility rather than automatically submit to ethical principles imposed "from without." For example, the editor of the prestigious daily *Haaretz*[12] claims that professional ethics in general—and especially journalistic ethics—is an elusive entity and that no code of ethics can take the place of the living editor, who determines ethical norms and guarantees adherence to them by his very

---

[11]J. Rosen, *Getting the Connections Right: Public Journalism and the Troubles in the Press,* New York, Twentieth Century Fund. 1996.

[12]The morning newspaper, founded in 1919, ranks as Israel's quality newspaper and among the world's most prestigious papers.

presence. He adds: "Journalistic ethics consists of constant self-flagellation. Every editor puts it to the test in countless cases engendered by changing social norms and various types of journalists."[13]

Conflicting conceptions among journalists regarding the need for M*A*S constitute only one of the pressures affecting these systems and their activities. Above all, the various types and degrees of pressure reflect the cultural-social environment in which the media operate. A conservative-traditional society will give rise to codes of ethics, written or otherwise, that reflect the social consensus, whereas in a liberal society there will develop much "softer" ethical codes. Social ecology also affects the political institution and other institutions in society, as well as pressure groups and the judicial system, each of which, in its own way, imposes pressure on the entire media institution and the media organizations that comprise it. The greater the external pressure on the media institution, the more it will attempt to formulate behavioral norms—of which accountability systems are only one practical manifestation—and impose them on its component organizations. In other words, external pressure on the media institution causes it to impose pressure and self-regulation on its component organizations.

Although studies tend to focus primarily on pressures imposed on the media institution by the political system or by advertisers, one cannot ignore the judicial system's effect on the media institution and its accountability systems. Legal decisions that interpret the law constitute normative signposts with which the entire media institution must align itself, even if they conflict with journalistic norms. The policy of "judicial legislation" effectively adopted by Israel may yield a situation in which not only legislators and the law, but also judges and their decisions impose pressure on the media. Such decisions are not limited to slander or invasion of privacy (which are covered by legislation in any case) but also include judicial interpretations of existing laws that themselves acquire the status of law.

One outstanding example is a decision handed down by the National Labor Court, determining that a newspaper owner has the right to tell the journalists who work for him not only *what to write about* but also *what to write*. The Court recognized that freedom of the press and freedom of expression are indeed lofty values, yet deemed the right of ownership no less important, indicating that it must not be affected adversely by intervention in the manner in which newspaper owners conduct their business.

Competition among media organizations is similarly worthy of attention. The prevailing claim is that business competition causes popularization of media content, lowers standards, and erodes professional and ethical norms. Relentless quests for scoops and exclusive photos led to the development of checkbook journalism and to the emergence of paparazzi, with all their atten-

---

[13]H. Marmari, "What is a Journalist?", *Haaretz,* Books Supplement, p. 1, 11 March 1998.

dant side effects. But one cannot deny that competition may also have the oppo-site effect, to improve accountability and develop professional and ethical norms—as demonstrated by the Israeli case.

For years, there was a kind of conspiracy of silence among the newspa-pers; each would publish only those IPC decisions concerning itself, avoiding publication of those involving other papers. Intuitively, one would expect news-papers to be eager to publish decisions concerning their competitors, thereby undermining their credibility. It thus emerges that the fiercer the competition, the greater the likelihood of credibility self-monitoring among the media, albeit for reasons other than those that inspired the development of accountability sys-tems and codes of ethics.

Similarly, the tough competition among media organizations need not necessarily be interpreted as negative. When a certain organization adopts accountability systems, including insistence on a code of ethics, it may be chart-ing a path for its competitors. For instance, in 1994, a Palestinian suicide bomber attacked a busload of passengers in the heart of Tel Aviv. The two tele-vision channels, as well as two popular newspapers, took a step unprecedented in the annals of Israeli journalism: they displayed photos of the grisly scenes of carnage. In the wake of the public furor that ensued, similar scenes of subse-quent disasters were not aired or published.

CONCLUSIONS

During the first few years after the establishment of the State of Israel, many of the media served as a mobilized and committed press, a phenomenon common in countries that have thrown off the yoke of colonial rule. In time, most committed press features disappeared and the Israeli media began adopting the professional and functional norms prevailing in Western democratic countries, including the creation and operation of accountability systems. In such countries, including Israel, political pressures are becoming less effective as modern technology dis-rupts well-established supervisory systems. On the other hand, increasing social pressure is being applied by various watchdog organizations (especially religious or right-wing groups) and by groups claiming to be the target of media discrimi-nation, which demand changes in both methods and content.

The emerging accountability systems have adapted—sometimes through trial and error—so as to cope with pressures originating outside the media institution, that is, in the political system or among pressure and interest groups. In contrast, appropriate systems and efficient methods have not yet been developed to deal with pressure originating within the media institution itself, namely those resulting from economic processes such as concentrated owner-ship and cross-ownership. In Israel and other countries, people are becoming increasingly aware that accountability systems, especially press councils, can protect freedom of the press not only from external threats and pressures but also from internal ones, especially those applied by media organization owners, whom some even call "the enemy within."[14]

The danger becomes far more intense when owners of media organizations are involved in additional economic ventures and the media they own are liable to find themselves having to promote their owners' overall business interests. Consequently, it is hardly surprising that media organization owners are none too happy about public disclosure of their business interests. Such disclosure may well be the cornerstone of the accountability concept, attesting to clean hands that have nothing to hide. It has already been pointed out that the press seeks full revelation and extensive discussion of public affairs, yet keeps its own interests private, closed and far from public scrutiny.[15]

Over the past few years, the issue of commercial transparency among media barons has been of some concern in Israel. During the mid-1990s, the IPC and its ethics courts even halted activity after publishers refused to satisfy journalists' demands to add a section to the Code of Ethics rendering commercial transparency mandatory. After months of extended discussions, a compromise was reached in which Section 15B of the code stipulated: "Once a year, the publisher and owners of a newspaper will publish in that newspaper appropriate disclosure of the substantive business and economic interests they maintain in the media field and outside it." The written words had no practical effect, however. About two years after the relevant Section was approved, and partly because the publishers were not adhering to the Code of Ethics, the National Association of Israeli Journalists announced its withdrawal from the IPC, thereby effectively terminating it. Ultimately, they resumed cooperation with the Council even though the issue was not fully resolved.

He who pays the piper calls the tune. Owners' involvement has a decisive effect on the existence, functioning, and efficacy of media accountability systems in Israel and elsewhere. If the owners so desire, they will support these systems, finance their activities, insist on enforcement of ethical principles, and censure violators. Alternatively, they may turn their backs on these systems, close the budget taps, turn a blind eye to ethical violations, and perhaps even encourage those violations that benefit their businesses.

The real danger, however, is not posed by such overt hostility, but rather originates in a kind of foggy situation in which owners ostensibly support accountability systems yet limit them to interests of the moment. The ambivalence is indeed fraught with danger, as the owners appear amenable to commercial and professional transparency, but in practice hide themselves and their interests behind thick (news)paper walls.

[14]M. Negbi, *The Enemy Within: The Effect of "Private Censorship" on Press Freedom and How to Confront It,* Harvard University, Discussion Paper D-35, 1998.
[15]Th. Glasser and S. Craft, "Public Journalism and the Prospects for Press Accountability," In J. Black (ed.), *Mixed News: The Public/Civic/Communitarian Journalism Debate* (pp. 120-134), Mahwah, NJ, Erlbaum, 1997.

CHAPTER 29
M*A*S in Estonia
Self-Regulation Rather Than State-Regulation

Urmas Loit

Unlike in many other new democracies, professionals in Estonia did not rush to draft a code of ethics. Estonia chose the way of case studies to establish the rules for journalism. It took six years of case-by-case approach within the Press Council until the media community dared write down the principles of good conduct. .

THE LEGAL SITUATION

It has always been difficult to explain to my colleagues from both East and West why, for a long time after we regained independence, there still was neither a media law nor a national code of media ethics in Estonia. In the eyes of my colleagues, too little regulation is closer to anarchy than to press freedom.

Most of Estonian media are against any kind of press law. Estonia used to have a print law during its pre-World War II period of independence. The law of 1923 was based on German and French models, quite liberal, which prohibited immorality, sedition, and subversion. Another law from the 1930s established censorship, due to the situation in Europe then. In its wake, the State Propaganda Department was formed. Fourteen kinds of articles were prohibited and all sentences concerning the president and the government had to be grammatically affirmative. Yet, compared to the overall European tendency towards authoritarian systems at that time, the Estonian system was liberal.

Soon after independence was recovered in 1991, Parliament tried to pass a press bill but, thanks to active opposition on the part of journalists, the draft never became a law. The absence of a press law does not mean there are no rules to regulate the media sphere. Several laws influence the operation of the media in different ways.

The Constitution of Estonia (1992) says that everyone has the right to get public information with no restraints (§ 44) and to express freely one's ideas, opinions, convictions, and any other information by all possible means (§ 45).

Dignity and privacy are protected by civil law and a person can sue anybody who has violated his/her rights. Estonian courts have made several decisions forcing offenders to pay quite large sums of money to injured parties. Thus, almost everyone in Estonia can be considered to be protected from libel and violation of privacy—even "public people," as the law makes no difference between "public" and ordinary people.

The Broadcast Law regulates radio and television in Estonia. This law guarantees freedom of operation, the protection of information sources, the right to register an objection (i.e., right of reply), morals and legality, protection of copyright, and so forth. Those same fields are unregulated as far as the print media are concerned.

JOURNALISM AND MEDIA ACCOUNTABILITY

Although the legal prescriptions are rather few, there is no anarchy in the Estonian media world. In 1997, a code of ethics was finally adopted. Until a national code was adopted, the codes of other European countries were studied and used.

According to media educators, lack of interpretation of experience and lack of discussion were the most negative features in media regulation at that time. In Estonia, the public has been involved too little. Court practice and the work of the Press Council have been explained superficially, with a focus on the decisions, not on the way they were reached. So there had to be a waiting period: the Estonian code could be introduced only when the society was ready to accept it. By 1997 Estonia reached that kind of readiness and the code generally started to work.

Moreover, the students in journalism at the University of Tartu had created an informal code of honor for themselves as early as the mid 1970s, and it is still endorsed by all students of journalism at the end of the first academic year. The 13 paragraphs of that informal, realistic code sounded extremely different from official propaganda all through the years of repressive Soviet occupation; they carry an important ethical value even today. For example:

2. I practice journalism not for myself and my boss, but for my nation.
4. I do not advocate values that I do not value myself.
9. I treat the protagonist as a human being not as raw material.

A written code does not work without support from the parties involved. Media accountability depends on the public agreement of journalists and audience rather than on formal printed texts.

There are no problems with such immediate responses as correction boxes and letters to the editor. It has become so self-evident that nobody is really able to imagine that they might not be there. Media criticism and polemics about the media in the media are somewhat newer features in the Estonian press and are thus having teething problems and providing work for the Press Council. Instead of discussing professional matters, the authors of criticism tend to attack colleagues personally and are sometimes even offensive.

The Press Council is the main institution among Media Accountability Systems in Estonia. It was founded in 1991. It expresses its views on all events that influence or could influence press freedom. Besides, the Council deals with complaints from the readers/listeners/viewers who have felt offended or injured by journalists. More than 200 cases have already been considered by the Press Council. Twenty a year may not seem like much, but it should be remembered that the total population is 1.4 million and that previously, under Soviet rule, people were scared to stand up for their rights—as it could be worth a free trip to Siberia. In 1999, the number of complaints was 37 (compared to 15 in 1996).

The Press Council was founded as a self-regulatory body to discuss matters before they went to court and to find out-of-court settlements. But it could play a much bigger role in foiling the state's attempts to control the press.

Up to April 1997 the Press Council was a department of the Estonian Newspaper Association, a publishers' association. A structural reform was then carried out in order to widen its importance and power base. The Association of Estonian Broadcasters, the Journalists' Union of Estonia, the Association of Media Educators and the Estonian Consumers' Association, plus public broadcasters (radio and TV) formed a new non-profit, non-governmental organization to run the new press council, reforming also the statutes and the rules of procedure. Later, the NGO Network, an Estonian federation, and the Council of Churches also joined in.

Most of the media associations in Estonia prefer general laws that apply to all rather than specific professional rules that would be set from above. In other words, there should be general rules for protection against libel in Civil Law; state secrets should be protected by some other law, and so forth. The only specific law concerning news media that exists is the Information Act that guarantees that every citizen (not just the media) has access to public information. It was enacted only in 2001.

Ethical rules do not fit into law, for most of the criteria in the field of ethics cannot be defined in legal terms. Often an ethical decision is called by some "inner voice," and the source is in feeling rather than objective judgment. A law could lead to the situation in which a state official would decide upon his/her impression and opinion whether the law has been broken or not. That would require highly qualified judges. At present, most Estonian judges lack this kind of qualification. If the decision were made by a bureaucrat, the results would be disastrous.

The Parliament of Estonia passed a law on advertising in June 1997 in which the dangers outlined above can be clearly observed. The Commission of Economic Affairs explained that the sector of advertising needed regulating. In their opinion, there is no good tradition of advertising in Estonia, which creates the need to enforce Western experience by law. The law sets rules that are based on the subjective impressions that someone might get from an ad. Usually it is an official's impression and if the impression is "bad" the fine can reach $5,600. The only means to avoid such effects has been to set up a co-regulatory body—a self-regulatory body that bases its decisions upon regulations established by law.

There is no guarantee that the possible press law would resemble the above mentioned Act. This is a good reason for having a strong media account-ability system and avoiding any kind of rules decreed from above. But when media fail to prove their accountability by sticking to the rules of self-regula-tion, when they fail to be open to public criticism, the general public may lose its trust in "simulated self-regulation" and politicans may be inclined to pass a law.

The role of media is almost settled in society. In 2002 there was no direct threat to the media and to freedom of speech in Estonia. But, according to polls, the reliability of media had decreased slightly.

Conclusion

After ranging over that panorama of media accountability systems, let us return to the three-pillared edifice. The market tells you to do whatever it takes to make money, within the limits set by the law. The law tells you what not to do in order to stay out of trouble with the police and the courts—and so does "self-regulation" but then you tell yourself. Ethics in the widest, noblest sense of the term tells you not just what to avoid, but also what to do so as to serve the public well.

Ethics covers territory covered by the law (such as respect for individual reputations) and, just as the law covers territory that has nothing to do with morality (such as the political organization of a country), ethics covers much ground outside the law, which lawyers in many countries find hard to accept. This appears clearly in the APME code (rev. 1995), one of the best codes in existence: ". . . The newspaper should serve as a constructive critic of all segments of society. It should reasonably reflect, in staffing and coverage, its diverse constituencies. It should vigorously expose wrongdoing, duplicity or misuse of power, public or private. Editorially, it should advocate needed reform and innovation in the public interest. . . ."

It was mentioned at the beginning of this book that news media had much improved over the 20th century. And just afterwards, it was made very clear that much improvement was still needed. Let us have a look at what has been accomplished and at what remains to be achieved—with the help of the triangular combination, but mainly with the M*A*S, the arsenal for democracy.

WHAT HAS ALREADY BEEN DONE

I have heard even such fierce critics as George Seldes and Ben Bagdikian acknowledge, in private, that media had greatly improved. They cannot now be as sensational, fraudulent, corrupt, partisan, racist, sexist, as they used to be. Far fewer facts and phenomena now get caught in the "spiral of silence" and escape public attention. One reason is that many more reporters are women or minorities. Another is that journalists are far better educated and aware of their mission. Just compare the average present-day newsman with the cynical protagonist of Hecht and MacArthur's play *The Front Page* (1928, movie 1931).

Has progress been due to the market forces? To legislation? History suggests an answer. During the "Gilded Age," the United States tried letting the market function in almost total freedom: you get an idea of the muck then excreted by looking at what Will Irwin raked in his series on American newspapers[1] for the magazine *Collier's* in 1911. On the other hand, the law without the market has also been tried, in every communist regime in the world, producing the worst media ever. And a great variety of combinations of law and market have been practiced in the 20th century. Now we know what the two can do— quite a lot—and what they cannot, also quite a lot.

In the improvement, other factors played a part. The *Technologies of Freedom*,[2] as Ithiel de Sola Pool called them, made the acquisition, the processing and the distribution of information, as well as the exchange of ideas, faster, more abundant, cheaper than ever. The communication revolution led governments to abandon their monopoly on broadcasting, in the whole of Europe and then in the rest of the world. It also made deregulation inevitable. The Internet is not ushering in utopia but is certainly bringing more good than harm, if only in countries with despotic regimes: what are a few Nazi sites in the West compared to millions of Chinese gradually getting access to the Web?

The fall of the Berlin wall and the subsequent collapse of the USSR destroyed the myth of a communist alternative to a capitalist press and so aided a revival of interest in "media ethics." Until then, the most notorious critics of the Western press (Herbert Schiller, Kaarle Nordenstreng, Ted Smythe, Armand Mattelart, etc.) kept totally quiet about the soviet media and suggested no third solution, so it seemed that the marxist model was an acceptable option. With the end of the Cold War, the Third World model, whatever that was, also stopped being mentioned.

In the 1990s, wars in many parts of the world—in the Gulf, in Africa, in the Balkans—and some spectacular events such the Simpson trial and the death of Princess Diana, all accompanied by serious breaches of journalistic rules, attracted attention to the misbehavior of media. Hence to ethics.

---

[1]Will Irwin, *The American Newspaper,* 1916, Ames, Iowa SUP, 1969.

[2]Cambridge, Harvard UP, 1983.

What of ethics? Attitudes have changed, in general, even if behaviors have not. That is a first stage in a slow process. It is interesting to compare the present view of media accountability with the screaming indignation or icy indifference that greeted the Hutchins report (1947) and its stress on the "social responsibility" of the press. Ethics may not yet dictate normal practice, but it is an accepted notion. The multiplication of j-school courses on ethics (68 in the United States in the late 1970s and 300 in the late 1990s) and of books on communication ethics (about 100) published[3] is a clear sign.

What of M*A*S? Experience with them has proved many of their opponents wrong. The fears of the libertarian critics have never been confirmed, even in India where the press council was set up by law: as mentioned before, when PM Indira Gandhi proclaimed a "state of emergency" (1975-1977), that is, when she suspended democracy, one of the three press measures she took was to suppress the press council.

M*A*S are slowly, very slowly, becoming a normal part of the picture, to the extent that some are not noticed anymore, such as many of the less spectacular M*A*S: correction boxes, letters to the editor, media pages, readership surveys, codes of ethics, books critical of the media, journalism education, and so forth. Most media seem to care more about their public than they used to, and they try to establish closer links with them: a striking (and controversial) illustration of that trend in the United States was the development of "public journalism." In France, many newspapers and magazines now publish letters to the editor, which was very rare before.

The United States is one country where the vague outline of a network of M*A*S has developed, involving criticism, monitoring, feedback, and training. Some of the best codes in the world were drafted and adopted by associations such as ASNE, APME, or SPJ-SDX, and a majority of newspapers now have their own charters. Three regional press councils operate in the United States and over 40 ombudsmen. Nearly all newspapers now have op-ed pages and letters-to-the-editor sections. Some have panels of readers they consult regularly; a few have free-press/fair-trial committees and/or joint staff-management groups. Good media employ good critics, such as David Shaw (of the *LA Times*) or Howard Kurtz[4] (of the *Washington Post*): the better dailies, such as the *New York Times* or the *Boston Globe*, practice regular criticism—as do the alternative weeklies and, of course, the many journalism reviews—not to mention a plethora of books. Last but not least, journalism schools in the United States are more numerous, more sophisticated, more productive than in any country on the planet.

---

[3]Clifford Christians and Edmund Lambeth, "The Status of Instruction in Communication Departments," *Communication Education*, July 1996, *45*(3), pp. 236-243. And Edmund B. Lambeth, Clifford Christians and Kyle Cole, "Role of the Media Ethics Course in the Education of Journalists," *Journalism Educator*, *49*(3), Autumn 1994, pp. 20-26.

[4]See *Media Circus: What's Wrong with America's Newspapers*, New York, Times Books, 1993.

University education for journalists has generalized even in the more refractory countries, such as Great Britain. Who will deny that the improvement of the press in the last generation is inseparable from the fact that almost 60% of news people and almost 80% of big city newspaper journalists are now college graduates? College courses in media accountability are now common in the United States—as are conferences, workshops and seminars on press ethics.

Everywhere, media research has greatly expanded, both in the scholarly and the commercial fields. No country can boast as much university and foundation research as the United States, whose results are presented in scores of journals (such as *Journalism Quarterly* and other publications of AEJMC). National organizations such as those of black and female journalists keep watch on the media microcosm. A number of partisan groups (such as FAIR and AIM) and local militant associations (such as the San Francisco Media Alliance) monitor media. So we now know much better what media do and don't do.

What has been achieved, in the United States and elsewhere, has been due to the three forces which in liberal democracies are in the service of the people: the law played its part, the market played its part. And lastly, ethics played a part by gradually changing the mentalities and some of the habits. It could play a far bigger role if the M*A*S were developed. To those who rightly argue that M*A*S are still much under-developed, let us say that those that do exist are both a sign and a factor of change. They stand as a signal that a medium no longer claims to be infallible, that it is ready to let outsiders look in, that it is willing to listen to them and render accounts. And M*A*S help it do that.

AGENDA FOR THE FUTURE

A New Journalism

"Journalism cannot be guided only by economic forces. [. . .] It should rather be felt as a sacred mission, knowing that powerful means of communication have been entrusted to you for the welfare of all, especially the weaker members of society," as Pope John Paul II declared to journalists on June 4, 2000. In other words, journalism has to change. And insofar as "media ethics" is understood to mean "good journalism," "good public service," this is an ethical issue.

A new definition of journalism is slowly emerging. Too much is obviously wrong about the journalistic tradition (see p. 7), including a mindless opposition to M*A*S. It needs to be overhauled. As breaking out of a mold always proves difficult, this will take time, but it should not be left to develop obscurely. It needs to be brought into the limelight, to be debated in newsrooms, in articles, radio and television programs, books, conferences—and in the classrooms of journalism schools.

Now that there is a corpus of scientific knowledge that they must learn in specialized schools, and professional associations with codes of ethics, journalists must pursue their evolution from trade to profession. And must keep as autonomous as possible from the media industry—on one side only of the mythic wall that is supposed to separate journalistic gate-keepers and business decision-makers.

Journalists must have acquired general culture, specialized knowledge, and a sense of priorities. They should be aware of the several functions of media in society (not just getting and packaging the news), aware of the obligations of news people to the population, aware of the rights of readers/listeners/viewers. They must distinguish between entertainment and information, between real events and fabricated events, between interesting and important news. They must strive to give a full and accurate report on what is happening, which means shedding the systematically pessimistic view of the traditional journalist. This means looking at the submerged part of the iceberg, not being content with obvious events, looking for phenomena developing under the surface of reality. They must cultivate an openness to, a curiosity for, new ideas, unexplored fields, foreign cultures, non-famous, non-powerful folk. And they must report all that in a style that is clear and attractive for their particular audience—that is, simplistic, even colloquial, if need be.[5] All this requires knowledge, competence, sophistication and dedication. This is not all: journalists must also cultivate confidence and humility so as to be capable of accountability.

Ethics and M*A*S

Libertarians believe that the only restraint on a journalist should be his/her conscience. Even if that were true, that conscience would have to be trained: children need to be taught virtue; journalists need to be taught professional morality. It is interesting that "mass communication ethics has quickened during and after periods of intense public media criticism that coincided with moments of growth in journalism education and in the university system generally—the 1890s and 1920s especially, and then the current activism, which began around 1980."[6]

Ethical behavior does not come naturally to all, even if they've been taught the principles and practices. Ethical rules need to be enforced, so devices must be created to encourage journalists to stay on the straight path. But, say libertarians, M*A*S endanger freedom. "Freedom" is a magic word, especially in the United States where many organizations are dedicated to press freedom—but not so many to "excellence in journalism." Freedom, however, is not the

---

[5]From the late 1930s to the early 1960s, the London *Daily Mirror* was a quality popular tabloid, making serious news palatable to an uneducated audience and mixing it with sex and crime.

[6]C. Christians and J. Nerone, *op. cit.*

goal. It is only a condition, an absolute condition, for reaching that goal: the goal is to serve the people well. Freedom too often means permission to make as much profit as possible—that is, the freedom from political restraints, not from economic restraints. Again, M*A*S have two missions: (1) improve the media directly and (2) make journalists more autonomous by obtaining for them the support of the public against both political and economic threats. Thus, M*A*S are not a limitation to press freedom but a fundamental means to preserve press freedom.

Another basic distinction to be stressed again is that between the little sins, mainly those of journalists, and the big ones, mainly those of media. It is all very well that a reporter check the accuracy of quotes, refuse gifts, respect people's privacy—but it is far more important that media do not dish out infotainment day after day, do not omit crucial information in order to please advertisers. What is often called "media ethics" today is like an antiseptic to cure some superficial infection. What is now needed is "in-depth ethics" aimed at fighting a deeper disease: the ugly transmutation of news media from public services into fountains of fun, vehicles for ads, cash machines.

So we get back to the triad, market/law/ethics. Both journalists and media users should be acutely aware that the law and the market cannot solve all problems and can create some very serious problems. So availing oneself of ethics is no longer an option, but an obligation. Maybe we should talk, not of morality, or social responsibility, or ethics (words that turn off some people), but of "quality control," which makes it clear to all—proprietors, news-people, and public—that everyone is to benefit from its use. This is becoming urgent at a time when a swarm of non-journalists, some malicious, generate piles of "information" on the Web: more than ever the public needs true professionals, competent and conscientious, armed with principles and rules, ready to render accounts.

ALLIANCE FOR PROGRESS

All the protagonists in social communication need to be involved because several M*A*S need to function together to produce an impact. And it is even better when many—if not all—M*A*S supplement and re-enforce each other. Besides, some of the more influential require a cooperation of all three fundamental groups.

Media Owners

That small group must absolutely be persuaded to go along. They have a crucial role to play in improving media quality. Only they can make it possible, or impossible, for journalists to behave ethically—if only by paying decent salaries. Money and publicity are vital for M*A*S to work efficiently—and those two resources are controlled by owners. Great figures among proprietors have demonstrated that their concern was not just the bottom line but also public service. In London, Roy Thomson spent millions modernizing first the *Sunday Times*, then the *Times*. Eugene Meyer transformed the mediocre *Washington Post* after buying it in 1933, and his children followed suit.

Why should owners be interested? One reason is obvious: they can suffer heavy losses in the case of a big violation of ethics, the kind that is covered by laws.[7] Secondly, media managers being accountable to share-holders, they need to keep in mind that quality pays. Admittedly, garbage can also pay, but in the entertainment business (where British tabloids belong)—not in the news business.

On a more lofty level, publishers and broadcasting bosses must acknowledge, unless they are total cynics, that they have a special responsibility towards their fellow human beings. Steering news media differs from manufacturing plastic flowers or dishwashers: news media constitute a major nervous system of society. Finally, there is a selfish reason: no one lives by money alone, especially if one possesses plenty of it. Prestige and influence count. Would one rather be remembered as the model for the infamous *Citizen Kane* or as the creator of the Pulitzer Prize? Would you rather be introduced as the publisher of the *New York Times* or that of the *Enquirer,* the supermarket weekly?

Journalists

The news professionals must fight in the front rank, of course, armed with their talents and their knowledge of the field. In their fight for independence they possess a kind of nuclear deterrent, the threat to strike—or even to quit collectively. That would make most publishers think twice before engaging in a major violation of ethics—if the threat were credible. But journalists (almost) never use it: it requires that the newsroom be in close communion over some fundamental values—which it rarely is—or that it be well organized by a single union.

The hard fact is that media professionals, who are relatively few, depend on media owners for their livelihood and career. They cannot expect politicians to give them disinterested assistance. They can only to turn towards voters-consumers who are extremely numerous and can put tremendous pressure on decision-makers. The public possesses the power that media people need to resist abuse by the authorities. Journalists reluctant to seek allies among the public should remember that when media users are not satisfied with the services of media, they tend to seek relief from government and a government, whatever its stripes, is always on the lookout for pretexts to restrict press freedom.

---

[7]Some years ago, the London *Sun* had to pay a million pounds for libeling Elton John.

The Public

Contrary to what some journalists claim, media ethics is not synonymous with self-regulation. The public has to be involved with M*A*S in various ways. Many social forces need to be converted to active participation in the improvement of media. One of them is consumers' associations, which should treat the media as they treat other sectors of the economy. Why do they test, evaluate, and compare TV sets, mobile phones, banks, or insurance companies, but never the products and services of the media industry? Another institution is the schools, whose efforts to train children in the smart use of media should be far greater.

Mainly, the masses of individual media users must be awakened, educated, stimulated, organized. Contrary to what intellectuals are fond of saying, the public is not stupid. It knows what good media are and it cannot be manipulated at will.[8] Georges Clémenceau[9] one day quipped that "war [was] something too serious to be entrusted to the military." The same, I believe, is true of media: they cannot be left to owners and workers of the industry. As it is, the public can do, and occasionally does, far more than it thinks itself capable of doing. For instance, by consuming one medium rather than another, it sends strong signals to its directors: in the late 1950s, the slumbering BBC-TV woke up when it realized that three quarters of its audience had switched to the lively new commercial network.

More directly, a motivated section of the public can apply pressure on legislators to obtain from government or from media owners that its needs be satisfied. That was the case in the United States when the Public Broadcasting Act (1967) was passed by Congress: it provided federal funds to help non-commercial TV take off. A more spontaneous example: 200,000 young Parisians took to the streets in 1984 to save radio station NRJ when it was threatened by government for violating technical rules. However, the improvement of media demands not scattered explosions, but continuous militancy. To obtain that from the public, news-people need to enjoy its confidence. By ethics and M*A*S they probably can get it.

A GLOBAL APPROACH

This book differs from most books on media ethics published in the United States in that it gives an international view. That is part of the message it carries. A globalization of minds must take place. The common remark that there

---

[8]About 60% of Americans still thought President Clinton was doing a good job after the media repeated for a year and a half that he was unworthy of, and should be removed from, the White House.

[9]Politician, publisher, pamphleteer, and prime minister of France during World War I (1917-1918).

are big differences in the appreciation of media behavior, and in codes, from one part of the world to another is simply not true. Everybody agrees on ethics and media quality—within democratic nations, of course. Actually, whoever reads codes from all over the globe is struck by the similarity: basic values are the same. Disparities are a matter of emphasis or limited to marginal matters— such as the sex life of politicians (not to be mentioned in France) or suicide (not to be mentioned in Sweden). Everywhere the same ideal is proclaimed. News is news, entertainment is entertainment, garbage is garbage in Sweden or Switzerland, Turkey or Taiwan. Quality and public service mean very much the same for the *Washington Post, Asahi Shimbun, The Guardian, La Repubblica, El Pais* and the *Times of India*.

Journalists must escape from local bondage. They have an obligation to concentrate on serving their community, but they should think in terms of the planet. They should stimulate in people an interest in the rest of mankind, both because of the growing interdependence of nations but also because of the need for human solidarity. One is tempted to see a connection between the poor coverage of the under-developed world by U.S. media and the fact that, as a percentage of its GDP per capita, U.S. foreign aid is far smaller than that of most industrialized democracies. An easy inexpensive way to cover the planet is to borrow material written or taped by foreign media for their own use: it informs on a foreign land and also can provide an original viewpoint on one's own country.

Exchanges should go further than that, but isolationism is rampant in most countries, especially in the United States. At a Salzburg Seminar in 1987, which Katharine Graham attended, I suggested at one point that U.S. media may have something to learn in Europe. Her curt reply was: "Certainly not!" I see a happy sign of change in that U.S. schools have been encouraging international exchange programs for both students and faculty.

In every nation, people should look for inspiration beyond the regional or national horizon, find what to imitate and what to guard against. Europeans, for instance, could do more U.S.-style checking of facts, separation of news and views, investigative journalism, precision journalism, academic research. And Europeans should guard against the United States obsession with violence, the spreading of sensationalism and celebrity worship from tabloid to quality press, foreign news shrinking almost to nothingness, and the cancerous growth of advertising.

DEVELOPING M*A*S

Ethics is nothing but hot air unless its rules are enforced, by one's conscience or under social pressure. As, very obviously, some people are not equipped with a very demanding conscience, there is a need for M*A*S. These have proved to be democratic, diverse, flexible, able to function at any level—individual publication, city, province, nation, region, planet. Allow me to repeat: the M*A*S are soft and powerful weapons to guarantee that a better service is given by the media to the public, so that journalists can recover the trust and the support of the public, so that they will find themselves able to withstand internal and external pressure.

Because everybody has heard about laws and market forces, because fewer people have heard about ethics and far fewer have heard about M*A*S, what is urgent is to start publicizing all the M*A*S, get them accepted, deployed, and used. At all levels, each kind must be tried and adapted until it reaches full development. Take press councils: they should exist at local, regional, and national levels and they should gradually assume every one of their functions. Achieving that is no easy task. Too much should not be expected from any one M*A*S. It seems important to me that a network of M*A*S be deployed to incite media to do their job well and to make it easier for them to do so.

But promoters of M*A*S should work patiently. Remember the slow evolution of the Norwegian press council. In Senegal, it took two years to set up a press council, before it even started operating. Only over 20 to 30 years does real change become visible. First, the attitudes change, then the speech, then the behavior. The development seems desperately slow to radicals. To the historian it is revealed to be exponential. Whoever fights for the introduction of some M*A*S will find it necessary always to concentrate on the half-full glass, on what exists, on what works—on the quality media, not on the garbage press, so as to keep the faith.

POSITIVE TRENDS

At the turn of the millennium, some positive signs could be observed. Here are a few examples picked in the United States. In 1996, the association of professors of journalism (AEJMC) gave itself a new division, Media Ethics. In June 1999, Gannett, the largest newspaper firm, issued a detailed code for its 73 dailies and, contrary to usage, it wanted the public to know about the code: "an important statement to our readers that they can trust and believe their local newspapers." In the same period, calls[10] were heard for a restoration of the code of the National Association of Broadcasters (NAB), which was abandoned in 1982 when the federal government inanely caused its cancellation in the name of anti-trust policy. Some time before, in 1997, there was a call by the Society of Professional Journalists (SPJ) for a revival of the News Council, and it was given a full page by *Editor and Publisher*,[11] the trade weekly. A little after that, a new council was established in Washington State.

---

[10]For example, by Newton Minow in the *Washington Post,* May 11 1999.
[11]March 29, 1997, pp. 8-9.

While in the year 2000 a large part of humans still did not enjoy freedom of expression, there were more democratic nations than ever (notably in Latin America and Eastern Europe). A consensus was spreading on human rights and on the twin evils of collectivism and excessive individualism. Pluralist democracy expanded in countries where it was still in the bud (India, Japan, black Africa). Within the old democracies, openness and tolerance increased.

Long before the fall of totalitarianism at the turn of the 1990s, the West has witnessed the rise of "rightism." Blacks, women, environmentalists, consumerists, homosexuals, various minority ethnic groups, and others have fought for their rights since the 1960s. They resent the domination of both Big Government and Big Business—yet would like the former to protect them against the latter. The rising level of sophistication has rendered much of the public better conscious of the media's role, more demanding and more militant. Also clearly, while people do take advantage of the correct information given them, they no longer yield to the influence of media, if they ever did. They want the media, new and old, to serve them.

As it boomed into an unforeseeable revolution, technology promoted ethics by having both a bad and a good impact. It makes it easier for more persons to distort the news even more (willingly or not) and, on the other hand, it democratizes the media, makes it (theoretically) possible for anyone to have access to public opinion. It makes some M*A*S much easier to set up and far less expensive than before—journalism reviews for example. The growing number of alternative outlets, weeklies, radio stations, websites—makes it more difficult for regular media to ignore ethics. *The Finger*, an alternative weekly in Los Angeles, triggered the Staples shopping center scandal (1999), which rocked the *Times* and made headlines nationally.

Deregulation and heightened competition make self-control or peer control or public control more needed. More and more people feel, will feel, the need for a quality label on the news they get, especially on the Internet. They will seek accrediting devices. Some discipline is needed. And because the market is now largely free, because cyberspace is not easy to regulate by law, ethics is left with a great responsibility.

Growing commercialization, too, may increase the temptations to distort news and vulgarize entertainment, but it makes media more responsive to public opinion. At the turn of the century, ethics was in the air. Media noted the improved performance of "ethical" investment funds[12] (one tenth of total investments in the United States), funds that stay away from armament, nuclear power, tobacco, alcohol, industries that pollute or are known for bad employment practices. Some of the funds were even applying pressure on companies to mend their ways and become "socially responsible." Nearly everywhere, some

---

[12]The first such fund started in 1970, an interesting period for M*A*S too.

media owners, in a context of increased competition, were tempted to follow the lead of some non-media businessmen, who decided to serve the public better and to show accountability—and then found that "ethics" paid.

NO OTHER WAY

The simple reason why we need to deploy the M*A*S arsenal and to make the "three-pillared system" work is that there is no acceptable alternative. State propaganda and commercial junk are not acceptable. Can you put total trust in the Law? Can you put total trust in the market? Can you trust both combined? Of course not. Whatever the failings and insufficiencies of "ethics and M*A*S" there is no choice. Thousands of words have been written and spoken to denounce the free market or the law or ethics and M*A*S—and many of the accusations are justified. But then what? Should we just sit and weep?

It would be absurd to expect the market spontaneously to produce quality media, and it would be hazardous to let government dictate what the media should do. Similarly, it is utopian to dream that media can be reformed simply by arousing the moral conscience of reporters and/or media moguls. Expecting too much of ethics and M*A*S would be no less dangerous than to dismiss them as gewgaws. Nowadays, the main threat on the freedom and the quality of media comes from the exploitation of communication channels by mega-companies such as Time-Warner/AOL or News International. Ethics and M*A*S cannot even dream of controlling the media giants that struggle on the world stage. Even if M*A*S appeared everywhere, at all levels, and if they all functioned in cooperation (which is unlikely in the near future), it would not be enough. There would still be a vital need for national and international laws and regulations, backed by sheer force.

So choice is impossible: we must combine Law + Market + Ethics and M*A*S, with a proportion of each that is bound to differ a little from one nation to the next, linked as it is to the ideology, the traditional vision of man and society, and to the existing media structures and practices. Whereas some nations, for instance, need an injection of freedom (France, Britain), others need more regulation (United States or Japan).

The three-pillar model, the combination Law + Market + Ethics and M*A*S might be called the "European model": on the Old Continent, in the 1980s, nations privatized and largely deregulated electronic media—but they have kept an ideal of public service. Everywhere now, the first two pillars in the triad are accepted and praised, in spite of the damage they can cause. Harmless as it is, the indispensable third tends to be ignored, although it is capable of limiting the abuse of the market and thus is capable of limiting the demand for legislation.

In that great fight for the welfare of mankind, that crusade for a better world in which are engaged all democrats, ecologists, civil rightists of every obedience, the M*A*S are some of the weapons to be used—an arsenal for democracy.

Bibliography

ADAMS Julian, *Freedom and Ethics in the Press*, New York, Rosen, 1983.

ADHIKARI G., *Press Councils: The Indian Experience*, New Delhi, Press Institute of India, 1965.

ALLEY Robert S., *Television: Ethics for Hire?*, Nashville (TN), Abingdon, 1977 [based on interviews with eminent producers].

ARANT David (ed.), *Perspectives: Ethics, Issues and Controversies in Mass Media*, St Paul (MN), Coursewise, 1999.

ARONSON James, *Packaging the News: A Critical Survey of Press, Radio, TV*, New York, International Publishers, 1971.

ARONSON James, *Deadline for the Media: Today's Challenges to Press, TV and Radio*, Indianapolis, Bobbs-Merrill, 1972.

BABB Laura L. (ed.), *Of the Press, By the Press, For the Press, and Others Too*, Boston, Houghton Mifflin, 1976 [self-analysis by journalists of the *Washington Post*].

BAGDIKIAN Ben H. *The Media Monopoly, Boston*, Beacon Press, 6th ed., 2000.

BAIRD Robert M. et al. (eds.), *The Media and Morality (Contemporary Issues)*. Amherst (NY), Prometheus Books, 1999.

BALK Alfred, *A Free and Responsible Press*, New York, Report to the 20th c. Fund, 1973.

BARNEY Ralph & Jay BLACK, *Communitarian Journalism*, Mahwah (NJ), Erlbaum, 1996.

BARRON Jerome C., *Freedom of the Press For Whom? The Right of Access to Mass Media*, Bloomington, Indiana UP, 1973.

BATES Stephen. *Realigning Journalism with Democracy: The Hutchins Commission, Its Times, and Ours.* Washington, DC, Annenberg Washington Program in Communications Policy Studies of Northwestern University, 1995. Available at www.annenberg.nwu.edu/pubs/hutchins.

BEAUCHAMP Tom L. & Stephen KLAIDMAN, *The Virtuous Journalist,* New York, Oxford UP, 1987.

BELSEY Andrew & Ruth CHADWICK (eds.), *Ethical Issues in Journalism and the Media,* London, Routledge, 1992 [British philosophers].

BERRY David (ed.), *Ethics and Media Culture: Practices and Representations,* London, Butterworth Heinemann, 1999 [British view].

BERTRAND Claude-Jean, *Media Ethics and Accountability Systems,* Piscataway (NJ) & London, Transaction, 2000.

BLACK, Jay. *Mixed News: The Public/Civic/Communitarian Journalism Debate,* Mahwah (NJ), Erlbaum, 1997.

BLACK Jay et al., *Doing Ethics in Journalism: A Handbook in Case Studies,* Needham Heights (MA), Allyn & Bacon, 1998.

BOGART Leo, *Commercial Culture: The Media System and the Public Interest,* Piscataway (NJ), Transaction, 1999.

BRADLEY H.J., *Press Councils of the World,* London, The Press Council, 1974 [mimeographed].

BRISLIN Tom (ed.), *Teaching Media Ethics,* Mahwah (NJ), Erlbaum, 1998.

BROGAN Patrick, *Spiked: The Short Life and Death of the National News Council,* New York, Priority, 1985 [U.S. National Press Council].

BROWN Lee, *The Reluctant Reformation: On Criticizing the Press in America,* New York, McKay, 1974.

BRUUN Lars (ed.), *Professional Codes in Journalism,* Prague, IOJ, 1979 [IOJ was a soviet front].

BUGEJA Michael J., *Living Ethics: Developing Values in Mass Communication,* Needham Heights (MA), Allyn & Bacon, 1995.

BUTTNY Richard, *Social Accountability in Communication,* London, Sage, 1993.

CASEBIER Allan & Janet J. CASEBIER, *Social Responsibilities of the Mass Media,* Lanham (MD), University Press of America, 1978.

CHADWICK Ruth. *The Concise Encyclopedia of Ethics in Politics and the Media.* Burlington, MA, Academic Press, 2001.

CHRISTIANS Clifford & Catherine L. COVERT, *Teaching Ethics in Journalism Education,* New York, Hastings, 1980.

CHRISTIANS Clifford & Mark FACKLER, *Media Ethics: Cases and Moral Reasoning.* New York, Longman, 5th ed. 1998 [76 case studies in a variety of fields].

CHRISTIANS Clifford, John P. FERRE & P. Mark FACKLER, *Good News: Social Ethics and the Press,* New York, Oxford UP, 1993 [philosophical approach].

CHRISTIANS Clifford & Vernon JENSEN, *Two Bibliographies on Ethics,* Minneapolis, University of Minnesota Press, 2nd ed., 1988.

CHRISTIANS Clifford & Michael TRABER (eds.), *Communication Ethics and Universal Values,* Thousand Oaks (CA), Sage, 1997.

CIRINO Robert, *Don't Blame the People: How the News Media Use Bias, Distortion and Censorship to Manipulate Public Opinion,* New York, Random House, 1971.

COHEN, Elliot D. (ed.), *Philosophical Issues in Journalism,* New York, Oxford University Press, 1992.

COHEN Elliot D. & Deni ELLIOTT, *Journalism Ethics: A Reference Handbook,* Santa Barbara (CA), Abo Clio, 1998.

COHEN-ALMAGOR Raphael, *Speech, Media and Ethics: The Limits of Free Expression.* New York, St. Martin's Press, 2000.

COLLINS Keith S. (ed.), *Responsibility and Freedom in the Press: Are They in Conflict?,* Washington (DC), Citizen's Choice, 1985.

Commission on the Freedom of the Press, *A Free and Responsible Press,* University of Chicago Press, 1947.

COOPER Thomas W., *Television and Ethics: A Bibliography,* Boston, G.K. Hall, 1988.

COOPER Thomas W. (ed.), *Communication Ethics and Global Change,* New York, Longman, 1989.

COUPRIE Eliane & Henry OLSSON, *Freedom of Communications Under the Law: Case Studies in Nine Countries,* Manchester, European Institute for the Media, 1987.

CRAWFORD Nelson A., *The Ethics of Journalism,* New York, Knopf, 1924; new ed. 1969.

CURRY J. L. et al., *Press Control Around the World,* New York, Praeger, 1982.

DAY Louis A., *Ethics in Media Communication: Cases and Controversies,* Belmont (CA), Wadsworth, 3rd ed., 1999.

DENNIS Everette E. et al. (ed.), *Media Freedom and Accountability,* New York, Greenwood, 1989.

DEWALL Gustav von, *Press Ethics: Regulation and Editorial Practice,* Düsseldorf, European Institute for the Media, 1997 [France, Germany, Italy, Sweden, United Kingdom].

DICKEN-GARCIA Hazel, *Journalistic Standards in Nineteenth Century America,* Madison, U. of Wisconsin Press, 1989.

DICKSON Thomas, *Mass Media Education in Transition,* Mahwah (NJ), Erlbaum, 1999.

DOWNING John et al., *Questioning the Media: A Critical Introduction,* Newbury Park (CA), Sage, 1990.

ELLIOTT Deni, *Toward the Development of a Model for Journalism Ethics Instruction,* Ann Arbor (MI), University Microfilms, 1984.

ELLIOTT Deni (ed.), *Responsible Journalism,* Troy (NY), Sage, 1986 [Nine essays by academics].

European Journalism Center, *Organising Media Accountability,* Maastricht, EJC, 1997.

FALLOWS, James, *Breaking the News: How the Media Undermine American Democracy,* New York, Pantheon, 1996.

FINK Conrad C., *Media Ethics: In the Newsroom and Beyond,* New York, McGraw Hill, 1988.

FLINT Leon N., *The Conscience of the Newspaper: A Case Book in the Principles and Problems of Journalism,* New York, Appleton, 1925.

FROST Chris, *Media Ethics and Self-Regulation,* Harlow (Essex), Longman, 1998 [Mainly about British national press].

FULLER Jack, *News Values: Ideas for an Informaion Age,* Chicago, University of Chicago Press, 1996.

GERALD J. Edward, *The Social Responsibility of the Press,* Minneapolis, University of Minnesota Press, 1963 [a classic].

GIBBONS William F., *Newspaper Ethics: A Discussion of Good Practice for Journalists,* Ann Arbor (MI), Edwards Bros., 1926.

GOLDSTEIN Tom, *The News at Any Cost: How Journalists Compromise Their Ethics to Shape the News,* New York, Simon & Schuster, 1985 [concrete cases].

GOLDSTEIN Tom (ed.), *100 Years of Media Criticism,* New York, Columbia UP, 1989.

GOODWIN Eugene, *Groping For Ethics,* Ames (IA), Iowa State UP, 1994.

GORDON A.D. & John M. KITTROSS, *Controversies in Media Ethics,* New York, Addison Wesley, 2nd ed., 1999.

GORLIN Rena A. (ed.), *Codes of Professional Responsibility,* Washington (DC), Bureau of National Affairs, 2nd ed., 1990.

GREENBERG Karen Joy (ed.), *Conversations on Communication Ethics,* Norwood (NJ), Ablex, 1991.

GROSS Larry & John STUART (eds.), *Image Ethics: The Moral Rights of Subjects in Photographs, Film and Television,* New York, Oxford UP, 1988.

HACHTEN William, *The Troubles of Journalism: A Critical Look at What's Right and Wrong With the Press,* Mahwah (NJ), Erlbaum, 1998.

HARMS L. S., J. RICHSTAD & K.A. KIE (eds.), *Right to Communicate: Collected Papers,* Honolulu, University Press of Hawaii, 1977.

HARMS L. S. & J. RICHSTAD (eds.), *Evolving Perspectives on the Right to Communicate,* Honolulu, East-West Center, 1977.

HASELDEN Kyle, *Morality and the Mass Media,* Nashville (TN), Broadman, 1968 [Christian viewpoint].

HAUSMAN, Carl, *Crisis of Conscience: Perspectives on Journalism Ethics,* New York, Harper Collins, 1992.

HEINE W., *Journalism Ethics: A Case Book,* London (Canada), University of Western Ontario, 1975.

HENNING Albert F., *Ethics and Practice in Journalism,* New York, Long & Smith, 1932.

HODGES Louis (ed.), *Social Responsibility: Journalism, Law, Medicine,* Lexington (VA), Washington & Lee University, 1978.

HOFFMANN-RIEM Wolfgang, *Regulating Media: The Licensing and Supervision of Broadcasting in Six Countries*, New York, Guilford, 1996.

HULTENG John L., *The Messenger's Motives: Ethical Problems of the News Media*, Englewood Cliffs, Prentice-Hall, 1976, 2nd ed., 1985.

HURST John & Sally A. WHITE, *Ethics and the Australian News Media*, South Melbourne, Macmillan, 1994.

IGGERS Jeremy, *Good News, Bad News: Journalism Ethics and the Public Interest*, New York, Worldview Press, 1998.

IOJ, *International Principles of Professional Ethics in Journalism*, Prague, IOJ, 1986 [IOJ was a soviet front].

IPI, *Press Councils and Press Codes*, Zürich, International Press Institute, 1964, 1967.

IRWIN Will, *The American Newspaper*, 1916, Ames, Iowa SUP, 1969.

ISAACS Norman E., *Untended Gates: The Mismanaged Press*, New York, Columbia UP, 1986.

JAKSA James A. & M. S. PRITCHARD, *Communications Ethics: Methods of Analysis*, Belmont, Wadsworth, 1988.

JENSEN Carl, *20 Years of Censored News*, New York, Seven Stories Press, 1997 [Monitoring media omissions].

JENSEN Joli, *Redeeming Modernity: Contradictions in Media Criticism*, Newbury Park (CA), Sage, 1990.

JOHANNESEN Richard L., *Ethics in Human Communication, 1975*, Prospect Heights (IL), Waveland Press, 4th ed., 1996.

JONAS Hans, *The Imperative of Responsibility*, Chicago, University of Chicago Press, 1984.

JONES G. Clement, *Mass Media Codes of Ethics and Councils*, Paris, Unesco, 1980 [intense Marxist bias].

JUUSELA Pauli, *Journalistic Codes of Ethics in the CSCE Countries*, Tampere, University of Tampere, 1991 [Synthetic study of Western and soviet codes].

KAPLAR Richard T. & Patrick D. MAINES, *The Government Factor: Undermining Journalistic Ethics in the Information Age*, Washington (DC), Cato Institute, 1995.

KEEBLE Richard, *Ethics for Journalists*, London, Routledge, 2001.

KESSLER Lauren, *The Dissident Press, Alternative Journalism in American History*, Beverly Hills (CA), Sage, 1984.

KIERAN Matthew, *Media Ethics: A Philosophical Approach*, Westport (CT), Praeger, 1997.

KIBERD Damien (ed.), *Media in Ireland: The Search for Ethical Journalism*, Dublin, Four Courts Press, 1999.

KINGSBURY Susan M., *Newspaper and the News: An Objective Measurement of Ethical and Unethical Behavior by Representative Newspapers, 1937*, New York, Johnson Reprint, 1969.

KLAIDMAN Stephen & Tom L. BEAUCHAMP, *The Virtuous Journalist*, New York, Oxford UP, 1987 [based on authentic situations].

BIBLIOGRAPHY

KNOWLTON Steven R., *Moral Reasoning for Journalists: Cases and Comments,* Westport (CT), Praeger, 1997.

KNOWLTON Steven R. & Patrick R. PARSONS (eds.), *The Journalist's Moral Compass: Basic Principles,* Westport (CT), Praeger, 1994.

KRIEGHBAUM Hillier, *Pressures on the Press,* New York, Crowell, 1972.

KUCURADI Ionna (ed.), *Ethics of the Professions: Medicine, Business, Media, Law,* Berlin, Springer, 1999.

KURTZ Howard, *Media Circus: The Trouble with America's Newspapers,* New York, Random House, 1994.

KURTZ Howard, *The Fortune Tellers: Inside Wall Street's World of Money, Media and Manipulation,* New York, Free Press, 2000.

LAMBETH Edmund B., *Committed Journalism: An Ethic for the Profession,* Bloomington, Indiana UP, 2nd ed., 1992.

LAND Richard D. & Frank D. YORK, *Send a Message to Mickey: The ABC of Making Your Voice Heard at Disney,* Nashville (TN), Broadman & Holman, 1998.

LEMERT James, *Criticizing the Media: Empirical Approaches,* Newbury Park (CA), Sage, 1989 [empirical research serving media].

LESLIE Larry Z., *Mass Communication Ethics: Decision Making in Postmodern Culture,* Boston (MA), Houghton-Mifflin, 2000.

LESTER Paul, *Photojournalism: An Ethical Approach,* Hillsdale (NJ), Erlbaum, 1991.

LEVY Philip, *The Press Council: History, Procedures and Cases,* London, Macmillan, 1967 [The British press council].

LIMBURG Val E., *Electronic Media Ethics,* Boston, Focal Press, 1994.

MacDONALD Barrie & Michel PETHERAM, *Keyguide to Information Sources in Media Ethics,* London, Lansell, 1998.

MacDOUGALL A. Kent (ed.), *The Press: A Critical Look From the Inside,* Princeton, Dow Jones, 1972.

MAKAU J. M. & R.C. ARNETT (eds.), *Communication Ethics in an Age of Diversity,* Urbana, University of Illinois Press, 1997.

MATELSKI Marilyn J., *Television News Ethics,* Boston, Focal Press, 1991.

McCULLOCH F. (ed.), *Drawing the Line,* Washington (DC), ASNE, 1984 [How 31 editors solved their worst ethical problem].

MEDVED Michael, *Hollywood vs. America,* New York, HarperCollins, 1992.

MERRILL John C., *The Imperative of Freedom: A Philosophy of Journalistic Autonomy,* New York, Hastings House, 1974 [hostile to "social responsibility"].

MERRILL John C., *The Dialectic in Journalism: Toward a Responsible Use of Press Freedom,* Baton Rouge, Louisiana SUP, 1989.

MERRILL John C., *Legacy of Wisdom: Great Thinkers and Journalism,* Ames (IA), Iowa SUP, 1994.

MERRILL John C., *Journalism Ethics: Philosophical Foundations for News Media,* New York, St. Martin's Press, 1997.

MEYER Philip, *Editors, Publishers and Newspaper Ethics,* Washington (DC), ASNE, 1983.

MEYER Philip, *Ethical Journalism: A Guide for Students, Practitioners and Consumers,* New York, Longman, 1987 [a classic].

MOORE Roy L., *Mass Communication Law and Ethics,* Mahwah (NJ), Erlbaum, 2nd ed., 1999.

MURRAY George, *The Press and the Public: The Story of the British Press Council,* Carbondale, Southern Illinois UP, 1972.

NORDENSTRENG Kaarle (ed.), *Reports on Media Ethics in Europe,* University of Tampere (Finland), 1995.

NORDENSTRENG Kaarle & Michael GRIFFIN (eds.), *International Media Monitoring,* Cresskill (NJ), Hampton Press, 1999.

OLEN Jeffrey, *Ethics in Journalism,* Englewood Cliffs (NJ), Prentice-Hall, 1988.

PATTERSON Philip & Lee WILKINS (eds.), *Media Ethics: Issues and Cases,* New York, McGraw-Hill, 1997.

PIPPERT Wesley G., *An Ethics of News: A Reporter's Search for Truth,* Washington, Georgetown UP, 1989 [personal experiences].

POLLAK Richard (ed.), *Stop the Presses, I Want to Get Off!,* New York, Random House, 1975 [anthology from the review [MORE]].

POSTMAN Neil, *Amusing Ourselves to Death,* London, Heinemann, 1985.

POTTER W. James, *Media Literacy,* London, Sage, 1998.

PRITCHARD David (ed.), *Holding Media Accountable: Citizens, Ethics and the Law,* Bloomington, Indiana UP, 2000 [very critical of M*A*S].

RIVERS Caryl, *Slick Spins and Fractured Facts,* New York, Columbia UP, 1996.

RIVERS William L. et al., *Backtalk: Press Councils in America,* San Francisco, Canfield, 1972 [US local press councils].

RIVERS William L. & Cleve MATHEWS, *Ethics for the Media,* Englewood Cliffs (NJ), Prentice-Hall, 1988.

RIVERS William, W. SCHRAMM & C. CHRISTIANS, *Responsibilities in Mass Communication,* New York, Harper & Row, 1957, 3rd ed., 1980.

ROBERTSON Geoffrey & Andrew NICOL, *Media Law: The Rights of Journalists, Broadcasters and Publishers,* London, Sage, 1985.

ROSEN Jay, *What Are Journalists For?,* New Haven (CT), Yale UP, 1999.

RUBIN Bernard (ed.), *Questioning Media Ethics,* New York, Praeger, 1978.

RUSHER William A., *The Coming Battle for the Media: Curbing the Media Elite,* New York, Morrow, 1988 [highly conservative viewpoint].

RUSSELL Nick, *Morals and the Media: Ethics in Canadian Journalism,* Vancouver, University of British Columbia Press, 1994.

SABATO Larry J. et al., *Peepshow: Media and Politics in an Age of Scandal,* Lanham (MD), Rowman & Littlefield, 2000.

SCHMIDT Benno C., *Freedom of the Press vs. Public Access,* New York, Praeger, 1976.

SCHMUHL Robert (ed.), *The Responsibilities of Journalism,* Notre Dame (IN), University of Notre Dame Press, 1984.

SCHWARTZ Ted, *Free Speech and False Profits: Ethics in the Media*, Cleveland (OH), Pilgrim Press, 1996 [Christian conservative].

SCHWARTZ Tony, *The Responsive Chord*, Garden City (NY), Doubleday, 1973 [ethics in broadcasting].

SEIB Philip, *Campaigns and Conscience: The Ethics of Political Journalism*, Westport (CT), Praeger, 1994.

SEIB Philip & Kathy FITZPATRICK, *Journalism Ethics*, Fort Worth (TX), Harcourt Brace, 1997.

SHAW Colin, *Deciding What We Watch: Taste, Decency and Media Ethics in the UK and the USA*, New York, Oxford UP, 1999.

SHAW David, *Journalism Today*, New York, Harper & Row, 1977 [anthology of critical pieces from the *Los Angeles Times*].

SHAW David, *Press Watch: A Provocative Look at How the Newspapers Report the News*, New York, Macmillan, 1984 [idem].

SHULTZ Julianne, *Democracy, Accountability and the Media*. Cambridge UP, 1999.

SINCLAIR Upton, *The Brass Check: A Study of American Journalism*, Pasadena (CA), 1919, reprinted by Arno Press, 1970.

SLOAN William David (ed.), *Makers of the Media Mind: Journalism Educators and Their Ideas*, Hillsdale (NJ), Erlbaum, 1990.

SMITH Ron F. & Eugene GOODWIN, *Groping for Ethics in Journalism*, Ames (IA), Iowa SUP, 1983, 4th ed., 1999.

SOLOMON Norman et al., *The Habits of Highly Deceptive Media: Decoding Spin and Lies in Mainstream News*, Monroe (ME), Common Courage Press, 1999.

SPARKS Colin & John TULLOCH (eds.), *Tabloid Tales: Global Debates over Media Standards*, Lanham (MD), Rowman & Littlefield, 2000.

SPG-SDX, National Ethics Committee, *Journalism Ethics Report*, Chicago, Society of Professional Journalists, yearly since 1981.

STRENTZ, Herbert. *News Reporters and News Sources: Accomplices in Shaping and Misshaping the News*, Ames (IA), Iowa State University Press, 1989.

STUHR John J., *Morals and the Media: Information, Entertainment and Manipulation*, Eugene, University of Oregon Books, 1990.

SWAIN Bruce M., *Reporters' Ethics*, Ames (IA), Iowa SUP, 1979 [problems faced by 67 journalists].

THAYER Lee et al. (ed.), *Ethics, Morality and the Media*, New York, Hastings House, 1980 [27 essays mainly by practitioners].

THOMAS, Helen. *Front Row at the White House*, New York, Scribner, 1999.

TRIKHA N.K., *The Press Council: A Self-Regulatory Mechanism for the Press*, Bombay (India), Somaiya Publications, 1986.

VAN DER MEIDEN Anne (ed.), *Ethics and Mass Communication*, Utrecht (NL), State University of Utrecht, 1980.

WEAVER, Paul H., *News and the Culture of Lying: How Journalism Really Works*, New York, The Free Press, 1995.

WHITNEY D. Charles, *Begging Your Pardon: Corrections and Correction Policies at Twelve US Newspapers*, New York, Gannett Center for Media Studies, 1986.

REVIEWS AND JOURNALS

American Journalism Review, University of Maryland, 1117 Journalism Bldg., College Park, MD 20742-7111. www.ajr.org

Columbia Journalism Review, Journalism Bldg., Columbia University, 2950 Broadway, New York, NY 10027. www.cjr.org

Ethics in Journalism, Washington & Lee University, Knight Professorship Program.

Journal of Mass Media Ethics, c/o Erlbaum, 10 Industrial Ave, Mahwah, NJ 07430-2262. *http://jmme.byu.edu*

Media Ethics, Department of Visual and Media Arts, Emerson College, 100 Beacon Street, Boston (MA) 02116. media_ethics@emerson.edu

On Line Journalism Review (OJR). www.ojr.org

St. Louis Journalism Review, 470 E. Lockwood, St Louis, MO 63119.

SOME INTERESTING WEBSITES
(most of which have many links to other interesting sites)

Accuracy in Media	www.aim.org
American JR	www.ajr.org
American Review	www.americanreview.net
American Society of Newspaper Editors (ASNE)	www.asne.org
Association for Practical and Professional Ethics	php.indiana.edu/~appe/home.html
Brislin, Tom, University of Hawaii	www2.hawaii.edu/~tbrislin/jethics.html
Cal State U. Fullerton	www.commfaculty.fullerton.edu/lester/ethics/ethics_list.html
Centre for Applied Ethics	www.ethics.ubc.ca/resources/media
Columbia JR	www.cjr.org
Cultural Environmental Movement	www.cemnet.org
Fairness and Accuracy in Reporting	www.fair.org
Indiana University J-School	www.journalism.indiana.edu/Ethics/
International Federation of Journalists	www.ifj.org
Media Ethics (Canada)	www.mediaethics.ca
Media Research Center	www.mediaresearch.org
ONO, Organization of News Ombudsmen	www.infi.net/ono
Pew Research Center for the People and the Press	www.people-press.org
Poynter Institute for Media Studies	www.poynter.org/research/biblio
Presswise (GB)	www.presswise.org.uk/ethics.htm
San Francisco's State University J-School's Ethics Links	www.journalism.sfsu.edu/www/ethics.html

Silha Center for the Study of Media Ethics
and Law   www.silha.umn.edu

Society of Professional Journalists (SPJ-SDX)   www.spj.org/ethics

University of British Columbia, Centre
for AppliedEthics   www.ethics.ubc.ca/resources/media

University of Oregon J-School   www.jcomm.uoregon.edu/about/
                                                                                         ethics/index.html

University of Tampere, Finland   www.uta.fi/ethicnet

WWW Virtual Library— journalism section   www.trainer.com/vlj.html

Yahoo - List of sites   http://dir.yahoo.com/
                                                                                         News and Media/Industry
                                                                                         Information/Media Ethics and
                                                                                         Accountability/

Profiles
of Contributors

THE EDITOR

Claude-Jean BERTRAND—PhD in English and U.S. studies. After teaching about British and U.S. Churches and media at the universities of Strasbourg and Paris-10 (Nanterre), he taught media studies at the Institut français de presse (University of Paris-2). He has written or edited a score of books devoted to British and U.S. Churches, to U.S. civilization, to U.S. media and, in more recent years, to media ethics. His articles have been translated into more than 15 languages.

CONTRIBUTORS

Britt BÖRJESSON—With a BA in media and communication studies, she lectures on media structure and media ethics at the Department of Journalism and Mass Communication of Göteborg University. She has done research on the history of Swedish press ethics. She is currently in charge of a survey of Swedish journalists, focusing on their attitudes to ethics.

Michael BROMLEY—Professor and Head of Journalism at Queensland University of Technology, Brisbane (Australia). In 2000-2001, he was Visiting Professor at the University of Michigan. A former newsman, particularly interested in the practices of journalists, he has written *An Introduction to Journalism* (1995); co-edited *A Journalism Reader* (1997) and *Sex, Lies and Democracy: The Press and the Public* (1998); and edited *No News is Bad News: Radio, Television and the Public* (2001). He is co-editor of the journal *Journalism*.

Clifford CHRISTIANS—He is professor of communications at the University of Illinois, after studying classical languages, theology, sociolinguistics and communicology. Having specialized in media ethics, he has become one of the top U.S. experts. His research has led him to publish numerous articles, special issues of reviews, and several books, among them *Teaching Ethics in Journalism Education* and *Good News: Social Ethics and the Press* (1993), *Communication Ethics and Universal Values* (with M. Traber) (1997), and *Media Ethics: Cases and Moral Reasoning* (6th ed., 2001).

Theodore L. GLASSER—A professor of communication and director of the Graduate Program in Journalism at Stanford University. A former vice president of the International Communication Association, he was elected in 2000 to serve as president of the Association for Education in Journalism and Mass Communication. His latest book, written with J. S. Ettema, is titled *Custodians of Conscience: Investigative Journalism and Public Virtue* (1998). He also edited *The Idea of Public Journalism* (1999) and, with C.T. Salmon, *Public Opinion and the Communication of Consent* (1995).

Benoit GREVISSE—A former journalist at the daily *La Libre Belgique,* with a PhD in social communication, he is now a professor at the Catholic University of Louvain, where he teaches comparative international media ethics. He is a member of the advisory board of the francophone Belgian equivalent of the FCC. Alone or in collaboration, he has published several books: *Écrire au quotidien* (1987, 1995), *Le Temps des Journalistes* (1997), *La presse écrite en Belgique* (1998), and *Prévention et réparation des préjudices causés par les médias* (1998).

Arnold ISMACH—He worked for 15 years in dailies before obtaining a PhD in communication. He was a professor at the University of Minnesota; then, from 1985 to 1994, dean of the journalism school of the University of Oregon. Very active in professional organizations that aim at improving the media and the training of journalists, he is the co-author of several books on the art of reporting and on big media issues (*Enduring Issues in Mass Communications,* 1978).

Al JaCOBY—He spent nearly 50 years in journalism, mainly at the *San Diego Union,* in La Jolla, California. He has occupied various positions, from mere reporter to editor of the Sunday edition, city editor, and deputy managing editor. In 1976, he became "readers' representative" for the daily and kept that post for seven years, until his retirement in 1992. JaCoby is writing a history of the *San Diego Union.*

Carl JENSEN—He was a reporter for the *Miami Daily News*, editor and publisher of a weekly newspaper, a public relations practitioner, a copywriter, then vice president of the BBDO advertising agency—and finally, from 1973 a professor of journalism at Sonoma State University in California, after obtaining a BA, MA, then a PhD in sociology from UC Santa Barbara. He retired in 1996. In 1976 he started Project Censored, a permanent research program on censorship in U.S. media.

Charles L. KLOTZER—In 1970 he founded, and then was for 26 years the publisher of, the monthly *St Louis JR*, the only survivor of the local journalism reviews launched (1968-1975) by working journalists to evaluate the media. Born in Berlin (1925), he fled Nazism to Shanghai (1939), arriving in the United States in 1947. He served as managing editor of a small weekly. He and his wife published an alternative magazine that evolved into a successful prepress and graphics company. They have never stopped devoting their time and money to progressive causes.

Yehiel LIMOR—Is a senior teacher in the Department of Communications of the University of Tel Aviv. Before teaching, he served for many years as a reporter and an editor at the daily *Maariv*. His publications include five books: *The In/Outsiders: The Media in Israel* (1998, with D. Caspi); *The Mass Media in Israel—A Reader* (1999, with D. Caspi. In Hebrew); *Journalism—Reporting, Writing and Editing* (1997, with R. Mann. In Hebrew); *The Media Institution* (1996, with D. Caspi. In Hebrew); *The Mediators: The Media in Israel 1948-1990* (1992, with D. Caspi. In Hebrew).

Urmas LOIT—After graduating from Tartu University with an MA in journalism, he entered Estonian national public radio where he was a reporter and editor. He has been a member of the Press Council since 1992 and its chairman since 1996. That same year he became managing director of the Association of Estonian Broadcasters.

Takeshi MAEZAWA—He has worked for *The Yomiuri Shinbun* daily newspaper as an investigative reporter (1956 to 1974), then as an editorial writer and a senior member of the Ombudsmen Committee. From 1987 and 1993, he was ombudsman for *The English Daily Yomiuri,* and wrote columns that were gathered into the book *Watchdog—A Japanese Newspaper Ombudsman at Work.* In 1991, he started teaching and since 1998, he has been a professor of communication at Tokyo Keizai University. He has written 20 books and many articles on mass communication and journalism.

Michel MATHIEN—After working as a journalist in the French regional press for 11 years, he obtained a PhD in Communication Sciences. He is now a professor at the Université Robert Schuman in Strasbourg. He has authored and co-authored 15 books among which are *La presse quotidienne régionale* (1986), *Le système médiatique: le journal dans son environnement* (1989), *Les journalistes et le système médiatique* (1992), *Les journalistes* (1995), and *Les agences internationales de presse* (1997).

Mario MESQUITA—A journalist since 1971, a member of Parliament (1975-1978), then the editor or publisher of two Lisbon dailies, vice-president of the press council (1984-1985) and first Portuguese ombudsman, for *Diário de Notícias* (1996-1997). A graduate of the University of Louvain (Belgium), he taught at the University of Coïmbra and since 1995, teaches media ethics and political communication at Universidade Nova in Lisbon. He has published six books, including *Portugal sem Salazar* (1973) and *O Jornalismo em Anélise: A coluna do provedor dos leitores* (1998).

Philip MEYER—A journalist at the *Miami Herald*, then its Washington correspondent for 16 years. At Harvard University in 1966-67, he developed his skills in the quantitative methods of the social sciences: his 1973 book (rev. 4th ed., 2002) *Precision Journalism: A Reporter's Guide To Social Science Research Methods* has become a classic. *Ethical Journalism* (1987) is a sign of his parallel interest in media ethics. Since 1981 he has taught as a professor at the University of North Carolina.

Kenneth MORGAN—He started his career as a journalist in 1944, working for newspapers and news agencies in Manchester, London, and Cairo. Then, for eight years he was secretary general of the British union of journalists (NUJ). From 1970, he was associated with the British Press Council, whose director he was for ten years (1980-1990), as he was of its successor, the Press Complaints Commission for its first year. He was a trustee of the wire service Reuters for 15 years and a governor of the English-speaking Union of the Commonwealth for seven.

Jim RICHSTAD—A journalist since 1960 for various dailies; earned a PhD in mass communication. He was a researcher from 1970 to 1982 at the East-West Center in Honolulu; a professor of journalism at the University of Oklahoma from 1982 to 1995; and five years teaching in China and Singapore. He has specialized in the "right to communicate" and international communication. He helped found the Honolulu Community-Media Council in 1969 and was active in it for 13 years, serving as executive secretary for five. He helped start the Pacific Islands News Association in the 1970s.

Jean SCHWOEBEL (1912-1994)—After getting a doctorate in law, he was hired by *Le Monde* in 1945, in the foreign news department, then in the diplomatic service. In 1951, he mobilized the newsroom to defend the founder of the daily and keep him as editor. He gathered the journalists into a "Société des rédacteurs" to prevent the repetition of such a crisis. He fought throughout his life for the independence of the press, then for better reporting on the Third World. His most famous book is *La Presse, le pouvoir et l'argent* (1968) [Press, Power and Money].

Michel SOUCHON—With a PhD in sociology, he did research within the public broadcasting monolith ORTF (1970-1975), then directed a study group at INA, the research, training and archives unit of public broadcasting. Later he was chief researcher for the two major TV networks, TF1 then Antenne 2 (1985-1989), after which he was a consultant to the president of public TV (1991-1995). His books: *La Télévision des adolescents* (1969), *Petit écran, grand public* (1980), *Trois semaines de télévision, une comparaison internationale* (1982), *L'Enfant devant la télévision des années 1990* (1991).

Barbara THOMASS—After studying communication, political science, and economics, working as a print journalist, and obtaining a PhD, she is now a researcher and lecturer at the University of Hamburg (Germany) and a scholar of the Deutsche Forschungsgemeinschaft. Her main fields are journalism, media ethics and media politics in Western Europe as well as media systems in Eastern Europe. She has published articles on media ethics, two books, *Journalistische Ethik. Ein Vergleich der Diskurse in Frankreich, Großbritannien und Deutschland* (1998) and *Medientransformation in Osteuropa* (with M. Tzankoff, 2001).

Lennart WEIBULL—At the turn of the century, he directed mass media research in the Department of Journalism and Mass Communication of the University of Göteborg, and served as dean of the School of Social Sciences. He has published books and articles on satellite television, on the history of the Swedish press/radio/television, on the Swedish public, on audience measurement methods, and so forth. His research is especially focused on media ethics in Sweden and the attitude towards it of professionals and users.

INDEX

Bishop, Ed, 226
Black JR, 206
Blair, Tony, 146, 307
Block, Eleanor S., 201
Boca Raton News, 287, 288
Bogart, Leo, 5
Bong!, 217
Bordeaux Statement, 66, 68
Boston Globe, 387
Bourdieu, Pierre, 337
Bourges, Hervé, 277
Bradlee, Ben, 67, 179
Brecht, Bertolt, 36-37
Brill's Content, 216
British JR, 217, 316, 329
British Press Council, 29, 113, 116, 118,
    119, 121, 123, 124, 126n, 127, 128,
    137-146, 372, 373
BRC / BRO (Japan), 302
BSC (Broadcasting Standards
    Commission-GB), 309, 310n, 311, 313,
    315, 370
Brown, John, 189
BSkyB, 316
Buncombe, 206
Burris, J., 214
Bush, Chilton R., 150n
Bush, George, 247
BVP, 342

C

Cairo (Illinois), 152, 154
Calcutt, David)/Calcutt Committee, 137,
    138, 140, 142, 144, 145
Caldwell, Earl, 205
Campaign for Freedom of Information, 317
Campaign for Press and Broadcasting
    Freedom, 318
Campbell, Cole, 226
Canard Enchaîné (Le), 217, 340, 346
Canon of Journalism, 116, 303, 304, 303n
Carcans-Maubuisson, 253
Carey, Jim, 183
Carles, Pierre, 339, 340
Carlton Television, 311
Carnegie, Andrew, 246
Carson, Rachel, 249

Carta di doveri del giornalista (Italy), 66,
    69, 71, 72, 73, 74, 75, 76, 77
Carter, Jimmy, 245
Catledge, Turner, 239
CBS Views the Press, 207
Centre de perfectionnement des journal-
    istes, 269
Chandler, R.W., 152
Chaparro, Carlos, 196
Charlotte Observer, 289
Charte des devoirs professionnels
    (France), 65, 68, 70, 71, 72, 76, 77
Chuma (Kiyofuku), 305n
Chicago Journalism Review, 202, 203,
    204, 205, 206, 208, 209, 210, 211, 213,
    214, 219, 220
Chicago Times, 240
Chiffres en folie, 337
Chipp, David, 143
Chiquita scandal, 15
Cincinnati Enquirer, 15
Citizen Kane, 391
Clark, Ruth, 285
Clémenceau, Georges, 392
Cleveland, Harlan, 160
Clinton, Bill, 8, 43, 245, 246, 392n
CNN, 21
CNRS, 339
Code of conduct (NUJ), 65, 68, 69, 70, 71,
    72, 73, 74, 76
Code of Practice (PCC), 68, 69, 70, 71, 72,
    73, 74, 75, 76, 310, 370
Colliers, 386
Columbia Journalism Review (CJR), 202,
    206, 209, 210, 213, 215, 216, 229, 246,
    262
Comment, 206
Comment manipuler les médias, 337
Commission on Freedom of the Press, 49
Commission nationale de la carte, 270,
    271n
Conscience clause, 12, 64, 104, 191
Conseil Supérieur de l'Audiovisuel
    (CSA-France), 21, 115, 122, 254n, 258
Consejo de prensa, 126
Conselho de Imprensa, 140, 191
Consumers' associations, 392
Cooke, Janet, 27